A WORLD BANK COUNTRY STUDY

Lithuania

An Opportunity for Economic Success

Volume 2: Analytical Background

The World Bank
Washington, D.C.

World Bank Country Studies are among the many reports originally prepared for internal use as part of the continuing analysis by the Bank of the economic and related conditions of its developing member countries and of its dialogues with the governments. Some of the reports are published in this series with the least possible delay for the use of governments and the academic, business and financial, and development communities. The typescript of this paper therefore has not been prepared in accordance with the procedures appropriate to formal printed texts, and the World Bank accepts no responsibility for errors. Some sources cited in this paper may be informal documents that are not readily available.

The cover illustration is *The Mechanism* (1996) by Klaudijus Petrulis, reproduced courtesy of the artist and Regimantas Skaržaukas. Photograph by Rimantas Ivoška.

ISSN: 0253-2123

Library of Congress Cataloging-in-Publication Data

Lithuania : an opportunity for economic success.
      p.   cm. — (A World Bank country study)
   Contents: v. 1. Main report — v. 2. Analytical background.
   ISBN 0-8213-4244-4 (v. 1). — ISBN 0-8213-4327-0 (v. 2)
  1. Lithuania—Economic policy—1991–   2. Lithuania—Economic
conditions—1991–   I. World Bank. II. Series.
HC340.6.L565 1998
338.94793—DC21
                                   98-23755
                                     CIP

CONTENTS

TABLES

FIGURES

BOXES

PREFACE

This report has been prepared by a World Bank team composed of Marcelo Giugale (team leader), Dana Cook (banking), Peter Kelly (energy), Jorge Martinez (municipal finance), William Meyers (agriculture), James Welch (privatization), Barbara Lee (infrastructure privatization), Peter Modeen (corporate governance, commercial judicial systems, private investors' perceptions), Ken Messere (tax administration), David Lindeman (pensions), Christopher Bender (pensions), Robert Pardy (securities markets), John Dawson (flow of funds), and Zhicheng Li (macro projections).

Valuable inputs and guidance were received from the following sector specialists at the Bank's Eastern Europe and Central Asia Vice-Presidency: Rodrigo Chaves, Csaba Csaki, Alexander Fleming, Louise Fox, Kristin Gilbertson, Philip Goldman, Marc Heitner, John Holsen, Vilija Kostelnikiene, Mantas Nocius, and Yoshine Uchimura. Useful comments from Ardo Hansson, Robert Holzmann, Dominique Lallement, Laszlo Lovei, Melinda Roth-Alexandrowicz, and Helen Sutch are gratefully acknowledged. Waleed Malik, Gary Stuggins, Samuel Talley, and Dimittri Vittas were the peer reviewers. Dagney Faulk and Midori Makino provided research assistance.

The report was carried out under the general direction of Basil Kavalsky and Pradeep Mitra. James Q. Harrison and Frank Lysy were the senior advisers to the report team.

The editorial staff, coordinated by Michael Geller and Marinette Guevara, included Armanda Carcani, Omar Hadi, David Robbins, and Jessica Rodriguez. Caroline McEuen was the principal editor.

The team wants to express its gratitude to the many officials and institutions in the Lithuanian government, academia, and business community whose cooperation made this report possible. In particular, special thanks are due the staff of the Bank of Lithuania; the Ministries of Agriculture and Forestry, European Integration, Finance, National Economy, Justice, and Social Security and Labor; the Auditing and Accounting Institute; the Lithuanian Securities Commission; the National Stock Exchange; the Central Depository; and the Judicial Training Center, all of whom provided extensive comments to early drafts of this report.

ABSTRACT

Lithuania could now consolidate and complete the achievements of its first structural adjustment effort, create an environment that will allow private entrepreneurs to thrive, and—within five years—become both the fastest-growing economy in the region and a sought-after, successful partner in Europe. In other words, *Lithuania does not have an immediate development problem—it has a unique development opportunity.*

For the country to make the most of that opportunity, this report proposes a policy agenda driven by two overarching objectives: the elimination of the remaining structural sources of macroeconomic imbalance and the rapid shifting of boundaries between the private and the public sectors—both in production and in investment and saving—as means to instill efficiency and to move the country to a higher long-term growth plateau.

To achieve the first objective, policymakers must end the direct and indirect fiscal drains associated with the resolution of pending banking problems, inefficient performance in state-controlled energy companies, poor municipal finance, and the remaining distortions in the agriculture sector. In other words, the first target of the new reform agenda should be to do away—permanently—with the operating deficit of the "quasi-public" sector (that is, the aggregate financial performance of the general government, the public energy sector, strategic public enterprises, farmers, pensioners, and the other sectors and interest groups that are, in effect, financially dependent on the state).

The second target of the new reform agenda—an efficiency-led increase in long-term growth—will require reforms in the legal, regulatory, and institutional frameworks, not only for privatization and private sector initiative, but also for the operation of the pension system and the development of the securities market. The core idea behind this element of the agenda is to place the allocation of the country's resources fully in the charge of profit-driven, private initiative. Freed to accumulate and invest their own long-term savings, private owners should, through their dealings in the securities market, put increased pressure on the managers of private and newly privatized firms to perform. The ensuing efficiency gains should bring the economy onto a faster growth path.

LITHUANIA–FISCAL YEAR

January 1–December 31

CURRENCY EQUIVALENTS

(as of 20 April 1998)
Currency Unit = Litas
4 Litai = US$1

WEIGHTS AND MEASURES

Metric System

ABBREVIATIONS AND ACRONYMS

ADR	American Depository Receipt	LPC	Lithuania Power Company
BFTA	Baltic Free Trade Agreement	LPG	Liquefied petroleum gas
BNM	Basic nontaxable minimum	MCF	Municipal Credit Facility
BoL	Bank of Lithuania	MEA	Minister of European Affairs
BSD	Bank Supervision Department	MFN	Most-favored nation
CAA	Court Administration Agency	MMPP	Minimal marginal purchase price
CEEC	Central and eastern European countries	MPARLA	Ministry of Public Reform and Local Authorities
CEFTA	Central European Free Trade Association	MoAF	Ministry of Agriculture and Forestry
CHP	Combined heat and power	MoJ	Ministry of Justice
CIS	Commonwealth of Independent States	MSL	Minimum Subsistence Level
CIT	Corporation income tax	MSSL	Ministry of Social Security and Labor
CSDL	Central Securities Depository	mtoe	Million tons of oil equivalent
DCF	Discounted cash flow method	MVV	Mannheimer Versorgungs-und
DH	District heating		Verkehrsgesellschaft NGH
DOD	Debt outstanding and disbursed	MW	Mega-watt
EFTA	European Free Trade Association	NAP	National Agricultural Program
EPC	Energy Pricing Commission	NDC	National Defined Contribution Accounts
ESR	Energy sector review	NOCs	Notional Defined Contribution Accounts
EBRD	European Bank for Reconstruction	NSEL	National Stock Exchange of Lithuania
	and Development	OECD	Organization for Economic Cooperation and
EU	European Union		Development
FDI	Foreign direct investment	PADP	Private Agricultural Development Program
FSU	Former Soviet Union	PAYGO	Pay as you go
GAO	Gross agricultural output	PIT	Personal income tax
GATT	General Agreement on Tariffs and Trade	PJ	Petajoules
Gcal	Giga-calorie	PPP	Purchasing power parity
GDP	Gross domestic product	PSD	Private sector development
GDR	Global Depository Receipt	PSEs	Producer Subsidy Equivalents
GoL	Government of Lithuania	RSF	Rural Support Fund
HOB	Heat-only boiler	SAL	Structural Adjustment Loan
IAS	International accounting standards	SEM	Small and medium-size
ICOR	Incremental capital output ratio	SODRA	Social Insurance Fund
IEA	International Energy Agency	SRP	Savings Restitution Plan
IFC	International Finance Corporation	TB	Treasury bills
INPP	Ignalina Nuclear Power Plant	Tcal	Tetra-calorie
IPO	Initial public offering	TMCF	Transitional Municipal Credit Facility
IPS	Interconnected Power System	TOE	Tons of oil equivalent
ISA	International Standards on Audit	Twh	Tetra-watt
KLASC	Klaipeda Stevedoring	UNDP	United Nations Development Program
ktoe	Thousand tons of oil equivalent	USAID	United States Agency for International
Kwh	Kilowatt		Development
LAAI	Lithuanian Auditing and Accounting Institute	VAT	Value added tax
LG	Lithuania Gas Company	VICA	Vilnius International Commercial Arbitration
LIA	Lithuanian Investment Agency	WTO	World Trade Organization
LISCO	Lithuanian Shipping	XGS	Exports of goods and nonfactor services
LLA	Lithuania Lawyers Association		

1

BANKING

Lithuania's banking sector has survived the (expected) difficult initial transition adjustments and has emerged stronger as a result of the process. The rapid increase in the number of banks following the collapse of the Soviet Union led to the creation of many "pocket" banks that were subsequently closed, with little systemic impact. In addition, in late December 1995, the largest private bank and three others, together representing a quarter of the total banking system's assets, were placed in "moratorium." Consolidation through failure has led to a greatly reduced number of much stronger banks.

After an initial period of excessive branch expansion, the remaining banks have begun a process of branch and staffing rationalization. With the help of twinning partners and other donor programs, management systems and asset generation quality have improved. Traditional sources of revenue—currency speculation and trading and high-margin lending—have been replaced by more traditional banking activities.

From a public policy viewpoint, several positive steps have enhanced the safety and soundness of the sector. The Bank of Lithuania (BoL) has received and absorbed invaluable training from advisers. The introduction of international accounting standards and Basle capital rules has been completed. The BoL has adopted more stringent large exposure and connected lending rules. All banks are regularly examined, and it is now BoL policy (in the absence of laws to the contrary) to revoke the license of any bank that fails to comply with prudential standards. The government and the banking sector have begun to fund a deposit insurance fund to protect individual deposits.

Despite this progress, several key policy issues remain unresolved. After an initial, partial privatization effort, the state-controlled banks continue to face major problems in corporate governance. The state banks are undercapitalized (Seimas having passed a law overriding the BoL regarding license revocation policy for banks on their way "to privatization") to some degree. The banks continue to be used as sources of government funding and programs. The government has decided to privatize the two remaining state banks, but it has not yet devised a plan to privatize the Savings Bank, which has the largest concentration of individual deposits in the country and is the largest buyer of treasury bills (TBs).

Undue political influence and interference still operate in the sector, influencing not only the investments and management of the state-controlled banks, but also BoL supervisory responsibility. BoL's independence is frequently threatened by actions of Seimas and the government that affect specific banks and banking issues.

The legal and institutional framework for the supervision of banks and their provision of services could be enhanced. The Central Bank Law and the Commercial Bank Law have been improved, but often in a patchwork fashion in a response to a given event. A comprehensive revision to both laws that focuses on impediments to supervisory action, problem bank resolutions, and the independence of BoL is warranted. Lithuania's credit laws are generally debtor-friendly. As banks have become more knowledgeable about lending techniques, these laws have restricted credit growth. Recent amendments to the Bankruptcy Law and the proposed establishment of lien registries are improvements. Other impediments remain. The inability of banks to take title to land in foreclosure and lengthy foreclosure processes for property (especially moveables) have caused banks to either not lend or to develop complicated alternatives. The deposit insurance fund is in its infancy. Recent amendments that expanded coverage with complicated coinsurance schedules may strain the ability of the sector to provide adequate reserves and avoid moral hazard. In addition, there is no statutory link outlining the fund's role in maximizing the recovery of expended funds in failed banks.

History and Recent Developments

Evolution of the Banking Sector

The banking sector has undergone dramatic change since 1994. Traditional sources of profitability, currency trading and exchange profits, have significantly diminished. Net interest margins appreciably declined as litas lending rates dropped from 80 percent to about 15 percent annually, and the cost of funds went from 70 percent a year and 18 percent a year (time and demand rates, respectively) to 10 percent a year and 3 percent a year. Loan-loss provisioning, both from the carryover from pre-1994 lending and from loans originated since 1994, eliminated most of the profit from the system. The first basic provisioning regulation, introduced by BoL in 1994, began the process of loss recognition. Strengthened enforcement of this regulation during 1995 and 1996 made transparent the dangerous depth of capital deterioration among banks. Fraud and other insider abuse, combined with socially and politically directed lending, added to the losses in the system. All of these factors reduced profitability to a point where high personnel costs and branch facility cost could no longer be supported.

That contraction in profitability forced a major consolidation in the industry through bank failures. At the beginning of 1994, there were twenty-seven operating banks in Lithuania; by April 1998, only ten banks remained in operation (State Commercial Bank was liquidated in March 1998 and its assets transferred to the Savings Bank, and in part to the work-out unit, Turto Bankas). While many of the banks that disappeared were small pocket banks, beginning in the summer of 1995, problems in larger banks became known to the public.[1] Depositors (including government) began to withdraw funds from weaker banks, and by late December 1995, a full banking "crisis" emerged. Two private banks (Innovation and Litimpeks), including the county's largest, were simultaneously unable to meet depositor liquidity demands. During the period from June 1995 to December 1995, moratoriums were placed on four private banks: Aura (Lt 100 million in deposits), Vakaru (Lt 200 million), Innovation (Lt 600 million), and Litimpeks (Lt 200 million). These banks represented a quarter of the post-crisis funding of the system. In addition, all other banks in the system, including the state-controlled banks, required capital infusions to remain solvent.

The public's response to the system's troubles was a flight to perceived quality, as local deposits moved to the perceived safety of the state-controlled banks (where their deposits were fully insured by the government). Foreign deposits without long-term commitment temporarily left the system.

---

1. Lithuania currently has one bank per 350,000 population, as compared with the following countries (population per bank; see Annex for other country comparisons): Argentina, 160,000; Bulgaria, 340,000; Canada, 550,000; Hungary, 280,000; Japan, 550,000; Latvia, 135,000; Russia, 75,000; Turkey, 900,000; United States, 25,000.

The government responded to the crisis with a three-pronged program: (a) the enactment of an emergency deposit insurance scheme providing limited coverage to individual deposits in all banks, (b) provision of limited liquidity support for banks, and (c) the granting of a full government guarantee of all deposits and creditors of two banks under moratorium (Innovation and Litimpeks). The government and BoL were unable to resolve the crisis involving the four troubled banks quickly, however, because there was no planned approach to deal with a banking emergency, the banking laws were deficient, and the constituencies of the four banks sponsored political interventions. Aura (with most of its depositors being government agencies) was transformed into Turto Bank, a government-owned workout unit, and its private depositors were fully compensated in the summer of 1996. Vakaru was placed into bankruptcy in September 1996, and its individual depositors were compensated according to the emergency deposit insurance law. Litimpeks reopened in May 1996, because enough depositors elected to convert their deposits to equity to meet the prevailing BoL capital rules, based on Lithuanian accounting practices. Nevertheless, the bank remained deeply insolvent under IAS (international accounting standards) and was unable to attract new business. BoL gave the bank until June 1997 to comply with prudential rules. The bank reached compliance, but it has been struggling to achieve profitable operations and to remain in compliance. Innovation's resolution was hampered by the law guaranteeing all deposits and the resulting fiscal cost to the government of its deep insolvency. In addition, the Seimas passed a series of laws, including one that required Innovation to reopen, one that required deposit conversion before the government could recapitalize, and, finally, one that established a new compensation scheme, overriding all previously passed laws. In the summer of 1997, Innovation's license was revoked; its depositors will receive minimal cash compensation and non-interest-bearing government bonds (with maturities of five to ten years, depending on the legal nature of the depositor).

BoL also began a program of enhanced regulation and supervision. New rules regarding large exposure, connected lending, and loan provisioning were introduced. ISA (international standard of audit) audits were demanded of all banks, and IAS and Basle capital rules were implemented as of 1 January 1997. While the previous Lithuanian accounting standards were in place as of 31 December 1996, BoL required all banks to publish IAS financial statements in the local press. In addition, BoL's Banking Supervision Department (BSD) has implemented an early warning system that evaluates the current status of the banking system and foresees trends. On-call audits are carried out by international audit firms at the instigation of the BSD on an on-going basis.

During the summer of 1996, the State Commercial Bank experienced liquidity pressure as an apparent result of the spreading news of a recent BoL examination. The government was forced to inject both capital and liquidity into the bank; it increased the bank's capital by Lt 165 million (146 million in treasury securities, the balance in cash and property). The government also ordered all state agencies to transfer their bank accounts to State Commercial. As a result, by the end of 1996, 65 percent (over Lt 475 million) of the funding of the bank was government or government-related. The bank continued to be subject to partial moratorium and its condition was becoming progressively worse. After two failed privatization efforts and unsuccessful discussions with EBRD about the rescue of the bank, in March 1998 the government was forced to decide about liquidation of the bank. Its good assets and all liabilities were tranferred to the Savings Bank. The government contributed Lt 180 million in nontradable restructuring bonds to equalize the transfer. Bad loans were transferred to the work-out unit.

While total funding of the banking system has grown by Lt 500 million since the end of 1995 (after a 20 percent growth in 1994), private sector funding has not increased. Ninety percent of the system's funding is from domestic sources, indicating a lack of confidence and/or interest by foreign-based bank customers. Similarly, while total fund deployment in earning assets has increased by Lt one billion since 1995, the entire increase is the product of bank investments in treasury bills and monetary instruments of foreign banks. Lending to the private sector has actually declined slightly in nominal terms (see table 1-1). This lack of real growth is the result of many factors, but most prominently: (a) the absence of depositor confidence following the banking crisis and the government's inability to quickly resolve insolvencies; (b) greater experience by the private bankers in evaluating credits and screening out bad borrowers; (c) strengthened prudential rules regarding provisioning; and (d) lack of an effective legal system for securing collateral and resolving troubled credits.

Table 1-1. The Lithuanian Banking Sector, 1994–March 1997: Selected Information

	1994	1995	1996	March 1997
Number of banks (1993 = 27)	22	12	12	12
Number of branches	253	250	232	239
Funding sources				
Nonbank public	542	378	278	292
Private sector	2,342	3,203	3,268	3,326
National and local government, central bank	956	1,480	1,537	1,763
Nonmonetary financial institution	47	39	28	34
Counterpart funds	28	53	59	55
Nonresident banks	87	157	416	239
Nonresident	244	235	389	382
Total selected funding sources	4,245	5,545	5,975	6,091
Utilization of funds				
Claims on nonresident banks	371	396	861	887
Claims on nonresidents	16	97	295	132
Claims on central government	241	510	862	1,002
Claims on local government	2	8	62	20
Claims on public enterprises	399	238	139	248
Claims on private sector	3,009	3,816	3,666	3,710
Claims on nonmonetary financial institutions	10	19	12	28
Total selected utilization	4,047	5,082	5,897	6,027

Industry Segments

The industry is divided into two segments, state-controlled banks and private banks. The state-controlled banks hold 58 percent of the total system funding, but this figure drops to 38 percent if government deposits are excluded. The government, by necessity in some cases, contributes a quarter of the funding of the entire system. While this appears to leave considerable room for the private banking sector, the state-controlled banks still hold three-quarters of individual deposits. The only major funding category that private banks control is private enterprise deposits (65 percent), and they hold almost all the foreign funding (albeit a very small amount; see table 1-2).

STATE-CONTROLLED BANKS. The Savings Bank is the largest retail bank in Lithuania. It has 44 branches, over 439 "subbranches," and 3,420 employees. During 1996, the bank closed 10 branches and 119 subbranches and reduced its employees by 408, and in 1997 the number of branches and employees was further reduced. The bank is 75 percent owned by the government, has total assets of about Lt 2.7 billion (including assets transferred from State Commercial Bank), and holds 60 percent of the individual deposits in the country. It serves as a distribution system for government payments. In August 1995, a special limitation on lending was imposed by the government (as owner). The liquidity created by this moratorium and a significant increase in individual deposits during the banking crisis have been invested primarily in TB and other bank instruments; the bank is currently the largest holder (and most active participant in the auction) of treasury bills. The chairman and the management board were replaced in August of 1997. At the end of 1997, the bank met BoL capital rules, but it is questionable whether the bank was capital-adequate under IAS. The government is increasing the capital of the bank to ensure IAS compliance. The bank showed a modest profit in 1997, but only after a write-up of certain government receivables, for which the IAS audit expressed a qualification (see table 1-3 for IAS financial statements for 1997).

Table 1-2. Lithuanian Banking System: Sources of Funding, March 1997
(Lt million)

Source	Commercial Bank	Savings Bank	Agriculture Bank	Total, state banks	Operating, private banks	Total system	State banks (percent)
Central Bank	19,976	0	68,222	88,198	63,940	152,138	58
Other banks	46,682	4,213	9,442	60,337	305,961	366,298	16
Government	524,116	43,201	509,859	1,077,176	356,623	1,433,799	75
State enterprises	52,026	8,657	50,129	110,812	85,442	196,254	56
Private, nonindividual	116,341	134,998	303,616	554,955	1,027,859	1,582,814	35
Private individual	90,231	953,673	219,434	1,263,338	418,395	1,681,733	75
Total funding	849,372	1,144,742	1,160,702	3,154,816	2,258,220	5,413,036	58
Funds in state-controlled banks[a]							38
Total funding, direct from government							26
Domestic versus foreign							
Central bank, government, and state enterprises	596,118	51,858	628,210	1,276,186	506,005	1,782,191	72
Domestic banks	1,218	4,196	9,437	14,851	123,862	138,713	11
Domestic private sector	198,082	1,088,671	522,504	1,809,257	1,165,186	2,974,443	61
Total domestic	795,418	1,144,725	1,160,151	3,100,294	1,795,053	4,895,347	63
Foreign banks	45,464	17	5	45,486	182,099	227,585	20
Foreign private sector	8,490	0	546	9,036	281,068	290,104	3
Total foreign	53,954	17	551	54,522	463,167	517,689	11
Total	849,372	1,144,742	1,160,702	3,154,816	2,258,220	5,413,036	
Domestic to total funding (%)	94	100	100	98	79	90	

a. Excluding government deposits.

The Agricultural Bank is the largest bank in Lithuania in total funding. It has 46 branches and 2,400 employees. The bank is 86 percent owned by the government, and has total assets worth Lt 1.5 billion. Almost half of the bank's funding is supplied by the government, including significant amounts earmarked to support special lending programs to benefit the agricultural sector. The bank suffered a loss of Lt 32 million in 1997. As a result, it did not meet the capital or large exposure regulations at the end of the year. According to qualifications expressed by the international auditors, the bank is capital deficient. A Lt 40 million capital increase is in progress. The prior management board has been replaced. These actions have hampered privatization efforts. Advisers have prepared a revised tender, which they have planned to have in place by June–July 1998.

PRIVATE BANKS. There are eight private banks in Lithuania. Vilnius Bank is the largest private bank, with over Lt 1,800 million in assets, and it has experienced significant growth since the end of 1995. Hermis Bank (Lt 1,200 million in assets) competes with Vilnius for both the individual and private enterprise customers in the Vilnius market and in other major commercial centers. Both banks, with

Table 1-3. IAS Financial Information (excludes failed banks), 31 December 1997

Item	Commercial	Agricultural	Savings	Hermis	Vilniaus	Ukio	Snoras	Litimpeks	Tauro	Siaulai	Medicino	Industry	Total
Balance Sheets													
Assets													
Cash	15,220	94,440	51,065	37,407	65,631	12,392	45,459	11,548	0	9,747	1,917	1,636	346,462
Balances due from BoL	19,233	35,138	127,421	104,408	173,846	30,043	12,955	20,157	0	12,446	4,566	11,014	551,227
Balances due from other banks	47,993	121,808	116,193	186,483	269,781	23,491	364,050	24,525	0	12,755	12,954	15,471	1,195,504
Reserve for loss	(17,910)	0	0										(17,910)
Loans	599,382	974,589	698,936	552,293	984,007	131,257	39,678	102,406	0	58,257	42,187	16,150	4,199,088
Reserve for losses	(309,623)	(221,551)	(26,838)	(39,829)	(62,305)	(45,403)	(4,518)	(27,551)	0	(4,328)	(12,666)		(754,612)
Short term government securities	147,314	253,803	503,690	163,664	209,659	7,184	43,525	4,217	0	15,153	2,740	13,978	1,364,927
Investments	166,006	16,905	105,649	6,007	76,914	0	2,215	566	0	2,491	1,189	1,005	378,947
Accrued income + other assets	33,763	84,037	61,470	70,685	20,569	37,074	28,901	19,705	0	14,717	7,098	2,152	380,171
Reserve for loss	(5,424)		(6,499)	0		(7,671)							(19,594)
Fixed assets	71,537	96,608	207,674	71,338	98,098	22,059	61,942	65,942	0	7,162	9,217	8,975	720,552
Total Assets	772,861	1,450,353	1,838,761	1,152,456	1,836,200	210,426	594,207	221,515	0	128,400	69,202	70,381	8,344,762
Liabilities and Capital													
Due to BoL	10,030	29,913	0	4,845	9,898	5,582		2,210		7,857			70,335
Due to other banks	98,689	16,908	3,020	139,190	432,138	14,083	43,185	6,233	0	15,981	16,853	6,000	792,280
Due to Lithuanian government	0	402,180	0										402,180
Deposits	769,430	904,619	1,663,529	834,343	1,164,209	156,934	477,173	171,222	0	66,747	34,699	36,962	6,279,867
Other liabilities	23,169	19,195	97,051	11,627	57,462	6,426	30,502	23,130	0	1,590	3,702	1,704	275,558
Subordinated debt	0		0		8,000		14,000	0					22,000
Total liabilities	901,318	1,372,815	1,763,600	990,005	1,671,707	183,025	564,860	202,795	0	92,175	55,254	44,666	7,842,220
Share capital	165,000	170,896	60,000	88,400	102,000	60,000	27,000	66,396	0	32,972	26,147	27,000	825,811
Reserve	(293,457)	(93,358)	15,161	74,051	62,493	(32,599)	2,347	(47,676)	0	3,253	(12,199)	(1,285)	(323,269)
Total capital	(128,457)	77,538	75,161	162,451	164,493	27,401	29,347	18,270	0	36,225	13,948	25,715	502,542
Total liabilities and capital	772,861	1,450,353	1,838,761	1,152,456	1,836,200	210,426	594,207	221,515	0	128,400	69,202	70,381	8,344,762

Table 1-3. IAS Financial Information (excludes failed banks), 31 December 1997 (continued)

Item	Commercial	Agricultural	Savings	Hermis	Vilniaus	Ukio	Snoras	Litimpeks	Tauro	Siaulai	Medicino	Industry	Total
Income Statements													
Interest income	56,345	118,324	109,514	72,995	110,712	13,284	41,523	9,658	0	9,392	4,596	2,850	549,193
Interest expense	31,278	41,963	45,145	23,173	32,103	11,246	26,769	9,122	0	3,821	2,139	475	227,234
Net interest income	25,067	76,361	64,369	49,822	78,609	2,038	14,754	536	0	5,571	2,457	2,372	321,959
Fees and commissions	7,851	17,562	42,997	25,823	47,739	6,048	7,223	3,096	0	523	1,031	552	160,445
Foreign exchange	4,437	7,412	10,420	10,042	18,650	5,532	20,289	5,432	0	1,503	1,693	391	85,801
Investment Activites	7,365	10,168					8,427						
Other operating income	1	12,912	379	155	(96)			161		(542)	(9)	2	12,963
Total income	44,721	124,415	118,165	85,842	144,902	13,618	50,693	9,225	0	7,055	5,172	3,320	581,168
Provision for losses	87,476	57,524	3,877	10,246	16,230	18,852	308	(6,393)	0	302	102		188,524
Salaries and wages	28,393	55,899	62,869	28,060	42,981	9,431	26,401	11,777	0	3,032	2,528	2,796	274,167
Depreciation	6,698	12,407	7,589	2,959	7,323	1,929	3,642	2,786	0	458	390	578	46,759
Other administrative expense	8,833	32,027	36,475	17,384	30,466	8,254	17,934	4,605	0	1,307	1,501	1,251	160,037
Valuation of foreclosed assets	(1,909)	(602)	2,149	(259)				(317)					(938)
Write-off of uncollectible assets	0	0	0			3,000							3,000
Profit before tax	(84,770)	(32,840)	5,206	27,452	47,902	(27,848)	2,408	(3,233)	0	1,956	651	(1,305)	(90,381)
Tax	0	0	0	0	324	0	1,320	0	0	0	262	0	1,906
Profit after tax	(84,770)	(32,840)	5,206	27,452	47,578	(27,848)	1,088	(3,233)	0	1,956	389	(1,305)	(92,287)

7

major institutional and strategic foreign investors, have been able to attract both customers and capital during the period following the banking crisis. Recently, Vilnius Bank applied to the Bank of Lithuania to acquire a 45 percent stake in Hermis Bank. The Bank of Lithuania has delayed approval of the application for somewhat dubious reasons. At the same time, Litimpeks and Ukio have suffered deposit declines and have generally fallen behind in the marketplace. Litimpeks still depends on partial government funding support. Snoras Bank, which has grown rapidly, primarily by investing in the foreign interbank market, has a sustained record of profitability. In an effort to attract more local consumer deposits, Snoras has recently opened the first group of unmanned banking kiosks at several locations, an innovation in the Lithuanian banking market. Siauliai Bank, located in Siauliai, primarily serves its unique geographic market. The remaining two banks are small institutions, primarily serving specific niches. (See table 1-3 for IAS financial statements for all private banks.)

Deposit Insurance Protection

Until the banking crisis in December 1995, the only legal basis for deposit protection was in the country's Civil Code, which provided 100 percent protection for individual deposits in state-controlled banks. Private banks' deposits were not afforded deposit protection. During the banking crisis, Seimas passed several laws related to deposit protection. First, it passed a measure insuring individual deposits in all banks up to a balance of Lt 5,000, with a 20 percent coinsurance provision. This law provided for the creation of a deposit insurance fund, a methodology for financing the fund, and membership criteria for qualifying banks. Second, Seimas passed a law fully guaranteeing the creditors (including deposits) of Innovation and Litimpeks "with all the assets of the state," but this law was rather vague concerning the method and time of payment. Third, a temporary law was passed to compensate all deposits up to Lt 5,000 (with a 20 percent coinsurance provision) in bankrupt banks. This law was intended to provide deposit protection for banks that had declared bankruptcy before the general deposit insurance law became effective, as well as (during the period of effectiveness of the law) deposits in banks that did not qualify for membership in the newly enacted deposit insurance fund. According to the Ministry of Finance, this law has expired.

The Seimas has since passed several laws that affected deposit insurance coverage. Late in the summer of 1996, it revised the special Litimpeks and Innovation law to remove coverage for Litimpeks deposits (the bank had been allowed to reopen) and to modify the Innovation provisions to provide for termination of the coverage unless 40 percent of the litas amount of deposits was converted to equity by 1 December 1996. In April 1997, the special provisions for Innovation were again amended, this time to provide for a payment mechanism. Individual depositors will receive up to Lt 8,000 in cash over a period ending in 1998, and any excess balance will be paid in five-year, non-interest-bearing bonds; nonindividual accounts would receive ten-year, non-interest-bearing bonds. In the spring of 1997, Seimas passed a law revoking the Civil Code provisions that granted 100 percent deposit protection for individual deposits in state-controlled banks, thus removing the unfair advantage of these banks over private institutions in the competition for individual deposits.

In May 1997 the government finally funded the deposit insurance fund. At the end of 1997, the fund had a balance of Lt 48 million (including Lt 21 million in insurance premiums paid by the banks). The government will contribute an additional Lt 20 million in 1998. Monthly insurance premiums are expected to be approximately Lt 2.4 million in 1998. The government will contribute Lt 30 million in 1998. Premium revenue is approximately Lt 2 million monthly based on current premiums of 1.5 percent of individual deposits. In July 1997 Seimas passed a law to increase the level of deposit coverage and decrease the premiums paid by banks. This new law introduces two sliding scales—first, the deposit coverage is increased, beginning at Lt 25,000 in 1998 and rising to Lt 65,000 in 2000; second, the amount of coinsurance is increased, depending on the amount of the deposit (the amounts differ for domestic and foreign currencies). For example, in the year 2000, the first Lt 25,000 will be 100 percent insured; the next 20,000, 90 percent insured; and the top 20,000, 70 percent insured. If the same deposit were in a foreign currency, the coverage would be 90 percent, 80 percent, and 60 percent, respectively. Premiums paid by banks are scheduled to be reduced to 1 percent of individual deposits in 2000.

Regulatory Structure

The banking system is regulated by BoL under the authority of the Law on the Bank of Lithuania. While several laws apply to the formation, operation, and liquidation of banks, the basic governing law is the Law on Commercial Banks. This law has been subject to constant and repetitive amendment since its introduction in 1994. BoL has the authority under many provisions to issue regulations to carry out the intent of the law.

Under the framework of these laws, BoL supervises banks through the operation of its BSD, which is staffed by fifty-three employees (increased from seventeen in 1993), twenty of whom are bank examiners (increased from five). The staff has received advice and training from on-site advisers, participated in a range of technical seminars, and received training abroad. The BSD is charged with the responsibility to examine banks and to report to the BoL board. This board, composed of fourteen members, is the decisionmaking body for any actions to be taken against banks. All examination reports, proposed administrative actions, imposition of restrictions on activities, and bank closings must be approved by the board.

The BoL has been aggressive in improving regulations since the end of 1995. The adoption of IAS (for all regulatory purposes) and the bank capital adequacy rules are most noteworthy. New, strengthened provisioning regulations and currency exposure reporting rules have been imposed. Large exposure and connected lending rules have been tightened, and the definition of borrower and connected person expanded.

Key Medium- and Long-Term Policy Issues

Excessive Political Interference in the Banking System

The banking sector remains subject to excessive political influence and control. This has seriously hampered BSD's ability to consistently supervise banks, allowed for inconsistent treatment of banks, undermined the transparency of the system, and thwarted privatization efforts. Politically and socially motivated lending, while reduced in volume, is still present. Laws and policies that favor or penalize specific banks, their depositors and customers, or their shareholders continue to be part of the system. That influence has taken several forms.

INDEPENDENCE OF THE CENTRAL BANK. The independence (both in principle and practice) of BoL is, at best, not apparent in Lithuania. The BoL board is structured to allow for government knowledge and influence. A few notable recent actions illustrate the situation:

- In 1997, BoL adopted IAS and tougher capital requirements and announced that any bank that did not meet the requirements would have its license revoked. The determination would be made on the basis of March 1997 data. In April 1997, Seimas passed a law exempting the state-owned Commercial Bank (then deeply insolvent) and the Agricultural Bank (undercapitalized) from the BoL rules, effectively eliminating the country's largest and fourth-largest banks (a quarter of the system's assets) from supervisory action until (and if) the banks are privatized.

- The BSD has proposed fourteen monetary sanctions against banks and bankers in the last year. Only two have been approved by the fourteen-member board of BoL. Those serving on the board include members of the business community and a representative of the Bankers' Association.

- BoL receives numerous inquiries from both government and Seimas for information. Some of these requests involve bank-specific information that by law and rule is not to be made public by BoL. Failure to respond to such requests, however, is viewed as noncooperation and incompetence on the part of BoL. Responding to such requests risks not only potential violations of law, but also inappropriate public disclosure of the information (often incomplete or inaccurately interpreted), which can lead to damage to the financial sector.

- In 1997 Seimas passed an amendment to the Commercial Banking Law regarding the duties and responsibilities of temporary administrators. The law specified that temporary administrators reported directly to BoL. Through the temporary administrator, the board of BoL assumed duties and responsibilities of the board and council (and in some matters, shareholders) of the administered bank. The law also provided, however, that all significant actions of a temporary administrator in a state-controlled bank must be approved by the government, thereby ceding significant supervisory and management authority to the government (which controlled the troubled bank council before the appointment of an administrator), while BoL retained all the responsibility.

- Government policies that limit compensation and expand background clearance of members of BoL's board and staff further undermine their commitment to act independently of political considerations.

BANK-SPECIFIC LAWS. The practice of proposing and enacting laws that target individual banks, and selected issues surrounding those banks, needs to be stopped. This practice creates the impression of a lack of foresight on the part of government, inadequacy in the existing laws, and/or political intrigue in the application of laws and policies. It also rewards inappropriate actions in the banking sector and raises competitive issues for well-run banks, ultimately promoting inequitable treatment of banks (explained further below).

The Innovation resolution is representative of this issue. After BoL placed a moratorium on Innovation Bank (a deeply insolvent bank), Seimas passed an emergency deposit insurance law partially insuring deposits in all banks up to Lt 5,000. At the same time, Seimas passed a law guaranteeing, in full, all creditors (including all deposits) in Innovation Bank. These two laws not only did not reassure the market (their alleged purpose) but also sent a clear signal that political forces were at work—forces that undermined the authority of BoL. The subsequent series of special Innovation laws, which required that Innovation be reopened (clearly giving preference to large, influential depositors) and its creditor guarantee be made contingent upon deposit conversion, as well as the eventual modification of its creditor compensation scheme in 1997, effectively foreclosed the mandated actions by BoL under the existing statutes. In the end, all of this prolonged the resolution of Innovation's problems through liquidation and created additional fiscal and political costs for the government.

In another notable example, BoL issued enhanced capital adequacy regulations in 1997 to strengthen the banking sector's solvency position. All banks knew of these new requirements well in advance of the effective enforcement date, including the possibility that BoL would revoke the licenses of any banks that failed to comply. The well-run private banks all met these new rules by raising capital in advance of the enforcement date. Yet, when it became apparent that two of the state-controlled banks would not meet the requirements, Seimas passed a law effectively exempting these banks from BoL corrective actions until they were privatized. The seeming reluctance of the government (as controlling shareholder) to assure compliance by its banks and the apparent will of the government (as regulator) to override internationally accepted banking standards creates, at the least, an uneven playing field for the banking sector. The rules apparently do not apply to the biggest players, and BoL can be overridden when it imposes the same discipline and cost on government (as a shareholder) as on the private sector. At worst, this indicates that political expediency overrides financial reality. In addition, such actions undermine privatization of state-owned banks. Overt political interference and lack of financial discipline decrease the willingness of market-oriented investors to buy equity in the banks in question.

FUNDING SUPPORT FOR TROUBLED BANKS. BoL has adopted more stringent guidelines on the use of its funding for troubled banks. These requirements, common in most industrial countries, include the requirement that BoL advances be collateralized; this renders BoL unable to fund the liquidity needs of a bank with uncollateralized advances, as was done in the cases of Innovation, Litimpeks, and other formerly troubled banks. In addition, the guidelines require short-term repayment of advances, which historically had not been repaid. Because these guidelines have removed a source of unsecured, long-term funding support, troubled banks have turned to the government.

For example, the government publicly committed not to provide any additional funding support for Litimpeks upon its reopening in 1996 and required the repayment of the outstanding government deposits by the end of 1996. Nevertheless, little repayment was received. While the government did not directly provide additional support, state-owned enterprises increased their funding, while the private sector withdrew funds. This could be understood by the market as either total disregard by the state-owned enterprises of the financial condition of the bank or political direction by the government—both perceptions could have resulted in a loss of funds or value to the government.

In another example, during 1996 the State Commercial Bank realized significant losses and experienced a funding crisis. When the bank's problem became known, the government ordered public authorities and agencies to move their deposits to the bank to minimize its liquidity problem. The effective funding of private sector deposit withdrawals with government deposits is essentially a full guarantee of the withdrawn private deposits and permits a "preference" (under the deposit insurance scheme) to the withdrawing depositors over both the remaining depositors and depositors of other banks. It can be argued that the funding was placed by the government in its role as shareholder—if so, the government should have placed significant funds in capital, as opposed to a deposit account, because the capital needs of the bank must also be met by the shareholder. As capital, the funds would allow the bank to meet prudential guidelines and permit the government to avoid the appearance of continuing to fund insolvent banks. Funds invested in capital would also represent a budget expenditure, however, something the government may have not been able to afford.

In at least two other cases (Aura and Tauro), the government and related agencies have concentrated deposits in banks so heavily that they became the banks' largest class of depositors. Such a high concentration of deposits without financial diligence on the part of the depositor (especially the government) or competitive bidding creates the impression of political motivation. Subsequent direct requests to BoL for information and assurances of the quality of the bank also impinge on BoL independence and could be perceived as a violation of law.

DIRECTED FUNDING. The government has historically directed funds to state-controlled banks for use in lending programs designed to support selected sectors of the economy. These programs were primarily directed toward agriculture and housing (as of 31 December 1996, 20 percent and 29 percent of State Commercial Bank and Agricultural Bank loans, respectively, were directed lending, and 20 percent and 30 percent, respectively, of the banks' funding was directed funding). The banks used these funds to provide loans that could not otherwise be obtained in the market to selected sectors—for instance, long-term loans for housing at subsidized interest rates. The bank could generally earn a spread of 5 percent over the cost of funding and would be responsible for the credit risk. Under these programs, the government has provided the funds at no, or low, interest rates. The banks historically had little or no say in the loan process. As a result, the maximum margin the bank could make was more than offset by credit losses. In one program, the government ordered a suspension of loan servicing to aid debtor farm processors. The agriculture programs were essentially stopped in 1997, with the government guaranteeing the remaining balance of program loans (by government decree, the bank could offset specific provisions against the funding balance). The housing program continues. Considering the credit losses, limited margin, and implied capital utilization, the banks do not see this activity as profitable. While most countries provide support for policy initiatives, such programs are usually structured so that the private sectors (in this case, banks) can choose to participate or not, and they can reasonably expect to earn a profit. Because the Lithuanian programs are carried out only in state-controlled banks, there is a strong presumption that government policy costs are being borne "off budget" at the expense of the banking system.

SALARY LIMITATIONS IN STATE-CONTROLLED BANKS. In June 1997, the government decreed that salaries of executives in state-controlled banks would be determined by a formula and tied to government employee salaries. The highest-paid bank employee (the chairman) could make approximately Lt 4,000 monthly (roughly the salary of an assistant department head in a private bank). This proposal affects virtually every board member of every state-controlled bank. All employees under long-term contracts at higher amounts were asked to renegotiate their contracts to bring their salaries into line with the new framework. Refusal meant facing the threat of dismissal, with relief from the courts for their contractual compensation. Bank directors owe a fiduciary responsibility, not to specific shareholders, but to the shareholders as a group, to the institution, and to the depositors. Representing one shareholder's interest against the best interest of the other constituencies is a serious breech of fiduciary duty. By dictating instructions to bank council members, the government undermines their ability to act in the best interest of the institution. By lowering salaries to civil service levels without consideration of the impact on the competitive position of the institutions, the government has placed the two largest banks in the country in potential financial peril, because experienced management will seek other opportunities. The government has indicated that the reason for the lowering of salaries was to bring cost/revenue ratios in line with the private sector and to reflect the lack of generally acceptable performance. The way to address these issues, of course, is through a strategic business plan, the hiring of professionally competent leadership at competitive compensation, and the removal of political operations from the banks, not through a wholesale reduction of board salaries that may lead to the mass resignation of competent senior management. In addition, major cost reduction is not to be found in cutting board salaries, but in a thorough evaluation of all staff and branch facility costs. If the council believes management salaries are too high, the council, not government, should compare them with the total compensation of similar positions in the industry, not in government. If a board member is not performing according to the bank's strategic plan, the proper action is to replace the individual board member, not to reduce salaries for the entire board.

Ironically, state-controlled banks covered by this proposal had one of their best performance years, and both the Savings and Agricultural Bank have begun implementation of branch and personnel rationalization programs. The present capital needs of the banks were not created by poor 1996 performance, but by growth and the adoption of IAS (which recognized long-standing problems). Finally, plans to privatize the state-controlled banks are undoubtedly jeopardized because experienced, quality management is a major asset to the purchaser. To cause a change in management and/or to create disenchantment among management is clearly not in the best interest of a shareholder (that is, the government) in the midst of a privatization process.

DIRECTED BANK INVESTMENTS AND LOANS. The state-controlled banks own more than half of the outstanding TBs. While holding securities is a normal part of banking operations, such a large concentration of ownership to the exclusion of other investment alternatives, combined with government ownership, could indicate a subsidy to the government at the expense of the bank. The nature of the TB auctions (the government, which owns some of the bidding banks, sets an undisclosed upper limit to the rate), the lack of participation of other domestic banks, and the (recently removed) restriction on lending at the Savings Bank (Savings Bank is the largest single owner, and its participation in the market began after the government imposed a lending moratorium on the bank in the summer of 1995) will inevitably be seen as a controlled purchase environment.

Directed lending to the energy sector provides further illustration of non-profit-maximizing decisions among state-controlled banks. In the fall of 1996, the government tried to reduce the level of energy payment arrears among its agencies and institutions at the control and municipal levels. Because the government did not want to fund this reduction "on budget" at the time, the Savings Bank (then under a lending moratorium) was asked to lend, and did lend, the enterprises the required funding. This not only represented use of public deposits to fund government, but also raised corporate governance issues on the part of the bank's councils. It hampered both the will and the ability of the government to privatize the banks. In the longer term, the government will not give up control of such a powerful policy tool and the private sector will not want to invest in banks that are instruments of government control.

GOVERNMENT RESTITUTION PROGRAMS. The government is in the process of developing restitution vehicles for citizens. The recently passed Savings Restitution Program includes two provisions that indicate possible government favoritism and political use of the banking system. The first provision calls for the establishment of accounts at the Savings Bank as the depository for funds received in the restitution process. The government envisions the eventual deposit of significant privatization-generated funds into these accounts. Nevertheless, these deposits could generate significant additional capital needs in the Savings Bank at a time when the government (as owner) has indicated no willingness to privatize the bank or to provide additional capital to the undercapitalized state banks. In addition, there is no indication of how the Savings Bank could profitably employ these funds or if the cost of servicing the accounts will exceed their value to the bank. Because the law establishes these accounts and specifies that they are to be held at the Savings Bank, there is no vehicle for competitive bidding by other banks. Since all banks (except state-controlled banks, which are effectively exempted by law) must meet higher supervisory standards, there is no reason banks should not compete for the opportunity to service restitution accounts.

The Savings Restitution Law also provides for the creation of a Savings Restitution Fund, which is allowed to borrow money to pay for restitutions, using the assets (or securities) listed for privatization as collateral (in an amount *not less* than 50 percent of the value of the assets). These loans will not be guaranteed by the government. Early drafts of the law indicated that the fund would borrow from the Savings Bank. The law, as passed, refers to "the Savings Bank and other banks" as possible lenders. Nevertheless, it is very likely that the government will borrow from the Savings Bank to accelerate the transfer of funds to the beneficiaries of the restitution scheme. The government's recent decision to allow the Savings Bank to reinstitute lending, its reluctance to privatize the bank and relinquish control of the council and board, and its history of directed lending further strengthen this possibility. Also, the requirement of not lending less than 50 percent of the value of an asset is a decision that should not be made by law, but by the lender. The banking system should be involved in the Savings Restitution Program only on a voluntary, profit-driven, and transparent basis, if it should be involved at all.

The Pace of Privatization of State-Controlled Banks

PROGRESS AND FUTURE PLANS. In February 1997, the government announced plans to privatize the State Commercial Bank and the Agricultural Bank. The plan envisioned the hiring of investment advisers for each bank through international tender. The investment adviser's role is to assist the government in preparing the banks for privatization by providing advice on privatization methods and assisting in the evaluation of proposals for purchasing bank shares.

As previously mentioned, the State Commercial Bank was liquidated in the spring of 1998, and most of its assets and liabilities were transferred to the Savings Bank. Originally, the bank was scheduled to be privatized by September 1997. There were no expressions of interest in buying the bank during two international tenders. Major private banks were not interested in the franchise, and foreign buyers were apparently concerned about asset quality, future profitability, and current capital deficiencies. The government's current plan for privatization of State Commercial Bank is based solely on a proposal for the European Bank for Reconstruction and Development (EBRD) to contribute Lt 120 million in capital in return for 35 percent of the bank's stock. EBRD's proposal contains several key conditions: completion of a due diligence examination; transfer of troubled assets to Turto; new management acceptable to EBRD; resumption of the twinning arrangements; and, most important, a "put option" to the government at cost (surely to be negotiated to include a minimal financial return) after a specified period if EBRD is not satisfied with the investment. The government would retain a 65 percent ownership position. The bank would be privatized after a period of two or three years.

The tender for advisers for the Agricultural Bank is complete; the government selected a consortium consisting of two international firms and a local brokerage firm. The bank is believed to have some investor appeal and could attract interest. The IAS information in table 1-3 indicates that the bank is solvent. Current plans envisage that this privatization will be completed no later than 30 June 1998.

The government has long hesitated to make a decision to privatize the Savings Bank. A variety of reasons were given for its reluctance to include the bank in privatization efforts. Some feel there is a public need for government ownership to provide a safety net for depositors. This reason has been significantly less important since the elimination of the special deposit protection provided by the Civil Code, the strengthening of the prudential rules (and their enforcement), and the increased stability of the major private banks. In addition, the perception of government ownership (even when the Civil Code provisions applied) did not stop a liquidity crisis at the State Commercial Bank. Others believe that the broad branch network of the Savings Bank provides the only alternative for banking services to small communities in the rural areas. While a valid concern, the Savings Bank has recently begun a branch justification program that is likely to eliminate smaller, unprofitable branches. There is also a belief that a government-controlled distribution system is needed to disburse government funds to participants in state-sponsored programs (such as social insurance, welfare, and unemployment). These programs could—and should—be handled through other mechanisms. The main issues of a distribution system are security of payments and cost. To have the banking system and its depositors fund the cost of the distribution system is inappropriate. If the Savings Bank were privately owned, it, along with other banks, could competitively bid to provide the government with that service, and the postal system could be employed as well. All factors considered, there appeared to be no justifiable reason not to privatize the Savings Bank, and, after discussion with the World Bank in May 1998, the government announced that the Savings Bank would be privatized within one year after the Agricultural Bank has been privatized.

IMPEDIMENTS TO PRIVATIZATION. The balance sheets and operations of the state-controlled banks create both policy and value maximization issues that should be addressed during the privatization process. Some issues are relevant to both banks, while others are unique to individual institutions.

First, large concentrations of government securities may be a disincentive to buyers (for example, the Savings Bank holds a quarter of all outstanding TBs, worth one-fifth of its assets). A buyer may be able to liquidate short-term securities through the market or normal maturity, but if a buyer chooses not to participate in future short-term security offerings, the government could be faced with an increased cost of borrowing, because the largest participants (the currently state-controlled banks) may choose not to participate. Longer-term securities (especially recapitalization bonds) may be discounted by a purchaser (resulting in a reduced sale price for the bank) because of inadequate yield and the lack of liquidity caused by the nontransferability of these assets.

Second, the government may not be politically able to afford the large discounts that potential buyers will require to buy the state-controlled banks in their current condition. Buyers generally form their own opinion of the quality of a bank's loan portfolio. Such an opinion is based on the buyers' methodology and judgment, not necessarily the same techniques and judgments formed by the bank's auditors and regulators. A buyer will also subtract from value any potential cost (both lost interest income and collection expense). Less uncertainty and suspicion are created when subquality loans are either removed or their quality enhanced by the seller of the bank. Subsidized and directed loans may not be attractive to a buyer, and below-market-interest-rate loans will be discounted. Directed credits will be reviewed with particular care for credit risk. A buyer will evaluate the cost of management and capital support for these programs in addition to the yield and loss risk.

Third, the banks in question have large government and state-owned enterprise deposits and other government-related funding. Government deposits (especially those in place for liquidity purposes) do not necessarily enhance, and may decrease, privatization value. A buyer will be concerned about the stability of these deposits after privatization and may request binding agreements governing their presence to protect the bank's liquidity. A buyer will be required to maintain capital to support these deposits and will look for an adequate return on this additional capital. If the deposits are to remain in the banks, the government should evaluate the impact that reduced interest rates and extended terms will have on government operations and budgets in order to enhance (or maintain) privatization values. Similarly, the deposits of state-owned enterprises, as well as deposits of municipal organizations, may also be subject to long-term arrangements to maintain privatization values, a process that the central government may find difficult to coordinate.

Fourth, the banks in question have a number of unprofitable branches and an excessive number of employees. Based on analysis by their own management, they range in size from 32 to 46 branches, 1,500 to 3,400 employees, and a deposit size for each employee of Lt 300,000–400,000. This can be compared with Vilnius Bank, the largest private bank, which has 15 branches, 745 employees, and Lt 1,000,000 in deposits for each employee. A buyer will analyze branch profitability, including the imbedded cost of facilities and the flexible cost of salaries. Too large a branch network and overstaffing will reduce privatization values. The banks are now in various stages of branch and employee rationalization programs. If significant adjustments are required, privatization values will be enhanced if these costs—including accrued branch closing and employee termination costs—are recognized before, or during, privatization. Excess facilities may be redeployed for other government activities and can be transferred to the government in return for a reduction in deposit balances.

Finally, a key element in enhancing privatization value is quality, experienced management. Lack of experienced management is a serious threat, not only to privatization, but also to the continued viability of the bank. The previously mentioned government decrees related to capping the salaries of management boards at civil service compensation levels in the state-owned banks has led to resignations and uncertainty at the other two banks. This action has jeopardized not only the privatization effort but also the future financial risk the government (as owner and as regulator) is accepting by not compensating senior management competitively.

The Need to Enhance the Legal and Institutional Framework

LEGAL AND REGULATORY FRAMEWORK DEFICIENCIES GOVERNING BANKING INSTITUTIONS. Since 1994, the Commercial Banking Law has been significantly improved. During this time, numerous amendments to the law have been incorporated, many in swift reaction to crisis or immediate need. As a result of this climate of change, a comprehensive review of this law and other laws related to banking has not been undertaken. There are currently several laws that govern the activities of banks and bankers. For instance, if not specifically overridden by provisions of the Commercial Banking Law, the Joint-Stock Company Act applies to corporate activities and governance of banks. Financially related crimes, fines, and penalties are covered in other statutes. Bankruptcy of banks and related liquidation procedures are defined elsewhere.

Recognizing that banks are different from other corporate entities because of the additional responsibility to depositors and the nature of the public trust, the general provisions of laws relating to corporations, corporate directors and officers, and bank customers are not adequate to meet the requirements of the unique banking environment. Bank management and bank employees have a special accountability to the public. Bank stockholders do not necessarily have the same accountability, but share the risk of reduced rights if the public trust is not honored by the council and management of the bank. As a result of their choice to be bankers and bank owners, these individuals may waive the normal property right protections, privacy standards, and other rights afforded by general law.

Provisions of general statutes have occasionally been difficult to apply or enforce in a banking context. For example, the Joint-Stock Company Act's securities issuance provisions have delayed the raising of capital when a bank has been critically undercapitalized. The act's shareholder rights provisions have also hampered the raising of capital. The Bankruptcy Act provisions can create administrative delays in distributing funds to depositors. There is no clear definition of insolvency suitable for the banking environment. Penalties for financial crimes are often inadequate when compared with the financial reward for committing the offense.

The Commercial Banking Law itself has also occasionally been difficult to apply because of its conflicting or ambiguous sections. For example, there is a view that BoL can hire, but not fire, a temporary administrator. The Commercial Banking Law is ambiguous regarding BoL's ability to supervise bank subsidiaries, or even to request certain financial information regarding those subsidiaries, a key issue as banks set up more operations (for instance, leasing) in subsidiaries. The information that regulators can request about bank officials is limited.

LEGAL AND PRACTICAL IMPEDIMENTS TO INCREASING THE VOLUME OF QUALITY LOANS. The Lithuanian legal framework is generally debtor-friendly. This bias has led to increased losses in banks, not only from credit losses but also through undue direct costs and losses of interest from delayed collection of residual values. More important, as banks have gained knowledge and experience (realizing that the borrower has a definite advantage over the lender), lending activity has been curtailed. Some profitable lending markets have failed to develop (for example, auto, office and plant equipment, and consumer goods) and banks have explored costly and laborious methods of creating quality loans (such as leasing and substitute collateral). Recent legal developments have improved the situation. The amendments enacted to the Bankruptcy Law assuring recovery to secured creditors to the extent of their collateral value have been a significant enhancement. The ability to perfect a lien through the enactment of lien registry provisions also indicates continued progress. Nevertheless, bankers still claim that it was better in many cases to make an unsecured loan and take the credit risk than to obtain collateral, register the lien, and repossess the collateral in the event of default.

The new lien registry system, while recently authorized, has not yet been implemented. The existing system for immovables did not fully protect against multiple pledging. In addition, the cost of registering was a percentage of the loan, and it was unrelated to the cost of registering. As a result, many banks did not register a lien (especially on large loans) until the loan experienced difficulties. The new law should be implemented expeditiously and a cost structure established that relates to the cost of the registry.

The process of debt resolution is still burdened by legal and procedural obstacles. The inability of Lithuanian corporations to own land has hampered the ability of banks to make loans backed by real estate.[2] If a bank makes a loan on an office building or house and the borrower defaults, the bank (as a corporation) cannot foreclose and take title to the land under the building, and temporary title to hold for eventual sale is unlawful. This results in a bifurcation of ownership. The law has also led to a long process for the acquisition of real property held as collateral; the transaction often extends for months after a borrower has defaulted. While the new Bankruptcy Law clarifies the secured creditor's priority in bankruptcy, it does not address the secured creditor's ability to remove the collateral from the bankruptcy process in a timely manner and recover the sale proceeds.

The repossession of moveables is equally complicated. For instance, bankers indicate it often takes three months to repossess a vehicle that is collateral for a loan. As a result, very few loans are secured by automobiles. By the time the bank has the right to possess the collateral, in most cases the collateral has been damaged or has disappeared. The result is an increase in the leasing of moveables; the bank retains title to the collateral until all payments are made. While apparently circumventing the collection (and lien registration) problem, this practice could subject the bank to liability from legal actions for loss or tort through the ownership of the moveable. For example, if an accident occurs in an automobile that a bank "owns," the bank may be held liable.

One method of stimulating quality credit on both a mass scale (that is, loans on identical terms and collateral) and for large projects is to create the legal framework for syndicated lending. For example, if a large project requires financing beyond the legal ability or risk tolerance of one bank, the bank could sell participation in (parts of) the loan to other banks or sophisticated investors. Not only is there no legal framework for this activity in Lithuania, but there is also a statutory prohibition against lending money unless granted a license by BoL. For instance, when the government established a troubled-debt work-out unit (owned by the government), it was necessary to create a limited-license bank to collect and restructure debts. This prohibition appears to prevent nonbanks from participating in major loans or any other kind of lending activity.

DEPOSIT INSURANCE COVERAGE AND PREMIUM ISSUES. The existing deposit insurance scheme is two-tiered. According to the Ministry of Finance, the recently funded deposit insurance fund will not afford deposit protection for a bank until the bank has paid at least one year of premiums. All operating

---

2. A law has been passed allowing legal entities to own land, but government decrees and detailed instructions are missing. The law has therefore not yet become effective, and there is some doubt that it will become effective in the near future.

banks have by now paid the required one year of premiums. The Temporary Law on Deposit Insurance, which covered deposits until the required premiums had been paid, has expired.

The overall cost of the fund is also a major issue for the domestic banking industry. The planned increases in coverage mentioned earlier raised the potential cost to the fund. At the same time, the current level of assessments to banks (1.5 percent of household deposits) exceeds the profitability of the sector for 1996. Even excluding the 1996 losses of State Commercial Bank, those assessments amount to a quarter of the system's profitability. (The sector currently has approximately Lt 1.6 billion in household deposits.)

RELATIONSHIP OF THE DEPOSIT INSURANCE FUND WITH OTHER GOVERNMENTAL UNITS. The responsibilities of the deposit insurance fund are limited to the compensation of depositors. According to the Ministry of Finance, the fund cannot file claims with the Bankruptcy Court to recoup funds advanced to depositors. The only claims the fund can file are those for expenses in administering depositor compensation.

The fund's relationship with other governmental units is not clearly defined. For example, interactions and communication between the fund and BoL and/or the Ministry of Finance are not specified. Under present law, revocation of license is the only way for BoL to close a bank. BoL may petition the Bankruptcy Court to place a bank in bankruptcy, but this does not technically close a bank. If BoL revokes a bank's license, then BoL no longer has authority over the institution, and the law is mute as to whether the fund can take over the liquidation of the failed bank. There is a possibility that a bank (now a former bank) can exist in regulatory limbo, with no government oversight and no automatic administrator (until the court can appoint a liquidator).

The government has yet to develop a policy regarding the best method to recover assets from failed banks. In most cases to date, the recovery has been left to the court handling the bankruptcy. In those cases, the court appoints a receiver and the receiver marshals assets and pays claims upon completion of the asset collection process. Bureaucratic court procedures, the lack of written policies or guidance, the rights of all creditors to appeal decisions, and other structural problems (debtor management appointed as administrators; government, by law, prohibited from writing off debts; lack of experienced and trained judges) cause prolongation of bankruptcy cases. To date, no bank bankruptcy case has been completed. In the case of Innovation Bank, the largest failure so far, the special law requires a liquidation outside bankruptcy. Innovation's assets were transferred to Turto Bank for management of the process of collection and sale (with the government retaining title to the assets).

Policy Recommendations

The main elements of continuing banking sector reforms will be a significant reduction of political influence, complete privatization of the government's ownership in the sector, an enhanced legal and institutional framework for bank operation, and an improved deposit insurance system. All of these reforms should be undertaken with the following goals in mind:

- Increasing the safety and soundness of the banking sector
- Insuring a level playing field for all sector participants
- Improving the transparency of government social and budgetary programs
- Increasing the quality and availability of credit and other services to bank customers
- Enhancing public confidence in the sector.

Reducing Political Interference in the Banking Sector

INCREASING THE INDEPENDENCE OF BOL. A critical element in improving public confidence and increasing the safety and soundness of the banking sector is the assurance of a well-governed, consistent, and fair supervisory function. This function should be independent of political influence. While political oversight and involvement in the legislative process related to banking is appropriate, and common in all countries, such political activity should normally be limited to establishing a consistent and viable legal framework for the operation of the banking sector. International practice (including EU directives) calls for the independence of the Central Bank and, in particular, the bank supervision function. A 1992 study[3] has rated central bank independence. Countries with a less independent central banks (Argentina, Brazil, Indonesia, Japan, and, most recently, Malaysia, Mexico, Sweden, Thailand, and Venezuela) have all experienced significant banking crises. Countries with more independent central banks (Canada, Germany, Greece, and South Africa) have generally remained crisis-free. The independence of a central bank's bank supervision function is usually determined by the extent to which external bodies (government, Seimas, the private sector) can influence (a) the consistency of the legally enacted policy framework under which the central bank operates, (b) the appointment and continued tenure of its chairman and board, and (c) the budget and operating policies of the central bank and its staff. Countries with central banks that report to the government and can have their chairman dismissed for policy reasons (such as Japan) have a much more dependent central bank than countries where the only possible reasons for dismissal are criminal offenses, illness, or conflicts of interest (such as Germany and the United States). Budgets and operating policies that are subject to political influence weaken the central bank (Japan). Still, legislative bodies have a review function to instill transparency (Germany, Sweden, and the United States). Some countries, notably New Zealand, have a system where the central bank's budget is approved by the legislative body, but for a five-year period instead of the normal one-year period of the government's budget, in order to remove short-term political influences.

While the current law alludes to BoL independence from the government, legal deficiencies and practices threaten the true independence of the bank. To increase the independence of BoL, the following changes in law are suggested:

- Explicitly stipulate that BoL is independent of Seimas. Provide for Seimas to receive reports of the activities of BoL and to review its budget, but to have no direct, required approval of the actions or budgetary issues of BoL.
- Give BoL the legal right (or option) to act under existing laws and regulations to resolve specific bank issues in lieu of bank-specific legislation by Seimas. Alternatively, require all changes impacting enforcement of the banking law or regulations affecting individual banks (rather than the sector as a whole) to have a minimum prospective effective date.
- Specify that Seimas cannot reduce a particular BoL board chairman's salary once the chairman is appointed.
- Provide that employees of BoL enjoy the same independence as board members.
- Prohibit BoL board membership of people whose immediate relatives are part of the council or board of a financial institution, or persons with a financial interest in, or who represent in any manner, a financial institution or group of financial institutions.
- Require documented abstention if a board member and/or his immediate family has direct or indirect (through partnerships or legal entities) borrowings from an institution under board consideration.

---

3. A. Cukierman, S. B. Webb, and B. Neyapri, "Measuring the Independence of Central Banks and Its Effect on Monetary Policy Outcomes," *World Bank Economic Review* 6, No. 3.

- Provide that the chairman of the board (or the board in its entirety) determine compensation levels for BoL employees.
- Specify that employee hiring decisions and related background investigations are to be a function of the BoL board or its designees. Ensure that government agencies with information necessary to make the decision are given authority to provide such information to BoL.
- Provide that selected, minimal data and information held by BoL are confidential. Allow BoL the continued authority to expand confidential treatment if it is necessary to protect the financial system.
- Provide for selected (but not all) bank supervisory actions to be determined by less than the entire board (that is, by an executive committee or bank supervision committee).

The government and the Seimas need to take immediate steps to reverse any laws and policies that hinder BoL independence, particularly provisions of the Bank Privatization Law that permit the Agricultural Bank to be exempt from BoL regulations and the recently enacted policies that place arbitrary limits on BoL staff compensation.

ADOPT RULES (OR LAWS) FOR PLACING GOVERNMENT DEPOSITS. The government should have explicit, definitive policies that govern the placement of its funds. The use of government funds to provide liquidity for troubled banks not only puts the funds at risk of loss, but may also deny their availability for normal government operations until the institution recovers. In addition, concentrations of government deposits in particular banks (troubled or not) creates liquidity risk to the bank if the government chooses to quickly withdraw funds. Consideration should be given to establishing criteria for the minimum standards a bank should meet to receive funds (perhaps higher than BoL standards) and limitations on concentrations based on the size of the bank (for instance, as a multiple of capital). Additional thought should be given to requiring collateralization for large government deposits (if they exceed an established standard) and developing a bidding system that allows qualified—and only qualified—banks to compete for deposits based on yield to the government. For instance, in the United States, most states require an open bidding (based on interest rate and services provided) from qualified banks. In addition, all deposits over a specified amount require collateralization (pledging) with acceptable securities (usually government or government-backed) in an amount in excess of the deposit. Lithuanian policy should at least specifically prohibit funding of banks that do not meet the requirements of government criteria.

REMOVE SALARY LIMITATIONS ON STATE-CONTROLLED BANKS. The imposition of the civil service salary scale on the boards of state-controlled banks should be ended. This action not only indicates political involvement, but also strengthens the appearance that the banks are not banks, but merely agencies of the government. More important, these banks, which are the largest in the sector, need to attract quality, motivated management to compete—and not repeat mistakes of the past. The government should survey the private banks, and perhaps other comparable private financial institutions in similar economies, to set an updated salary scale and incentive program.

DEVELOP POLICIES TO REDUCE THE INFLUENCE OF THE STATE-CONTROLLED BANKS IN THE SECURITIES MARKET. Steps should be taken to minimize the influence of these banks in the TB auctions to improve transparency and to avoid the appearance that the profits of the state-controlled banks are subsidizing government borrowing costs or that depositors are indirectly funding government borrowings. Because the banks are currently viewed by the government as a government agency (see salary limitations, above), TB purchases by state-controlled banks could be viewed as government buying in its own auction. Thus, the government should consider limiting state-controlled banks to noncompetitive bids.

ADOPT NEW POLICIES REGARDING SUBSIDIZED AND DIRECTED LENDING PROGRAMS. The government should consider amending the current subsidized lending programs to (a) increase the permitted margin to allow banks to achieve reasonable profit; (b) guarantee a portion, or all, of the credit exposure; (c) allow all banks to participate in the program; or (d) a combination of all of the above. A properly designed program will prompt all banks to participate. Directed lending for special purposes at the bank's own risk (that is, on their balance sheets) should cease immediately.

ELIMINATE THE ABILITY OF THE GOVERNMENT'S RESTITUTION PROGRAMS TO BORROW FUNDS. Borrowing from state-controlled banks to finance restitution programs (even when collateralized on assets to be privatized, and especially when based on the valuations of government valuation experts) could be characterized as a connected-party transaction—the owner of the bank causes an entity of its creation to receive the proceeds of a loan secured by assets valued by the owner. It is also anticipated that the government will not guarantee the loans, no matter what kind of bank, public or private, grants them. Most banks in arms-length transactions require some entity or person to be responsible for repayment of loans if the collateral turns out to be insufficient. Since the spirit of the restitution program is to distribute the proceeds of privatization, not the proceeds of loans, there is no need to borrow funds for distribution other than for political appeasement. If operating funds are needed, they should be obtained from the government's budget, not from bank borrowings. Therefore, it is suggested that the relevant law be amended to prohibit borrowing by restitution programs and agencies.

OPEN THE PROCESSING OF GOVERNMENT RESTITUTION AND DISTRIBUTION PROGRAMS TO PRIVATE BANKS. The exclusive right of state-controlled banks to handle restitution accounts and other government payment distribution programs is both a market distortion and an unfair competitive privilege. If the cost of handling these programs exceeds the profits a bank can make from utilization of the funds, it represents a subsidy to the government, funded by the public's deposits. In contrast, if the bank is profiting from the relationship, it represents a subsidy from the taxpayers to the bank. In either case, the process suggests that state-controlled banks are government agencies that compete against the private sector. It is also probable (but unclear in law) that funds deposited in these programs are covered under the deposit insurance fund, something that could eventually spread the cost of restitution across all the depositors in the system (not improbable, because it is state-controlled banks that do not fully meet all regulatory standards). The government should consider allowing other banks in compliance with regulations to bid competitively for these services.

Privatization of the Government's Ownership in the Banking Sector

SALE OF THE GOVERNMENT'S MINORITY POSITIONS IN PRIVATE BANKS. The government should proceed immediately with the sale of all its (and that of state-owned enterprises) minority stock in private banks. Most could be sold in a short period of time in the open market. Other positions could be sold in private transactions with other bank shareholders. These small positions clearly represent a nonstrategic asset on the part of government, and it is not the role of government to speculate in equity securities. In the case of state-owned enterprises, the cash generated from the sale could be better used in their core businesses and would remove the appearance of undue influence on the banks.

CONCLUDE THE IMPLEMENTATION OF THE AGRICULTURAL BANK PRIVATIZATION PLAN. The government should proceed with the current privatization plan. Key issues that need to be addressed in the near future are the impact of the bank's excessive personnel and branches on ultimate privatization values; the remaining subsidized lending program, residual loans, and funding for terminated lending programs; and foreclosed shipping assets. Determination of possible modification of these programs and transfers of assets (including subquality loans) before the actual privatization process may enhance values. As mentioned earlier, the impact of the government's policy on board compensation should be seriously considered.

DEVELOP A STRATEGY AND TIMETABLE FOR PRIVATIZATION OF THE SAVINGS BANK. Although the Savings Bank will be privatized only within a year of the privatization of the Agricultural Bank (scheduled to be accomplished in the fall of 1998), the government should immediately prepare a detailed plan for the privatization of the bank. The government should proceed to address the structural problems in the bank and to hire investment advisers well in advance of the start of the privatization process. The bank and the government are presently codependent in many areas. On the asset side of the balance sheet, the bank owns a significant amount of TBs, recapitalization bonds, and government notes issued in return for its claim on the former Soviet Foreign Trade Bank. These assets may not be attractive to prospective purchasers and could detract from the value of the bank. In addition, the bank has several foreclosed assets (including one large asset) that may require transfer before privatization to avoid lessening proceeds. A careful evaluation, similar to the evaluation performed on the State Commercial Bank, should begin as soon as possible. As in the other state-owned banks, reconsideration of the government policy on compensation is needed.

Enhancing the Legal and Institutional Framework for Banking

The government and BoL should study the special nature of banking in the context of the public trust that banks must honor. In doing so, the government and BoL should consider adopting a comprehensive banking law that clarifies the issues discussed above. Special attention to corporate statutes, consolidated supervision, bankruptcy and liquidation, and access to information is warranted. The review should consider, along with the other potential improvements identified, the following actions:

- Combine the laws that regulate banks into one statute. For example, the Joint-Stock Company Act provisions relating to capitalization, shareholder rights, and the like could be incorporated and modified to meet banking needs.
- Incorporate a definition of insolvency into the law that will permit BoL to close a bank (and under current law, petition for bankruptcy). Include in the definition of insolvency (that is, permitting BoL to petition for bankruptcy) the inability to meet liquidity demands.
- Incorporate bankruptcy provisions for banks into the Commercial Banking Law to allow expedited resolution. Adopt bank-specific resolution (liquidation) processes in coordination with the deposit insurance fund.
- Codify penalties and fines for financial crimes involving banks, including appeal procedures in the Banking Law.
- Clarify that BoL can regulate, establish standards, and examine bank subsidiaries. Require consolidated reports to be filed with BoL.
- Allow banks to classify doubtful assets according to BoL's approved procedures and include specific provisions in expenses (to make them tax deductable).

The review should seek to identify areas in which regulatory actions are limited by the ability of shareholders, councils, or boards to utilize the Commercial Banking Law or other statutes to deny or delay BoL authority. For example, work already in progress to amend the law relating to the authority of temporary administrators should be completed or included in this overall review. Temporary administrators should clearly report to BoL. While it is not necessary (and probably not preferable) that they be BoL employees, temporary administrators should work under BoL direction and policy, and BoL should have the authority to dismiss them.

Several other legal and institutional modifications can be utilized to create an environment more conducive to improved credit quality and to minimize losses and costs in the credit process. Recently proposed registry laws for both moveables and immovables are a significant improvement. The new Bankruptcy Law allowing for priority claims for secured creditors is also a very positive development. The government, in conjunction with the banking sector, should continue this progress through the following initiatives:

- The registries envisioned in the new laws should be established quickly, with a view toward ease of process and efficiency. Fee schedules, if any, should relate to cost recovery and not be viewed as a tax or revenue source.
- The law allowing banks to own land should be brought into force by issuing necessary decrees and instructions. At a minimum, banks should be allowed to own land acquired through foreclosure until the credit is resolved.
- Laws should be adopted to allow lenders to seize collateral quickly if a borrower defaults on a loan. Adequate post-seizure remedies for wrongful seizure can be provided (appeals to court for financial damages for unjustified or illegal seizure).
- The Bankruptcy Law should be amended to ensure that secured creditors (with judicial consent) have the right to remove collateral from the bankruptcy process, liquidate the collateral to the extent of their claim, and return excess collateral or funds to the court.
- Laws and processes should be adopted to allow syndicated lending, both within and outside the banking system.

Improving the Deposit Insurance System

The initial funding of the deposit insurance fund is a notable achievement. Combined with the new, strengthened prudential regulations, that step should lead to enhanced depositor confidence. Also, recent amendments to the Deposit Insurance Law have almost entirely eliminated moral hazard among individual depositors.

AMEND THE LEVEL OF DEPOSIT INSURANCE PROTECTION. The recently passed law significantly increases deposit protection for individual deposits (from Lt 5,000 to Lt 65,000 by the year 2000). In addition, the new law introduces three levels of coinsurance for litas deposits, three different levels of coinsurance for foreign currency deposits, and a three-year phase-in schedule. The government should consider amending this law to ensure (a) that the levels of coverage are appropriate for the Lithuanian situation (the BoL coverage of Lt 10,000 will safeguard 98 percent of the individual depositors), (b) that the insurance levels can be supported by bank assessments without overburdening the paying banks' profitability, (c) that the coinsurance levels for foreign currency deposits meet EU standards (EU requires homogeneous coverage across currencies), and (d) that the new coinsurance levels will comply with EU standards in the year 2000 (EU requires higher coinsurance levels). Consideration should be given to investigating whether compliance with EU standards is essential. With a proposed compensation level in 2000 of three times the current per capita income, the levels of compensation would exceed those of most developed countries (with exceptions, notably the United States and Japan) and would also exceed those of most developing nations. In addition, only a few major countries (the United States and Norway being two notable examples) include foreign currency deposits in their insurance coverage.

REEVALUATE THE LEVEL OF DEPOSIT INSURANCE ASSESSMENTS. The current level of assessments on banks is 1.5 percent of individual deposits. This level represents 25 percent of the 1996 profits of the system (excluding the loss of State Commercial Bank). This level is to be maintained during 1998–99 and reduced to 1 percent of deposits in 2000. This rate of assessment is among the highest in the world (compare Argentina, 0.36 to 0.72 percent; the Czech Republic, 0.5 percent;

Germany, 0.03 percent; Hungary, 0.2 percent; Nigeria, 0.937 percent; the United States, 0.24 percent). Separate statutes also provide for the proceeds of bank privatizations to be contributed to the fund. The current law has no targeted minimum funding, or the flexibility to reduce assessments if the fund reaches a given targeted level. In setting targeted minimum funding, the government should consider the new enhanced supervisory regime in determining risk to the fund. The law should be amended to allow the fund the flexibility to reduce premiums if a targeted minimum level of funding is achieved.

LINK THE DEPOSIT INSURANCE FUND WITH THE ASSET RECOVERY PROCESS. It is unclear in the law whether the fund has the right to file claims in bankruptcy proceedings to recover money advanced to pay depositors; the law should be amended immediately to make clear that this right of substitution exists. Previous recommendations have indicated a need for a statutory scheme to improve the liquidation process of failed banks. In developing this scheme, the fund should have authority over the process to maximize the amount of funds recovered and to minimize recovery time. Among the methodologies used in other countries are (a) having a fund-appointed administrator of the bankrupt estate, (b) having the fund legally represent all depositors in the process, and (c) having the fund control the work-out unit that manages the asset resolutions. The government should incorporate the needs of the fund when developing the statutory scheme to address the unique issues of bankrupt banks. The law should be clear, so that all parties (shareholders, depositors, government, and Seimas) know the process beforehand and, except in rare cases, the process is not modified to suit any party's special interest. In the United States, for example, when the primary regulator revokes a license, the bank is immediately placed in bankruptcy. The fund is immediately (within the hour) appointed administrator for the bankrupt estate, with wide discretionary powers over all matters (including asset security and disposition, employee retention, and depositor payment). The only significant involvement of the bankruptcy court is the final resolution of the bankrupt estate. There is no delay, no issue of who is responsible, and no chance of asset stripping by interested parties.

2

ENERGY

There have been major achievements in reforming Lithuania's energy sector since the end of 1996. These have included the establishment of an autonomous and powerful Energy Pricing Commission, a study of the wider regulatory environment, the settling of the government's debts to the Lithuanian Power Company, the enforcement of energy payment discipline on the part of public bodies, the decentralization of the district heating sector, and an accelerated privatization program. Nevertheless, several key reforms have yet to be accomplished. Among them are the future of district heating after decentralization; the creation of competitive market conditions in the electricity industry; improved corporate governance; commercialization and privatization of Lithuanian Power Company and Lithuanian Gas Company; and a heightened emphasis on energy conservation.

The financial and market performance of Lithuanian Gas are not supportable in the medium term. The company appears to be in a policy vacuum. The government intends to privatize the enterprises, but there is no clear strategy, either in relation to the company or to the natural gas market. Following the transfer of the district heating business, Lithuanian Power Company is in a much stronger position than in the past, but its costs are too high and its profits too low. Although the government intends to unbundle the electricity generation, transmission, and distribution businesses, nothing has yet been done to put fair and transparent market mechanisms in place. A strategy for the privatization of Lithuanian Power Company or its parts has not yet been developed, and there is an urgent need to put appropriate governance structures in place in both Lithuanian Power and Lithuanian Gas to oversee strategic development and efficiency improvements.

The district heating businesses, now in municipal hands, face major challenges arising from their weaknesses in the technical, market, managerial, and governance areas. Large financial expenditures are required if the state's existing investment in potentially economical systems is to be protected. The case for continued price regulation in the sector is dubious.

The government has established useful policies and institutions to maximize use of native and renewable energy sources and to promote energy conservation. There are, however, deficiencies in relation to the financing of the Energy Saving Fund, public information, regulation of industrial and commercial concerns, and energy waste by the energy companies.

Main Recommendations

The government should issue a new *Statement of Energy Policy and Strategy* that emphasizes the importance of completion of the regulatory framework for energy, the establishment of a competitive electricity market, the unbundling of Lithuanian Power, governance standards for all publicly owned energy companies (including the district heating networks), the privatization of the state's remaining ownership positions in the sector (except Ignalina Nuclear Power Plant), and the setting of standards and targets for energy conservation and the development of new energy sources. Key overall objectives for the sector should be set, accompanied by transparent performance measures.

The state's fiscal exposure to the energy sector should be explicitly terminated, and the current subsidies to low-income households should be phased out. The government should carry out an urgent study of the municipalities' district heating investment needs and design and put in place a financing program. It should specify by law the governance standards to be met by district heating companies, publish "league tables" of performance, and phase out price regulation in the sector.

The ongoing review of the regulatory environment should be speedily completed, and electricity market structures selected and established in accordance with European Union (EU) norms. Each of Lithuanian Power's generating stations and distribution utilities should be separately incorporated, and private investment should be sought. Before privatization of Lithuanian Power, performance indicators should be established for the company, an appropriate board appointed, and barriers to commercial rates of management remuneration, the use of incentives, and measurement removed. The total privatization of Lithuanian Gas should be placed immediately in the hands of advisers.

The Energy Saving Fund should be adequately funded. An enhanced program of public energy awareness should be established and financed. Rules and standards for energy conservation should be applied to industrial, commercial, and institutional energy consumers, including requirements for energy audits. Publicly owned energy companies must accept their prime responsibility to minimize losses and waste of energy, and this should be a key performance indicator applied to their boards.

Principal Features of Lithuania's Energy Sector

The Demand and Supply Balance

ENERGY DEMAND. As in all of the other countries of the former Soviet Union, the salient feature of Lithuania's energy sector since the reestablishment of independence has been a collapse in demand. Between 1990 and 1996, total demand (measured in final energy consumption) fell by 58 percent, from 10.7 to 4.5 million tons of oil equivalent. The primary cause of such a marked reduction was the demise of the centrally planned Soviet economic system, which led to widespread closures of industrial enterprises and rapid energy price increases.

While every class of energy consumer was compelled to reduce usage (table 2-1), the reduction was most marked in manufacturing industry, agriculture, and construction, the sectors most directly affected by the collapse of central economic planning. In relative terms, households and services, including transport, exhibited less severe reductions in consumption. Households are now the largest consumers of energy in Lithuania, followed by the transport sector. Industry and the household sector are major consumers of all three kinds of energy—electric power, heat, and organic fuels—while the transport and agriculture sectors depend primarily on oil products.

The economy has now bottomed out. The future evolution of domestic energy demand will be determined by the expansionary effects of economic growth, moderated by the effects of tariff increases and conservation efforts.

Table 2-1. Final Energy Consumption, by Sector

Sector	1990 (ktoe)	1996 (ktoe)	Change (percent)	Share, 1996 (percent)
Industry	3,839.7	1,050.8	-72.6	23.6
Construction	204.9	35.9	-82.5	0.8
Transport	1,725.5	1,241.6	-28.0	27.8
Agriculture	890.8	180.6	-79.7	4.0
Services	1,027.4	499.9	-51.3	11.2
Household	1,884.5	1,334.0	-29.2	29.9
Other	1,085.7	118.4	-89.1	2.7
Total	10,658.5	4,461.2	-58.1	100.0

Note: ktoe: Thousand tons of oil equivalent.
Source: Lithuanian State Statistics Department.

SUPPLIES: INDIGENOUS ENERGY RESOURCES.   Lithuania has negligible native supplies of primary energy. The largest component of domestic supply in 1996 was firewood (half the total), followed by crude oil. Efforts are being made to increase the supply of energy from indigenous sources, and the progress being made is illustrated in table 2-2. The most notable development has been the increased contribution of indigenously exploited crude oil, which in 1996 amounted to more than 4 percent of total crude oil supply.   The government expects further small increases in the indigenous proportion of primary energy consumption by 1999, and it intends to prepare a national program for the production and utilization of biofuel and bioenergy.

Table 2-2. Indigenous Primary Energy Production

Energy source	1990 (ktoe)	1996 (ktoe)	Change, 1990–96 (percent)
Peat	13.9	17.7	27.3
Firewood	142.2	223.5	57.2
Other solid fuel	24.5	44.9	83.3
Crude oil	4.0	155.4	3,785.0
Hydropower	35.6	28.1	-21.1
Total	220.2	469.6	113.3

Note: ktoe: Thousand tons of oil equivalent.
Source: Lithuanian State Statistics Department.

SUPPLIES: ENERGY IMPORTS.   The most significant imported energy resources are crude oil, natural gas, oil products, and nuclear fuel.   Russia is the principal source of energy imports by an overwhelming margin, and is effectively a monopoly supplier of both nuclear fuel and natural gas.   The dislocations in the economy consequent to the break-up of the Soviet Union dramatically affected the scale of Lithuania's energy trade (table 2-3). Not only did domestic demand fall, but export possibilities were also reduced by falling demand and foreign exchange shortages in neighboring countries, and imports fell as a result.

It can be seen that the fall in import requirements between 1990 and 1996 was absorbed primarily by oil and natural gas. Nuclear fuel imports fell less sharply because production levels at the Ignalina Nuclear Power Plant (INPP) were not solely dependent on Lithuanian domestic demand, but responded to export demand as well, curtailed though this may have been by the economic difficulties of Lithuania's neighbors.

Table 2-3. Imports of Primary Energy Resources

Energy source	1990 (ktoe)	1996 (ktoe)	Change (percent)
Coal	758.4	248.4	-67
Other solid fuel	44.6	6.5	-85
Crude oil	9,511.0	3,736.7	-61
Orimulsion	0.0	32.6	—
Natural gas	4,822.7	2,165.3	-55
Nuclear energy	4,438.8	3,633.2	-18
Oil products	7,397.2	1,722.7	-77
Electricity	390.7	360.1	-8
Total	27,363.4	11,905.5	-56

Note: ktoe: Thousand tons of oil equivalent.
Source: Lithuanian State Statistics Department.

FINAL CONSUMPTION. Table 2-4 illustrates the overall effect of these developments on the make-up of Lithuania's final energy consumption.

Table 2-4. Final Energy Consumption, by Fuel

Energy source	1990 (ktoe)	1996 (ktoe)	Change, 1990-96 (percent)	Share, 1996 (percent)
Coal	721.2	181.6	-74.8	4.1
Peat	8.9	13.1	-47.2	0.3
Firewood	137.6	214.6	56.0	4.8
Other solid	48.0	18.4	-61.7	0.4
Oil and oil products	4,538.0	1,670.2	-63.2	37.4
Natural gas	666.5	370.9	-44.4	8.3
Electricity	1,265.3	560.9	-55.7	12.6
Heat	3,273.0	1,431.5	-56.3	32.1
Total	10,658.5	4,461.2	-58.1	100.0

Note: ktoe: Thousand tons of oil equivalent.
Source: Lithuanian State Statistics Department

The severe fall in the consumption of oil products reflects the importance of the (declining) industrial sector to these fuels. It is notable that the only fuels to show increases in their share of final consumption (albeit from a very low level) were peat and firewood, which are almost entirely indigenous in origin.

Within the consumer categories, some noteworthy developments took place in the shares of different fuels:

• The share of *oil products* in the total energy consumption of *industry* fell from 31 percent in 1990 to 15 percent in 1996; the slack was taken up by electricity and heat.

• In the *agricultural* sector, the opposite phenomenon can be observed. The share of oil products rose from 43 percent in 1990 to 65 percent in 1996, while consumption of heat fell from 21 percent of the total in 1990 to 9 percent in 1996.

• Among *households,* the share of oil products in total final energy consumption fell from 23 percent to 5.3 percent, while the combined share of *peat and firewood* increased from 5.1 percent in 1990 to 14.2 percent in 1996, and *heat's* share rose from 40 percent to 52 percent.

THE ELECTRICITY SECTOR. The capacity of Lithuania's electricity generation system is about 5,800 megawatts (MW). Peak demand in 1996 was just under 2,000 MW, which explains many of the peculiarities of the Lithuanian electricity sector, particularly the huge export potential provided by these generation assets, the heavy costs imposed by the maintenance of generating capacity (represented by the thermal plant at Elektrenai, for example) that is rarely used, and the difficulties inherent in the establishment of effective market mechanisms. Table 2-5 shows the evolution of supply and demand in recent years.

Table 2-5. The Electricity Balance

Activity	1990 (TWh)	1996 (TWh)	Change, 1990–96 (percent)	Share, 1996 (percent)
Production	28.4	16.8	-41	—
Imports	4.5	4.2	-8	—
Total supply	32.9	21.0	-36	—
Exports	16.5	9.3	-43	—
Domestic consumption	16.4	11.6	-29	—
Use				
Energy system	0.2	3.4	1,600	—
Losses	1.6	1.8	15	—
Final consumption	14.7	6.5	-56	—
Industry	8.0	2.7	-65	42
Construction	0.3	0.1	-72	1
Transport	0.2	0.1	-58	1
Agriculture	2.9	0.4	-85	7
Services	0.7	0.9	37	14
Households	1.8	1.6	-9	25
Other	0.8	0.6	-22	10
Total final consumption	14.7	6.5	-56	100

Note: Twh: terawatt hour.
Source: Lithuanian State Statistics Department.

The very great increase in the consumption of electricity by the electricity sector itself is a feature of the tables. The particularly sharp fall in agricultural demand is also notable, but it was in line with the 80 percent reduction in that sector's overall energy consumption. The reduction in exports has had implications for both the finances of the energy companies and the balance of payments.

Final domestic electricity consumption increased by 4 percent in 1996 over 1995. This was the first increase in several years, and it was driven primarily by a recovery in industry. The trend was maintained in 1997. Exports also increased in 1996, by 17.5 percent, but are thought to have reverted to 1995 levels in 1997.

The dominant asset in the Lithuanian electricity industry is INPP. With a capacity (derated) of 2,500 MW, it provides 43 percent of national capacity. In recent years INPP has been able to supply between 80 and 90 percent of domestic demand, and it also makes possible the large export trade in electricity. Many economic, financial, managerial, and safety issues surround the operation of INPP, which is the subject of G7 monitoring under a Nuclear Safety Agreement administered by the European Bank for Reconstruction and Development (EBRD). These issues, however, are outside the scope of this chapter.

THE NATURAL GAS SECTOR. Lithuania has an extensive natural gas network that distributes gas, primarily purchased from Russia, throughout the country. As in the case of electricity, there is a substantial surplus of capacity over demand: 1996 gas consumption was 2.7 billion cubic meters, while the designed capacity of the transmission network is 8 billion cubic meters. Table 2-6 illustrates the evolution and current status of supply and demand.

Table 2-6. The Natural Gas Balance

Category	1990 (million cubic meters)	1996 (million cubic meters)	Change, 1990–96 (percent)	Share, 1996 (percent)
Imports	5,991.0	2,693.5	-55	—
Exports	181.0	0.0	-100	—
Domestic consumption	5,810.0	2,693.5	-54	—
Use				
Energy system	4,165.0	1,494.0	-64	—
Losses etc.	18.0	57.6	220	—
As raw material	799.0	681.1	-15	—
Final energy consumption	828.0	460.7	-44	—
Industry	327.0	174.0	-47	37.8
Construction	8.0	1.3	-84	0.3
Transport	32.0	4.3	-86	0.9
Agriculture	34.0	8.6	-75	1.9
Services	147.0	45.1	-69	9.8
Household	274.0	226.1	-17	49.1
Other	6.0	1.3	-78	0.3
Total final consumption	828.0	460.7	-44	100.0

Source: Lithuanian State Statistics Department.

It is clearly demonstrated in the table that the dominant use of natural gas in Lithuania is in the energy sector itself, as a feedstock for power and heat plants. The relatively small decline between 1990 and 1996 in *household* consumption of natural gas probably reflects the efforts of the private sector to diversify its energy sources away from the district heating systems.

Apart from the 2.0 million tons of oil equivalent (mtoe) in natural gas consumed, some 100,000 tons of oil equivalent of liquefied gas, a product of the oil industry, is also used. Of this amount, 20 percent is used to fuel vehicles; of the remainder, virtually all is used by households for domestic heating and cooking.

THE OIL SECTOR. Oil and oil products still constitute the largest single component of Lithuania's final energy consumption, despite the exceptionally severe reductions in consumption since 1990 (table 2-7).

Virtually all crude oil consumed in Lithuania is used to produce oil products. Of these, motor fuel and diesel oil are the dominant products.

THE DISTRICT HEATING SECTOR. Most Lithuanian households, especially in post-war housing developments, are connected to district heating systems, as are many industrial, commercial, and institutional consumers. The district heating systems are major consumers of primary energy, and heat is the most important single energy product at the final consumption level. Table 2-8 sets out the supply and demand configuration.

Table 2-7. The Oil Balance

Category	1990 (ktoe)	1996 (ktoe)	Change, 1990–96 (percent)	Share, 1996 (percent)
Crude oil production	4.0	155.4	3,785	—
Imports	9,511.0	3,736.7	-61	—
Exports	0.0	122.9	—	—
Stock changes	11.0	6.2	-44	—
Domestic consumption	9,526.0	3,763.0	-60	—
Use				
Fuel for energy	2.0	5.5	175	—
Raw material	9,368.0	3,725.2	-60	—
Losses	154.0	25.3	-84	—
Final energy consumption	2.0	7.0	250	—
Oil products				
Final energy consumption	4,694.9	1,663.2	-65	100.0
Industry	1,208.9	158.7	-87	9.5
Construction	95.9	26.3	-73	1.6
Transport	1,663.0	1,226.6	-26	73.7
Agriculture	378.7	116.5	-69	7.0
Services	154.3	55.5	-64	3.3
Household	436.0	71.3	-84	4.3
Other	758.1	8.3	-99	0.5
Total final consumption	4,694.9	1,663.2	-65	100.0

Note: ktoe: Thousand tons of oil equivalent.
Source: Lithuanian State Statistics Department.

A feature of the heating figures is that in a period when every other economic sector sharply reduced its consumption of heat, the *household* sector maintained its level of usage. Given that the 1990–96 period was one of rising domestic heating tariffs, this may reflect the absence of viable alternative heating systems for most domestic consumers. It also highlights the scale of the energy conservation task in Lithuania. The year 1996 was the first in which total household consumption of heat fell below the 1991 level.

Table 2-8. The Heat Balance

District heating	1990 (000 Tcal)	1996 (000 Tcal)	Change, 1990–96 (percent)	Share, 1996 (percent)
Production	34.2	19.7	-42	—
Used in energy systems	0.0	1.1	—	—
Losses	1.4	4.3	201	—
Final consumption	32.7	14.3	-56	—
Industry	16.5	4.9	-70	34.3
Construction	0.7	0.0	-98	0.1
Transport	0.1	0.0	-98	0.0
Agriculture	1.9	0.2	-92	1.1
Services	4.3	1.8	-57	12.7
Household	7.5	7.0	-7	48.6
Other	1.8	0.5	-74	3.1
Total final consumption	32.7	14.3	-56	100.0

Note: Tcal: tetra-calories.
Source: Lithuanian State Statistics Department.

The Energy Intensity of the Lithuanian Economy

Like those of other FSU countries, the Lithuanian economy is highly energy-intensive. Energy supply is characterized by a large degree of overcapacity at the secondary level, most notably in power generation and natural gas distribution, and demand is marked by a slow adjustment to the realities of world energy prices. These features dominate policymaking in the sector and are at the root of many of the difficulties the government has faced in seeking to bring about much-needed energy economy and the rationalization and commercialization of energy enterprises.

Extravagant consumption of energy was a feature of the economy of the FSU, and was unaffected by the oil shocks of the 1970s. To illustrate this phenomenon, between 1972 and 1990 the energy intensity of the Organization for Economic Cooperation and Development (OECD) countries fell from about 520 to 400 tons of oil equivalent (toe) for each US$1 million in GDP. During the same period, the average energy intensity of the countries of the FSU *rose* from 720 to 820 toe for each US$1 million in GDP. Lithuania's energy intensity was about 1,400 toe for each US$1 million in GDP in 1990, more than three times the intensity found in market economies. Even with the reduction in energy demand since the restoration of independence, which was driven partly by the collapse of inefficient industry and partly by the inability of both residential and industrial consumers to pay higher prices, energy intensity in 1996 was only slightly lower, at about 1,200 toe for each US$1 million in GDP. In 1994, Lithuania's intensity was slightly higher than Estonia's, and 85 percent greater than that of Latvia. While the differences can be partly explained by differences in economic structure (for example, Lithuania is more industrialized than either of its Baltic neighbors) and Lithuania's production of electricity for export, such a high level of intensity compounds the adjustment problems of the Lithuanian economy and underlines the need for more rapid progress in achieving improved energy conservation.

The Main Institutions in the Energy Sector

Since the end of 1996, the ministry responsible for policy and planning in the energy sector has been the Ministry of Economy, which embraces the functions of three former ministries: the Ministry of Economy, the Ministry of Industry and Trade, and the Ministry of Energy.

Five specialized agencies are of particular importance to the energy sector:

- VATESI. This is the state nuclear safety inspection agency. Its guidelines for operation were formulated by the International Atomic Energy Agency.
- The Energy Agency. This body is responsible for the preparation and implementation of energy sector development programs and projects, the drafting of normative acts for the energy sector, and international cooperation.
- The Lithuanian Energy Institute. This group carries out fundamental and applied research in all fields of energy technology and economics.
- The State Energy Inspection. This body carries out technical supervision of the energy sector and controls industrial safety issues.
- The State Commission for Pricing of Energy Resources and Energy Activity Control (commonly known as the Energy Pricing Commission, or EPC). The members of the EPC are appointed by presidential decree, and it serves as the ultimate arbiter of electricity, gas, and heat prices.

In addition, the Ministry of Finance is responsible for the implementation of government policy in a number of areas of significance to the energy sector. These include the payment of production subsidies to the Lithuanian Power Company (necessitated by tariffs that, until recently, did not cover costs), the management of consumer subsidies to low-income households, and the imposition of payment discipline on state and municipal energy consumers.

The Ministry of European Affairs has a coordinating role in relation to governmental programs that affect Lithuania's application for membership of the European Union (EU). These responsibilities touch on the privatization strategies to be adopted in relation to the state's ownership of energy sector assets.

The main gap in the institutional structures that deal with energy is a comprehensive regulatory agency that would handle the licensing of operators, the quality and security of supply, customer protection, safety, and other important aspects of a developed, market-based energy sector. (This need is currently being addressed through an EU-PHARE–sponsored study, and it is expected that the necessary legislation will be brought forward during 1998.) In addition, the commercialization of Lithuania's electricity industry will highlight the need for new institutional and regulatory arrangements in the power market. (This issue had not been addressed in detail at the time this chapter was written.)

The State Energy Companies

Most of the assets comprising the Lithuanian energy sector are in state hands, although plans for the privatization of several of these assets are at an advanced stage. Table 2-9 summarizes key operational and financial data for the principal state energy companies.

The figures given for the Lithuanian Power Company in table 2-9 should be interpreted with care. After the end of 1996, two developments—the repayment of production subsidies from the 1994–96 period by the state and the separation of the district heating business, which has been transferred to municipal ownership—render the configuration not strictly comparable with the current situation. The distorting effect of the considerable amount of intertrading among companies—for example, all of INPP's sales, and nearly 65 percent of the sales of Lithuanian Gas (LG), are to Lithuanian Power Company—on the aggregate figures should be taken into account.

Table 2-9. Key Indicators, Energy Sector Companies

Company	Business	Authorized capital (Lt million)	State share (percent)	Employees (numbers)	Sales, 1996	Net profit, 1996
Lithuanian Power Company	Power/heat utility	2,849	91	21,167	2,440	-99
Ignalina Nuclear Power Plant	Electricity generation	2,127	100	5,120	714	10
Mazeikiai Oil	Oil refining	581	91	3,580	998	-18
Lithuanian Gas Company	Natural gas distribution	334	91	4,516	729	-23
Lithuanian Fuels	Oil product distribution	179	73	1,852	320	-10
Klaipeda Oil	Oil terminal	158	72	619	95	57
Birzai	Oil pipeline	63	90	274	76	34
Geonafta	Exploration	16	81	340	23	11
Total		6,307	93	37,468	5,395	-11

Source: Accounts of companies.

The significance of the energy sector in the Lithuanian economy is underlined by the figures. More than 2 percent of the employed population, and 7 percent of public sector employees, work in these eight companies. The low aggregate return on the very large capital investment is a source of concern to the government.

PRIVATIZATION. INPP, LPC, and LG are on the list of special purpose companies. Companies that carry this designation cannot have greater than 30 percent nonstate participation, and by a 1995 law they must retain this status until the year 2000. In the case of LG, a current share issue will bring the private proportion of shares to about 25 percent. LPC is in the process of being restructured following its divestiture of the district heating business, and while it is expected that separate companies will be established to handle electricity generation, transmission, and distribution, there is no immediate plan to introduce private capital in these activities.

Privatization plans are more advanced in the oil sector. Both the Mazeikiai Oil Refinery and the Geonafta Exploration Company are on the list of enterprises to be privatized by international tender in 1997–98. The government has also decided to privatize Lithuanian Fuels.

Since 1 July 1997, the district heating networks previously owned by LPC have been in the hands of municipalities. The assets of the networks include the combined heat and power plants in Vilnius and Kaunas, which are significant suppliers of electricity to the National Grid at selected times. There has been no decision regarding the introduction of private capital to the district heating sector.

The Role of the Private Sector

While electricity supply is still a state monopoly, and district heating is largely in the hands of regional monopolies, private sector participation in other parts of the energy sector is significant, and growing. The LG monopoly in gas is limited to transmission and distribution. Of the 3 billion cubic meters of natural gas transported by the company in 1996, 48 percent was the property of other companies, sold to customers in competition with LG. In liquefied gas, the company's share of the market has fallen, from 100 percent in 1992 to 67 percent in 1996. Lithuanian Fuels, which distributes oil products throughout Lithuania, already faces competition from several established Western companies.

The privatization of Mazeikiai Oil Refinery will greatly increase the scale and influence of private sector participation in Lithuania's products sector and will provide opportunities for accelerated development of facilities and management.

The private sector will also have a growing presence in the heating market. The removal of producer subsidies from suppliers of district heating will open up a competitive market for other forms of heat, including boilers, fueled by natural gas and electricity in individual buildings.

Energy Pricing

The pricing of oil products has been deregulated and has essentially been determined by the market since 1993. Tariffs for electricity, natural gas, and district heating (including hot water) are determined by suppliers in cooperation with the EPC. In practice, disagreements about price are settled by the EPC.

The commission approved tariffs for electricity, gas, and heating in July 1997 that are calculated to recover the full cost of generation, transmission, and distribution. The establishment and full resourcing of the EPC, which was achieved by the government during 1997, is seen as a major step forward in the reform of Lithuania's energy sector.

The general tendency in recent years has been for tariffs to move toward full cost coverage.

Table 2-10 illustrates the effects of this trend on electricity and heat tariffs. The table illustrates the extent of the reduction that has been made in cross-subsidization between consumer groups, evidenced by the steep increases in tariffs for households, particularly in the case of heat. Table 2-11 puts two important Lithuanian energy prices into a Baltic perspective.

Table 2-10. Electricity and Heat Tariffs
(US cents)

Customer category	Unit	Average, 1995	Average, 1996
Electricity			
Industry	kWh	3.29	3.45
Households	kWh	3.95	4.21
Other	kWh	4.00	4.38
Heat			
Industry	Gcal	18.88	20.78
Households	Gcal	12.94	22.44
Other	Gcal	18.56	20.22

Note: kWh: Kilowatt hour; Gcal: giga-calorie.
Source: Lithuanian Power Company.

Table 2-11. Average Energy Prices in Baltic States, January 1997
(US cents)

Commodity	Unit	Estonia	Latvia	Lithuania
Electricity	kWh	3	6	4
Petrol (A93)	litre	41	50	38

Source: Lithuanian State Statistics Department.

As a result of the introduction of tariffs that cover costs, no further subsidies to energy producers are expected, and none have been provided in the 1997 state budget. Subsidization of the energy sector is now limited to a system of consumer subsidies that are available to low-income households with heat and hot water bills that exceed a set proportion of their incomes; eligibility is determined according to a complex set of rules. These subsidies are expected to cost the state around Lt 200 million in 1997.

Energy Strategy of the Government of Lithuania

The government's strategy for the reform of the energy sector is set out in the 1995 Energy Law of the Republic of Lithuania. Article 3, under the heading of Energy Policy Objectives, states:

The main state energy policy objectives shall be:

1) Energy saving
2) Effective usage of primary energy resources
3) Decreasing comparative energy expenses for production of national product
4) Trying to find and guarantee access to reliable local sources of energy supply as well as to import fuel from more than one foreign country with regard to the need for demonopolization and decentralization
5) Encouraging energy producers and consumers to use local, recovering, and secondary energy resources in the most effective way
6) Reliable, high-quality production and supply of fuel, electric, and heating energy at the lowest possible costs in different energy systems
7) Minimizing energy production adverse impacts on the environment

8)   Creating favorable legal and economic conditions for investment
9)   Encouraging competition and participation of private capital to increase economic efficiency.

After a period of seemingly slow progress toward these objectives, there has been very significant and positive change during 1997. The formal objectives of the Energy Law have been supplemented by a series of governmental and ministerial initiatives and statements that have set out a very clear agenda for continuing reform, restructuring, and commercialization. These initiatives and intentions, in their focus and strategic direction, can be summed up as follows:

- Achieve economic pricing for all energy products and terminate energy subsidies.
- Attract private capital into the sector.
- Commercialize and privatize energy enterprises.
- Diversify both indigenous primary energy resources and sources of imports.
- Create competitive energy markets wherever possible.
- Heighten the emphasis on energy conservation.
- Increase attention to the protection of the environment.
- Establish an unambiguous regulatory environment designed to achieve long-term security of supply and equitable treatment for energy producers and consumers.
- Achieve conformity of energy laws and markets with EU norms.

A new and up-dated energy strategy is in preparation that will take into account the changes to date and identify the challenges of current circumstances.

Recent Reform Progress

THE ACHIEVEMENTS OF 1997. The arrival in office of a new government in December 1996 led to the transformation of the energy policy environment. After several years in which implementation of reform lagged far behind intentions, a series of decisions, backed up by implementation measures, has created a much more positive reform environment than seemed possible a year ago.

The *Energy Pricing Commission* was established on a basis of complete autonomy and with the power to be the ultimate arbiter of heat, gas, and electricity prices. Commissioners of standing have been appointed by presidential decree, and they have been provided with sufficient funds from the state budget to commence their work satisfactorily. The EPC approved new energy tariffs as of 1 July 1997. Because there had not been enough time to undertake a thorough inquiry into all the costs of energy supply, possible efficiency improvements, and the short- and long-term investment needs of the energy supply companies, the EPC approved tariffs that generally accepted the current cost levels of suppliers, but made no allowance for the financing of investments. This was a holding action on the part of the EPC. Over the longer term, it intends to analyze costs and efficiencies in detail and to use the tariff methodologies to put downward pressure on the costs it considers to be excessive and that should not be borne by consumers. The EPC will make demand forecasts for energy products and, working with the energy companies, examine models of future supply and investment needs, and methods of financing these needs, including the place of investment costs in energy tariffs.

The wider question of *regulation in the energy sector*, including licensing, consumers' rights, security of supply, and other important issues, is also recieving attention. Studies are under way and legislation is expected in 1998.

The *buildup of losses in the Lithuanian Power Company*, primarily caused by inadequate tariffs in the past, has also been addressed. During 1997, the government made payments to LPC and took over some of its debts, to a total value of Lt 776 million. This covers the estimated amount of these losses from January 1994 to September 1996. The government has also committed itself to compensate LPC for losses arising from inadequate heat tariffs for the period from October 1996 to June 1997, when LPC's responsibility for district heating was terminated.

Concerted action has been taken to deal with the problem of *the energy arrears of public authorities*. These have included direct budgetary measures (diverting the budgetary transfers of delinquent municipalities to the energy companies), disconnections, and the imposition of sanctions on budgetary organizations and their management. The effects of these measures on electricity arrears have been dramatic (table 2-12); similar effects can be seen in the arrears for gas and district heating.

The *restructuring of the power and heat subsectors* has commenced. On 1 July 1997, the district heating business of LPC was transferred to the ownership and management of municipalities. As part of the transfer, two significant combined heat and power plants, in Vilnius and Kaunas, passed out of LPC's ownership, creating at least the possibility of competition in electricity generation. The minister for economy has announced his intention to separate LPC's remaining generating business from its transmission activities and to incorporate a number of separate regional electricity distribution companies.

Table 2-12. Consumer Arrears for Electricity

	Days' billing				Percent of total,
Customer category	*11/1/96*	*5/1/97*	*11/1/97*	*5/1/98*	*5/1/98*
Industry	11	10	9	12	35
Agriculture	61	39	34	34	15
State budgetary	92	36	26	15	6
Municipal budgetary	41	51	17	29	10
Household	9	6	5	5	7
Other	28	25	21	22	26

Source: Lithuanian Power Company.

The pace of *privatization of state energy companies* has quickened. Mazeikiai Oil Refinery and Geonafta are on the 1997–98 privatization list, and they are currently being offered for sale. It is likely that Lithuanian Fuels will soon follow.

Key Medium- and Long-Term Issues Facing Lithuania's Energy Sector

The salient point regarding the state-owned energy infrastructure in Lithuania is that it was never conceived as a set of Lithuanian assets. On the contrary, all the networks and facilities—power stations, high-voltage transmission lines, gas and oil pipelines, the oil refinery—were centrally planned as part of the highly energy-intensive economic strategy of the FSU. Electricity capacity, for example, was planned and built to meet the regional power requirements of the integrated northwest part of the Interconnected Power System (IPS) of the FSU. Installed peak capacity is more than three times peak demand, and the theoretical *annual* capacity of Lithuania's electricity industry is about six times final domestic demand. This large overcapacity in comparison with Lithuania's domestic needs, an artifact of the Soviet strategy, particularly by the 2,500, MW (derated) capacity of INPP, provide a significant export capability. Net electricity exports in 1996, primarily to Russia and Belarus, exceeded 30 percent of domestic production.

The scale of INPP's capacity and its cost advantage in comparison with fossil fuel generators combine to make it the producer of the bulk of the electricity generated in Lithuania—83 percent in 1996. In contrast, some of the thermal plants, notably the large oil- and gas-fired station at Elektrenai, run at extremely low levels of capacity utilization. The overall load factor is less than 20 percent. To put this in perspective, Lithuania has about as much electricity generating capacity as Hungary, with one-third of its population. One of the cost burdens borne by the energy sector is that while domestic energy demand shrank by 45 percent between 1991 and 1996, the energy infrastructure is the same as it was in the past in its capacity generate, transmit, distribute, supply, and manage facilities and related costs.

Progress is being made in commercializing and privatizing the main companies in the energy sector and in putting in place an appropriate regulatory framework. Nevertheless, difficult problems lie ahead for the authorities. Among them, the future of nuclear power in Lithuania is critical, but in light of the many geopolitical uncertainties surrounding a potential decision to close INPP, it is not covered in this Policy Note. Equally important for policymakers is the future structure, ownership, and governance of the publicly owned companies that operate in the district heating, electricity, and gas sectors because of the very large investment requirements of these businesses, the need to promote competition at every feasible level, and the weak competitive position of some district heating networks.

Altogether, just under 50 percent of Lithuania's final energy consumption is supplied by these enterprises, which are virtually monopoly suppliers in the domestic market. For this reason, policies that affect these enterprises are of much greater significance than policies governing the other state-owned energy companies in the oil subsector, which are already exposed to competition. The emphasis in this chapter is thus on policy issues that affect the district heating, electricity, and gas companies.

As in the banking industry (discussed in a Chapter 1 of this volume), the key underlying questions are how to disentangle the role of the state as owner of most of the energy sector with that of the state as regulator, and how to deal with the implied transition period (of perhaps two or three years) in which the government must act to achieve better management of publicly controlled assets in the interests of consumers, taxpayers, and the employees of these enterprises, and also in the interest of maximizing ultimate privatization proceeds later on.

The Forthcoming Problems of the Newly Decentralized District Heating Sector

More than 80 percent of buildings in the residential and commercial sectors are connected to district heating (DH) systems. Although there are about 2,000 producers of heat in the country, including industrial, commercial, and other large concerns that have their own heat-generating capacity, most consumers are connected to one of the pipeline networks previously controlled by LPC, but owned by sixteen municipalities since 1 July 1997. These supplied over 70 percent of the 20 Tcal of heat consumed nationally in 1996. This investment, the economic and environmental costs of developing alternatives, and the energy economy that should—in principle—be available in such systems are all reasons that the future of DH should be of concern to policymakers.

The recently implemented decentralization of the DH system should encourage greater economy, efficiency, and effectiveness in the provision of an essential utility. There are several reasons for this. Heating is a local resource. There is no concept in DH like a national grid that requires management at the national level. The technical characteristics of heat exclude national dispatching. Local authorities can maximize welfare in their areas by responding directly to local needs instead of accepting a centrally designed service model that may not suit all municipalities. The ensuing costs can be assigned to smaller units, with management accountability tied to cost and financial objectives. Managers can be closer to customers, and thus understand local market trends better. In addition, investment, tariff, and service decisions can be tailored to local conditions.

The decentralization of the DH networks, together with the important combined heat and power (CHP) plants at Vilnius and Kaunas, also marks an important step in the restructuring of the sector because it is accompanied by new pricing arrangements. Under the terms of the legislation, prices are set by regional municipal groupings, subject to the approval of the EPC. Until early 1997, government policy regarding heating tariffs had two main elements. First, it set tariffs at levels that did not cover costs and met the deficit out of public funds (in 1996, the last full year in which deficits were expected to be met out of budget funds, costs exceeded sales revenues by Lt 440 million. Second, low-income households were directly subsidized through a limitation on the amount a household could be charged for heating to 25 percent (5 percent for hot water) of household income. This limit was also subject to rather complex criteria based on the size of families and dwellings. The state then paid for consumption in excess of that proportion (Lt 203 million is provided for the purpose in the 1997 budget).

Tariffs approved by the EPC for the 1997/98 heating season show some regional variations. For example, an increase was approved in Vilnius that raised the old national tariff for householders of Lt 103.97/Tcal to Lt 114.9/Tcal (excluding value added tax), an increase of 10.5 percent. For Siauliai, the increase approved brought the rate to Lt 147.1/Tcal, an increase of 41.5 percent. In the smaller municipalities, which can set their own prices, increases ranged from 21 percent (Mazeikiai) to 146 percent (Skuodo).

The power of the EPC to approve tariffs that cover legitimate costs would appear to assure the financial viability of the new municipal entities. On this basis, it would be reasonable to expect that from the 1997/98 heating season forward, the only subsidy required in the heating sector would be the direct consumer subsidy to low-income households, which can legitimately be regarded as a social welfare provision. (Although from the standpoint of national policy, the present system of subsidizing low-income households is extremely inefficient, offering no incentives for economy, and inferior to more direct income-support measures.)

On the debit side, decentralization could also carry some costs arising from the general shortage of qualified and experienced staff in key management areas (such as finance) in Lithuania. It has been the general experience in other countries that the benefits of decentralizing the management of companies competing in local markets tend, after what may be a difficult adjustment period, to exceed the costs. "Empowerment" of regional and local enterprise management has been seen to be effective in sectors as diverse as food retailing, banking, and public administration. It has also been effective in the energy sectors of countries of western, central, and eastern Europe. In Poland, for example, the district heating industry has been decentralized to forty-nine municipal groupings, which are operating with increasing effectiveness in a deregulated market. In the Czech Republic, the larger networks have been privatized and are moving rapidly toward normal financial targets.

Nevertheless, the DH systems operating in Lithuania suffer from many problems, problems that can cause serious imbalances in the finances of their municipal owners, and ultimately in the finances of the central government. Four of these problems stand out.

The systems have massive investment needs. Lithuania has an unbalanced (by international standards) heat generation structure. DH systems usually take advantage of the heat produced as a by-product of electricity generation in CHP plants, and use heat-only boiler (HOB) plants only to meet peak demand and at the peripheries of networks. The dominance of INPP in Lithuania's electricity supply profile means that there is less scope for CHP plants. As a result, 70 percent of the heat supplied to the DH networks comes from HOB plants, most of which are more than twenty-five years old and fitted with outdated equipment and obsolete control systems. A significant reduction in the role of INPP in electricity generation could enhance the case for investment in CHP plants. In the meantime, HOB plants badly need to be upgraded to improve economy.

The transmission (pipeline) network is obsolete and inefficient. The heat distribution networks suffer from high heat and water losses because of poor design, construction, and maintenance (and also because of inefficient operation, according to 1994 World Bank data). Heat losses from water leakage and poor insulation have been estimated at about 30 percent of supply, costing about Lt 250 million annually at 1996 consumption levels. To ensure satisfactory performance, about 4–5 percent of the total pipe length should be replaced each year, but financial constraints have prohibited adherence to this practice in recent years. In a typical year, LPC replaced less than 1 percent of its heat pipelines. The result, presented in table 2-13, below, has been a progressive and serious deterioration in the efficiency of the system. To put the figures in perspective, heat losses in Swedish DH networks are about 6 percent. If present trends were allowed to continue, Lithuania would have virtually no working DH systems within a decade.

Table 2-13. Heat Losses in DH Networks, 1990–96
(percent)

Year	Loss
1990	7.3
1991	7.5
1992	9.0
1993	12.2
1994	14.0
1995	20.9
1996	31.1

Source: "Energy in Lithuania '96," Lithuanian Energy Institute.

Physical controls are inadequate. There is a lack of flow and temperature controls at district heating substations. Roughly half of domestic consumers are unmetered, which complicates the efforts of suppliers in billing, collection, and customer relations, while depriving consumers of control over their own energy expenditures. The metering issue has assumed prominence in Lithuania largely because of the very high energy intensity in the economy, coupled with the rather low awareness of conservation matters on the part of consumers. It is interesting that in Finland, which has an energy intensity that is not excessive for such a cold climate, district heating is metered and charged to buildings rather than to individual households. It may well be that in Lithuania some of the costs of installing individual metering arrangements could be avoided through public education and better insulation of buildings. The cultural dimension of issues such as this can not be ignored.

The investment needs described above (heat-only boiler dependency, deteriorated pipelines, and poor physical controls) will tax the municipalities' financial capacity. The cost of all of the necessary investments in the DH sector nationally was estimated at Lt 3 billion (US$750 million) in the December 1993 "Energy Master Plan for Lithuania State Power System." Recently, international consultants supplied Vilnius Municipal DH company with an estimate of Lt 240 million (US$60 million) as the cost of making the necessary improvements *inside* the city's apartment buildings—about Lt 1,500 for each household. This estimate did not include the cost of the necessary improvements to the transmission and distribution pipeline networks or the HOB plants. To put the cost for each household in perspective, Lt 1,500 is equivalent to over four months of income for the average household member. A current World

Bank case study in Kaunas estimates the cost of replacing the entire Kaunas DH network grid over a period of ten years at US$114 million with the conventional pipe system, which would have an estimated life of between three and twenty years (average, ten years). The cost would be US$210 million if preinsulated pipe were used, which would have an estimated life in excess of thirty years.

By any measure, Lithuania's municipalities face very costly investment programs if their DH networks are to be modernized, but the return from such investment could be high. Lithuania's 1994 *Energy Sector Review* (ESR) called for a DH rehabilitation program that could achieve energy savings of about 25 percent. Given that fuel costs alone in LPC's heat networks amounted to Lt 726 million nationally in 1996 (US$181.5 million), the potential for worthwhile investment seems clear.

Heating tariffs, of course, could and should include provision for the remuneration of necessary investment, and should, over time, help pay for it. However, financing that investment will be a major challenge. There are three main reasons for the difficulty of this project. First, it is extremely unlikely that the DH companies would be able to borrow the necessary funds on their own; municipal government intervention and/or guarantees would be needed. And, as explained in another part of this report, the municipal governments face serious financial problems of their own. It seems inevitable that the central government will have to play a role, compromising its own fiscal accounts. Second, EPC takes the view that much can be done by the DH enterprises to reduce their operating costs, and that until this has been done, it would be unjust to expect consumers to pay higher tariffs to finance investments. There is merit in the EPC's view. While Lithuania's DH companies are money-losing operations, there are nine Czech DH enterprises with mixed municipal and private ownership that produce an aggregate rate of return on net assets of about 11 percent, even though they apply a household tariff of US¢1.925 per kWh, more than 10 percent less than the average household tariff in Lithuania (US¢2.15 per kWh). Poland is another example. As a consequence of the reform measures undertaken in four Polish cities (which include both institutional and technical components), energy losses have been reduced to about a third of the level before the reforms; significant management capacity has been created within DH enterprises; and direct subsidies to residential consumers have been reduced from almost 70 percent of cost in 1991 to virtually zero. Similar programs in Lithuania should yield comparably attractive benefits. Finally, as discussed below, it is not certain that the new tariff structures will be enforceable or competitive.

Weak mechanisms to enforce payment discipline are the second major problem the newly decentralized DH companies will face. While a more local management focus and autonomous customer relations strategies can help improve the payment collections of DH entities, they and their municipal owners will undoubtedly have political difficulties within their own constituencies when raising heat and hot water tariffs (as an example, tariff adjustments ranging up to 41 percent were needed in Siauliai, and even larger ones were required in smaller municipalities). A particular problem is posed by the heating arrears of state budgetary organizations. In September 1997, these organizations owed Lt 32 million to LPC (then the owner of the DH network) for heat—almost 30 percent of LPC's total receivables for heat. Half of this figure was owed by *municipal* budgetary organizations, whose debts were equivalent to fifty-six days worth of billing. (A year earlier, these debts amounted to 190 days worth of billing, and only fiscal measures taken by the central government in October 1996 and March 1997 prevented them from returning to such levels.) In other words, the new DH companies, now municipal entities, are likely to find that their biggest consumer debt problems will be caused by their sister organizations under municipal control. It is moot whether they will be able to enforce payment discipline on such bodies, especially because disconnections of electricity supply to defaulting heat consumers will no longer be possible in the post-decentralization environment.

The third key problem inherited by the DH companies is *their limited capacitiy to compete with alternative sources of heating*. Once tariffs are adjusted and enforced to cover economic cost—and, thus, to include provisions for necessary investments—consumers may switch to heating provided by electricity and natural gas at an increasing rate. The price elasticity of heat demand in Lithuania has not been systematically measured. A study in the Czech Republic concluded that price elasticity of DH heating was low, and that the negative effects of even large price increases would be outweighed in the medium and long term, in the case of industrial users, by a perception that DH was the cheapest heating source. In 1996, Lithuanian consumers responded to an average tariff increase (for householders) of 73 percent by reducing their purchases of heat by 11.5 percent, confirming a rather low level of elasticity. This may, however, have been assisted by two factors that are likely to change in the next few years.

First, for consumers still benefiting from the heat subsidy to low-income households, the increased tariff was of only academic interest because their heating expenditures are capped at a set proportion of their income. Once the subsidy is phased out (or converted into a direct income support tool), the reactions of those households may change dramatically. Second, for other consumers, the relationship between consumption and cost is insufficiently transparent, not least because only half of all households have meters. The prevalence of domestic bathtubs and sinks without plugs, the thermal inefficiency of many buildings, and poor building maintenance procedures are telling examples of the current attitude. Cost-covering price increases, however, will eventually bring home to consumers the value of economy in the use of heat and hot water and a deeper awareness of alternative sources of supply.

Once each network faces sufficient competition from electricity and natural gas in the heating market in their area, the overall purpose of EPC regulation of heat price will come into question because the free working of the market will prevent any one supplier from extracting rents. In the medium term, district heating could (and should) be removed from the purview of the EPC. Country examples help illustrate the actual and potential intensity of competition in the heat market. In Poland, as of January 1998, the new Energy Law provides that heat prices are to be left to the market. In the Czech Republic, price control on heat is being gradually liberalized. In Sweden, the government has been forced to provide grants for extensions to district heating systems. In Denmark, the Heat Supply Act has been amended to ban the conversion to electric heating of existing buildings located within a district heating or natural gas supply network.

Finally, *the newly decentralized DH companies lack adequate governance and management structures*. It is unclear if the improvements in governance, management, and cost control that should be associated with decentralization will be realized quickly in Lithuania. Although studies were carried out before the actual decentralization of DH, little has been done to prepare municipal authorities for their new responsibilities.[1] For example, structures of governance have not been put in place in municipalities that would ensure efficient management control. The companies have not prepared business plans that would clarify the likely levels of their immediate financial performance and anticipate the financial impact of their future investment needs. While the DH enterprises in larger cities will have management and technical capabilities, the business "culture" of these entities may not be conducive to profitable operation, and the smaller entities may be lacking in the most basic skills and facilities. In such circumstances, better cost control, investment planning, and treasury and financial management will not be easily achieved.

There are several reasons why these are important, and potentially serious, negative factors. In

---

1. For instance, the consulting arm of the German utility Mannheimer Versorgungs-und Verkehrsgesellschaft mbH (MVV), *Decentralization of District Heating for Lithuania,* in 1996.

the first place, the current management of DH networks will, in most cases, remain in place after the networks have been transferred to municipal ownership and control. This is a positive factor—DH managers have a thorough knowledge of their business and strong technical skills. At the same time, they have not yet been required to work in a rigorously commercial environment, and they are accustomed to receiving support from corporate management in LPC. To make a successful transition to profit-driven, market-aware modes of operation will require not only effort on their part, but also a framework of strategic direction and support from the municipality.

That support should be provided by a board that is a blend of political, economic, and commercial acumen, as well as consumer representation. This is normal practice in the Scandinavian countries, for example. Such a board can provide the best assurance that, on the one hand, the municipal owner's prerogatives are respected, while on the other hand, corporate management of the DH enterprise is provided with the legal basis for resisting attempts to exercise unreasonable control against its best interests. In Germany, for example, the supervisory board of MVV (the Mannheim DH entity) discharges the normal functions of any corporate board (hiring and evaluating the chief executive, approving budgets, approving major investment plans and financing, and the like). It also approves major expansions of the network, tariff applications, and large contracts. Legally constituted supervisory boards of this nature can, in the Lithuanian DH context, act as necessary insulation between the commercial imperative and the political expedient. They can also represent an important element of the barrier that should be put in place between the DH companies and the municipalities to guard against both subsidization of DH by the municipalities and the local-level expropriation of DH cash flows that should be retained for investment in the networks. The information at hand, however, is that no such boards have been put in place in Lithuanian DH entities, and that governance is essentially a matter for the elected local authorities and municipal officials.

In sum, urgent investment needs, difficulties enforcing payment, loss of competitiveness, and weak governance will plague Lithuania's DH companies in the short and medium term. Some of them will be less equipped than others to deal with these issues because of their economic circumstances, the capabilities of their management, or the political environment in their parent municipalities. In some cases, this will lead to corporate failures in the coming years. To the extent that there is a competitive market for heat, with other operators standing ready to fill the gap, this should not be a dramatic problem. Indeed, such failures might be a fast route for private capital to become involved in the heating industry, with consequent improvements in efficiency for the economy as a whole.

The Future Role of the State in Power and Gas

THE LITHUANIAN POWER COMPANY. LPC's accounts for 1995 and 1996 are summarized in Annex 2-1. In 1996 the company had some 21,000 employees; 1.3 million electricity customers; and just under 0.5 million consumers for heat. Apart from 9 percent of its shares that were distributed to employees and are now quoted on the Vilnius Stock Exchange, its equity is owned by the state. As in the case of LG, it is governed by a supervisory board of five members—all civil servants—and by a management board chaired by the director general (it is understood, however, that the supervisory board, which has never operated effectively, is to be abolished).

This important company—the largest corporation and the largest employer in Lithuania, even after the decentralization of DH (the largest private sector employer, AB Ekranas, an electronics manufacturer, employs 25 percent of LPC's numbers)—is in a state of transition. LPC as it stood at the end of 1997 is a very different corporate entity from what it was six months earlier. It is the operator of Lithuania's national electricity grid and the monopoly distributor and supplier of electricity. It is now a relatively small player in electricity generation, albeit with very substantial reserve capacity. It is no longer significantly involved in heat supply or in businesses unconnected with electricity. It has a relatively strong balance sheet, with a debt-to-equity ratio of only 15:85. Payment discipline on the part of its consumers has improved, partly because of government action, and cost-covering tariffs for its product have been approved by the new, independent, EPC.

Many of the company's unprofitable ancillary activities have been closed or disposed of, while all the remaining ancillary activities, save the Elektra Hotel in Vilnius (to wit, the TENA procurement subsidiary and four maintenance and construction units), are in the process of being incorporated as "closed" companies that will be independently managed and sold during the next two years. In accordance with government policy, LPC's electricity business is to be separated into discrete business units for generation, transmission, and distribution and supply.

Table 2-14 illustrates the key features of LPC as forecast for 1998: this is not comparable to Annex 2-1 because of the changes in corporate structure described above. It demonstrates, however, the new, healthier situation that policy planning for LPC should take into account. (The forecast assumes a continuation of the tariffs set on 1 July 1997, which LPC believes are inadequate to finance its operations or to contribute to investment costs.)

There is a widespread perception that LPC is inefficient, that it imposes unreasonable costs on the economy, and that it is a burden on the budget. A Management Performance Review and Improvement Program is under way in LPC. Among the objectives of this project will be an analysis of LPC's technical, marketing, managerial, and financial performance, with comparisons against international norms. Even without the results of this study, however, it is possible to indicate the general status of LPC's financial performance. The rate of return on total capital employed in 1992 was in the range of 13–15 percent for three U.K. companies, 3–8 percent for three Norwegian companies, and 7–14 percent for eleven Swedish companies (return on capital employed in LPC was negative in 1996). The net profit margin (profit to turnover) in the companies surveyed was generally in the range of 9–16 percent (negative in LPC). The debt-to-equity ratios of the Swedish companies ranged between 90:10 and 50:50; for the U.K. companies, around 50:50; and for the Norwegian companies, between 65:35 and 10:90 (LPC, 24:76 on 31 December 1996 and forecast to be 14:86 on 31 December 1998). Similarly, the eight regional electricity distributors in the Czech Republic (which are quoted on the Prague Stock Exchange) had an average ratio of net earnings before tax to net assets of exactly 10 percent in 1996. The principal Czech generator earned a return on net assets of nearly 17 percent.

The "new" LPC has total assets of Lt 2.3 billion. It would not be unreasonable for the state to expect LPC to earn 7.5 percent on this figure—that is, Lt 172 million before taxes. This would imply a margin on sales of about 13 percent. These ratios are in line with international experience, which also suggests that the company should be able to support additional borrowings to finance necessary investments. LPC is currently not earning such returns on its electricity business, according to the company's own pro forma accounts. This failure is probably the result of a combination of factors, including the following:

- Domestic tariffs, until recently, have been too low to allow profit on electricity sales, (although LPC's export trade has probably been profitable).
- Personnel numbers are excessive.
- Fuel costs for LPC's own generation have been increased by the company's inability to finance purchases at the most opportune time.

- Finance has been scarce, for even high-yielding investments in the upgrading of electricity networks.

Table 2-14. Summary Features of LPC, 1998 (forecast)

Item	Unit	Amount
Income statement		
Sales		
Home sales	GWh	7,390
Export sales	GWh	1,000
Total sales	GWh	8,390
Revenue		
Home revenue	Lt million	1,175
Export revenue	Lt million	100
Total revenue	Lt million	1,275
Purchased power	Lt million	635
Fuel	Lt million	74
O+M costs	Lt million	503
Depreciation	Lt million	141
Interest	Lt million	49
Total costs	Lt million	1,402
Noncore results	Lt million	-10
Net profit	Lt million	-137
Balance sheet		
Current assets	Lt million	121
Fixed assets	Lt million	2218
Total assets	Lt million	2,339
Current liabilities	Lt million	309
Net assets	Lt million	2,030
Loans	Lt million	283
Shareholders' funds	Lt million	1,747

Against this background, several issues remain to be addressed by the government. The first is *the regulation of the electricity market*. The market is currently opaque, partly because of a lack of transparency in LPC's operations, but more generally because INPP, which produces most of the electricity consumed in Lithuania, as well as an important export element, is not subject to the kind of reporting arrangements being adopted by other state-owned enterprises, including financial disclosure that meets international accounting standards. This issue is likely to become controversial now that the large CHP plants in Vilnius and Kaunas have been transferred to municipal ownership. The operators of these plants are likely to contend that they can supply electricity to the National Grid at a price below INPP's full cost. Furthermore, as the Lithuanian economy expands, and with closure of one INPP reactor a possibility in the medium term, the prospects of much greater diversity of supply in the electricity sector and of the growth of an active power market will emerge.

Just how a transparent and efficient electricity market can be created should be of immediate concern to policymakers The EU's Directive No. 96/92/EC of 19 December 1996 concerning common rules for the internal market in electricity stipulates that there should be separation of the accounts for the different parts of an integrated electricity business; an independent transmission system operator; and access to the system for producers, suppliers, and eligible customers. Within these general provisions, several approaches are possible. Argentina, Australia, Chile, Sweden, and the United Kingdom favor the "pool" model, in which there is open access by all generators to a continuous marketplace. This, in the short term, yields the lowest prices. In Lithuania's current circumstances, however, INPP will be the lowest bidder under almost all conditions, which would mean bankruptcy for LPC's Elektrenai Plant, an essential national reserve capacity. The alternative is the "single buyer" model in use in several other European countries. In this arrangement, a monopoly buyer negotiates supply agreements with all available generators, and "availability" contracts with all stations considered to be necessary to the country's overall power strategy. At first examination, this would seem to offer the best route for Lithuania, and the closure of even one of INPP's reactors would allow a lively electricity market to develop. While no new capacity is needed in today's conditions, an INPP closure would create openings for new private generators. It is relevant that technological change has meant that a unit as small as 250 MW can now be as competitive in cost as a 1,000-MW unit.

The way the electricity market is eventually regulated will be critical for the second pending policy issue affecting LPC—*the strategy for its privatization*. Most of the successful transformations of previously state-owned power companies around the world have followed the model of privatization first, *then* internal reorganization. The United Kingdom electricity industry is a good example of this approach, where private sector attitudes and management skills have succeeded in achieving radical change in culture and performance. Rather fewer countries—France and Ireland are examples—have chosen to reform and reconstruct their electricity sectors while keeping them in state ownership, although at least in Ireland, later privatization is a strong possibility. In Lithuania, market realities—the capacity and demand equation and the dominance of INPP—seem to make early and full privatization unlikely, at least in generation. In these circumstances, policymakers may be forced to push for reform to enhance internal efficiency now, and to keep the privatization timetable open.

An important related issue is the selection of companies that would be preferred partners in the electricity industry. The government has a choice between seeking strategic investors with expertise in the industry or simply selecting those with the necessary financial capacity. Given the outdated nature of much of LPC's generating and transmission/distribution plant, there would be advantages in attracting the interest, for example, of Scandinavian or German power companies, in both generation and transmission.

Another policy matter in the possible sale of LPC is whether its power generation assets should be privatized as one or as several entities. LPC management believes there is competitive strength in keeping the stations in one entity. The arguments in favor of this do not seem compelling, and indeed such a model could provide a continuing screen for inefficiency.

The government will also need to decide whether to corporatize and privatize the regional distribution utilities as seven companies (the present number), divide them into a greater number, or convert them into one national network. While managerial competition would confer benefits, there might also be costs arising from the loss of critical mass. It is relevant that in Ireland, which has approximately the same geographical area as Lithuania and where the number of electricity customers is 1.4 million (LPC's is 1.3 million), the government, after extensive study, has decided to retain the distribution and supply network as a single business (naturally, with regional divisions). European experience seems to bear out the belief that a regional distribution utility needs about 250,000 customers to be viable. This suggests that Lithuania should have no more than five such utilities. Such a number would offer the opportunity for development of a strong, competitive supply sector, with management competition in performance, customer interests at the forefront, and management that can be rewarded from market returns.

Finally, before privatization is achieved, other corporate issues will require government attention. For example, it will need to decide how much freedom LPC should have to reinvest funds liberated by the sale of subsidiaries and ancillary businesses. Given the need of the company to invest in the rehabilitation of its assets, a case could be made that it should be allowed to retain the proceeds of the disposal of noncore assets on the basis of investment plans approved by the government-appointed supervisory board.[2] Yet, if further unbundling of LPC—into generation companies, a national grid/national dispatch company, and a number of distribution utilities—precedes privatization, it may be advisable that the proceeds from the sale of separate corporate units revert to the government and other shareholders, not to the company.

The third pending policy issue is the *promotion of efficiency enhancements in the period leading to privatization*. While from a policy point of view, an adequate management incentive structure is the best tool to seek efficiency in the use of public assets, some nonfuel costs deserve immediate attention from the government as owner. For example, the ratio of personnel costs to fuel costs in LPC has risen by over 60 percent in three years—from 22 percent in 1994 to an estimated 36 percent in 1997. The extremely high staff numbers in the company cannot be overlooked. In 1996, approximately 11,000 staff worked in the electricity business of LPC, as well as over 5,000 in INPP. There were, therefore, approximately twice as many employees for each 1,000 customers in the Lithuanian electricity sector as there were in the comparably sized Irish industry.

The emphasis placed on efficiency improvements by the management of an enterprise may be affected by their perception of the rewards they receive. In this respect, LPC (and LG; see below) suffers from government restrictions placed on the remuneration of senior executives. The civil-service-linked pay structure for such executives is not capable of offering incentives for exceptional effort and performance. Senior financial staff, furthermore, is aware of the very much higher salaries available to well-qualified and experienced accountants and financial analysts in growing private sector enterprises and have no incentive to remain in worse-paid public sector employment.

Issues of the kind outlined here (immediate efficiency-promoting steps) are exactly the sorts of issues that should concern the board of a company. They require a cost-cutting program from management, provision of management incentives, and the improvement of financial management. They are at the heart of corporate governance as described earlier. LPC, as well as LG and other energy companies, lacks such a board.

THE LITHUANIAN GAS COMPANY. LG transported 3.06 billion cubic meters of natural gas in 1996; its own sales represented 1.59 billion cubic meters of this total. Allowing for the 422 million cubic meters transshipped to Kaliningrad, LG's share of domestic Lithuanian consumption was 60 percent. The company provided transmission services to the suppliers of the other 40 percent, half a dozen importers that are primarily suppliers for LPC, and a number of large industrial users. LPC was the buyer in 65 percent of LG's sales, and 34 percent of the sales of other suppliers of power and heat generation. The company also supplies 67 percent of the LPC market, the balance of the market being in the hands of about 60 small, regional distributors.

LG's pipelines have a capacity at the Lithuanian border of 12 billion cubic meters annually, so

---

2. A first step should be to require professional valuations of these businesses, which comprise, inter alia, the TENA procurement subsidiary, a concrete fabrication plant, the Kruonis construction company, two power line maintenance operations, and the Hotel Elektra in Vilnius. Total employment in these operations is about 1,200 people.

current capacity utilization is about 25 percent. The company believes that investment in gas storage facilities would permit more flexible gas purchasing arrangements, and thus improve their competitive position. (The company's estimate of the cost of storage facilities for five months' supply is $250 million.) LG operates the natural gas business through seven regional distribution subsidiaries and has 4,600 employees. Its financial data are listed in table 2-15.

Table 2-15. Lithuanian Gas Company
(Lt million)

Item	1996	1995
Sales	729	712
Profit (loss) before tax	(13)	62
Taxation	5	18
Profit (loss) after tax	(17)	44
Net assets	502	442
Long-term debt	101	78
Financing and accrued charges	76	
Capital and reserves	325	364

Source: Lithuanian Gas Company, *Annual Report*, 1996.

The state faces several policy issues regarding this company, both as owner and as regulator. The first is *the need to elicit efficiency until privatization*. LG is a stable company. Nevertheless, it is facing difficult competitive conditions in its LPG business. Given its generally dominant position in its markets, particularly in natural gas, its financial performance is unacceptable. While the 1996 accounts, prepared to international accounting standards, were the first for some years to show a net loss, the return on assets in previous years has generally been far too low—2 to 3 percent, compared with 10 percent or more in western European gas companies. The National Energy Strategy estimated LG's necessary capital expenditures at US$569 million (Lt 2.3 billion) in 1994, to be spent primarily on the pipelines and other elements of the gas distribution system. A fifteen-year investment program was envisaged, suggesting average annual expenditures of Lt 150 million. A more recent gas sector development program prepared by the company envisages capital expenditures averaging Lt 100 million annually over the 1997–2000 period. In recent years, internal cash flow has not exceeded Lt 60 million each year. Clearly, financing such a level of investment requires either a major improvement in operating performance or the injection of significant new equity or loan capital. The present debt-to-equity ratio is on the order of 25:75, which means that new loan funding is certainly a possibility. But new capital, whether it is equity or debt, will require remuneration, which implies, once again, a major improvement in operating profitability.

The reasons for LG's low profitability are unclear, and no objective analysis is available. There is reason to believe that the company's cost structure is excessive for the amount of business it does, but until an independent cost audit is completed (something that has never happened), it is impossible to be certain. Nevertheless, some crude comparisons with the smaller Irish natural gas monopoly are interesting (table 2-16).

Comparisons of this sort are hazardous given the differences in operating conditions between the enterprises, but the figures given above suggest that there is a *prima facie* case that LG is overstaffed. If this is the case, or if other costs are excessive, this is not a supportable situation in the medium term. LG may have a monopoly in natural gas distribution in Lithuania, but its product is in a competitive market where customers will be increasingly aware of options.

Table 2-16. A Comparison of the Lithuanian and Irish Gas Systems

Item	Lithuanian Gas Company	Irish Gas Board
Customers	484,000	267,500
Transmission lines (km)	1,400	1,030
Distribution lines (km)	4,100	5,000
Employees	4,500	733
Sales ($ million)	178	379
Net profit (loss) ($ million)	-4.3	117

Source: Lithuanian Gas Company, Bord Gais Eireann.

Second, that lack of efficiency is compounded by *serious corporate governance problems*. Management is supposedly overseen by a supervisory board. In theory, this board includes five members, all civil servants, but in practice it appears to play no independent role. The latest information is that it is to be disbanded, and no alternative mechanism is under discussion. It should be noted that in other European countries such boards are becoming the norm in state-owned enterprise, as they have long been among private sector companies. Ireland's Electricity Supply Board, which strongly resembles LPC as a state-owned, vertically integrated power monopoly undergoing a painful change process, is controlled by a board of twelve, none of whom is a civil servant.

Third, *there is an obvious policy vacuum regarding LG's privatization*. Nine percent of LG's shares are in private ownership and are traded on the Vilnius Stock Exchange, while the remaining 91 percent are held by the state. The government has approved the issue of additional shares with a nominal value of Lt 66 million to Russian gas suppliers, bringing the total private shareholding to 25 percent. These shares are being issued at a premium of 65 percent, and will therefore yield Lt 109 million to the company. The rationale for the sale strategy is unclear. It would have been preferable to have sold the shares by international tender. It would also have been advantageous for the government to have sold some of its existing shareholding rather than issuing fresh shares, which will leave the proceeds in the company's hands rather than with the government.

The full privatization of the company is envisaged in the medium term, although a firm privatization timetable and plan have not yet been established, despite the evident interest in the company by several overseas gas enterprises. More immediately, the company is currently contemplating spinning off its seven regional distribution utilities into joint ventures with municipalities (in this respect, a pilot study is under way in Kaunas municipality). It is evident from these developments, and from similar suggestions that have been made in relation to electricity distribution, that some municipalities envisage a future in which they will control integrated utilities for their regions (electricity, heat, gas, and water distribution). No economic, strategic, or financial case has been made for such integrated utilities.

Although it is understood that the government intends to fully privatize the company, nothing concrete has happened. Three company-specific factors seem to be delaying LG's privatization. First, while the government appears to be committed to the sale of the company (with necessary safeguards in place because of the strategic importance of the pipeline and supply network), there is disagreement in the Seimas about the proportion of equity the state should retain, although there is no obvious benefit in retaining any part of LG in public ownership. Second, the creation of regional integrated utilities, which is apparently under consideration, could make the company less attractive. (The example of LPC would not inspire confidence in the conglomerate model.) Third, privatization initiatives are being effectively left to company management. While management has an important role to play in supplying government with information to aid decisionmaking, the initiative should be firmly in the hands of the shareholders (the government in particular) and their representatives, the supervisory board.

Fostering Energy Conservation and Renewable Energy

The Lithuanian energy sector is characterized by a number of features (some already described above) that are detrimental to economy in the consumption of scarce, imported and expensive energy resources. These features include:

- Financial arrangements and management cultures have insulated energy companies from the needs of their consumers.

- Until recently, tariffs failed to reflect the full cost of energy.

- There have been high levels of power losses (technical and nontechnical) from the electricity distribution networks and massive leaks from the DH hot water networks.

- In DH, there has been excessive reliance on HOBs, which are old and inefficient.

- There has been a lack of flow and temperature controls at DH substations.

- Heat is not metered.

- Buildings are thermally inefficient (Soviet norms permitted heat transmission values five times those of Sweden).

- Building maintenance is poor or absent, partly because of uncertainty over property rights and responsibilities.

- A preexisting culture attached little importance to energy conservation, partly because energy was so "cheap" in the FSU.

The high energy intensity of the economy, largely attributable to these factors, is not difficult to illustrate. For example, average heat consumption in households was estimated in 1993 to be 300 kWh per square meter, which was two-to-three times the average in Denmark. Hot water consumption per capita was 40 percent higher than in Sweden. The reduction in heat consumption since 1993 does not materially affect the point.

The government has put considerable effort into changing these features in recent years. Public awareness—and sharply increased heat and electricity tariffs—have started to bring home to the community the benefits of conservation and the high rates of return produced by conservation measures. Policies have been drafted covering the subsidization of conservation investments, the improvement of the legal environment affecting the ownership of property, and the establishment of building standards. An important initiative was the establishment, within the then Ministry of Energy, of an Energy Conservation Program with two key responsibilities: (i) drafting of further legislation on energy conservation and (ii) promoting the greater utilization of local, renewable energy sources. A program objective is to increase indigenous production of primary energy (mainly peat and timber) enough to reduce imports of primary energy by 14 percent by the year 2010.[3] If achieved, this would reduce Lithuania's annual import bill by Lt 450 million (US$112.5 million) at 1996 prices. In order to promote this objective, an Energy Saving Fund has been established with ECU 3 million of EU-granted funds. The fund is similar to Energy Efficiency Funds established in the Czech Republic, Latvia, Slovakia, Slovenia, and Romania. The government has promised to add Lt 10 million to the fund, but the relevant line was struck out of the 1997 budget before it was passed by the Seimas.

In general, the government appears to have clear policy objectives in the conservation area, and is rightly giving priority to demand-side measures in residential, industrial, commercial, and institutional

---

3. Moneys from the fund are devoted to grants to aid specific projects, whether exploration of renewable energy sources or projects to improve (for example) the energy efficiency of buildings. The program also engages in a publicity campaign to heighten public awareness of conservation issues.

buildings and in industry, transport, and agriculture. In gross terms, these are the areas where the greatest savings can be made. The government has commissioned studies of energy-saving and resource-diversification possibilities, and has been assisted in this by the World Bank and other agencies. It is paying particular attention to building codes and investments in existing buildings.

There are four areas where further development of policy, or the more forceful expression of existing policies, appears necessary. The most important of these relates to an area where the responsibility of the state is most clear: in the operations of the energy companies owned by the state or by municipalities.

The government's national energy efficiency program, originally issued in 1992 and published in revised form in 1996, estimates that the total annual saving potential through the implementation of all measures is 24.7 TWh (equivalent to the output of two INPPs). Of these potential savings, 5.3 TWh—21 percent of the total—are in the generation and distribution of electricity and heat, activities that are currently controlled by publicly owned enterprises. The approximate value of such savings, in terms of imported fuel and associated variable costs, is Lt 600 million (US$150 million). This estimate includes an assumption that losses from the DH system would be at the 1994 level of about 14 percent. Since 1994, however, these losses have risen to over 31 percent; using the higher figure would add up to Lt 200 million to the annual saving. The program estimates the investments needed to secure such savings at Lt 7 billion. Here, the financial interests of the state parallel the economic case for conservation, not to mention the environmental benefits—an example of what the International Energy Agency (IEA) has called "no regret" actions. It can be very crudely estimated that the state budget's exposure to the energy sector will be in the region of Lt 500 million in both fiscal 1998 and 1999, falling to less than Lt 400 million in 2000 and 2001, and heading toward zero thereafter as the remaining consumer subsidies are (presumably) phased out. Rapid and effective implementation of energy-saving investments by publicly owned energy companies could thus greatly ease the impact of these costs, particularly through increased levels of technical efficiency in the generation, transmission, and distribution of electricity and heat.

The second area where greater force and consistency of policy is required is in relation to the Energy Saving Fund. The failure of the government to meet its commitments to the fund gives the wrong message to consumers and does not seem economically justifiable.

Third, little direct pressure is placed on large industrial and commercial consumers to examine their energy-using practices. Energy-efficiency audits are all but nonexistent.

Finally, there is evidence that consumers are generally still not as conscious as they should be of the costs of wastefulness in energy consumption or of the benefits to be gained from economy. According to a social assessment carried out in connection with the World Bank's Energy Efficiency/Housing Pilot Project, 45 percent of householders interviewed in Vilnius and Kaunas either thought that energy saving was a waste of time or had no opinion, while 80 percent felt that to reduce their consumption further would inflict hardship on their families. It seems that, despite the commendable efforts of the Energy Conservation Program, the message may not have gotten through. The IEA specifically recommends the use of information policies to show consumers how they can save money by saving energy.

Policy Recommendations

Overall Strategy and Principles

The *Statement of Energy Sector Development Policy and Strategy* adopted by the government in 1994 remains valid. Considerable progress has been made in implementing important elements of that policy and strategy—for example, in DH decentralization, in establishing the EPC, in planning the overall regulatory environment, in achieving pricing transparency, and in attracting private capital. Important shortfalls persist, however, in other areas of energy policy. These relate primarily to the performance of state-owned energy companies, the future role of the state as owner, the development of energy market mechanisms, and energy conservation. In all of these areas, new policy approaches are needed so that Lithuania may realize its overall objectives of efficiency in energy production and consumption; reliability and quality of supply; diversity of energy resources and sources; protection of the environment; and, critically, the financial independence of the energy sector from the state.

The main tools to achieve those objectives are (1) fiscal policy, to support the principle that the level, nature, and effects of any explicit or implicit subsidies to energy producers or consumers should be controlled; (2) governance, to support the principle that the overall strategic role of the state as owner (as far as this role lasts) should be clearly separated from the direction and management of commercial enterprises; (3) conservation policy, to support the principle that fiscal, pricing, investment, and other incentives and penalties should be deployed to encourage economy on the part of energy producers and users, and to accelerate the development of indigenous renewable primary energy sources; (4) regulatory policy, to support the principles of consumer protection, long-run economy of supply, and the operation of the market; and (5) privatization, to support the principle that private sector involvement in the energy sector will contribute to long-term improvements in efficiency and customer service.

Although the 1995 Energy Law remains valid, progress has been slow in some important areas that should receive special attention from government. It is therefore recommended that the government adopt a new, time-bound Plan of Action formulated along the lines of the Plan of Action appended to the 1994 *Statement of Energy Sector Development Policy and Strategy*, but recognizing the changes in circumstances over the past four years and, consequently, adopting a different emphasis. The new plan should (1) set a date by which the regulatory framework for the energy sector will be complete, with the necessary agencies staffed, resourced, and at work; (2) state how a competitive electricity market will operate; (3) provide a firm schedule for the unbundling of LPC into transparent corporate entities; (4) provide a firm schedule for the privatization of all the state's investments in the energy sector (except INPP); (5) set out comprehensive governance rules for energy enterprises controlled by the state or by municipalities and specify the duties, prerogatives, and membership guidelines for supervisory boards of such enterprises; and (6) set targets for energy conservation, the diversification of energy sources, and the exploitation of renewable energy resources, and proclaim the measures (including incentives and sanctions) being taken to achieve the targets.

A statement of the type recommended above should be accompanied by the selection of a series of key objectives for the energy sector, and the establishment of measurable monitoring indicators for each. These should relate to the principal areas of government concern, including overall energy intensity, diversity of fuel sources, development of indigenous and renewable energy forms, levels of subsidization, financial performance of state-controlled utilities, and the like. The objectives should include, inter alia, (1) reduction of energy intensity of the economy by 10 percent annually (such reductions have been achieved by several European countries over short periods); (2) reduction of import dependency by 10 percentage points by the year 2000 (for example, Denmark reduced its import dependency from 47.4 percent in 1990 to 28.8 percent in 1994); (3) reduction in the proportion of oil supplies sourced from Russia to less than 80 percent by 2000; (4) phasing out of consumer heat subsidies over three years; (5) earning annual dividends (or interest) from remaining state-owned energy companies equivalent to 5 percent of net assets (all such enterprises had a combined book value in 1996 of slightly more than Lt 10 billion; a 5 percent rate of return would have implied aggregate profits of Lt

500 million, whereas the enterprises incurred an aggregate loss of about Lt 50 million); and (6) increasing the private sector share of electricity generation to 5 percent of the total by 1999.

Performance targets of this type should be supplemented by similar targets at the utility or company level, covering the principal measures of technical, managerial, and manpower efficiency. (Annex 2-2, which is drawn from World Bank Technical Paper No. 243, *Improving Electric Power Utility Efficiency*, suggests some appropriate headings for setting targets for LPC; similar targets might be set for the other energy companies.)

Making Viable the Transfer of District Heating to Municipal Ownership

Two general principles should be protected in designing policy to meet the new DH environment: the state budget's exposure to the DH sector must be completely eliminated, and the government's overall energy objectives and strategy must continue to be supported in the new ownership environment.

In 1997 the state was fiscally exposed to the DH sector through the consumer subsidy for low-income households and through the inclusion in the budgets of the municipalities of provision for DH deficits. As economic growth resumes and heating tariffs are being set at cost-recovering levels, it should be feasible for the government to evaluate the impact on households of reducing that subsidy progressively over a (small) number of years, with the intention of eliminating it altogether by a target date—the year 2000, for example.

As regards operating deficits, it is inevitable that these will be incurred in 1997. There is no justification, however, for any future provision for heating losses, in the 1998 budget or subsequently. It is important that the advantages achieved by securing municipalization of the sector should be maximized without delay. For that purpose, the government should make it absolutely clear that it will not finance deficits in the future, as it did in the past when DH was under LPC control. It is the responsibility of the municipal authorities to make whatever changes are necessary in their DH entities to secure profitable operation within the tariffs approved by the EPC.

There is one dilemma that the municipalities will face that merits government involvement in solving. This relates to the weakening competitive position of many DH networks. Technical deficiencies are compounded in consumers' eyes by large tariff increases. Yet the investment funds required to upgrade DH facilities and strengthen the competitive position of the networks, by reducing future (maintenance and other) operating costs, are enormous. The weaker the DH networks become, the more consumers will turn to other forms of heating. In many cases, this will be a suboptimal development because the efficiency of the alternative system will be significantly less than that of an (efficient) DH system. The consequences will be manifested in Lithuania's balance of payments, in industrial costs, and in environmental effects. The financial costs of the necessary investments, large though they may be, could probably be recovered through tariffs, but only over a long time-scale. Suitably structured borrowing would appear to offer a solution, but Lithuania's municipalities have no real borrowing capacity, no track record in bond markets, no suitable collateral to offer to lenders, and no experience of evaluating and preparing projects of this scale (see the chapter on municipal finance in this volume).

It is therefore recommended that the government provide assistance to municipalities in two ways:

•   By carrying out an urgent study of the investments needed on a municipality-by-municipality basis (estimated to be Lt 3 billion nationally over the period 1995 to 2010, an average of Lt 200 million a year, in the 1993 Energy Master Plan for Lithuania State Power System)[4]

- By negotiating and coordinating a borrowing program to obtain the necessary finance to implement a major rehabilitation program for the entire DH sector, concentrating on those projects that are estimated to yield the best combination of economic and environmental benefits.

The Municipal Development Project currently under consideration by the World Bank envisages the establishment of a Municipal Credit Facility (MCF), initially amounting to $32.5 million, for on-lending to municipalities for a variety of capital purposes, mainly infrastructural. The suggested MCF seems to provide a structure that would be perfectly appropriate to the financing of investments in the DH systems. The emphasis that it places on local capacity building and institutional development—and the fact that successful MCF lending operations would greatly ease subsequent bond market or other credit operations of the municipalities—fully supports overall energy sector development in Lithuania. It is questionable, however, whether the scale of the MCF being considered is adequate for the substantial DH investment program that is required. It may be necessary to consider a separate operation specifically for the municipal DH enterprises. The funds made available by such an operation could be supplemented by a special temporary levy on tariffs that would divert into investment a proportion of the cost savings achieved through the investment program and other cost efficiencies. Whether the instrument used is the proposed MCF or a custom-made alternative, the conditionalities attached to lending to municipalities should include requirements in relation to the governance of DH entities (see below) to ensure that they can operate in a fully commercial manner, as businesses rather than as departments of the municipal administration.

It is equally important that the state use the powers at its disposal to insist upon the highest standards of management and governance in the DH sector. The work of the EPC, and the expected establishment of a broad regulatory agency for the energy sector, will contribute toward this objective. However, there are additional measures that the government could usefully adopt:

- Provisions that are currently being applied on an effective temporary basis to compel state budgetary organizations to pay their DH bills promptly should be made permanent.
- The structure of governance that applies to DH entities should be specified through legislation, including the powers and membership of boards, which should include, as in similar companies in western Europe, a majority of "outside" (nonmanagerial) representation such as consumers, financial experts, and business people, as well as representatives of the municipalities.
- Regular "league tables" should be published ranking DH entities in terms of their performance against a range of indicators, including profit ratios, tariffs, cost per customer, market share in their areas, heat losses, thermal efficiency, receivables overdue, use of indigenous and renewable fuels, and the like.
- Finally, a date should be set by which the heating sector should be freed from price regulation; this process should go in tandem with the introduction of private capital, on an unrestricted basis, to the DH sector.

Toward the Privatization of LPC and LG

The first principle that must inform policy in relation to these two important and influential companies is that decisions about their future ownership, regulation, and financial objectives are for the government, not the companies' management, to make, and that the latter's role is only to implement policy and to

---

4. Perhaps building on the work already being done in Kaunas by the Bank's ESMAP program.

achieve the financial and service objectives set. This has two important implications: there must be clear lines of demarcation between the government as shareholder, the government as regulator, the government as customer, and the utility's management; and the government as controlling shareholder must make clear decisions about the future of the companies, and must establish organs of corporate governance to ensure implementation of these decisions. These organs should include supervisory boards that contain a majority of outside members, including economists, financial experts, successful figures from the private sector, and representatives of consumers (industrial and commercial as well as residential; as mentioned earlier, the five-member supervisory boards appointed to LPC and LG in April 1997 consist exclusively of civil servants).

Thus, it is recommended to:

- Complete the current review of the regulatory environment for energy with a view to having a comprehensive regulatory agency, responsible for all key issues such as the licensing of operators and the specification and monitoring of supply standards (in addition to the EPC's existing role in the tariff area), fully resourced and operational.

- Following full analysis of the options, and in conformity with European Union policies, put in place electricity market mechanisms that will provide for competition between, and fair remuneration of, electricity generators (whether the assets under their control are characterized as base load, peak load, or reserve capacity) for efficient bulk trading with distribution utilities, and long-run minimalization of the cost of electricity to consumers.

- Establish each of LPC's remaining generating stations as a separate state-owned company, its shares controlled by the Ministry of Economy and reporting directly (through its board) to that ministry, until privatization takes place.

- Establish each of LPC's seven regional electricity distribution utilities as a separate subsidiary of LPC, incorporated under company legislation and with municipal representation on its supervisory board, again until privatization takes place.

- Remove all barriers to fully commercial operation in LPC, in particular by replacing the members of the present supervisory board with a board of seven to nine persons, consisting of one executive of the company (the general director), one civil servant, and five to seven others who might include a private sector business person, a banker, a financial expert, a consumer, an economist, and an LPC employee elected by the workforce (all of these would be appointed and accountable to the ministry, but their remit on the board would be to ensure the highest possible standards of efficiency, service, and financial performance).

- Appoint boards, selected along similar lines, to the generating and distribution companies.

- Establish a series of performance indicators for LPC to achieve, based on the framework shown in Annex 2-2.

- Engage experienced international financial advisers to attract private capital into the electricity industry and to develop a plan for the ultimate privatization of the generation and distribution/supply sectors (the transmission activity, the National Grid, should remain in public ownership).

- Place the total privatization of LG immediately in the hands of duly selected international advisers; assuming the regulatory agency is in place before the sale is concluded, there should be no need for the government to retain a "golden share."

- Remove all obstacles, such as the present proviso that the maximum salary in LPC may not exceed five times the average pay in the company, to the establishment of performance-related remuneration of energy sector managers in line with managers carrying similar responsibility in the Lithuanian private sector. (On the basis of studies in thirty-two developing countries, a recent World Bank policy research report, "Bureaucrats in Business," 1995, concluded that performance contracts between government and the managements of state-owned enterprises could help to speed the reform of such enterprises if incentives are aligned appropriately.)

Capturing More of the Benefit of Energy Conservation

Although government has shown a considerable degree of commitment to the principles of energy conservation and the development of Lithuania's indigenous sources of renewable energy, further efforts are needed.

The Energy Saving Fund should be adequately funded, initially by the government making good on its commitment of Lt 10 million. This is essential if the government is to be perceived by consumers as serious in its commitment to energy economy. Without such financial resources, the fund will be unable to make its intended contribution to conservation.

The government, and in particular the Ministry of Economy through its Energy Conservation Program, must examine defects in its efforts to educate Lithuania's consumers in the benefits of conservation and must allocate the resources necessary for the program to mount a much more effective and continuing public education and information campaign. This should include setting up information and advice centers, "Energy Information Kiosks" (as are widely used in Belgium, for instance), greater use of the media, and special modules in primary school curricula. Other devices, such as a "National Energy Awareness Week," as in Ireland in 1994, would help to "plant" ideas in the public's mind. The cost of such measures should be met out of energy tariffs.

Industrial, commercial, and institutional consumers (starting with large consumers) should be required by law to carry out energy audits according to standards set by the Energy Conservation Program. Public procurement rules should incorporate energy-saving technologies among their criteria.

Finally, the government must make it clear to the supervisory boards of state and municipal energy companies that progress in replacing energy-wasteful equipment and methods will be considered a key performance indicator. State funds for that purpose should not be used, or indirectly committed to these companies. All categories of such companies, on present tariffs, should be able to structure their finances to make energy-preserving rehabilitation investments possible without government guarantee or support, since all will earn continuing financial benefits from making these investments. The government should seek an understanding with the EPC that tariffs will take account of the need for conservation investments over a lengthy period, and that the tariffs will encourage companies, rather than penalize them, for making these investments.

ANNEX 2-1

Financial Statements of Lithuanian Power Company, 1996
(Lt millions)

Item	1996	1995
Profit and loss account		
Revenues	1,568	1,282
Expenses		
Purchased power	710	469
Fuel	144	102
Depreciation	125	85
Salaries, wages, and social security	151	106
All other expenses	391	285
Total expenses	1,521	1,047
Operating result of continuing operations	47	235
Other income/expenses	(83)	(70)
Interest on debt	(112)	(45)
Penalties and overdue interest	49	12
Other	(146)	(103)
Income (loss) from continuing operations	(99)	132
Subsidy income	819	95
Net result of discontinued operation	(362)	(442)
Net income (loss)	358	(215)
Balance sheet		
Fixed assets	3,061	2,975
Subsidies receivable from the government	730	—
Current assets	679	728
Total assets	4,470	3,703
Shareholders' equity	2,477	2,105
Long-term debt and deferred revenue	528	700
Long-term debt to be assumed by the government	226	—
Current liabilities	890	898
Obligations to be canceled by the government	349	—

Note: Financial statements were prepared to international accounting standards.

ANNEX 2-2

Sample Performance Indicators for LPC

Qualitative Indicators—General

Does LPC have clear and consistent objectives?	
Has management the right to hire and fire?	
Is there an appropriate management information and reporting system?	
Is management held accountable for its performance?	
Is LPC's training program adequate?	
Are daily operations insulated from external political pressure?	
Does management control salaries?	
Is there continuous monitoring of ongoing projects?	
Are performance-based incentives in place for employees?	

Quantitative Indicators

Human resources

Turnover of manpower/average workforce	
Training costs per employee	
Number of employees/customers	
Rate of absenteeism	
Employees per MWh sold	

Commercial and accounting

Accounts receivable/months billing	
Bad debts/accounts receivable	
Billing lag in days	
Accounts more than 3 months overdue/total accounts receivable	
Service connection lag in days	

Financial

Rate of return on assets	
Debt-service ratio	
Average revenue from electricity sales	
Self-funding ratio	

Technical

Forced outage rate	
Plant availability hours/8760	
System cost of power produced	
System load factor	
Technical losses	
System own use	
Reserve margin	
System fuel cost	
Staff years per MWh generated	
System losses	
Nontechnical losses	

Source: World Bank, *Improving Electric Power Utility Efficiency*, Technical Paper No. 243 (Washington, D.C.).

3

MUNICIPAL FINANCE

This note reviews developments in Lithuania's fiscal decentralization policy since the World Bank report *Lithuania: Municipal Finance Report* of April 1995 and suggests an agenda for further reform. The rationalization and modernization of the system of municipal finances will play a significant role in placing Lithuania's public accounts on a sustainable path. Close to a third of consolidated public sector spending is at the municipal level, and key public services such as education and public utilities are primarily the responsibility of municipal governments. Municipal governments also play a significant role in social protection. With no taxing powers of their own of any significance, and with no clear borrowing guidelines, the financial balance of municipalities is a crucial element in the stability of the country's macroeconomic framework, because the central government implicitly plays the role of payer of last resort.

After a spate of new laws and reforms in 1993–94, followed by the *Municipal Finance Report* and an ensuing government task force, the process of municipal reform would appear to have come to a halt. During 1995 and 1996 the system of municipal governments continued to operate within a faulty framework characterized by lack of revenue autonomy; perverse incentives for expenditure efficiency, revenue mobilization, or cost recovery; and a budgeting system that was still anchored in the gap-filling system inherited from the central planning era.

Fortunately, in July 1997, the Seimas approved the Law on Methodology for Establishing Municipal Budget Income. This law has returned Lithuania to an innovative and creative path of reform. It set in place a system of formula-driven transfers for equalization purposes that does much to address the perverse incentives and uncertainties that have plagued the country's municipal finances during the transition years.

Nevertheless, the design and implementation of an efficient system of municipal finance for Lithuania remains incomplete, and in some areas seriously flawed. The government's agenda for future reform will need to encompass a long list of issues, including the structure of decentralized governments, the clarification of assignments for capital investment responsibilities, the long-term viability of decentralized district heating companies, the increase in revenue certainty and autonomy of municipal budgets, the improvement in the design of equalization and categorical transfers, the regulation of borrowing activities by municipalities and the facilitation of long-term credit, and the complete overhaul of the budgeting process at the local level.

Main Features of Municipal Finance in Lithuania and Recent Developments

The Structure of Decentralized Governments

At the time of independence, the structure of decentralized governments in Lithuania consisted of eleven cities with "republican" subordination, forty-four rayon (or county) governments, and a third tier of rural settlements or villages subordinated to the rayon governments. This vertical structure of government was too complex and lacked optimal scale at the third tier of rural settlements. The old structure also lacked adequate democratic representation at the rayon (or county) level. The Law on Local Administrative Units and their Boundaries of July 1994 reformed the decentralized structure of government by introducing a single tier consisting of fifty-six municipalities.[1] The urban or city municipalities represented 44 percent of all municipal expenditures in 1996. The level of concentration has not been as pronounced in Lithuania as in other small countries, such as Estonia and Latvia. The two largest municipalities, Vilnius and Kaunas, represent approximately one-quarter of all municipal expenditures, and the six largest municipalities account for close to 40 percent.

Among the Baltic states, Estonia, like Lithuania, has only two tiers of government, the central government and 255 municipalities. The municipalities in Estonia have a considerably lower average size in population than those in Lithuania. Latvia is now in the process of reforming its vertical structure of government, moving from three to two tiers of government and consolidating local governments into 150 to 200 municipalities. These new municipalities, on average, would also be significantly smaller than those in Lithuania. Most eastern European countries and those of the former Soviet Union have three levels of government, as is the case in most Organization for Economic Cooperation and Development (OECD) countries. However, some smaller OECD countries and quite a few small developing countries have only two tiers of government. Although there are significant variations in the average size in population of local governments in these countries, Lithuania's average municipality would be above the international average.[2]

An important part of the 1994 reform in Lithuania was the elimination of an intermediate, decentralized level of government, the rayons (or counties). In their place, the Law on Administrative Units created ten regional, deconcentrated administrative units (or counties), which operate as arms of the central government ministries to deliver central government services in a deconcentrated fashion throughout the national territory. In addition, there are plans to expand the number of municipalities. (This issue is discussed in the section entitled "Key Medium-Term Policy Issues," below.)

Local government interests are represented by an Association of Municipalities, which is officially recognized by the government.[3] The association has some positive features. Membership is voluntary and funding comes entirely from contributions of the member municipalities.[4]

---

1. In addition to the fifty-six municipalities, there are about 500 neighborhoods (seniunijos), essentially the former rural towns and settlements, that are headed by an officer appointed by the mayor of the municipality. These neighborhoods, however, do not have administrative unit status.

2. See, for example, Richard M. Bird, Robert D. Ebel, and Christine I. Wallich (eds.) *Decentralization of the Socialist State: Intergovernmental Finance in Transition Economies* (Washington, D.C.: The World Bank, 1995).

3. For example, the 1997 Law on the Methodology for Establishing Municipal Budget Income names the Association of Municipalities as part of the dialogue with the Seimas and the government for determining the size of the municipal budgets in the general government budget.

4. There is only one municipality (Klaipeda) that is not a member of the association.

The core governance institution in the municipalities is the council, which is democratically elected every two years and operates through a series of area-specific committees, including Budget and Finance, Labor and Social Issues, Culture and Education, Ecology and City Development, Economy, and Health and Sports. The Council appoints the mayor, two vice-mayors, and the chief executives or heads of departments; the latter appointees report to the mayor.

The Significance of Local Government Budgets

Local governments have played, and continue to play, a significant role in Lithuania's public sector and in the overall economy. In 1996, municipal budgets represented slightly over a third of the national budget (central plus local government) and a quarter of the general government consolidated budget (including social security and extrabudgetary funds). The average share of subnational budgets in the general consolidated budget in OECD countries tends to be higher than is the case in Lithuania; only quite centralized countries such as France and the United Kingdom have a lower share than Lithuania (see Annex table 3-28). Among the transition countries, Poland and Romania also have a lower share of subnational government expenditures in the general consolidated budget.[5]

As a reference point, municipal expenditures in Lithuania in 1996 exceeded all central government expenditures on the economy and social affairs combined. Over the past six years, however, the relative importance of the local government sector has declined somewhat (by roughly 9 percentage points) in reference to the national and the general government consolidated budget (table 3-1). That drop in the relative importance of municipal budgets was most pronounced in 1995 and, to an even greater extent, 1996. Municipal governments now handle expenditures worth about 6 percent of gross domestic product (GDP), half the level of the early years of independence. In real terms, both central government and local government expenditures decreased in the early years of the transition, but, while in recent years real central government expenditures have decreased minimally, or actually increased, real municipal expenditures have generally continued to decrease (table 3-2). It is difficult to offer a simple, straightforward interpretation of these trends. To some extent, the decrease in the share of local governments in the national budget reflects a realignment of national expenditure priorities—the Seimas has cut local expenditures more deeply than central government expenditures. During this period, however, there have also been complex changes in the role of government and the assignment of responsibilities among the levels of government, and those changes are reflected in the historical trends.

Table 3-1. The Relative Size of Municipal Budgets and National Budget Expenditure
(percent)

Year	National budget/GDP	Municipal budget/GDP	Municipal budget/national budget	Municipal budget/ total expenditure, general government
1991	26.4	11.6	43.9	33.4
1992	24.0	10.9	45.5	34.8
1993	24.3	9.9	40.7	31.3
1994	25.6	11.1	43.3	32.4
1995	27.7	10.9	39.3	30.0
1996	25.3	6.6	35.4	26.2

5. See Bird, Ebel, and Wallich, "Decentralization of the Socialist State."

Table 3-2. Municipal and Total National Expenditures
(Lt million)

	1992	*1993*	*1994*	*1995*	*1996*
In nominal terms					
Municipal expenditures[a]	370	1,100	1,860	2,494	2,657
Total national expenditures	1,060	3,402	5,920	8,228	10,132
In constant 1992 litas[b]					
Municipal expenditures	370	216	212	219	188
Annual change in real terms (percent)		-42	-2	3	-14
Total national expenditures	1,060	667	675	722	717
Annual change in real terms (percent)		-37	1	7	-1

a. Excludes expenditures of municipal enterprises other than subsidies from municipal budget.

b. Based on annual average inflation rates according to the IMF: 1993, 410 percent; 1994, 72 percent; 1995, 30 percent; and 1996, 24 percent.

Source: Updated from World Bank, *Lithuania Municipal Finance Report*, 1995.

Composition of Municipal Budgets

EXPENDITURES. Traditionally, the most important component of local expenditures has been social services, which include education, culture and recreation, health, and social assistance. In 1996, expenditures in social services represented four-fifths of total municipal expenditures; education accounted for half of the total, and health care for a little over a quarter. The other major component of the municipal budget in 1996 was "housing and municipal economy," which represented 13 percent of total municipal expenditures. For 1997 (through July 1), over half of all municipal expenditures were in education alone (table 3-3). The other two most important expenditure categories were welfare and housing, each representing approximately one-tenth of overall expenditures. The figures for 1997 already reflect the recently decreed shifting of health service responsibilities from local governments to the state's Health Insurance Fund.

Table 3-3. Lithuania: Composition of Municipal Expenditures, 1997
(Lt million)

Category	Total	Percentage of total
General administration	47.3	3.5
Social security and public order	10.2	0.8
Education	719.0	53.3
Health care	66.7	4.9
Welfare	145.9	10.8
Housing and municipal economy	151.6	11.2
Culture and recreation	56.2	4.2
Fuel, energy, and supplies	39.0	2.9
Agriculture	0.0	0.0
Other expenditures	113.8	8.4
Total expenditures	1,349.6	100.0

Note: The figures are based on expenditures up to 1 July 1997.

Source: The figures are compiled from data provided by the Ministry of Finance.

The relative importance of expenditures on social services in Lithuania's local budgets has been increasing during the transition, as shown in table 3-4. This reflects a change in priorities, especially toward education and health.[6] As real budget resources have decreased over the years, including the resources of local governments, social services have been spared the major cuts. Note, however, that real GDP has declined over the transition period; consequently, real resources spent on the social sectors have also declined. Real expenditures in 1992 litas were lower in 1996 than in 1992.

Table 3-4. Lithuania: Social Expenditures as a Share of the Municipal Budget, 1992–97

Year	Social expenditures (Lt million, 1992)	Real social expenditures (Lt million, 1992)	Total municipal budget (Lt million, 1992)	Social expenditures	
				Percentage of municipal budget	Percentage of GDP
1992	215.3	215.3	369.3	58.3	6.7
1993	638.8	155.8	1097.9	58.2	5.3
1994	1,203.6	170.7	1857.9	64.8	5.5
1995	1,466.9	160.1	2253.7	65.1	4.7
1996	2,136.1	188.0	2654.5	80.5	5.3
1997[a]	987.8	n.a.	1349.6	73.2	n.a.

n.a. Not available.
Note: Social expenditures include health, education, social assistance, and culture.
a. Based on actual expenditures through 1 July 1997.
Source: Ministry of Finance.

There are two other important ways to look at the composition of municipal expenditures. The first is the economic classification of expenditures—that is, what kinds of economic inputs are purchased through the budget—and the second is the variation of expenditure levels across municipalities. The economic classification of municipal, central, and national government budgets for 1996 is shown in table 3-5. Both the municipalities and the central government spend approximately one-tenth of their budgets on capital expenditures and the rest on current expenditures. This share of capital expenditures has recorded an increase in 1996 from the level of the transition years. Capital public expenditures are low as a percentage of GDP, however, and more important, they are quite inadequate given the postponed infrastructure investment, maintenance, and rehabilitation of the past five years. The main items among current expenditures are wages and salaries (plus social security contributions) and subsidies and transfers. Wages and salaries represented a third of total expenditures of municipal governments in 1996, and one-quarter of central government expenditures. The difference is largely explained by the greater responsibilities of municipalities in the area of social services, which tend to be labor-intensive. Nonetheless, these figures are not high by international standards. For subsidies, the largest amounts go to fuel and energy at both levels of government, closely followed by subsidies to transport and communications.[7]

The variation of per capita expenditures across municipalities is quite considerable. As updated in table 3-6, total expenditures per capita ranged in 1996 from a minimum of Lt 534 to a maximum of Lt 3,869, over a sevenfold difference. The disparities across municipalities, as measured by the coefficient of variation, are quite consistent across most functions.[8] Although some of the variation is no doubt the

---

6. The reform of the health sector in 1997 has meant a sharp decrease in health expenditures in the local budgets. Historically, the relative importance of education and health in the local budgets may also have been a reflection of the lack of efficiency in public expenditures, especially because these sectors have been characterized by excess capacity. (See the World Bank, *Lithuania: Municipal Finance Report*, 1995; and *Public Expenditure Review*, 1994.)

7. A further breakdown of the composition of subsidies is presented in Annex 3-1.

8. Individual municipality data are presented in table 3-20 in Annex 3-1.

result of reporting issues, as appears to be the case for health services, it is still too large to be ignored. For example, education expenditures per capita differ sixfold across municipalities. In addition, the disparity in expenditure per capita across municipalities does not appear to follow a systematic pattern. This is shown in table 3-7, where per capita municipal expenditures[9] are regressed on a measure of fiscal capacity (per capita general revenues collected in the jurisdiction), a measure of need (percentage of the population not of working age), a measure of scale (population of the municipality), and a dummy variable that distinguishes between urban and rural municipalities. The only two explanatory variables that are statistically significant are population and the dummy variable. Expenditures per capita tend to decrease with the size of the municipality, and they are consistently larger in urban municipalities compared with rural municipalities. The regression, however, only explains 17 percent of the variation in the dependent variable, per capita municipal expenditures.

Table 3-5. Economic Classification of Budget Expenditures in 1996 at the Municipal and Central Government Levels

	National expenditure		Central government		Municipalities	
	Thousand litai	Percent	Thousand litai	Percent	Thousand litai	Percent
Total expenditure	7,510,191	100.0	5,332,794	100.0	2,852,500	100.0
Current expenditure	6,700,107	89.2	4,789,988	89.8	2,556,677	89.6
Goods and services	5,382,695	71.7	3,214,402	60.3	2,168,293	76.0
Wages and salaries	2,310,281	30.8	1,282,012	24.0	1,028,269	36.0
Social security contributions	652,806	8.7	357,703	6.7	295,103	10.3
Other	1,236,603	16.5	996,965	18.7	239,638	8.4
Interest payments	296,228	3.9	292,785	5.5	3,443	0.1
Outside general government	217,592	2.9	214,149	4.0	3,443	0.1
Abroad	78,636	1.0	78,636	1.5	—	—
Subsidies and other transfers	1,021,184	13.6	1,282,801	24.1	384,941	13.5
Subsidies	396,449	5.3	252,560	4.7	143,889	5.0
To nonfinancial institutions	303,730	4.0	165,785	3.1	137,945	4.8
Transfers among government levels	n.a.	n.a.	646,558	12.1	—	—
Transfers of households	619,787	8.3	379,752	7.1	240,035	8.4
Scholarships	68,417	0.9	68,417	1.3	—	—
Capital expenditure	807,827	10.8	542,806	10.2	265,021	9.3
Acquisition of fixed capital assets	785,491	10.5	520,470	9.8	265,021	9.3
Construction	499,765	6.7	275,815	5.2	223,950	7.9
Land reclamation and expansion	125,267	1.7	125,267	2.3	—	—
Purchase of tangible assets	153,429	2.0	118,096	2.2	35,333	1.2
Lending minus repayments	2,257	0.0	—	—	2,257	0.1
To nonfinancial public enterprises	257	0.0	—	—	257	0.0
To financial institutions	2,000	0.0	—	—	2,000	0.1
Transfers to the state budget	n.a.	n.a.	—	—	28,545	1.0

n.a. Not available.
Source: Government Finances of the Republic of Lithuania, Vilnius, 1996.

REVENUES. The most important source of municipal revenues in 1996 was the personal income tax (PIT). Revenue sharing from this tax represented 57 percent of all revenues when transfers are included in total revenues, and 75 percent when transfers are excluded. (Transfers from the central government amounted to about one-fifth of total municipal revenues for 1996; see table 3-8.) Among other taxes, the corporate income tax (CIT) was the second most important source of revenue, representing 8 percent of total revenues, followed by taxes on property (the land tax, enterprise assets, and land rental), which together represented about 7 percent. All other income sources are very small.

---

9. The results for per capita transfers in this table are discussed in a separate section.

For 1997 (through July 1), the composition of revenues does not change drastically see (table 3-8). The most notable changes are the decrease in the relative importance of revenue sharing in PIT, which is down to 48 percent, and the increase in the relative importance of transfers from the central government, which are up to a third of total municipal revenue.

Table 3-6. Descriptive Statistics for per Capita Local Expenditures, 1996
(litai)

Region	Mean	Unweighted mean	Coefficient of variation	Minimum	Maximum
General administration	23.4	32.3	0.799	10.2	202.3
Social security and public order	4.2	6.3	0.649	0.0	18.8
Education	301.3	336.6	0.488	234.2	1,496.4
Health care	174.0	185.1	0.537	70.5[a]	657.6
Welfare	74.1	79.5	0.198	37.0	119.4
Lodging and municipal economy	95.5	118.2	1.765	9.9	1,543.7
Culture and recreation	26.8	40.9	1.100	8.8	352.3
Fuel, energy, and supplies	16.6	20.1	1.680	0.0	188.9
Agriculture	0.2	0.3	5.950	0.0	12.7
Total expenditures	716.0	819.2	0.539	534.8	3,869.2

a. Three city municipalities (Vilnius, Klaipeda, and Visaginas) reported zero or close to zero expenditures on health during 1996.

Source: Computed from data supplied by the Ministry of Finance.

Table 3-7. Regression of Transfers and Municipal Expenditures on Fiscal Characteristics, 1996

Item	Per capita transfers	Per capita local expenditures
Constant	-1,525.30*	118.50
	(2.20)	(0.78)
Per capita general revenues (capacity)	-0.021	.011
	(0.60)	0.23)
Population not of working age (%)	36.64*	8.43
(Need)	(1.87)	(0.69)
Population	-0.001*	-0.001*
	(1.67)	(2.09)
City dummy	339.60*	525.60*
	(2.14)	(2.43)
R-squared	0.18	0.17

Note: Absolute values of *t*-statistics are in parenthesis. * Indicates statistically significant estimate at the 10 percent level. City dummy equals one for cities; variable equals zero otherwise.

The composition of revenues for local governments has undergone major changes over the past five years. These changes mainly reflect reforms in revenue assignments (discussed later in this chapter). As shown in table 3-9, the importance of shared PIT revenues increased, especially after 1995, when municipalities stopped receiving revenue sharing in the value added tax (VAT). The CIT, in contrast, has consistently declined as a source of revenue for municipalities; in 1998, it will be assigned entirely to the central government.

There is also considerable disparity in per capita revenues across municipalities. As shown in table 3-10, total revenues per capita before transfers in 1996 ranged from Lt 259 to Lt 1,786, close to a sevenfold difference.[10] In individual sources of revenue, disparities as measured by the coefficient of

10. The data by individual municipality are presented in Annex 3-1.

variation tend to be smaller for sources that were "regulated" (through changes in the sharing rates) than for sources of revenue assigned 100 percent to municipalities (such as taxes on property) or generated by the municipalities themselves. Remarkably, when transfers from the central government are added to municipal revenues, disparities generally increase. This is shown by the higher coefficient of variation for total revenues per capita after transfers (and by the wider range between minimum and maximum revenues per capita), now equivalent to an eightfold difference.

Table 3-8. Composition of Municipal Revenues, 1996 and 1997
(Lt million)

Source	Total	Percentage of total
	1996	
Personal income taxes	1,514.8	57.0
Corporate income taxes	216.5	8.1
Property taxes	177.4	6.7
Other taxes	90.2	3.4
Income from municipal property	0.8	0.0
Penalties	33.1	1.2
Other nontax revenues	73.6	2.8
Income from purchased LT assets	0.1	0.0
Transfers from state	550.6	20.7
Total revenue	2,657.0	100.0
	1997	
Personal income taxes	655.0	48.5
Corporate income taxes	60.1	4.4
Property taxes	85.7	6.3
Other taxes	24.3	1.8
Income from municipal property	17.0	1.3
Income from purchased LT assets	0.0	0.0
Other nontax revenues	94.2	7.0
Transfers from state	404.4	29.9
Total revenue	1,350.7	100.0

Note: Based on actual collections up to 1 July 1997.
Source: Compiled from data provided by the Ministry of Finance.

The post-transfer increase in revenue disparity is indeed remarkable, for one of the explicit objectives in creating the transfer system was to reduce disparities in the distribution of resources across municipalities. In 1996 there were two traditional types of transfers. The first were lump-sum, gap-filling transfers to municipalities that could not cover their minimum required expenditure budgets, even after collecting 100 percent of the regulated taxes. The second was the special purpose transfer, received by a smaller number of municipalities for capital construction projects and other objectives such as environmental protection.[11] To the extent that the latter type of transfer may be unrelated to need or capacity and the gap-filling transfers may have negotiated elements, it would appear that the system of transfers in 1996 was not an equalizer. This hypothesis is partially supported by the regression of per capita transfers on a measure of fiscal capacity, a measure of need, a measure of scale, and a dummy variable that distinguishes between urban and rural municipalities, as shown in table 3-7. Transfers per capita are not correlated with the measure of fiscal capacity. They increase with the measure of need, however, making the system of transfers a more effective tool for equalizing fiscal disparities across

---

11. The transfers received by individual municipalities are also shown in table 3-19 in Annex 3-1.

municipalities, which has been a main objective of the reforms introduced in 1997 that are discussed below.

Table 3-9. Sources of Municipal Revenues, 1992–97
(percent of municipal revenues)

Source	1992	1993	1994	1995	1996	1997[a]
Corporate income tax (CIT)	20.6	18.2	16.4	15.2	10.7	6.3
Land tax and other property taxes	1.4	3.3	2.9	8.7	8.8	9.1
Fees and other [b]	10.7	9.4	10.1	6.7	5.0	15.4
Personal income tax (PIT)	56.9	48.3	47.1	69.4	75.4	69.2
VAT	10.4	20.8	23.5	0.0	0.0	0.0
Total	100.0	100.0	100.0	100.0	100.0	100.0

Note: For 1992–94, the table excludes revenues from local service fees collected by local governments, representing 2–5 percent of total municipal revenues.

a. Based on collections through 1 July 1997.

b. Court fees, car inspection fees, market fees, taxi licenses, alcohol licenses, fines, confiscations, and the like. From 1995, fees defined as "state fees" are a shared revenue source (30 percent to local governments).

Source: Updated from World Bank, *Municipal Finance Report* (Washington, D.C., 1995), with data provided by the Ministry of Finance.

Table 3-10. Descriptive Statistics for per Capita Local Revenues, 1996
(litai)

Source	Mean	Unweighted mean	Coefficient of variation	Minimum	Maximum
PIT	408.6	372.5	0.333	190.0	867.3
CIT	58.4	57.9	0.798	13.8	223.5
Property taxes	47.9	53.4	1.054	17.1	434.1
Other taxes	24.3	21.1	1.014	6.0	149.3
Income from municipal property	0.2	0.3	3.909	-0.2	6.2
Penalties	8.9	8.3	0.545	1.3	21.2
Other nontax revenues	19.8	25.7	1.535	0.3	236.9
Income from purchased LT assets	0.0	0.1	3.388	0.0	1.0
Total revenues (before transfers)	568.2	539.0	0.439	259.9	1,786.2
Transfers	148.5	283.0	1.154	0.0	2,243.3
Total revenue	716.7	822.0	0.566	550.3	4,029.5

Source: Computed from data supplied by the Ministry of Finance.

Assignment of Expenditure Responsibilities

The assignment of expenditure responsibilities has not changed significantly since it was reviewed in the World Bank's *Lithuania: Municipal Finance Report* (1995). This section focuses on some recent alterations. For the most part, the assignment of expenditure responsibilities between municipalities and the central government in Lithuania obeys generally accepted principles. Local governments are responsible for the provision of public services of direct benefit to local residents that have small, or no, benefit spillovers to residents of other municipalities (such as transportation, garbage collection and solid waste disposal, and water and sewerage). The central government, in turn, is responsible for the provision of services with nationwide benefits, such as national defense or public order and safety. An important exception in this area is district heating (DH), which was the responsibility of a state (central government) enterprise, but was decentralized to the municipal level (and ownership) in July 1997. Given the significance and complexity of the DH issues, this reform is discussed in a separate section below.

Municipal governments have also played a significant role in the provision of social services, including education, culture and recreation, health, and social welfare services. These functions have been shared with the central government and, not surprisingly, have been a source of confusion, in part because some of these functions have been declared as delegated (as opposed to devolved) from the central government, with the implication that the central government has retained the right to intervene, and it has done so through sectoral laws. This has been the case in education services, for example. In other cases, such as health services, the murkiness in assignment of responsibilities has been rooted not only in the concept of delegation, but also in the complexity of operating some facilities. In other instances, confusion in the assignment of responsibilities has not been in the delivery of the service, but in determining the level of government that is responsible for its actual financing, as has been the case with some social welfare services.

A good way to understand the division of expenditure responsibilities is to examine actual expenditures by function at the two levels of government. This differentiation is shown in table 3-11. In 1996, municipalities accounted for over two-thirds of total expenditures on education, for 60 percent of health services, for virtually all expenses in housing and community amenities, and for a third of social welfare services.[12] In contrast, municipal expenditures represented only 2 percent of national expenditures on public order and safety.

Lithuania's division of expenditure responsibilities between the central and local governments is quite similar to that of the average OECD country, as shown in Annex table 3-28. International experience indicates that there is no absolute best blueprint for the assignment of expenditure responsibilities. Countries with centralized regimes tend to have lower expenditures on education, and especially on health, at the subnational level. The provision of health serviced through a separate, extrabudgetary fund at the central level, of course, also affects its relative importance in the local budgets. All OECD countries listed in table 3-28 (except Austria and the United States) also assign most housing expenditures to the subnational level, as in Lithuania. In contrast, Lithuania assigns more welfare expenditures at the local level than is the case in most OECD countries, where this redistributive function is considered more the role of the central government. One important exception to this pattern is Denmark, where over 90 percent of welfare expenditures are disbursed through local budgets.

Revenue Assignments

Three stages are clearly identifiable in revenue assignment policy during the past seven years of transition in Lithuania. The first stage was the revenue assignment contained in the Law on Budget Structure of 1990. In this stage, the three major tax sources (VAT, PIT, and CIT) were shared with local governments on a derivation basis (that is, taxes are shared with the community where they are actually "derived" or collected) and generally at "regulated" (customized by municipality) rates. In the case of CIT, local governments were allowed to retain 100 percent of tax revenues from "municipal enterprises." Local governments also retained 100 percent of the revenues of taxes on property (which included the land tax, the land rental tax, and the enterprise assets tax). In addition, local governments were assigned a list of fees and charges.

The second stage followed the amendment to the Law on Budget Structure in 1995. The most important change was the assignment of all VAT revenues to the central government. Revenues from PIT and CIT continued to be shared with local governments; in the case of CIT, distinctions were no

---

12. A further breakdown in the composition of these three services is shown in tables 3-15 to 3-17 in Annex 3-1.

longer made between revenues from municipal enterprises and those from other contributors.

Table 3-11. Budget Expenditure by Function of Government in 1996

	National		Central government		Municipalities		Local as
	Thousand litai	Percent	Thousand litai	Percent	Thousand litai	Percent	percentage of national
Total expenditure	7,510,191	100.0	5,332,794	100.0	2,852,500	100.0	37.9
Expenditure on the economy	1,525,205	20.3	1,040,675	19.5	484,530	17.0	31.7
Housing and community amenity affairs and services	352,984	4.7	531	0.0	352,453	12.4	99.8
Fuel and energy affairs and services	296,699	4.0	234,985	4.4	61,714	2.2	20.8
Agriculture, forestry, fishing, and veterinary affairs and services	631,695	8.4	631,594	11.8	101	0.0	0.0
Mining (fuel excluded), manufacturing, and construction affairs and services	31,401	0.4	31,401	0.6	—	—	—
Transport and communication affairs and services	168,170	2.2	98,525	1.8	69,645	2.4	41.4
Other economic affairs and services	44,256	0.6	43,639	0.8	617	0.0	1.4
Expenditure on social affairs	3,821,972	50.9	1,685,832	31.6	2,136,140	74.9	55.9
Education affairs and services	1,712,880	22.8	595,773	11.2	1,117,107	39.2	65.2
Health care affairs and services	1,072,669	14.3	427,657	8.0	645,012	22.6	60.1
Social security and welfare affairs and services	746,299	9.9	471,775	8.8	274,524	9.6	36.8
Recreational, cultural, and religious affairs and services	290,124	3.9	190,627	3.6	99,497	3.5	34.3
Expenditure on other functions of government	2,163,014	28.8	2,606,287	48.9	231,830	8.1	10.7
General public services	553,189	7.4	466,572	8.7	86,617	3.0	15.6
National defense affairs and services	177,805	2.4	177,805	3.3	—	—	—
Public order and safety affairs	829,744	11.0	814,258	15.3	15,486	0.5	1.8
Expenditure not classified by major group	602,276	8.0	1,147,652	21.5	129,727	4.5	21.5

Source: Government Finances of the Republic of Lithuania, 1996.

The third stage started with the adoption of the Law for Establishing Municipal Budget Income in July 1997. The major change in this law is that 100 percent of CIT revenues are now retained at the central level, and at the same time, revenues from the PIT are assigned to municipalities, with some important qualifications. According to the new law, tax revenues for the municipalities are:[13] (i) PIT revenues, after the contributions to the Compulsory Health Insurance Fund are subtracted;[14] (ii) land tax; (iii) rent for state land and water reservoirs; (iv) assets tax on enterprises and organizations; (v) the stamp fee (based on the Law on the Stamp Fee); (vi) the trade outlet fee; (vii) estate tax (on inheritances and

---

13. This same assignment appears in the Law on Amendment of the Law on Budget Structure of July 1997.

14. These contributions, stated as a percentage of collections in each municipality, are defined in the Law on Health Insurance. In addition, as discussed below, municipalities with higher than average per capita PIT collections will have to make forced contributions to the new system of equalization transfers. The new law also makes it clear that the PIT remains a regulated tax, with a customized sharing rate to be established annually by the Seimas.

gifts); and (viii) other income from taxes as provided by law (at present, none).[15]

A historical overview of the actual revenue sharing between the central and local governments is shown in table 3-12. Shared revenues from PIT have gained importance as the main financing source of local governments; this importance will increase even further in 1998 because CIT revenues are no longer shared with municipalities. The second most important source of revenues is transfers.

Table 3-12. Municipal Share of National Revenues, 1992–96

Revenue source	Percentage of total revenues					1996 Revenues (million litai)	
	1992	1993	1994	1995	1996	National	Municipal
Personal income tax (PIT)	80	66	53	74	73	2,087	1,514
Corporate income tax (CIT)	25	24	39	50	37	587	216
VAT	10	20	26	–	–	2,280	–
Excise taxes and customs	–	–	–	–	–	836	–
Other tax and nontax revenue	10	11	13	10	11	3,497	377
"Subsidies" and other support	15	7	27	37	26	–	550
Total	46	42	47	32	29	9,287	2,657

Source: Updated from World Bank, *Lithuania Municipal Finance Report* (Washington, D.C., 1995).

Transfers

Over the past five years, the system of transfers from the central to the local governments has been simple, and had not changed much from the methodology used in the Soviet Union. The main form of transfer has been the gap-filling lump-sum transfer to local governments that are unable to finance the minimum expenditure budget, as determined by the Ministry of Finance, through their own and shared revenue.[16] Conceptually, these transfers have been used as fiscal equalization tools in support of the equalization already undertaken through the regulated rates for shared taxes. To the extent that the minimum required budget was formulated in a nontransparent and, at times, negotiated fashion, the gap-filling transfers have also been nontransparent. As the regression analysis of table 3-7 showed, it is also questionable whether or not the end result of the transfers was truly equalizing.

The gap-filling transfers were complemented by transfers for capital investment purposes, an echo of the previous regime, which viewed all capital investment in public infrastructure as the responsibility of the highest level of government. In recent years, capital transfers have taken the form of transfers to the municipal budgets for single investment projects over Lt 5 million, individually approved by the Seimas, and for several central government programs (such as land development or environmental protection). These are categorical grants, and the municipalities have little or no discretion in their use. The system of transfers for equalization purposes has recently been completely overhauled by the Law of Establishing Municipal Budget Income. (The new system is discussed below: "Key Medium-Term Policy Issues.")

---

15. The new law also lists nontax revenue sources for municipalities as: (i) local levies and fees (in accordance with the Law on Local Levies), (ii) penalties and income from confiscated assets, (iii) income from municipal assets, (iv) income from municipal enterprises, and (v) other incomes. Both tax and nontax revenues are supposed to be transferred directly to the municipal budgets by the State Tax Inspectorate.

16. The budgeting process and the concept of the minimum expenditure budget are discussed below.

Borrowing

The current legal framework for municipal borrowing is ambiguous.[17] The Local Government Law (article 15) regulates the use of bank credit. There are no explicit limits on the level of borrowing, however, nor are there provisions for bankrupt and nonpaying local governments, collateral provisions to permit escrowing of revenue streams, or the pledging of municipal assets to guarantee repayment of loans.[18] Some observers have argued that municipal borrowing is prohibited by article 27 of the Law on Budget Formation, which states that municipal budgets must be balanced. Finally, the new Law for Establishing Municipal Budget Income (article 8) states that municipalities have the right to borrow "according to the procedures and conditions established by the government." But none has yet been issued.

The new law also stipulates that the central government can issue loans in the event of a temporary shortage in municipal budgets. This practice is already in place: the central government has provided bridge financing at zero interest to municipalities for liquidity management purposes.[19] Other than these short-term loans, there has been little borrowing. No municipality appears to have issued bonds, and there are no prospects for such activity anytime soon. Borrowing from commercial banks is taking place, but on a small scale. Banks have been less than eager to lend because of the lack of collateral and the inability of most municipalities to pay their arrears to state entities and suppliers. Examples of bank borrowing are provided by the city of Vilnius, which was granted loans by the State Commercial Bank and the Agricultural Bank (two state-controlled banks) for a total of less than Lt 20 million in 1997 (see Annex table 3-18). The City of Kaunas also recently borrowed Lt 3 million for parking meters from a commercial bank at 10 percent annual interest; all revenues from parking in the city commercial district were escrowed to the repayment of this loan.

Key Medium-Term Policy Issues

Structure of Decentralized Governments

The current vertical government structure of two levels, central government and municipalities, and ten deconcentrated administrative units within the central government, appears to fit the needs and size of Lithuania, and it seems to be a settled issue. What is not settled is the composition of local governments, particularly by the number of municipalities. The Seimas has passed a resolution providing for a second phase of territorial administration reform that calls for the preparation and approval of criteria and procedures for the establishment of new municipalities.[20] This process of enlargement is envisioned to

---

17. Issues in municipal borrowing are discussed in more detail in C. Bareikien and V. Sukys, "On the Possibilities of the Use of Credit and Loans by Local Government Institutions" (Proceedings from the National Seminar on Fiscal Decentralization in Lithuania [FDI-CEE], Vilnius, May 1966); and T. H. Cochran, "Building a Hard Credit Culture with Lithuanian Local Authorities and Municipal Enterprises" (New York: The Institute of Public Administration for the Lithuania Municipal Development Project, for The World Bank, May 1997).

18. See Cochran, "Building a Hard Credit Culture."

19. For example, Vilnius and Kaunas recently borrowed from the Ministry of Finance to pay teachers' salaries during the summer vacation.

20. The legal framework through 1996 is reviewed in N. Puteikis, "Report on the System of Local Self-Government in Lithuania" (paper presented in the National Seminar on Fiscal Decentralization in Lithuania [FDI-CEE], Vilnius, 1 May 1996).

take place over time; the target number of municipalities mentioned varies from 80 to 112.[21] There is interest in the Seimas in increasing political representation through further fragmentation among rural municipalities, but the executive branch has decided to move slowly in this area. This is probably the right approach, one that will provide stability and continuity.

Whatever final number of municipalities is agreed upon, Lithuania will face major municipal finance issues over the next three years. If unattended, these issues could have serious repercussions on the country's macroeconomic framework. These issues are addressed below.

Expenditure Assignments

Several events in the recent past have helped make the assignment of expenditure responsibilities less convoluted in Lithuania's system of decentralized government. First, the provision of all health services became the exclusive responsibility of the national Health Insurance Institute in July of 1997.[22] The decentralization of district heating (DH) services to the municipalities is also a step in the right direction. These services, of such a clear local benefit, had been misassigned by the central government. Further, the passage of time and increased practice have begun to lessen the responsibility-assignment confusion of earlier years.

Yet, important problems remain in the assignment of expenditure responsibilities. The most critical among them is the determination of capital investment responsibilities for local services, especially in light of the vast needs for infrastructure investment at the local level (in turn, arising from lack of maintenance or new undertakings during the past five years).[23] Policy in this area is less than clear. Municipalities are, in principle, responsible for all the capital investment necessary for the services assigned to them. This is theoretically the right approach, but the central government is responsible for all capital investments above Lt 5 million.

These contradictory policies are largely the result of compromise forced by the lack of developed credit markets or institutions that would allow municipalities to borrow for long-term investments. In other words, this is a problem of a lack of credit, not a lack of revenue autonomy. Although revenue autonomy at the local level is a desirable feature in its own right, as emphasized throughout this note, revenue autonomy is not necessary for local governments to be able to borrow or invest in infrastructure. The ability of a municipality to repay a loan is enhanced by autonomous sources of revenue, although municipalities can certainly use funds from general revenue sharing and lump-sum transfers to repay any loans. Thus, the solution to the problem of capital investment responsibilities hinges on the solution to the issue of borrowing at the local level. (This issue is addressed separately in this Policy Note.)

A second issue that will require attention in the assignment of expenditure responsibilities is that of unfunded government mandates. Unfunded mandates from the central government are a common problem in all decentralized systems of government, and Lithuania is no exception. In principle, Lithuania's Law on Local Self-Government offers the right solution. It states that municipal functions delegated by the state shall be financed by special transfers form the state budget to the municipalities. Delegated functions currently include civil registry, registry of enterprises and organizations, and

---

21. The administrative reform of 1994 had two versions, one with 56 municipalities and the other with 112.

22. During the transition, some large municipalities may still have obligations for the maintenance of hospitals.

23. See the World Bank, *Lithuania: Public Expenditure Review* (March 1994); and *Lithuania: Municipal Finance Report* (April 1995).

management of state parks. Other functions, such as public order, civil safety, and fire protection also appear to be on the list of delegated functions. The new Law on Municipal Budget Income (article 16) rules out unfunded mandates from the central government to the municipalities. What is needed is adherence to the principle of explicit compensation for mandates as a matter of practice for *all* mandates.

The Decentralization of District Heating

The government decentralized the ownership and responsibility for DH to municipalities in July 1997. Prior to that change, DH was the responsibility of the Lithuanian Power Company (LPC), which operated six regional DH networks located in large municipalities.[24] Smaller municipalities managed their own DH facilities, in some cases inherited from bankrupt enterprises and collective farms. There are also state-owned enterprises with their own boilers, which provide heating for adjacent buildings.[25] The coverage of DH varies across areas and is, of course, less prominent in rural areas or areas with single, detached homes as opposed to high-rise buildings.

The DH operations of LPC and those of municipalities were subsidized by the central government. Tariffs for DH were controlled, and direct subsidies to the producers covered about half of the operating costs of the companies.

The decentralization of DH has broken up the former LPC operation into six new companies. These will be owned jointly by several municipalities, but in most cases it is expected that the largest municipality in the area will play a dominant role in running the company.[26] Smaller municipalities will continue their own DH operations. As part of the reform, tariffs will be set by a newly created Energy Pricing Commission (EPC), and the understanding is that the new tariffs will allow full cost recovery for the new DH companies. The DH operations of the smaller municipalities will not be forced to use EPC-set tariffs. As part of the reform in DH, the government will discontinue direct subsidies to producers; it is planning to introduce a means-tested cash subsidy program for low-income households in its place.

Municipalities have inherited a trouble-filled service that has been plagued by low tariffs, low collection rates, obsolete and outmoded physical infrastructure, significant operating losses, and debt. The transfer of responsibilities for DH to municipalities under these conditions could be interpreted as a maneuver to transfer the financial imbalance from the central to the local level; the DH subsector was the main drain of resources for LPC in the recent past. It is clear that simply transferring ownership of assets and responsibility for provision of DH to the municipalities should not lead to any changes in the bottom line. Without further changes, the financial shortfall that has plagued the LPC could continue to trouble the municipalities. The fundamental question for the future is whether or not current plans are sufficient to avert the problems of the past.

On the plus side, decentralization could lead to improved management and organization, including improved cost recovery for services rendered. On the minus side, the list is much longer. Cost recovery continues to be uncertain. The general goal is to set tariffs at cost recovery, but the higher tariffs may also lead to many more customers not paying their bills. The threat to cut off heating to nonpayers at times may not be credible because of the adverse impact it would have to other users in the

---

24. These are Vilnius, Kaunas, Klaipeda, Siauliai, Panevezys, and Alytus.

25. In most cases, these enterprises are eager to divest this responsibility.

26. The number of new companies in the breakup of LPC is determined by the technical requirements of the existing distribution networks.

building. The main problem with the new cost recovery strategy is the lack of metering for heating.[27] In the past, LPC had the leverage of threatening to cut off electricity to individual nonpayers of heating bills, because electricity was metered, but municipalities will not have this power.

Other changes introduced in the system may also make things more difficult for municipalities. A means-tested cash subsidy is, on balance, the most desirable way to address the problem of the impact of higher tariff rates on low-income households. It will give them not only the means to pay the higher bills but also an incentive to conserve energy and to introduce energy-efficient renovations. The fear among municipalities is that poor recipient households will use the money for other, more immediate, needs, such as buying food, and will not pay the DH bills.

A further threat to the municipal DH companies is that as tariffs rise, the customers that are more able to pay will be, at least marginally, converting to alternative sources of heating (natural gas and electric heating). To the extent that this happens, the municipal DH companies may get into a vicious cycle of higher per customer costs that will require higher tariffs, which in turn will induce more conversion to alternative modes of heating. This would leave municipal companies primarily with customers who can neither switch to alternate modes nor pay.

There are other institutional issues that will affect the performance and viability of the new municipal DH companies. First, the role of EPC in setting tariffs and standards needs to be clarified. Second, it is unclear what level of government (municipalities or central) will be ultimately responsible for covering operating deficits arising from low-income or other nonpaying customers. Municipal officials appear to believe that this will be a responsibility taken over by the central government. Finally, there will be an immediate need for new capital investment and rehabilitation of the infrastructure of the new DH companies, but it is less than certain where this financing will originate.[28]

Remaining Issues of Revenue Assignment

The evolution of revenue assignments in Lithuania has both positive and negative features. On the positive side, revenue sharing has been restricted to revenues that are most easily shared on a derivation basis. Retaining 100 percent of VAT revenues at the national level has been the right policy decision. VAT is debited and credited throughout the nation, and it is difficult, if not impossible, to identify how much tax is actually generated in a single local jurisdiction. Similarly, the apportionment of CIT revenues gets complicated when enterprises have economic activity in several jurisdictions.[29] PIT and property taxes are, in theory, the best taxes to share with local governments, if taxes are to be shared. The tax bases of the property tax and PIT are the least mobile, they are unlikely to lead to tax exporting, and they establish a link with those directly benefiting from municipal services. An added positive effect of the evolution in Lithuania's revenue sharing arrangements is that the tax bases for PIT and property taxes are less volatile in relation to changes in economic activity than those for CIT and VAT. If sharing rates are kept stable in the future, the current choice of sharable taxes should provide greater revenue

---

27. The problem is less acute for the distribution of hot and cold water, for which there is almost 100 percent metering.

28. A nonexhaustive list of other issues that have not been resolved includes adequate corporate governance institutions for the new companies, appropriate incentives to managers, and means to retain the advantage of the centralized purchase of heating oil.

29. The apportionment of CIT revenues is implemented in other countries through the use of formulas based on the share of the sales, labor, and/or property of enterprises in each jurisdiction.

stability and certainty for municipal governments. This is significant, given the dearth of both in recent years.

On the negative side, the evolution of revenue assignments in Lithuania has not provided any significant degree of revenue autonomy to local governments.[30] As argued elsewhere in this note, the ability of local governments to raise their own revenues in some marginal but significant amount is a fundamental pillar of a well-developed system of decentralized government. With very few exceptions, the structure of subnational government revenues in OECD countries shows that from one-third to two-thirds of these revenues come from taxes assigned to local governments (Annex table 3-25). Depending on whether or not property taxes are counted as local taxes, the share of own-taxes in Lithuania's local government revenues is between 3 and 10 percent.[31]

Another negative feature of revenue assignments in Lithuania has been the lack of certainty that it has generated for local governments, something that has contributed to poor planning and inefficiencies in public expenditures at the local level. Although the scope for uncertainty decreased after revenue sharing was restricted to PIT revenues, the reform of July 1997 failed to provide a fixed sharing rate to municipalities that was stable over time because, as pointed out earlier, the Seimas has retained the right to determine the annual PIT sharing rates. In addition, the Seimas is to legislate the fixed share of the PIT collected in each municipality that will go to finance the new Health Insurance Fund.[32]

The New System of Transfers

The system of transfers has been the subject of a far-reaching reform in the Law for Establishing Municipal Budget Income of July 1997. This law introduces a system of formula-driven transfers for equalization purposes. It also lists other transfers from the central government, including (i) transfers for capital investments in municipalities as provided in the Public Investment Programs; (ii) transfers for compensation for restitution of houses and apartments to former owners; (iii) transfers for the purchase of housing for returning Lithuanian political prisoners and exiles; and (iv) transfers for housing.

Missing in the new system of transfers are conditional grants that would allow the central government to pursue or encourage municipal expenditure in areas of national priority or importance, or in areas that exhibit significant externalities across municipalities. Perhaps this omission is linked to the lack of tax autonomy at the local level. Local governments, however, have considerable discretion in the spending of shared tax revenues and general transfers, and thus a matching grant program could be

---

30. Local governments have the freedom to impose local fees and charges, but these cannot generate significant amounts of revenue. Municipalities also have some degree of discretion, but only to lower their revenues either by reducing the rate of the land tax from its maximum statutory rate of 4 percent or by granting tax holidays to local enterprises for revenues shared by the municipality. Ironically, this latter is a form of discretion that should be discouraged or limited.

31. PIT, shared at 100 percent with the municipalities, is not considered a local, own-tax. PIT remains a central government tax, since local governments have no discretion over the rate or any other aspect of the tax. Strictly speaking, shared taxes are a form of government transfer.

32. Although it may have been politically expedient, financing the Health Insurance Fund with earmarked revenues from PIT retained at the local level is a complicated and nontransparent arrangement with little or no economic logic. It is not good budgetary practice to earmark tax revenues for any particular kind of expenditure program, unless there is an explicit linkage between payments and services, as may be the case, for example, between social security contributions and pension payments. No such connection exists between personal income tax and national health insurance benefits.

effective in the future, even if no revenue autonomy is granted. It is quite common for central governments to use conditional grants, often with matching arrangements, to encourage and channel subnational government expenditures into priority areas. It has also become more common for nations to use formulas for the distribution of transfers for equalization purposes. The degree of sophistication and effectiveness of these formulas varies significantly. The reforms of 1997 for equalization transfers put Lithuania ahead of many other countries in transition.

Nevertheless, the new system of equalization transfers for Lithuania's municipalities introduced in the Law for Establishing Municipal Budget Income of July 1997 is complex. In order to understand its properties and how it may be further improved, we examine the steps in the formulas in detail in the following paragraphs and use the mathematical notation employed in the law. (A detailed examination is also justified because the formulas are new, and they have not been explained elsewhere.)

The first step is the determination of the total pool of funds to be distributed as grants or as an "overall state budget grant." The pool of funds (D) is calculated according to the following formula:

$$D = A - B - C$$

where A is the forecast level of expenditures for all municipalities for the planned year, B is the forecast of total revenues from tax and nontax sources for all municipalities, and C is the total amount of specific grants from the central government to the municipalities for the planned year.

Two important rules are employed that tend to minimize the perverse impact of this gap-filling approach on incentives. First, rather than using the normative approach of the past, the forecasted amount of expenditures for the entirety of municipal budgets is politically determined (in a dialogue among the central government, the Seimas, and the Association of Municipalities) as a percentage share of total expenditures of the national budget. Also important in minimizing the perverse incentive effects on revenue collection efforts by the municipalities, the level of nontax revenues is determined as a fixed percentage share of the tax-income forecast for all municipalities.

The overall pool of transfer funds (D) is subdivided into three subfunds and distributed through three separate windows: (a) "Reserves for Extraordinary Events" ($D1$); (b) "Equalization of Tax Revenues" ($D2$); and (c) "Equalization of Expenditure Needs" ($D3$).

FIRST WINDOW: RESERVES FOR EXTRAORDINARY EVENTS. The total size of $D1$ is determined politically at budget time as a percentage share of the overall pool of transfer funds (D). The purpose of this window is to help municipalities with realized or actual tax revenues that fall below the forecast for the budget year. The grant, therefore, is given toward the end of the current fiscal year. $D1$ is apportioned according to the relative claim of each municipality in the group, calculated as the fraction of the municipality shortfall to the shortfall of all municipalities.[33]

To avoid free-riding by municipalities, the figure for actual revenues is augmented by the forgone revenues implied by the tax exemptions and special treatments granted by the municipal council. This first window presents two problems, however. First, how will forecasted revenues be defined, and by whom? Second, transfers are still aimed at filling a gap ex-post, and thus lower the incentive of

---

33. Thus, for each municipality *(i)* with a shortfall, the amount of funds received from the first window, $D1i$, is: $D1i = D1 * (xif - xi) / \Sigma(xif - xj)$, where x_i is actual and xif forecast tax income in municipality i, and $\Sigma(xjf - xj)$ is the summation of shortfalls across all municipalities.

municipalities to collect their own revenues.

SECOND WINDOW: EQUALIZATION OF TAX REVENUES. Again, the total size of *D2* is determined politically at budget time as a percentage of the overall pool of funds, *D*. The goal of this window is to bring municipalities with per capita forecast tax revenues below the national average closer to the average. The gap between the municipality's forecast per capita tax revenues (pcx_{if}) and the national average forecast per capita tax revenues for all municipalities (*PCX*) is closed only by a given percentage (*H*). The actual number of qualifying municipalities under the second window can also be adjusted by means of a scaling coefficient (*K*) for the national average per capita tax revenues.[34] Note that as *K* decreases from a value of one down, the number of municipalities qualifying for a transfer will decrease.[35]

The perverse incentive to collect less revenue is addressed in this window by using forecast revenues rather than actual revenues.[36] This still poses the problem of how forecast revenues will be determined, and by whom. In theory, these forecasts will be carried out by the Ministry of Finance. If the forecasts are based on past collections, the mechanism may not be time-consistent because municipalities may affect the forecast for next year with collection efforts in the current year.

THIRD WINDOW: EQUALIZATION OF EXPENDITURE NEEDS. The goal of this window is to account for expenditure needs beyond the direct control of the municipalities. The total level of funds available for this window (*D4*) comes from two sources—that is, *D4 = D3 + P*. The first component (*D3*) is the funds left over from the partitioning of *D* to the first two windows; thus *D3 = D – D1 – D2*. The second component (*P*) is formed by mandatory contributions from PIT collections from municipalities with forecast per capita collections (pcy_{if}) that are higher than the national average for all forecast per capita collections of municipalities (*PCY*). This is a "fraternal system," also known as a "Robin Hood" system of funding, which is used by most Scandinavian and some central European countries. The contributions from better-off municipalities are automatically computed by the State Tax Inspectorate and deposited directly in the State Treasury Account. As in the case of the second window, only a share (*h*) (note that this differs from parameter *H*) of the difference between the municipality's per capita collections and the national average is actually contributed to the fund. In addition, the national average figure (*Y*) used in the formula can be adjusted by a scaling coefficient (*k*) (note that this differs from parameter *K*) that affects the number of municipalities that will be contributing to the fraternal fund.[37]

The overall funds in the third window (*D4*) are allocated to the municipalities according to a

---

34. The claim to *D2* for a qualifying municipality is given by the formula: $d2i = Gi * H * (K * PCX - pcxif)$, where *Gi* is the population of municipality *i*.

35. Even though the "next step" is not clearly stated in the text of the law translation, the actual amount of the grant received by a qualifying municipality in the second window should be $D2i = D2 * (d2i / \Sigma d2j)$. Actually, article 12 of the law calls the expression for *d2i* in the previous footnote the share of the grant allocated to a municipality. This formula as stated in the law, however, does not guarantee that when all shares are added, the total will be equal to the amount available (*D2*). The "next step" we discuss in this footnote should be incorporated in the law.

36. Conventionally, equalization formulas use a measure of fiscal capacity (tax bases) rather than actual revenues to avoid the problem of perverse incentives toward tax effort.

37. The complete formula for the determination of P_i is: $P_i = G_i * h * [pcy_{ij} - (k * PCY)]$, where, as before, G_i is the population in the *i*th municipality, and the total transfer fund is: $P = \Sigma P_i$.

relative measure of need based on three demographic variables that are determined for each 1,000 inhabitants. The demographic variables are number of children under eighteen years of age, denoted by ($r1$); number of disabled persons, denoted by ($r2$); and number of pension-age persons, denoted by ($r3$).

The amount of transfer actually received by a municipality from the third window is given by the formula:

$$D4_i = D4 * E_i$$

where E_i is the demographic index for the ith municipality, computed as the ratio of the weighted average of needs in the ith municipality to the sum of weighted average needs for all municipalities.[38]

The formalization of the third window includes a flaw: it does not take into account the relative size of the population in a municipality in relation to the rest of the country. As a result, small municipalities may receive larger need-based transfers than much larger municipalities. For example, while Vilnius is 200 times more populous than Neringa, the latter municipality may receive a larger amount of need-based transfers under the third window. The culprit here is the way the demographic factors (r_i, $i = 1, 2, 3$) are defined by 1,000 inhabitants. For example, if Neringa has twice as many children (and the other demographic variables) per 1,000 inhabitants as Vilnius, it tends to receive twice as much in transfers from the third window. There are several simple ways to correct this problem. Two possible methods are described in the simulations of the new system of transfers in Annex 3-3, in which the demographic factors (r_i, i = 1, 2, 3) are defined as type of population in a municipality in relation to the nation as a whole.

The flaw in the population scale has important consequences for the actual distribution of municipal revenues. Summary statistics are shown in Annex table 3-24 for the distribution of municipal revenues that would result from several simulations. The table also presents summary statistics for the distribution of (forecast) revenues for 1997 before the transfers and the distribution of actual revenues for 1996. The disparities in the distribution of municipal revenues, measured by the coefficient of variation, is larger for the simulation with a literal application of the text of the law (Municipal Budget Income) than for the distribution before the equalization transfers or the distribution for 1996. Changing the methodology to take the scale of population into account produces distributions of municipal revenues that show considerably smaller disparities.

The simulations presented in Annex table 3-24 also sound a cautionary note about the computation of the fraternal reserve fund. The size of the municipalities' payments into the fund is determined by two parameters, h and k. As explained above, parameter k determines how "wealthy" municipalities must be, as determined by PIT collections, in order to pay into the fund. Parameter h

---

38. The formula is given by:

$$E_i = \sum_i Mr\,(r_i - min.r_j) \Big/ \sum_j \sum_i Mr\,(r_i - min.r_j)$$

where Mr is the weight attached in the formula to each of the three demographic variables (r_i, i = 1, 2, 3). Note that while the numerator of the formula is added across the three weighted demographic components for one municipality, i, the denominator of the formula is added across the three weighted components and for *all* municipalities. Only if a single municipality has the minimum figure for all three variables would it fail to receive any transfer from the third window. In any other case, the municipality will get a positive amount.

determines the share of "excess revenues" (per capita revenues minus $k*$ per capita average revenues) that municipalities must pay into the fund. The extent of equalization is extremely sensitive to the level of these parameters. Our simulations show that increasing h from 0.5 to 1.0 reduces the coefficient of variation in the distribution of revenues tenfold.

SETTING AND APPROVAL OF TRANSFER FORMULA PARAMETERS. The Law on the Methodology for Establishing Municipal Income distinguishes between two sets of parameters, depending on whether they are set for a period of three years or set every year in the annual budget. The list of parameters, which was negotiated by the Ministry of Finance, the Ministry of Municipal Affairs, and the Lithuanian Association of Municipalities, and eventually approved by Seimas, includes: (i) the share of consolidated municipal budget expenditures in total national budget expenditures; (ii) the fixed share of municipal nontax income as a percentage of municipal tax income; (iii) the gap coefficient (H) in the second window; (iv) the adjustment coefficient (K) in the second window; (v) the gap coefficient (h) in the third window; (vi) the adjustment coefficient (k) in the third window; and (vii) the weights (Mr) for the demographic variables in the third window.

The list of parameters set in the budget *each year* includes: (i) the share of the total pool of transfer funds from the central government budget (D) destined for the second window for equalization of tax revenues ($D2$); (ii) the share of the total pool of transfer funds from the central government budget (D) destined for the third window for equalization of expenditure needs; and (iii) the specialized or targeted grants.

It should be noted that these provisions appear to contradict earlier elements in the law, which stated that grant funding for the third window (equalization of expenditure needs), or $D3$, is to be computed as a residual from overall funding (or the "overall state budget grant"), minus the funding for the first and second windows, or $D3 = D - D1 - D2$. With respect to the first window, the law states that after three-quarters of the budgetary year have passed, the Seimas will establish the sum of funds for the first window for "Reserves for Extraordinary Events" ($D1$). This creates a timing problem and is probably the cause of the inconsistency in the text of the law regarding the determination of $D3$.

The distinction between parameters determined for a period of three years and those set annually is a positive step toward more predictability and stability in municipal revenues. The magnitudes of the equalization transfers (D, $D1$, $D2$, and $D3$), however, will vary annually. Given that the revenue sharing rates for PIT could also vary annually, as will targeted grants, only modest progress has been made in the Law for Establishing Municipal Budget Income to provide municipalities with more predictable sources of revenue. At the least, the shares dividing the annual pool of funds (or "overall state budget grant") into the three different windows could also be fixed for a period of three years. The same should be done for the municipalities' sharing rates in PIT.

Borrowing Issues

The municipalities' inability to engage in long-term borrowing in any significant amount is a critical issue, given the vast need for capital infrastructure investment at the local level. Furthermore, borrowing is the right way to finance long-lived infrastructure. It addresses the otherwise impossible liquidity problems of financing investments out of current savings and it distributes the payment for infrastructure services among the generations of taxpayers that will benefit from them. The government needs to issue regulations and limits for municipal borrowing and to facilitate the development of commercial credit for municipalities. (Some specific options are discussed in the Policy Recommendations section.)

Budgeting Process at the Municipal Level

Although generally not discussed under intergovernmental relations, the existence of proper budgetary institutions is central to effective decentralization. The realization of the benefits of decentralization—increasing the efficiency of public expenditures by making government more responsive and accountable to the needs and preferences of taxpayers—is impossible without budgetary autonomy and good budget practices. Because of the length and complexity of budget process issues at the local level in Lithuania, these issues are addressed separately in Annex 3-2.

Policy Recommendations

REFORM THE NUMBER OF LOCAL GOVERNMENTS. There appears to be room in the future for increasing the current number of municipalities to enjoy the benefits of increased representation and accountability without sacrificing the principle of a minimum desired scale.[39] Although the minimum scale for some services should remain a concern, the administrative costs of a larger number of municipalities will probably represent a minimum amount. As shown in table 3-13, administrative expenditures as a percentage of total local expenditures have remained almost the same throughout the transition period. Ironically, it rose slightly only after the administrative reform of 1994 that consolidated all local governments into only fifty-six municipalities. If new municipalities are created, the benefits from economies of scale in some services should be preserved through the arrangement of special districts or the creation of companies that provide services to several municipalities. This is the approach now being followed in the decentralization of DH, and it should be imitated for other services with significant economies of scale in production, such as water or sewerage treatment plants.

Table 3-13. Lithuania: Administrative Expenditures as a Share of the Municipal Budget, 1992–97 (Lt million)

Year	Administrative expenditures	Total municipal budget	Administrative expenditures as percentage of total	Administrative expenditures as percentage of GDP
1992	9.7	369.3	2.6	0.3
1993	26.1	1,097.9	2.4	0.2
1994	46.6	1,857.9	2.5	0.2
1995	59.7	2,253.7	2.7	0.2
1996	86.6	2,654.5	3.3	0.2
1997[a]	47.3	1,349.6	3.5	n.a.

n.a. Not available.
a. Based on actual expenditures through 1 July 1997.
Source: Ministry of Finance.

CLARIFY THE ASSIGNMENT OF CAPITAL EXPENDITURE RESPONSIBILITIES. Current policy on the assignment of capital expenditure is inadequate. Municipalities are theoretically responsible for all capital infrastructure for the public services assigned to them, but at the same time, the central government has become responsible for all public investment in infrastructure projects with costs over Lt 5 million. International practice varies with respect to the level of involvement of central governments in the provision of capital infrastructure at the subnational level. From a first-best, theoretical viewpoint, the principle of assigning responsibility for infrastructure to local governments is the right one.

---

39. A chief objective of the 1994 administrative reform was to reach a minimum size of municipalities of 10,000 inhabitants to realize economies of scale. There are currently only nine municipalities with populations under 30,000.

Maintenance, operation, and capital investment for infrastructure should all be assigned to the level of government that is responsible for the delivery of the public service involved. Assigning responsibility for operation to one level of government and capital investment to another tends to lead to a lack of maintenance and inefficient investment choices.

From a practical viewpoint, direct involvement of the central government in the provision of capital infrastructure at the subnational level may be needed when local governments do not have the financial means to invest in infrastructure. This is the case in developing and transitional countries with incomplete credit markets and weak intergovernmental finance systems. Although direct involvement of the central government may be temporarily justified in Lithuania, it also carries risks. The dichotomy between operation and investment has often been singled out as the main cause for the poor state of capital infrastructure in the former Soviet Union. At the same time, indirect involvement of national governments through matching grants or similar arrangements is quite common internationally, and it is also desirable in light of interjurisdictional externalities and equity considerations.

In the medium term, as sources of credit are developed for long-term borrowing by municipalities, the central government should have the option of phasing out the current policy of financing projects over Lt 5 million and let municipalities take charge of these responsibilities. In addition, the funds currently used at the central government level for projects over Lt 5 million could be used for conditional or categorical grants from the central government in support of well-developed policies of national relevance or with significant externalities, as is the case now for drainage projects for land development, wastewater treatment, and other environmental purposes. The funds could also be used to provide partial financial support to poorer municipalities or to capitalize a municipal credit facility, as discussed below.

PUT DECENTRALIZED DH COMPANIES ON A FINANCIALLY SUSTAINABLE PATH. To strengthen the viability of the new DH companies, the government should take several measures. Foremost is the issue of metering, which must be dealt with up front. Postponing the introduction of metering saves much-needed resources in a sector that faces considerable demands for capital infrastructure renovations, but international experience clearly shows that it is unlikely that attempts at cost recovery will be sustainable without the eventual introduction of metering. Conservation and efficiency gains are likely to be minimal until metering is introduced; otherwise, the actions of an individual customer will not be linked to the utility bills they pay.

There is also a need for a better understanding of the tariffs that must be set for DH to make alternate modes of heating provision feasible or profitable. Considerable insight can be gained from studying the experience of other countries where there has been conversion to natural gas or electric heating. If tariffs are set too high too quickly, the switch to alternate modes may make the process irreversible. Finally, it would have been desirable to have tested the switch from direct subsidies to producers to means-tested subsidies to low-income households through a pilot project in order to better handle nonpaying customers. To compensate for this lack of experience, the new companies should share experiences in this area soon—and as often—as possible.

INTRODUCE MORE REVENUE CERTAINTY AT THE LOCAL LEVEL. One of the most distorting factors in municipal finances during the transition years has been the uncertainty local governments have experienced regarding their revenue sources. This has led to poor planning and diminished efficiency levels in public expenditures. Some degree of uncertainty has been unavoidable given the shrinking of traditional tax bases associated with economic restructuring and downsizing; but a significant degree has been generated by unstable revenue assignment policies. Recent reforms in revenue assignments have been in the right direction: both VAT and CIT are assigned entirely at the central government level, and revenue sharing in PIT and property taxes are now the main sources of tax revenue for municipalities. Unfortunately, recent legislation has left considerable uncertainty about what share of PIT a municipality can expect. The uncertainty continues because the Seimas can still change the sharing rate for each municipality annually and because a set percentage of PIT collections will be dedicated to funding the Health Insurance Fund.

Two measures to improve revenue certainty at the municipal level are recommended here. First, the funding of the Health Insurance Fund should be decoupled from any revenue sharing with the municipalities. As argued earlier in this note, the current arrangement has no economic merit or rationale. The Health Insurance Fund should be financed from general revenues or from earmarked payroll taxes, depending on the health insurance scheme adopted. Most countries with public health insurance plans use earmarked payroll taxes for financial support. The government could consider this option to cover the costs of health services provided to employed contributors and their families, while the costs of health services to the poor, unemployed, and the elderly should be financed, as in most countries, by transfers from the general budget. These changes should be accompanied by complementary measures on revenue sharing that adjust the overall level of funding for municipalities downward to reflect the decrease in their expenditure responsibilities in health services.

Second, the government should consider providing stable sharing rates in PIT for all municipalities for a period of three years. The timing for the review of these rates by the Seimas could be synchronized with the review of the formula coefficients in the new system of transfers that determine the contribution of better-off municipalities to the "fraternal reserve fund" for the equalization of expenditure needs across municipalities. Revenue certainty for municipalities will also be heightened if all other parameters in the new system of equalization transfers were set for a period of three years. This would leave only the overall pool of funds for equalization purposes to be determined on an annual basis. It is a common international practice to fix transfer formula parameters into a law, and sometimes empower a commission to review these parameters every three years or so, rather than leaving the recurrent decisions to political institutions.

INCREASE REVENUE AUTONOMY AT THE LOCAL LEVEL. The lack of any significant degree of revenue discretion is among the most important problems left on the agenda for reform of intergovernmental relations in Lithuania. As a consequence, many of the efficiency gains associated with decentralization have not been realized. The failure to grant tax autonomy to municipalities is rooted in what appears to be a widespread interpretation of the Constitution that bestows the power to introduce taxes exclusively on the Seimas.[40] This constitutional mandate, however, does not seem to contradict the practice in many unitary countries (for example, Denmark, Estonia, Spain, or the United Kingdom) of parliamentary delegation of power to local governments to raise taxes on their own within set rules and margins. Annex table 3-26 shows the significant reliance on local taxes in OECD countries with both unitary and federal systems. The two most commonly used taxes with revenue significance at the local level are the property (real estate) tax and a (subnational) personal income tax. Local sales and excise taxes are also quite important in some of these countries.

Economic efficiency and political accountability at the local level in Lithuania could be greatly

---

40. Within this interpretation, municipalities would have the right to reduce tax burdens (as long as they have budgetary consequences only for the municipality itself), but would not have the right to increase any tax.

enhanced by providing local governments with discretionary revenue authority.[41] In seeking these goals, the government has essentially two choices: to introduce taxes that are exclusively assigned to local governments, giving them discretion to vary rates within predetermined bands, and/or to introduce surtaxes (or piggyback taxes) on PIT, with some discretion over rates. The latter is the simplest and most effective means of providing municipalities with the potential for discretionary revenues. Again, international experience varies. Some countries provide decentralized governments with both options (locally assigned taxes and a local surtax on personal income), and other countries tend to rely more on one of the two options. Local surtaxes on personal income are common in western European countries (such as Austria, Denmark, Germany, or Sweden).

Under the first option of exclusively assigned local taxes, the clearest candidate is the introduction of a real estate property tax that would include in its tax base not only the value of land and structures of commercial and industrial properties, but also those of residential properties. Many OECD countries have some form of locally assigned real estate property tax. The government has plans to introduce such a tax, although it is unclear if there are plans to give limited discretion over rates to the municipalities, even to give them the option to set their rates between a minimum and maximum set by the Seimas. The introduction of this tax presents significant challenges, such as the accurate valuation of property at market values and the dispersion of property registration.[42] The most important and immediate task is the preparation of fiscal cadasters with clear identification of property (land and structures), current owner, and updated market value. In the medium term, this tax should be administered by the State Tax Inspectorate, but the eventual development of local tax administrations should be considered.

A second candidate for providing municipalities with revenue discretion is an annual tax on motor vehicles. This tax is common in OECD countries and in many developing countries. Following international practice, this tax could be based on the value of the vehicle, as proxied by model and age, for example, and could also give discretion to the municipalities to set their own rates within margins established by the Seimas. To facilitate enforcement, the tax would be paid annually with the renewal of registration of motor vehicles in the place of residence of the owner.[43]

IMPROVE THE DESIGN OF THE NEW SYSTEM OF TRANSFERS. The reform in the system of transfers introduced in the Law for Establishing Municipal Budget Income of July 1997 is a significant accomplishment. It represents a radical departure from the gap-filling approach to equalization of the past and it provides a solid foundation in a critical area of intergovernmental finances. It is a rare event in

---

41. Discussions of decentralization issues in Lithuania seem to miss the point that efficiency at the local level is enhanced by allowing municipalities to exert greater tax pressure if local residents so desire. The emphasis should not be on uniformity, but rather on the ability of citizens to tax themselves according to their own preferences to provide public services at the local level. At the desired level, the greater or lesser taxes paid by residents are balanced against the services actually provided. Fundamentally, this concept of efficiency is not unlike that associated with private markets, which let individuals decide on their own how much and for what purpose to spend their incomes. It would be difficult to argue that, in general, citizens would be better-off if their freedom to make these decisions were restricted.

42. The registry for urban land is kept by the Ministry of Justice; for rural land, by the Ministry of Agriculture; and for buildings, by the Ministry of Housing. Liens on real estate property are kept in a completely different registry.

43. One potential problem is that owners may try to register their cars in lower tax municipalities, something that has been addressed quite effectively in other countries by, for example, requiring that car owners show proof of their place of residence. This approach, however, requires compliance by all municipalities.

any country that a new and complex law does not include areas that need revision and modification, and there are aspects of the new law that will need reassessment by the government.

Any system of equalization of transfers must address two issues: disparities in fiscal capacity or ability to generate tax revenue and differences in expenditure patterns arising from the incidence of population groups with special needs or other elements that affect the costs of service provision. These two issues are generally addressed by windows two (equalization of tax revenues) and three (equalization of expenditure needs), respectively, of the current system. Window one (reserves for extraordinary events) of the new system, in contrast, appears to be a remnant of the old, gap-filling approach, except that the gap is generated ex-post. Nevertheless, the perverse consequences on the revenue mobilization effort are unchanged. Municipalities that make less of an effort to raise their own revenues will get larger transfers. The new system of transfers would be improved with the elimination of window one.[44]

Similarly, the use of forecast revenues in a municipality for equalization in relation to the national average in window two (equalization of tax revenues) helps with the problem of perverse incentives to raise own-revenues, but if forecasts are actually based on past collections, the incentive problem will reappear over time. Collecting less actual revenue this year yields lower forecast revenues next year, and therefore creates the hope of larger transfers. In the medium term, the solution should be to base equalization in window two (equalization of tax revenues) on fiscal capacity as approximated by measures of tax bases. This approach, based on capacity rather than forecast or actual collections, will become imperative, if and when municipalities are granted true tax discretion.

The choice of parameters in window three (equalization of expenditure needs) for the development of the fraternal pool of funds will require great care, given the sensitivity of the results to the parameters set. In addition, as discussed at length earlier, the definition of the formulas for the equalization of expenditure needs will have to take into account the scale effect of municipality size to avoid unfortunate results in the distribution of transfers.

Finally, for categorical grants with objectives other than equalization, the government should follow best international practices for using matching grants to promote and leverage central government resources with municipal resources in areas of national priority, such as education, or areas with otherwise significant externalities across municipalities, such as environmental protection.

REGULATE BORROWING AND FACILITATE ACCESS TO LONG-TERM CREDIT BY LOCAL GOVERNMENTS. The main solution to the severe need for capital infrastructure at the local level is for municipalities to engage in long-term borrowing for worthy projects. The government, however, needs to be aware that irresponsible borrowing behavior by municipalities may arise in an unregulated environment, and such borrowing could easily threaten fiscal stability at the national level. At the same time, municipalities willing and able to borrow for worthy projects now find it difficult to get credit because of the lack of developed credit markets and institutions.

The tasks ahead for the central government in this regard are twofold: regulate and facilitate municipal credit. In regulation, international experience (for example, western European countries for successful experiences and Latin American countries for generally unsuccessful ones) provides a time-tested set of rules:

---

44. This window may have a weak justification, however, because window two is based on forecast, rather than actual, revenues.

- Municipalities should only borrow for capital investment purposes.[45]
- There should be strict borrowing limits. For example, for long-term debt for capital investment purposes, debt service (interest and repayment of principal) should at no time exceed 15 or 20 percent of the municipal "recurrent revenues" (which exclude special grant funds and borrowing proceeds).
- If the municipality issues debt guarantees, these guarantees should be included in the 15 percent ceiling.
- Borrowing should also be allowed for short-term cash or liquidity management. In this case, annual borrowing should not exceed 5 percent of projected revenues, and all loans should be reimbursed at the end of the year.
- International borrowing should require previous approval by the Ministry of Finance.
- There should be strict reporting requirements to the Ministry of Finance and credible and effective sanctions for noncompliant municipalities. The Ministry of Finance should maintain a public debt registry for outstanding local government debt.
- Municipalities with outstanding long-term loans should be subjected to external audit every year. Loan nonpayment (or default) situations should be clearly defined to automatically trigger a financial rehabilitation plan supervised by the central government authorities.

Facilitating the development of credit sources for municipalities will be a more difficult proposition. This issue has been ably analyzed in Cochran,[46] and his conclusions are worth repeating here. Given the lack of a credit market and the unwillingness or inability of banks to lend to municipalities, the best bet in the immediate future for developing a sustainable credit line for municipalities is to create a transitional municipal credit facility (TMCF). This entity would lend directly to municipalities and municipal enterprises within a strict "hard credit" culture and could be capitalized by borrowing from the IBRD and from other potential sources.[47] Later on, this entity could launch other financing models, including a "loan to lenders" model that will permit TMCF to lend to a small number of banks willing to accept long-term municipal credit risk. At some later date, the municipal credit facility could also be authorized to operate as a bond bank to facilitate the development of a municipal bond market. The municipal credit facility should incorporate "sunset" provisions and not interfere with the development of private credit markets for municipal governments.[48]

IMPROVE THE BUDGET PROCESS AT THE LOCAL LEVEL. The budget system and fiscal management process at the local level have lagged behind in the reform. While other components of the system of decentralized governance have been the subject of continuous reform, changes in the budgeting process have been scanty. The process is still regulated by the Budget Formation Law of Lithuania of 1990, an antiquated legal framework that has limited the efficiency of local governments. The current

---

45. Borrowing to service debt should not be allowed. Borrowing to roll over or convert debt, however, is permissible.

46. T. H. Cochran, "Building a Hard-Credit Culture with Lithuanian Local Authorities and Municipal Enterprises" (mimeo, 1997).

47. Independence of the TMCF from government intervention will be an essential element of its success. This is a critical issue, especially given the current record of political intervention in the credit decisions of not only public banks, but also private banks, with the objective of "directing" funds toward public policy objectives. See M. Giugale, "Lithuania: Macroeconomic Issues and Prospects for a Transition Country at a Junction" (presented at Lithuania's Agricultural Strategy Conference, Vilnius, April 1992).

48. International experiences with what systems have worked and have not worked are discussed in Cochran, "Building a Hard-Credit Culture."

budgetary process presents serious deficiencies at all stages of the budget cycle, including budget preparation and revenue forecasting, budget execution, and ex-post audit and evaluation.

A key policy measure in the medium term is thus the drafting and approval of a Municipal Budget Law. This law should program budget preparation, not from the perspective of expenditure needs, but rather from the perspective of revenue availability; introduce a modern treasury function for budget execution; introduce budget evaluation; and strengthen current institutions of control and audit. More specific recommendations for the reform of the budget process are offered in Annex 3-2.

ANNEX 3-1
Data Tables

Table 3-14. Subsidies Granted from Budgets, 1996

Category	National		State		Local	
	Thousand litai	Percent	Thousand litai	Percent	Thousand litai	Percent
Subsidies	396,469	100.0	252,550	100.0	143,889	100.0
The economy	329,659	83.1	205,951	81.5	123,678	86.0
Housing and community amenity affairs and services	6,426	1.6	—	—	6,426	4.5
Fuel and energy affairs and services	218,834	55.2	157,090	62.2	61,714	42.9
Agriculture, forestry, fishing, and veterinary affairs and services	2,062	0.5	2,062	0.8	—	—
Transport and communication affairs and services	102,189	25.8	46,756	18.5	55,433	38.5
Other economic affairs and services	148	0.0	43	0.0	105	0.1
Social affairs						
Recreational, cultural, and religious affairs and services	693	0.2	—	—	693	0.5
Other functions of government						
Expenditure not classified by major group	66,117	16.7	46,599	18.5	19,518	13.6

Source: *Government Finances of the Republic of Lithuania, 1996.*

Table 3-15. Budget Expenditure on Education Affairs and Services, 1996

Category	National		State		Local	
	Thousand litai	Percent	Thousand litai	Percent	Thousand litai	Percent
Total expenditure on education affairs and services	1,712,880	100.0	595,773	100.0	1,117,107	100.0
Preprimary establishments	246,549	14.4	—	—	246,549	22.1
Comprehensive and vocational schools	978,024	57.1	232,468	39.0	745,556	66.7
Comprehensive primary basic and secondary schools	755,584	44.1	15,985	2.7	739,599	66.2
Boarding schools and child care homes (families included)	97,824	5.7	91,867	15.4	5,957	0.5
Vocational schools	124,616	7.3	124,616	20.9	—	—
Higher schools	310,503	18.1	310,503	52.1	—	—
Higher schools (after graduation, a university diploma is awarded)	229,438	13.4	229,438	38.5	—	—
Special secondary schools	81,065	4.7	81,065	13.6	—	—
Other educational institutions	88,246	5.2	10,837	1.8	77,409	6.9
Support for nonstate educational institutions	1,129	0.1	112	0.0	1,017	0.1
Preschool establishments	437	0.0	—	—	437	0.0
Comprehensive schools	580	0.0	—	—	580	0.1
Special secondary schools	112	0.0	112	0.0	—	—
Other educational functions	76,751	4.5	31,799	5.3	44,952	4.0
Maintenance of central and municipal institutions	5,864	0.3	4,240	0.7	1,624	0.1
Research and research institutions	842	0.0	842	0.1	—	—
Socioeconomic programs	4,972	0.3	4,972	0.8	—	—

Source: Government Finances of the Republic of Lithuania, 1996.

Table 3-16. Budget Expenditure on Health Care Affairs and Services, 1996

Category	National		State		Local	
	Thousand litai	Percent	Thousand litai	Percent	Thousand litai	Percent
Total expenditure on health care affairs and services	1,072,669	100.0	427,657	100.0	645,012	100.0
Hospitals and polyclinics	731,479	68.2	116,526	27.2	614,953	95.3
General	525,155	49.0	12,796	3.0	512,359	79.4
Specialized	149,646	14.0	78,133	18.3	71,513	11.1
Maternity centers	8,203	0.8	—	—	8,203	1.3
Nursing and convalescent homes	28,474	2.7	25,597	6.0	2,877	0.4
First aid stations	20,001	1.9	—	—	20,001	3.1
Clinics (specialized)	219,935	20.5	219,935	51.4	—	—
Other health care institutions	58,997	5.5	43,030	10.1	15,967	2.5
Prosthetics and other medical equipment	21,465	2.0	15,303	3.6	6,162	1.0
Other health care functions	34,798	3.2	27,255	6.4	7,543	1.2
Maintenance of central and municipal institutions	2,276	0.2	1,889	0.4	387	0.1
Research and research institution	1,172	0.1	1,172	0.3	—	—
Socioeconomic program	2,547	0.2	2,547	0.6	—	—

Source: *Government Finances of the Republic of Lithuania, 1996.*

Table 3-17. Budget Expenditure on Social Security and Welfare, 1996

Category	National Thousand litai	National Percent	State Thousand litai	State Percent	Local Thousand litai	Local Percent
Total expenditure on social security and welfare affairs and services	746,299	100.0	471,775	100.0	274,524	100.0
Social security affairs and services	508,378	68.1	277,772	58.9	230,606	84.0
Special pensions	808	0.1	343	0.1	465	0.2
State pensions of the first and second class of the Republic of Lithuania	4,616	0.6	4,616	1.0	—	—
State pensions of casualties	88,900	11.9	88,900	18.8	—	—
State pensions to interior officers	19,641	2.6	19,641	4.2	—	—
State pensions to officers of national defense	1,175	0.2	1,175	0.2	—	—
State pensions to officers of national security	45	0.0	45	0.0	—	—
State pensions to officers of prosecuting magistracy	215	0.0	215	0.0	—	—
State pensions to scientists	5,399	0.7	5,399	1.1	—	—
Social pensions	156,947	21.0	156,947	33.3	—	—
Social benefits	77,171	10.3	—	—	77,171	28.1
Family and child allowances	108,353	14.5	—	—	108,353	39.5
Funeral grant	21,311	2.9	—	—	21,311	7.8
Other social assistance welfare affairs and services	23,797	3.2	491	0.1	23,306	8.5
Social welfare	131,749	17.7	98,336	20.8	33,413	12.2
Children's residential institutions	27,785	3.7	15,312	3.2	12,473	4.5
Old persons' residential institutions	31,337	4.2	21,558	4.6	9,779	3.6
Handicapped persons' residential institutions	61,510	8.2	59,008	12.5	2,502	0.9
Other residential institutions	5,427	0.7	2,458	0.5	2,969	1.1
Institutions delivering home visiting and housekeeping	5,690	0.8	—	—	5,690	2.1
Other functions of social security and welfare	97,207	13.0	91,695	19.4	5,512	2.0
Maintenance of central and municipal institutions	7,665	1.0	2,672	0.6	4,993	1.8

Source: Government Finances of the Republic of Lithuania, 1996.

Table 3-18. Vilnius: Municipal Budget Loans and Loans Scheduled for Repayment
(Lt thousands)

Borrower	Amount of loan	Term of loan	Paid back by 97/01/01	Planned to repay in 1997	Purpose of loan
State Commercial Bank	15,198	1/4/11	1519.8	3,039.6	85 percent import agreement for purchase of trolleybuses
State Commercial Bank	15,131.2	2002	0	3,026.2	85 percent import agreement for purchase of buses
Agbank	2,671.5	97/11/07	0	2,671.5	To repay 15 percent of bus purchase agreement
Ministry of Finance	35,000	99/11/01	0	10,937.5	To repay loan to Savings Bank for energy and heating
Ministry of Finance	4,000	99/11/01	0	1,250	To cover the 996 short-term loan from the MoF
Ministry of Finance	3,600	4/1/16	0	0	Renovation of education institution
Total	75,600.7		1,519.8	20,924.8	

Note: Repayment of the 36,000,000 Lt loan for renovation of the education institution shall begin in the year 2001.
Source: City of Vilnius.

Table 3-19. Lithuania: Municipal Revenue by Municipality, by Source, 1996
(Lt thousands)

Region	PIT	CIT	Asset taxes	Other taxes	Income from Mun. prop.	Penalties	Other nontax revenues	Income from LT assets	Transfers from state	Total revenue
Vilnius	284,497.0	27,844.0	32,783.0	16,501.0	14.9	6,460.0	9,761.0	0.0	0.0	377,860.9
Alytus	43,858.7	7,214.9	5,217.2	1,434.6	0.0	686.9	858.8	0.0	0.0	59,271.1
Birstonas	1,969.2	494.0	264.9	61.6	0.0	36.3	180.5	0.0	1,546.0	4,552.5
Druskininkai	11,456.4	1,228.8	1,062.4	619.7	2.5	253.3	750.4	2.8	3,783.0	19,159.3
Kaunas	206,414.0	30,460.7	19,016.7	13,410.9	0.0	3,376.0	4,210.2	0.0	0.0	276,888.5
Klaipeda	100,689.2	12,254.7	11,413.1	13,040.0	23.3	4,032.1	6,148.3	0.0	0.0	147,600.7
Marijampole	20,530.0	2,766.8	3,527.1	1,819.2	0.0	864.4	176.0	0.0	0.0	29,683.5
Neringa	2,306.2	204.0	1,154.3	397.0	1.6	56.4	630.0	0.0	5,965.0	10,714.5
Palanga	11,235.5	1,643.5	3,105.4	420.6	-3.4	302.6	2,535.2	11.0	7,791.0	27,041.4
Panevezys	55,838.4	7,344.0	7,964.0	5,066.9	213.1	835.3	10,987.2	0.0	0.0	88,248.9
Siauliai	82,216.0	9,315.0	6,784.0	4,890.0	10.0	1,004.0	1354.1	0.0	0.0	105,573.1
Visaginas	15,715.1	1,245.5	612.4	1,099.8	158.8	227.1	35.0	0.0	0.0	19,093.7
Akmene raj.	13,314.9	3,632.8	2,112.5	496.5	2.2	187.5	396.2	0.0	2,343.0	22,485.6
Alytus raj.	9,056.4	789.7	1,192.4	237.3	0.0	54.4	545.8	7.4	28,018.0	39,901.4
Anyksciai raj.	13,357.0	6,827.2	1,396.0	421.0	0.0	72.5	4,542.6	0.0	13,703.0	40,319.3
Birzai raj.	15,729.3	8,610.2	2,084.0	706.6	0.0	331.9	2,155.6	0.0	0.0	29,617.6
Ignalina raj.	7,597.4	686.4	1,696.2	262.1	1.8	437.2	49.4	0.0	11,054.0	21,784.5
Jonava raj.	30,663.4	2,073.8	3,447.7	872.5	0.0	742.3	2,802.1	35.9	0.0	40,637.7
Joniskis raj.	11,170.7	1,518.6	2,216.2	609.3	0.5	272.5	77.3	0.0	6,658.0	22,523.1
Jurbarkas raj.	11,389.5	652.0	1,720.9	774.0	0.0	302.1	375.7	0.0	14,933.0	30,147.2
Kaisiadorys raj.	20,050.6	2,810.2	2,825.6	513.7	0.0	162.9	11.1	0.0	0.0	26,374.1
Kaunas raj.	24,394.0	2,088.0	2,824.0	647.0	0.0	739.0	118.9	0.0	17,831.0	48,641.9
Kedainiai raj.	30,408.1	9,355.0	4,800.2	858.6	0.0	271.4	977.8	0.0	6,567.0	53,238.1
Kelme raj.	9,779.7	662.7	1,127.5	529.7	0.0	258.3	1,352.4	0.0	19,032.0	32,742.3
Klaipeda raj.	18,103.0	9,660.0	2,415.0	537.0	0.0	488.0	555.4	0.0	10,361.0	42,119.4
Kretinga raj.	13,624.3	1,852.0	1,785.1	638.5	-0.5	333.8	26.1	0.0	13,648.0	31,907.3
Kupiskis raj.	9,138.5	894.3	1,542.3	504.1	0.0	306.8	1,513.4	25.7	6,413.0	20,338.1
Lazdijai raj.	8,199.0	1,041.7	687.5	1,267.1	0.0	395.0	421.9	0.0	11,328.0	23,340.2
Marijampole raj.	14,605.2	1,932.0	2,000.5	523.8	0.0	355.4	1,009.5	0.0	29,681.0	50,107.4
Mazeikiai raj.	35,261.9	6,238.3	5,548.7	1,476.8	1.9	989.8	2,750.6	0.0	0.0	52,268.0
Moletai raj.	7,711.7	753.2	1,179.4	314.3	0.0	193.4	153.2	0.0	7,916.0	18,221.2
Pakruojis raj.	8,997.6	1,211.1	1,978.1	516.8	1.1	110.0	1799.6	0.0	10,400.0	25,014.3
Panevezys raj.	14,489.2	1,773.5	2,405.1	746.2	0.0	102.6	993.6	0.4	9,269.0	29,779.6
Pasvalys raj.	11,010.5	987.8	1,925.4	693.8	-0.7	223.5	150.8	0.0	9,967.0	24,958.1
Plunge raj.	17,470.0	1,929.0	1,662.0	783.0	4.0	246.0	16.8	0.0	14,020.0	36,130.8
Prienai raj.	11,585.0	1,212.7	1,238.4	403.2	13.0	279.1	933.7	0.0	14,322.0	29,987.1
Radviliskis raj.	20,420.0	1,489.3	1,825.1	825.5	0.0	231.8	264.0	1.3	9,088.0	34,145.0
Raseiniai raj.	13,355.6	1,656.1	1,682.7	573.8	0.0	180.8	378.8	0.0	18,705.0	36,532.8
Rokiskis raj.	16,301.0	5,270.0	2,656.0	437.0	0.0	118.0	248.4	2.0	9,907.0	34,939.4
Skuodas raj.	5,423.4	691.0	640.0	410.0	16.0	131.0	143.3	0.0	13,590.0	21,044.7
Sakiai raj.	10,154.3	872.3	1,884.2	531.3	0.0	177.8	794.2	1.7	16,327.0	30,742.8
Salcininkai raj.	9,975.0	1,145.0	689.0	490.0	0.0	142.0	205.3	0.0	19,424.0	32,070.3
Siauliai raj.	15,395.0	2,863.0	1,799.0	832.0	0.0	650.0	1,520.9	0.0	5,622.0	28,681.9
Silali raj.	6,328.1	716.9	804.6	244.3	0.8	239.3	321.0	0.0	15,038.0	23,693.0
Silute raj.	19,019.6	2,216.9	2,376.7	699.5	4.9	592.0	193.9	0.0	23,591.0	48,694.5
Sirvintos raj.	6,198.8	299.4	841.9	358.7	0.0	116.5	284.2	0.0	9,804.0	17,903.5
Svencionys raj.	13,099.2	912.5	1,044.4	216.0	0.0	260.5	506.6	0.0	10,111.0	26,150.2
Taurage raj.	16,585.0	1,100.0	1,958.0	1,115.0	0.0	549.0	748.4	0.0	14,576.0	36,631.4
Telsiai raj.	18,601.0	4,029.0	1,856.0	759.0	0.0	79.0	32.0	0.0	15,267.0	40,623.0
Trakai raj.	32,960.6	7,305.2	2,863.8	1,238.4	0.0	572.5	1,562.5	0.0	18,922.0	65,425.0
Ukmerge raj.	18,034.4	2,210.5	1,876.9	667.9	0.2	329.6	148.0	0.0	13,463.0	36,730.5
Utena raj.	28,840.0	5,931.0	2,402.0	826.0	335.9	741.0	2,642.1	0.0	0.0	41,718.0
Varena raj.	13,519.3	1,418.6	1,202.6	350.4	0.0	287.4	885.1	1.0	9,299.0	26,963.4
Vilkaviskis raj.	14,207.5	1,295.7	1,770.1	3819.1	5.3	429.4	564.4	0.0	15,531.0	37,622.5
Vilnius raj.	24,083.3	2,750.6	1,825.1	1,349.5	14.6	1,008.7	604.5	0.0	19,727.0	51,363.3
Zarasai raj.	8,422.5	1,102.3	716.8	358.0	5.2	254.9	157.4	4.6	16,076.0	27,097.7
Total	1,514,756.2	216483.4	17,7430.1	90,195.6	827.0	33,081.0	73,561.2	93.8	550,617.0	2,657,045.3

Source: Ministry of Finance.

Table 3-20. Lithuania: Municipal Expenditures by Municipality, by Category, 1996

(Lt thousands)

Region	General administration	Social security and public order	Education	Health care	Welfare	Lodging and mun. econ.	Culture and recreation	Fuel, energy, and supplies	Agriculture	Total expenditures
Vilnius	11,412.6	0.0	153,085.6	93,052.5	35,466.6	78,379.4	5,117.6	2,868.7	0.0	379,383.0
Alytus	2,304.0	0.0	33,403.2	100.0	7,866.2	11,598.6	4,411.7	100.4	0.0	59,784.1
Birstonas	359.3	5.1	1,775.6	286.1	228.8	1,343.1	404.2	0.0	0.0	4,402.2
Druskininkai	590.4	0.0	7,149.2	5,937.1	1,478.3	2,609.1	616.0	0.0	0.0	18,380.1
Kaunas	5,043.7	0.0	108,137.0	84,718.2	27,471.7	44,897.7	5,476.1	5,184.7	0.0	280,929.1
Klaipeda	2,067.9	0.0	63,503.2	49,575.3	10,076.0	12,221.2	4,782.1	0.0	0.0	142,225.7
Marijampole	787.2	77.0	17,705.1	0.0	3,214.2	8,823.6	1,238.9	237.1	0.0	32,083.1
Neringa	537.8	0.0	3,979.0	592.1	137.8	4,104.6	936.8	0.0	0.0	10,288.1
Palanga	706.9	0.0	7,763.4	4,522.5	1,651.8	9,810.4	565.7	61.7	0.0	25,082.4
Panevezys	2,347.7	186.0	40,909.3	9,403.4	9,575.6	15,695.3	4,376.7	30.7	0.0	82,524.7
Siauliai	1,608.0	0.0	46,728.5	12,355.5	10,368.4	18,065.7	3,436.3	121.0	0.0	92,683.4
Visaginas	575.2	0.0	13,653.7	0	1,240.4	819.5	1,630.1	1.1	0.0	17,920.0
Akmene raj.	1,045.4	179.8	10,456.3	7,332.0	3,281.3	1,306.7	723.6	7,372.8	0.0	31,697.9
Alytus raj.	1,157.5	625.7	10,324.7	21,897.5	2,523.5	2,261.0	1,834.4	894.2	0.0	41,518.5
Anyksciai raj.	1,113.9	332.0	11,954.3	15,592.5	3,176.0	4,130.7	1,909.4	4,488.1	68.2	42,765.1
Birzai raj.	1,090.7	260.9	11,130.9	7,485.8	2,992.8	3,108.1	1,673.9	256.1	0.0	27,999.2
Ignalina raj.	925.7	310.3	8,334.9	4,309.3	1,993.9	1,870.7	1,168.6	0.0	0.0	18,913.4
Jonava raj.	1,295.4	250.9	17,268.1	9,847.3	5,459.9	4,397.0	1,387.0	1,208.2	0.0	41,113.8
Joniskis raj.	918.5	302.0	9,847.7	6,349.0	3,276.2	4,341.9	864.2	0.0	0.0	25,899.5
Jurbarkas raj.	1,314.3	182.9	13,400.2	6,733.9	3,988.7	1,802.4	1,557.0	1,338.2	0.0	30,317.6
Kaisiadorys raj.	1,322.6	378.4	11,429.2	6,248.5	2,346.5	1,586.2	1,430.7	1,368.8	0.0	26,110.9
Kaunas raj.	2,329.8	764.0	23,493.4	8,143.1	5,816.8	5,399.7	1,510.3	3,162.3	0.0	50,619.4
Kedainiai raj.	1,705.1	569.5	20,485.9	11,844.4	5,115.9	9,736.7	2,543.7	3,008.7	0.0	55,009.9
Kelme raj.	1,108.6	321.6	12,101.2	7,032.2	4,190.9	5,785.2	1,233.8	0.0	0.0	31,773.5
Klaipeda raj.	1,278.8	376.2	15,330.2	12,948.2	3,750.3	4,324.8	1,917.4	0.0	0.0	39,925.9
Kretinga raj.	1,170.8	210.0	14,013.3	8,901.3	3,385.8	2,497.9	1,578.7	177.1	0.0	31,934.9
Kupiskis raj.	906.5	275.8	7,891.5	4,600.7	1,821.6	2,167.6	1,132.3	90.4	0.0	18,886.4
Lazdijai raj.	1,091.2	442.1	9,709.7	5,516.8	3,138.6	1,882.8	953.6	499.2	0.0	23,234.0
Marijampole raj.	1,530.9	507.0	13,651.6	22,454.8	3,771.8	3,931.5	1,739.3	1,916.3	0.0	49,503.2
Mazeikiai raj.	1,409.2	271.9	22,217.2	12,845.3	6,227.0	1,278.6	1,741.8	215.9	0.0	46,206.9
Moletai raj.	907.8	242.0	8,106.7	4,598.6	2,047.3	1,416.4	1,092.8	231.3	0.0	18,642.9
Pakruojis raj.	1,368.4	199.8	10,228.8	6,829.0	3,177.3	2,083.7	1,316.4	147.8	0.0	25,351.2
Panevezys raj.	1,298.4	355.8	13,142.4	6,239.2	3,455.8	1,799.1	1,433.4	1,519.7	0.0	29,243.8
Pasvalys raj.	1,389.1	316.8	9,828.2	7,000.7	2,743.6	2,163.0	1,375.5	725.2	0.0	25,542.1
Plunge raj.	1,537.8	508.0	17,821.7	10,226.7	4,538.3	3,178.3	1,927.1	88.7	0.0	39,826.6
Prienai raj.	1,623.3	435.7	12,278.0	6,840.4	3,184.8	2,928.1	1,592.0	827.5	0.0	29,709.8
Radviliskis raj.	1,452.3	294.5	15,547.8	7,673.1	4,775.4	1,895.1	1,682.7	2,516.5	0.0	35,837.4
Raseiniai raj.	1,121.3	223.2	12,615.6	8,728.5	4,371.6	7,862.5	1,078.0	733.0	0.0	36,733.7
Rokiskis raj.	1,110.1	520.7	15,830.4	9,806.3	3,406.8	2,388.9	2,002.4	2,041.0	0.0	37,106.6
Skuodas raj.	975.1	178.9	8,613.5	5,098.9	2,868.4	1,739.6	987.1	2,167.0	0.0	22,628.5
Sakiai raj.	1,443.9	251.8	12,694.1	8,053.7	3,443.0	2,940.6	1,145.5	942.2	0.0	30,914.8
Salcininkai raj.	1,520.1	432.6	14,633.2	7,973.3	3,576.1	5,585.0	1,283.7	0.0	512.2	35,516.2
Siauliai raj.	1,654.2	232.9	12,208.3	7,698.9	3,913.5	1,322.0	1,505.3	936.2	0.0	29,471.3
Silali raj.	1,279.5	267.2	9,677.7	5,534.4	3,976.1	1,210.0	915.6	0	0.0	22,860.5
Silute raj.	1,980.9	433.7	22,536.6	10,531.8	6,965.7	7,440.0	1,952.9	1,758.2	0.0	53,599.8
Sirvintos raj.	723.1	140.5	7,678.1	4,533.8	1,957.7	1,139.2	807.8	0.0	36.9	17,017.1
Svencionys raj.	1,087.5	289.5	10,585.5	7,390.6	2,876.1	2,415.8	2,001.6	0.0	0.0	26,646.6
Taurage raj.	1,240.3	261.7	15,071.7	8,001.0	5,622.6	1,879.5	1,122.2	0.0	0.0	33,199.0
Telsiai raj.	1,378.8	317.6	16,651.8	10,265.9	5,572.9	4,221.8	2,383.7	0.0	0.0	40,792.5
Trakai raj.	2,322.6	486.9	35,157.5	12,511.6	5,276.3	4,672.1	1,778.3	0.0	0.0	62,205.3
Ukmerge raj.	1,280.1	420.7	15,020.2	7,320.8	3,967.4	7,039.2	1,275.6	1,460.5	0.0	37,784.5
Utena raj.	1,239.7	423.9	17,451.7	9,651.7	2,832.3	5,969.7	2,384.7	0	0.0	39,953.7
Varena raj.	1,003.9	388.3	11,587.9	6,955.4	3,154.9	1,473.3	1,704.3	713.9	0.0	26,981.9
Vilkaviskis raj.	976.3	265.3	16,967.6	9,181.8	4,536.6	3,010.0	1,764.9	1,079.9	0.0	37,782.4
Vilnius raj.	2,669.9	478.1	25,203.5	8,758.4	5,361.0	2,540.5	1,436.5	9,025.3	0.0	55,473.2
Zarasai raj.	977.5	290.3	9,135.4	6,982.7	1,889.6	3,458.5	1,654.9	198.9	0.0	24,587.8
Total	866,17.5	154,85.5	1,117,107.0	645012.5	274,524.4	353949.6	99,496.8	61,714.5	617.3	2,654,525.1

Source: Ministry of Finance

97

ANNEX 3-2. Municipal Budgeting Issues

The realization of benefits from decentralization—increasing the efficiency of public expenditures by making government more responsive and accountable to the needs and preferences of taxpayers—is not possible without budgetary autonomy and good budget practices. This Annex first examines the existing level of budgetary autonomy at the municipal level in Lithuania. The last three sections of the Annex review the current practices in budget preparation, execution, and audit, and recommend directions for reform.

Extent of Budgetary Autonomy

Lithuania is a unitary state, and all the budgetary authority of subnational governments is delegated by the state. Article 121 of the Constitution gives local authorities the right to draft and approve their own budgets, charge fees, and provide for the "leverage of taxes and duties at the expense of their own budget." In addition, the Budget Formation Law of 1990, which, with many amendments, remains the key legal framework for the budget process, grants autonomy to local governments from interference from the central government budget.

Despite the declarations of municipal budget autonomy, the budgets at the municipal level are hierarchically interlinked with the central government budget. In practice, budgetary autonomy requires several things. First, local governments must be able to formulate their budgets separately from (the budgetary cycle of) the central government, including the approval of their budgets, even when the central government budget has not been approved. This demands stability and certainty in funding sources of subnational governments. Second, local governments must have the means at their disposal to increase their budgets, at least at the margin, through autonomous sources of revenues, even if revenue sharing and transfers from the central government are the main sources of revenue. Third, local governments must have the freedom to allocate most resources to budget programs as they see fit and should be able to produce and deliver public services using the techniques and input combinations they consider most appropriate.

By these standards, the scorecard for Lithuania's decentralized government is mixed. Municipal budgets are not yet independent of the budgetary cycle of the central government and there is very little revenue autonomy to raise revenues at the margin. Nevertheless, with the important exceptions discussed below, municipal governments have discretion to spend their funds as they see fit.

It is necessary to underscore the importance of revenue autonomy, an issue that appears to be misunderstood in Lithuania. Over the past seven years, considerable discussion and effort has gone into the form of revenue sharing and transfers. But without some degree of tax autonomy at the municipal level, the form central government funding takes is in some ways irrelevant because the central government has always adjusted revenue sharing or transfers to meet the funding level predetermined by an independently estimated "minimum required" budget. The reaction of some municipal officials to the new Law for Establishing Municipal Budget Income of 1997 was precisely that nothing would change from the past because the Ministry of Finance would find a way to restrict overall funding to what it deemed to be a "minimum required" budget. [49]

In practice, municipal budgetary autonomy in Lithuania has been reduced by the lack of a stable method of financing local governments, annual changes in revenue sharing, and poor revenue forecasts. The uncertainty associated with funding sources reduced, if it did not eliminate, the municipalities' ability to plan their expenditures. The new Law for Establishing Municipal Budget Income is an important attempt to improve on past practices. Until now, municipal governments received almost all their funds from revenue sharing and subventions from the central government, and these were changed every year, their amounts unknown until the central government budget was approved. The new law increases the certainty of revenue streams by fixing a number of parameters in the transfer formulas for a period of three years. Some other important parameters in these formulas, however, will still be determined every year. But of greater consequence, revenue sharing of PIT, the most important source of revenue for municipalities, will still be determined every year, and the sharing rates can be "regulated" or customized for each individual municipality.

On the other side of the budgetary autonomy debate is the criticism that municipalities may be abusing their current powers, because they continue to be too heavily involved in "economic development" activities, acting to the detriment of private initiative. Furthermore, the lack of national rules for local codes and regulation for certification processes has led to fraud and corrupt practices. There would appear to be a long agenda for the Ministry of Public Administration Reform and Local Authorities (MPARLA) "to regulate the regulatory activities" of municipal governments. In the view of some observers in Lithuania, these practices in municipal governance have given decentralization a bad name and contributed to the delay of reform.

Issues in Budget Preparation and Structure

OVERALL APPROACH TO BUDGETING. An important problem in budget preparation in Lithuania has been, and continues to be, the overall approach to budgeting from a perspective of needs rather than from a consideration of which programs are feasible given current revenue sources.

The tradition inherited from the previous regime was that the first step in the budget process is to put together a minimum required (expenditure) budget for each municipality. The methodology used by the Ministry of Finance and the municipalities to arrive at this minimum required budget has evolved in recent times, but conceptually remains the same as in the past—required budgets were developed bottom-up on the basis of an extensive list of budgetary norms. More recently, the minimum required budget was built on the basis of the past-year budget, adjusted for inflation. After the minimum expenditure budget is determined, it may be scaled down further to fit the availability of funds. At the same time, the Ministry of Finance produces a forecast for own municipal revenues. [50] The funding gap for each municipality is filled through revenue sharing. Because tax bases differ across municipalities, the sharing rates for some

---

49. The "minimum required" budget is a concept inherited from the previous regime, when budgets were formed on the basis of physical and cost norms that pretended to quantify minimum expenditure needs of governments. In practice, the budgets constructed on these bases became maximum budgets, and actual fund allocations were rarely large enough to finance the minimum expenditure need established by the norms. This issue is discussed further below.

50. In the process of budget determination, each municipality must accept the Ministry of Finance's estimates of both revenue and expenditure projections, although the municipalities are free to make their own projections. In other countries in transition, this process has been more subject to negotiation between central and local governments.

taxes are regulated or customized so that the municipality does not receive more funds than allowed in the minimum required budget. Poorer municipalities with lower tax bases receive 100 percent of the collections from shared taxes, and if this is not enough to cover the minimum required budget, they receive a lump-sum transfer for the remaining gap.

The new Law for Establishing Municipal Budget Income of July 1997 takes some significant steps toward a budgeting approach based on available means rather than needs, but it stops short of breaking with the past. This new law brought more budget certainty to municipalities by introducing formula-driven transfers, but it retains the expenditure-need approach to budgeting in two fundamental ways. First, revenue sharing from PIT will continue to be set annually, and supposedly "regulated" by an assessment of budgetary needs of the municipality by the Ministry of Finance. Second, the first window of the new system of transfers is still based on the notion of gap-filling for municipalities with actual revenues that fall short of those forecast. In theory, these forecast revenues will be the counterpart of a minimum required budget.

The approach to budgeting based on a minimum required budget has been criticized for putting emphasis on the fulfillment of needs by maintaining existing capacity and programs rather than by asking the hard questions of whether or not some expenditures should be continued, or if there is a more efficient way to achieve the same results. The discontinuation of the use of physical and cost norms and the reality of significant real budget cuts, however, have eroded the severity of these problems. A more enduring problem is the notion that the central government should still provide the means for fulfilling some minimum expenditure needs. This has had a negative impact on the search for efficiency and in the mobilization of revenues at the local level.

On the agenda for future reform in the municipal budget process in Lithuania is the development of a local budget law that, among other things, develops an approach to budgeting based on the principle that the budget is an instrument for implementing programs within available means, not an instrument for fulfilling predetermined needs.

REVENUE FORECASTS. Poor revenue forecasts have been a source of difficulty in budget preparation at the local level. The normal difficulties in forecasting in an unstable environment may have been exacerbated by the lack of trained staff. There is also a possibility that the authorities ignored more realistic revenue forecasts and included optimistic revenue projections in the budget for political reasons. Either poor forecasting or political pressures have led to unrealistic budgets and to the use of budget sequestering during budget execution, as discussed below. Although municipal governments, by law, are supposed to operate with balanced budgets, in reality they have been running significant deficits in the form of arrears.

The extent of the revenue projection problem is illustrated in table 3-21, where forecast revenues are shown side-by-side with actual revenues for 1994, 1995, and 1996. The problem has varied from year to year, but except for a few municipalities, it has not been disastrous. During 1994, only 84.3 percent of the forecast revenues were realized for the consolidated municipal sector. Some municipalities, such as Alytus and Varena, barely realized half of their forecast revenue. Performance was much better during 1995, when actual revenues for the entire sector exceeded forecast revenues by about 10 percent, but here again, there were municipalities, such as Visaginas, that barely collected half of forecast revenues. Aggregate actual revenues during 1996 were 94 percent of forecast revenues, and many municipalities collected 80+ percent of their forecast revenues.

Both the Ministry of Finance and municipalities must understand the significance of improved revenue forecasts, and therefore the need to invest resources in achieving these results. The new revenue assignment of CIT, which tends to be among the most unstable sources of revenue at the central level, should make it possible to produce better forecasts for municipal revenues.

Table 3-21. Municipal Budget of Cities and Regions of the Republic of Lithuania, 1994–96 (Lt thousands)

Region	Estimated revenues	Actual revenues, 1 Jan. 1995	Fulfillment (%)	Estimated revenues	Actual revenues, 1 Jan. 1996	Fulfillment (%)	Estimated revenues	Actual revenues, 1 Jan. 199⁻	Fulfillment (%)
Vilnius	256,999	180,701	70.3	330,077	347,428	105.3	402,835	361,625	89.8
Alytus	32,680	18,492	56.6	41,791	41,991	100.5	65,616	57,726	88.0
Birstonas	1,959	1,983	101.2	2,314	2,640	114.1	3,349	2,790	83.3
Druskininkai	9,811	24,080	245.4	11,153	11,874	106.5	14,938	14,368	96.2
Kaunas	203,300	186,177	91.6	230,953	262,393	113.6	297,315	269,301	90.6
Klaipeda	88,708	83,740	94.4	106,029	114,968	108.4	145,457	137,396	94.5
Marijampole	15,911	15,695	98.6	20,639	27,763	134.5	29,291	28,642	97.8
Neringa	3,159	2,486	78.7	2,312	3,228	139.6	3,772	4,061	107.7
Palanga	12,856	13,643	106.1	12,351	14,455	117.0	18,045	16,405	90.9
Panevezys	45,911	40,817	88.9	60,732	89,139	146.8	81,358	76,212	93.7
Siauliai	60,301	55,139	91.4	81,213	90,164	111.0	118,191	103,205	87.3
Visaginas	n.a.	n.a.	n.a.	13,244	6,858	51.8	19,180	18,672	97.4
Akmene	20,891	15,294	73.2	16,888	18,819	111.4	23,305	19,556	83.9
Alytus	10,892	8,171	75.0	7,835	8,506	108.6	10,434	11,275	108.1
Anyksciai	21,876	18,946	86.6	16,449	17,452	106.1	22,042	22,001	99.8
Birzai	22,775	26,052	114.4	21,996	22,979	104.5	27,861	27,131	97.4
Ignalina	24,100	31,403	130.3	12,324	10,640	86.3	9,704	10,241	105.5
Jonava	24,072	11,407	47.4	30,107	38,973	129.4	35,208	37,058	105.3
Joniskis	14,720	17,131	116.4	13,392	14,864	111.0	17,766	15,515	87.3
Jurbarkas	12,341	11,329	91.8	9,909	12,566	126.8	16,023	14,537	90.7
Kaisiadorys	17,220	15,735	91.4	18,006	21,513	119.5	26,571	26,201	98.6
Kaunas	28,898	21,547	74.6	26,664	23,048	86.4	29,203	29,953	102.6
Kedainiai	30,229	21,648	71.6	29,435	33,694	114.5	39,586	45,421	114.7
Kelme	13,231	10,522	79.5	10,340	12,606	121.9	14,927	12,100	81.1
Klaipeda	20,974	23,082	110.1	17,827	22,780	127.8	28,091	30,715	109.3
Kretinga	17,319	16,359	94.5	14,259	14,846	104.1	17,981	17,899	99.5
Kupiskis	12,666	8,932	70.5	8,252	10,858	131.6	13,131	12,079	92.0
Lazdijai	10,848	9,517	87.7	7,859	9,854	125.4	11,987	11,195	93.4
Marijampole	16,955	15,074	88.9	13,867	15,831	114.2	17,639	19,061	108.1
Mazeikiai	25,477	23,415	91.9	33,217	32,515	97.9	44,480	48,527	109.1
Moletai	10,584	9,115	86.1	9,772	9,040	92.5	11,218	9,958	88.8
Pakruojis	12,996	10,452	80.4	9,838	11,031	112.1	12,992	12,704	97.8
Panevezys	17,035	11,912	69.9	13,178	15,440	117.2	19,236	19,413	100.9
Pasvalys	16,175	11,573	71.5	13,424	14,053	104.7	17,486	14,619	83.6
Plunge	26,165	21,674	82.8	19,230	20,516	106.7	26,499	21,844	82.4
Prienai	13,362	9,957	74.5	9,063	12,934	142.7	15,580	14,440	92.7
Radviliskis	20,713	17,652	85.2	18,291	22,262	121.7	27,373	24,559	89.7
Raseiniai	19,197	13,885	72.3	15,168	15,418	101.6	19,004	17,269	90.9
Rokiskis	22,555	17,359	77.0	18,461	20,401	110.5	25,141	24,664	98.1
Skuodas	7,718	6,823	88.4	5,297	5,578	105.3	7,160	7,164	100.1
Sakiai	11,527	10,348	89.8	9,329	11,023	118.2	13,027	13,440	103.2
Salcininkai	16,105	11,716	72.7	12,071	10,588	87.7	13,463	12,299	91.4
Siauliai	21,002	15,695	74.7	15,013	19,057	126.9	23,545	20,889	88.7
Silale	8,437	6,110	72.4	5,764	6,577	114.1	8,016	8,094	101.0
Silute	24,102	26,034	108.0	21,998	21,045	95.7	26,498	24,314	91.8
Sirvintos	8,472	6,731	79.4	7,975	6,420	80.5	8,082	7,699	95.3
Svencionys	15,248	11,533	75.6	11,428	12,935	113.2	16,045	15,272	95.2
Taurage	21,772	15,782	72.5	16,736	17,512	104.6	22,281	20,758	93.2
Telsiai	24,459	17,809	72.8	21,162	20,792	98.3	25,882	25,245	97.5
Trakai	34,097	23,098	67.7	31,233	34,517	110.5	41,552	44,369	106.8
Ukmerge	24,261	20,455	84.3	19,499	21,784	111.7	26,882	22,789	84.8
Utena	28,393	23,520	82.8	33,361	35,922	107.7	39,368	37,999	96.5
Varena	15,734	7,982	50.7	13,039	14,439	110.7	18,078	16,491	91.2
Vilkaviskis	18,428	19,486	105.7	13,787	15,843	114.9	19,545	21,093	107.9
Vilnius	27,266	21,641	79.4	20,819	23,394	112.4	29,400	30,009	102.1
Zarasai	11,962	13,367	111.7	7,747	8,375	108.1	10,318	10,602	102.8
Total	1,554,844	1,310,226	84.3	1,614,117	1,782,141	110.4	2,128,957	1,998,864	93.9

n.a. Not available.

Source: Ministry of Finance, updated by World Bank staff.

EXTRABUDGETARY FUNDS. There are two kinds of extrabudgetary funds at the local level; first, those shared with the central government, such as the Environmental Fund, the Privatization Fund, and the Road Fund; and second, local extrabudgetary funds properly financed by municipal service fees. The size and number of subnational extrabudgetary funds are not known, and there are no reporting requirements for them. Their relative importance is said to differ by municipality.

The undesirability of extrabudgetary funds is well known. They break the principles of universality and integrality of the budget. They are not subject to the same level of scrutiny as regular budget funds, which means that they generally lack adequate accountability. The use of multiple extrabudgetary funds decreases the careful consideration of priorities in the allocation of public resources. With the exception of social insurance and pension funds, which can be justified as being outside the budget at the central level, all other extrabudgetary funds, including those of municipalities, should be fully integrated into the regular budgets.

CAPITAL INVESTMENTS. The management of the investment program for municipalities remains a weak point; funds are still allocated to individual investment projects for municipal investments over Lt 5 million.[51] The Ministry of Economy is responsible for evaluating the requests from the municipalities. The selection criteria are not transparent, and the choice of a Lt 5 million threshold may discriminate against smaller but more efficient projects, and perhaps against smaller municipalities.[52] The majority of the proposals approved by the Ministry of Economy involve the completion of unfinished projects, and these proposals do not always seem to be subject to a rigorous economic analysis.[53]

It would be desirable to improve the planning framework and time horizon for these expenditures. The large number of programs that remain incomplete at the local level is a clear reflection of these needs. One option would be to pool the funds into well-defined sectoral programs with clear guidelines for eligibility, perhaps with cofinancing by the municipalities.

Issues of Budget Execution

EFFECTIVENESS OF EXPENDITURE CONTROLS AND BUDGETARY ARREARS. Among the most serious problems in budget execution is the lack of efficient control of expenditures. The municipalities still rely on the control of cash release to spending units as the primary mechanism for expenditure control. Once the spending unit has been credited the funds, it can write checks up to the maximum authorized in the budget. The unit is supposed to report the actual balances drawn from the account monthly, but this can differ from the expenditures the spending unit has accrued during the period. This is how substantial arrears are possible within the budget system.

We have direct evidence of arrears only in the two largest municipalities, Vilnius and Kaunas. These municipal governments appear to be using arrears, or the postponement of payments due, as a source of regular financing. Arrears can be quantified by the difference between cash payments and payment obligations. Arrears are also created by delaying the processing of incoming bills prior to the writing of payment orders. In the case of Vilnius, half of the arrears are in the nonpayment of social security contributions and withheld PIT to the State Tax Inspectorate. Other arrears are in wages, heating bills, and other services (table 3-22). The actual size of the arrears at the consolidated municipal

---

51. This issue was addressed in the World Bank, *Lithuania: Public Expenditure Review* (Washington, D.C., 1994).

52. For projects under Lt 5 million, municipalities have to use their own funds.

53. It is not clear how much weight is given to the option of leaving the unfinished projects as sunk costs.

level is not known, but it could be considerable.[54]

Table 3-22. City of Vilnius Arrears, 1996 and 1997
(Lt thousands)

Item	1996	1997[a]
Total arrears	72,030.6	98,673.6
Wages	8,009.1	8,965.9
Individual income tax	9,616.5	34,576.9
Social security contributions	7,570.9	16,454.7
Heating	21,460.5	4,639.1
Community services	29.0	81.5
Transportation expenses	1,034.8	980.7

a. For the first six months.
Source: City of Vilnius.

Part of the solution to the expenditure control problem is the adoption of a treasury function at the local level. This will permit the control of expenditures in three stages: (a) the commitment of expenditures, meaning that budget appropriations are authorized, contracts are signed, and procurement is initiated; (b) the verification stage, in which work is completed, bills received, and the obligation to pay is verified by each spending unit; and (c) the payment stage. Part of the current problem is that control of expenditures is done at the payment stage rather than at the time of commitment. The effective constraint on expenditures is actually exercised by limiting the amount of fund transfers to the spending units. This means that there are no checks or information flows on spending until the payment obligation has been generated.

The introduction of a treasury function at the local level may not stop all arrears (for example, social security and PIT payments), but it will stop many. A modern treasury function will also help with other aspects of budget execution, including cash and debt management, accounting, and procurement. From a practical viewpoint, carrying arrears may only provide municipal governments with temporary relief.[55]

IMPLEMENTATION FLEXIBILITY. Another important issue in budget execution is giving spending units the necessary flexibility to implement the budget. Municipalities are subject to rigid national wage scales, and Seimas requires that the wage fund be no larger than the amount spent last year in wages, plus an adjustment for inflation. The lack of flexibility in wage setting has caused a high turnover among employees, who are looking for better-paid jobs in the private sector. The problem is more acute in special skills. In the longer term, GoL should give freedom to municipal governments to set wages and salaries at levels that can compete with the private sector within the geographical area.

Another persistent problem of budget implementation flexibility is that municipalities cannot close facilities or reorganize them without prior permission from the line ministry. For example, the municipality cannot close a school without official permission from the Ministry of Education. Of

---

54. If, on average, all municipalities have arrears proportional to those of Vilnius, the level of arrears for all municipalities would have have been close to Lt 400 million in 1996 (about 1 percent of GDP) and Lt 520 million (1.10 percent of GDP) in 1997.

55. Prices charged by suppliers will tend to be adjusted upward to compensate for the additional financial costs of delayed payment. More often than not, total costs for governments will be higher when significant arrears are carried. It should be noted that arrears to private providers tend to be less than those to public entities because many private vendors demand to be paid on delivery.

course, these rules severely limit the budgeting implementation efficiency of local governments. Municipalities should have complete discretion to manage the hiring of inputs to deliver the public services assigned to them. The constraints set by the central government on the use of funds for targeted capital transfers, however, are entirely reasonable and should be kept.

BUDGET SEQUESTERING. An important development in budget execution procedures has been the linking of expenditure payments to actual cash collections through sequestering. Although such responsible budget practices are laudable, these practices also carry the risk of significant perverse results. Without a detailed plan from policymakers setting priorities for all items in the budget, sequestering de facto empowers those officials in charge of budget execution with the right to redirect budget priorities.[56] It would appear, however, that in many instances sequestering priorities are dictated by the municipal councils. At some point of budgetary shortfall, it becomes more desirable to adopt a revised budget plan.

The only way to get rid of the need for budget sequestering is to formulate more realistic budgets. The Budget Formation Law of 1990 is silent on how to proceed in the implementation of sequestering. A future local budget law should regulate budget sequestering and introduce explicit rules for triggering a formal process for revision of the overall budget.

Issues of Budget Control, Audit, and Evaluation

In theory, three different budget compliance functions are required in this phase of the budget cycle. First, internal control and an audit are carried out by the government agencies themselves, to check the legality of disbursements. Second, external audit is carried out ex-post by an independent institution or one that responds exclusively to the legislative branch of government to verify the legality and correct use of funds by the spending agencies in the executive branch. Third, the evaluation of budget programs is carried out by several institutions, with an emphasis on outcomes and performance, and with the purpose of improving the effectiveness of government expenditures. These three modes of compliance are complementary and reinforcing.

Budget compliance measures, except for internal control, lack tradition in Lithuania. Internal audit and control practices were strong and effective under the previous regime. Ex-post monitoring and audit is incipient at the municipal level. External ex-post audit at the municipal level is carried out by the comptroller, who is appointed by, and reports to, the Municipal Council. In addition, the State Comptroller's Office, which performs the audit of central government accounts, can audit municipal government accounts as requested by central authorities. Because there is no separation of powers at the municipal level (the mayor is not elected directly, but rather is appointed by the Municipal Council), there may be an issue with the proper detachment and independence of the municipal comptroller. The main charge of the comptroller is to prevent and uncover inappropriate or fraudulent use of funds.

Little or no budget evaluation is now carried out. The focus of the evaluation function is on the effectiveness of public expenditure programs; this allows reexamination of the relevance of the program objectives in the context of the problems and needs initially identified, and of the correspondence between the resources allocated to the program and final performance.

The strengthening of ex-ante internal control will be accomplished by the creation of a treasury function at the municipal level. Internal control should also be reinforced by (i) the adoption of administrative sanctions based on shared responsibility for infractions or for fraudulent use of funds, and

---

56. The room for distortion is larger, the smaller the share that is eventually executed out of the planned budget.

(ii) the establishment of explicit rules and regulations for the management of public funds, procurement, and conflicts of interest.

There also seems to be consensus on the need to complete and reinforce the external audit function. Independent audits of municipal finances by private accounting firms is an option that should be considered in the drafting of a future local budget law. There is also a need for an effective budget evaluation function. The comptroller and budget departments of the municipalities should be trained in budget and program evaluation techniques.

ANNEX 3-3. Simulations of Equalization Transfers: A Description of the Methodology

The simulations performed in this Annex are based on the newly introduced Law on Municipal Government Revenues for 1997. They assume that funding from the central government is set at Lt 332,438 thousand, which is all allocated to Window II. Resources from the fraternal reserve fund are allocated in Window III. Because the allocation of funds in Window I is determined ex-post upon shortfalls of forecast revenues, no funds are allocated to Window I in the simulations. A summary of the three windows, with definitions of terms and symbols, is presented in box 3-1.

Simulation results are presented in tables 3-23 and 3-24. Table 3-23 shows the allocation of resources to all municipal governments, depending on one specific set of assumptions, which are stated in the footnote to the table.

Table 3-24 presents the descriptive statistics for several simulations based on varying assumptions. For comparison purposes, table 3-24 also presents descriptive statistics on the level of per capita revenues before transfers for 1997, as well as the distribution of revenues for 1996 using the old method of gap-filling transfers. That is, for 1996, municipal revenues were generated from own-sources, shared revenues, and subventions based on gap-filling principles. Table 3-24 shows five additional simulated distributions of revenues for 1997. These simulations are the result of different assumptions concerning the parameters in the fraternal sharing formula and the definition of the demographic factor formula.

Window I

According to the new legislation, the allocation of resources in Window I is based on the difference between actual and forecast levels of municipal revenue collections. For the purpose of these simulations, no funds are distributed in Window I, thus $D_1 = 0$.

Window II

In the simulations presented in this note, all central government funds are allocated to this window (thus $D = D_2$). The allocation of resources in this window depends on two parameters, K and H. These parameters are set at $K = 0.95$ and $H = 0.95$. This means that regions that collect less than the benchmark of 95 percent of average per capita revenues will receive a transfer of 95 percent of the gap between per capita regional revenue collections and the benchmark. The simulated distribution of funds in Window II is based on forecasts of municipal revenue collections for 1997. The amount allocated to this window (Lt 332,438 thousand) is exactly equal to the amount necessary to finance equalization of the poorer regions up to 95 percent of the benchmark level.

Window III

FRATERNAL POOL. The fraternal fund is allocated fully to Window III (thus $D_3 = P$). Unless stated otherwise, the parameters used in these simulations are $k = 1.1$ and $h = 0.5$. This would mean that only regions that have per capita collections more than 10 percent above the national average pay into the reserve fund. These parameters would result in a reserve fund of Lt 151,743 thousand. Alternatively, when the parameter values are adjusted to $k = 1$ and $h = 1$, a reserve fund of Lt 400,669 thousand is produced.

DISTRIBUTION OF FUNDS. Several variations of need-based equalization were simulated as a result of the flaw in the recently enacted equalization law. First, this window was simulated using the need-equalization according to the actual (flawed) law adopted for 1997. In addition, two alternative measures of fiscal need are explored: method I and method II. All three methods are similar in that they are weighted averages of several need indexes. All simulations are based on indexes for two need factors: children and senior citizens. Each of the need factors is assigned a weight of 0.5.

METHOD FOR 1997 (AS IN THE NEW LAW). In the simulated distribution of resources using the method for 1997, the simulation follows the steps in the new law, as discussed in the main text of this note.

METHOD I. This method consists of three steps:

(1)   The relative need for each region equals its share of the need factor compared with the national total. For example, if a region contains 20,000 children out of a national total of 1 million, its relative need—based on this factor—would be 0.02.

(2)   The relative claim for each region equals the difference between the relative need for each region and the lowest relative need observed among all regions.

(3)   Using step (1) and step (2) in this method, the need-based transfer for each region is then defined as:

$$Need\text{-}Based\ Transfer\ for\ Region\ i\ =\ Fund\ \bullet\ \frac{Rel.\ Claim\ for\ Region\ i}{\sum_{j} Rel.\ Claims}$$

METHOD II. This method consists of two steps:

(1)   The relative need for each region equals its share of the need factor compared with the national total. For example, if a region contains 20,000 children out of a national total of 1 million, its relative need—based on this factor—would be 0.02.

(2)   Using step (1) in this method, the need-based transfer for each region is then defined as:

$$Need\text{-}Based\ Transfer\ for\ Region\ i\ =\ Fund\ \bullet\ \frac{Rel.\ Need\ of\ Region\ i}{\sum_{j} Rel.\ Needs}$$

Therefore, the difference between method I and method II is that in method I, an intermediate step is taken to normalize the relative need in each municipality in relation to the minimum observed relative need in all municipalities by subtracting the relative need of each region from the lowest relative need observed among all regions. This additional step is more in keeping with the spirit of the current description of Window III in the Law for Establishing Municipal Budget Income of July 1997 than is method I.

Box 3-1. Summary of New System of Equalization Transfers

The total pool of funds (D) or "overall state budget grant" is calculated as $D = A - B - C$, where A is the forecast level of expenditures for all municipalities for the planned year; B is the forecast revenues from tax and nontax sources; and C is the total amount of specific grants.

The total pool of funds (D) is then divided into three subfunds, or three separate windows: $D1$, $D2$, and $D3$.

Window I: "Reserves for Extraordinary Events." Total funding ($D1$) is determined politically at budget time and it is apportioned among those municipalities with tax revenues below forecast revenues in the budget, and distributed according to the formula $D1_i = D1 * (x_{if} - x_i) / \sum (x_{if} - x_i)$, where x_i is actual and x_{if} is forecast revenues in the budget.

Window II: "Equalization of Tax Revenues." Total funding ($D2$) is determined politically at budget time. The purpose of Window II is to bring municipalities with per capita forecast tax revenues below the national average closer to the average, and distribution is according to the formula:

$$D2_i = D2 * (d2_i / \sum d2_j), \text{ where } d2_i = G_i * H * [K * PCX - pcx_{if}],$$

and where:

G_i	=	population of municipality i
H	=	scaling coefficient gap in *difference* with national average
K	=	scaling coefficient for the national average *level*
PCX	=	average forecast per capita tax revenues among all municipalities
pcx_{if}	=	per capita forecast revenues in municipality i.

Window III: "Equalization of Expenditure Needs." The two sources of fund for this window ($D4$) come from ($D3$) and (P) so that $D4 = D3 + P$,

where: $\qquad D3 = D - D1 - D2$ and $P = \sum P_i$

and: $\qquad P_i$ = contribution from PIT collections from municipalities with forecast per capita collections (pcy_{if}) higher than the average (PCY), and determined as:

$$P_i = G_i * h * (pcy_{if} - kPCY)$$

where:

h	=	scaling coefficient for how much of the *difference* between pcy_{if} and PCY will be contributed
k	=	scaling coefficient for the national per capita income tax
G_i	=	population of municipality i.
pcy_{if}	=	PIT forecast per capita collections for municipality i
PCY	=	average PIT forecast per capita collections.

The overall funds in Window III are allocated to the municipalities according to relative measures of need based on three demographic variables defined in terms of 1,000 inhabitants:

$r1$	=	number of children under 18
$r2$	=	number of disabled persons
$r3$	=	number of pension-age persons.

The amount received by each municipality $D4_i$ is

$$D4_i = D4 * E_i, \text{ where } E_i = \sum_i (r_i - min.r_j) / \sum_j \sum_i Mr (r_i - min.r_j)$$

where Mr is the weight attached to each of the three demographic variables (r_i, $i = 1, 2, 3$), and min.r_j is the minimum value of the demographic variable j ($j = 1, 2, 3$) across all municipalities.

Table 3-23. Lithuania: Simulated Equalization Transfers for 1997 Based on the Law of Municipal Budget Income (Lt thousands)

Region	Local tax revenue	Payment into reserve fund	Transfer for Window I	Transfer for Window II	Transfer for Window III	Local revenue after transfers
Vilnius	530,278	90,550	0	0	21,373	461,101
Alytus	57,239	5,336	0	0	2,762	54,664
Birstonas	2,090	0	0	0	64	2,154
Druskininkai	11,665	0	0	0	826	12,491
Kaunas	265,152	6,560	0	0	16,438	275,030
Klaipeda	185,208	31,427	0	0	7,797	161,577
Marijampole	34,266	1,493	0	0	1,993	34,766
Neringa	3,967	1,183	0	0	0	2,784
Palanga	14,882	1,507	0	0	708	14,083
Panevezys	98,101	8,918	0	0	5,107	94,290
Siauliai	89,556	538	0	0	5,647	94,665
Visaginas	11,215	0	0	5,894	1,035	18,143
Akmene raj.	14,410	0	0	5,590	1,667	21,667
Alytus raj.	9,626	0	0	7,300	1,648	18,574
Anyksciai raj.	13,965	0	0	5,515	1,805	21,285
Birzai raj.	15,754	0	0	4,057	1,740	21,551
Ignalina raj.	10,445	0	0	2,565	1,132	14,142
Jonava raj.	36,231	1,682	0	0	2,053	36,602
Joniskis raj.	12,140	0	0	5,482	1,460	19,081
Jurbarkas raj.	13,082	0	0	7,710	1,783	22,576
Kaisiadorys raj.	21,815	0	0	0	1,756	23,571
Kaunas raj.	24,744	0	0	16,950	3,338	45,032
Kedainiai raj.	34,089	0	0	2,229	2,972	39,290
Kelme raj.	10,199	0	0	11,693	1,978	23,869
Klaipeda raj.	18,590	0	0	4,702	1,933	25,226
Kretinga raj.	14,354	0	0	9,155	1,977	25,486
Kupiskis raj.	9,914	0	0	3,511	1,161	14,587
Lazdijai raj.	8,030	0	0	8,605	1,610	18,245
Marijampole raj.	15,181	0	0	10,829	2,376	28,386
Mazeikiai raj.	43,766	2,548	0	0	2,571	43,788
Moletai raj.	8,640	0	0	4,948	1,213	14,801
Pakruojis raj.	10,635	0	0	5,202	1,332	17,169
Panevezys raj.	15,137	0	0	6,239	1,914	23,290
Pasvalys raj.	12,340	0	0	6,601	1,650	20,591
Plunge raj.	18,288	0	0	10,746	2,532	31,566
Prienai raj.	12,114	0	0	7,739	1,810	21,663
Radviliskis raj.	20,356	0	0	7,846	2,464	30,666
Raseiniai raj.	14,091	0	0	9,664	2,111	25,866
Rokiskis raj.	17,406	0	0	6,398	2,123	25,927
Skuodas raj.	5,934	0	0	8,079	1,223	15,236
Sakiai raj.	10,797	0	0	10,641	1,957	23,394
Salcininkai raj.	10,319	0	0	10,080	1,728	22,126
Siauliai raj.	16,326	0	0	10,229	2,305	28,861
Silali raj.	6,508	0	0	10,264	1,493	18,265
Silute raj.	19,975	0	0	15,876	3,095	38,945
Sirvintos raj.	6,675	0	0	4,383	926	11,984
Svencionys raj.	12,722	0	0	5,615	1,617	19,954
Taurage raj.	17,506	0	0	11,069	2,395	30,970
Telsiai raj.	18,847	0	0	12,416	2,679	33,942
Trakai raj.	33,103	0	0	8,010	3,255	44,368
Ukmerge raj.	18,564	0	0	7,774	2,286	28,624
Utena raj.	30,787	0	0	0	2,263	33,050
Varena raj.	13,379	0	0	5,571	1,681	20,631
Vilkaviskis raj.	15,454	0	0	11,551	2,374	29,378
Vilnius raj.	24,003	0	0	19,750	3,510	47,263
Zarasai raj.	8,751	0	0	4,005	1,103	13,858
Total	2,028,611	151,743	0	332,483	151,743	2,361,094

Note: The simlation is based on the following assumptions:

Equalization Fund is Lt 332,483 thousand, allocated to Window II; where $K = 0.95$ and $H = 0.95$.

Payments into 'fraternal' Reserve Fund are based on $k = 1.1$ and $h = 0.5$, allocated to Window III.

Funds in Window III are allocated based on method I.

See the text for a complete description of the equalization mechanism.

Table 3-24. Lithuania: Comparison of Municipal Revenues after Simulated Equalization Transfers in per Capita Terms, 1997

Transfer method	Local revenues before transfers, 1997	Local revenues for 1997, 1996 method	Local revenues method, in the new law	Method I (using k = 1.1, h = 0.5)	Method II	Method I (using k = 1, h = 1)	Method II
Mean	435.9	723.5	702.1	591.9	593.8	629.4	634.4
Standard deviation	223.9	433.3	429.4	87.2	90.5	16.9	11.8
Coefficient of variation	0.514	0.599	0.612	0.147	0.152	0.027	0.019
Minimum	195.4	541.1	539.5	541.5	543.3	547.2	596.9
Maximum	1,491.9	3,709.3	3,644.6	1,046.9	1,085.2	657.9	660.5

Note: See text in this Annex for list of assumptions.

Source: Computed using data supplied by the Ministry of Public Administration Reform and Local Authorities (MPARLA).

ANNEX 3-4

International Comparison Tables

Table 3-25. International Comparison of Government Revenues and Composition of Subnational Revenues (percentage of total subnational revenues)

Economy	Total 1993 consolidated government revenues as percentage of 1993 GDP[a]	Share of subnational governments in total consolidated revenues (1993)	Tax revenues	Nontax revenues	Transfers	Capital revenues
Australia 1995	42.7	44.5	35.2	22.6	38.4	3.8
Austria 1994	55.7	33.7	48.4	23.5	27.3	0.8
Belgium 1994	51.0	12.0	37.5	8.8	53.6	
Canada 1993	52.9	60.4	57.0	14.9	28.1	
Denmark 1995	74.6	44.2	46.9	8.3	43.1	1.7
Finland 1990	34.6		46.5	13.0	35.1	5.5
France 1995	51.0	19.2	43.8	19.3	36.4	0.5
Germany 1995	54.8	42.0	51.1	23.2	24.0	1.7
Iceland 1993	39.1	23.6	70.6	19.2	9.9	0.4
Ireland 1993	53.4	25.5	6.3	16.0	74.2	3.5
Italy 1989	43.3		10.2	8.1	79.5	2.2
Luxembourg 1994	55.1	14.8	32.2	26.5	38.8	2.5
Netherlands 1995	67.8	25.2	10.3	13.8	70.2	5.8
Norway 1994	66.4	32.7	44.6	16.3	38.5	0.6
Portugal 1994	40.0	9.6	29.2	15.1	49.4	6.2
Spain 1993	47.4	31.7	29.5	8.2	61.4	1.0
Sweden 1994	65.1	40.2	69.0	10.4	19.4	1.3
Switzerland 1993	49.4	49.1	49.6	24.6	25.1	0.8
United Kingdom 1995	47.7	26.4	10.8	12.5	72.9	3.8
United States 1994	40.7	51.4	46.4	23.1	30.4	0.05

a. *World Tables* (Washington, D.C.: World Bank, 1995).

Note: Consolidated revenues are defined as revenues of central, regional, and local governments.

Source: Government Finance Statistics Yearbook (Washington, D.C.: World Bank, 1996).

Table 3-26. International Comparison of the Composition of Subnational Tax Revenues
(percentage of total subnational tax revenues)

| Economy | Tax on income, profits, and capital gains | | Property tax | Domestic tax on goods and services | Social security contributions | Other taxes |
	Total	Individual				
Australia 1995			39.4	40.0		20.5
Austria 1994	40.4	33.0	5.4	40.7	3.3	10.1
Belgium 1994	75.7	60.4		19.0	5.3	
Canada 1993	33.7	30.0	22.2	29.5	11.6	2.9
Denmark 1995p	93.4	91.9	6.5	0.1		
Germany 1993	66.1	47.9	7.9	26.0		
Iceland 1993	59.0	54.2	17.6			23.4
Ireland 1993			100.0			
Japan 1989	63.4	28.7	23.1	12.6		0.9
Luxembourg 1994	98.9	98.9		1.1		
Netherlands 1995			37.5	3.7	58.8	
Norway 1994	90.1	81.8	9.3	0.6		
Portugal 1994	14.0		66.9	19.1		
Spain 1993	16.8	13.4	36.9	41.8	0.01	4.5
Sweden 1994	100.0	100.0				
Switzerland 1993	81.0	71.1	14.7	4.3		
United Kingdom 1995			1.4			98.6
United States 1994	24.5	20.2	32.8	40.9	1.8	

Source: Government Finance Statistics Yearbook (Washington, D.C.: IMF, 1996).

Table 3-27. International Comparison of Government Expenditures and Composition of Subnational Government Expenditures (percent)

Economy/year	1993 consolid. general expenditures as percentage of 1993 GDP[a]	Share of subnational governments in general consolid. expenditures, 1993	Subnational government expenditures as percentage of total subnational expenditures							
			General public services, public order, and safety	Education	Health	Welfare	Housing and community amenities	Recreation, cultural and religion	Transportation and communication	Other expenditures
Australia 1995	47.3	41.5	17.4	24.2	16.5	4.8	5.6	4.2	11.1	16.3
Austria 1994[b]	60.1	31.2	12.8	22.1	20.2	22.8	4.3	2.8	5.1	9.9
Canada 1993	60.8	58.3	9.7	24.2	19.9	16.7	4.6	2.5	5.7	16.7
Denmark 1995p	77.2	43.6	3.6	11.1	14.8	58.2	2.2	3.0	3.1	3.8
France 1993	57.1	17.6	12.8	19.5	2.3	17.6	24.0	7.6	3.6	12.5
Germany 1991	33.6		12.7	17.0	10.4	20.7	9.9	3.9	5.3	20.1
Iceland 1993	43.4	23.9	5.9	14.3	1.0	16.7	6.7	16.8	11.0	27.6
Ireland 1993	55.8	24.1	4.3	11.2	45.9	6.1	12.0	2.1	12.5	6.0
Luxembourg 1994	53.1	16.1	13.8	15.7	0.3	6.7	20.9	11.8	13.3	17.5
Netherlands 1995	71.5	24.6	12.8	17.9	2.6	22.6	20.0	5.8	6.7	11.6
Norway 1994	69.2	31.5	6.1	21.3	28.5	17.6	7.7	4.5	5.5	8.9
Spain 1993	55.9	29.6	5.2	25.1	31.7	5.5	4.2	3.5	5.0	19.7
Switzerland 1993	52.5	48.4	9.7	25.4	17.5	12.2	4.9	3.5	9.1	17.6
United Kingdom 1995	55.1	22.8	19.1	29.2		13.2	21.2	3.4	5.5	8.5
United States 1994	44.2	46.0	10.7	36.2	17.0	13.5	1.2	1.7	7.1	12.7

a. *World tables* (Washington, D.C.: IMF, 1995).
b. The composition of subnational government expenditures contains only the regional level.
Source: *Government Finance Statistics Yearbook* (Washington, D.C.: IMF, 1995).

119

Table 3-28. International Comparison of Expenditure Assignment by Level of Government
(percent)

Economy	General public services		Education		Health		Social security and welfare		Housing and community amenities	
	Central	Subnational	Central	Subnational	Central	Subnational	Central	Subnational	Central	Subnational
Australia 1995	43.9	56.1	31.1	68.9	53.9	46.1	91.0	9.0	24.5	75.5
Austria 1994	76.2	23.8	68.4	31.6	76.9	23.1	91.0	9.0	74.6	25.4
Canada 1993	43.2	56.8	7.5	92.5	14.3	85.7	63.9	36.1	13.7	86.3
Denmark 1995p	76.4	23.6	51.7	48.3	6.6	93.4	48.6	51.4	48.0	52.0
France 1993	73.9	26.1	62.8	37.2	97.8	2.2	91.3	8.7	18.3	81.7
Germany 1991	51.5	48.5	6.8	93.2	71.7	28.3	77.5	22.5	8.4	91.6
Iceland 1993	82.7	17.3	72.5	27.5	98.6	1.4	81.6	18.4	33.0	67.0
Ireland 1993	86.1	13.9	78.5	21.5	49.4	50.6	93.5	6.5	36.3	63.7
Luxembourg 1994	84.7	15.3	74.9	25.1	97.4	2.6	97.7	2.3	43.0	57.0
Netherlands 1995	70.0	30.0	65.8	34.2	94.9	5.1	84.2	15.8	32.2	67.8
Norway 1994	71.0	29.0	40.6	59.4	21.8	78.2	81.8	18.2	30.6	69.4
Spain 1993	81.0	19.0	39.3	60.7	42.9	57.1	96.5	3.5	31.8	68.2
Switzerland 1993	33.8	66.2	9.8	90.2	55.5	44.5	80.8	19.2	10.3	89.7
United Kingdom 1995	55.9	44.1	36.5	63.5			88.9	11.1	22.2	77.8
United States 1994	50.2	49.8	4.8	95.2	55.2	44.8	71.5	28.5	70.9	29.1

Source: *Government Finance Statistics Yearbook* (Washington, D.C.: IMF, 1996).

120

Table 3-29. International Comparison of Expenditure Assignment by Level of Government (percent)

Economy	Recreation, culture, and religion		Transportation and communication		Other (including defense)	
	Central	Subnational	Central	Subnational	Central	Subnational
Australia 1995	25.8	74.2	20.3	79.7	73.7	26.3
Austria 1994	59.2	40.8	79.3	20.7	88.2	11.8
Canada 1993	17.3	82.7	27.2	72.8	60.9	39.1
Denmark 1995p	40.5	59.5	50.0	50.0	91.3	8.7
France 1993	27.4	72.6	57.7	42.3	88.9	11.1
Germany 1991	9.3	90.7	55.8	44.2	64.4	35.6
Iceland 1993	35.2	64.8	70.9	29.1	70.4	29.6
Ireland 1993	41.7	58.3	51.4	48.6	96.4	3.6
Luxembourg 1994	37.4	62.6	79.9	20.1	81.5	18.5
Netherlands 1995	17.7	82.3	59.6	40.4	86.1	13.9
Norway 1994	41.6	58.4	69.2	30.8	98.1	1.9
Spain 1993	43.9	56.1	75.8	24.2	88.5	11.5
Switzerland 1993	8.2	91.8	43.7	56.3	87.6	12.4
United Kingdom 1995	32.7	67.3	51.1	48.9	94.0	6.0
United States 1994	15.6	84.4	30.2	69.8	76.2	23.8

Source: *Government Finance Statistics Yearbook* (Washington, D.C.: IMF, 1996).

4

AGRICULTURE

As it was in other Baltic countries in the pre-Soviet period, agriculture was one of the most significant components of the Lithuanian economy. Lithuania, like the other Baltic countries, went through a rapid period of industrialization and collectivization of agriculture under Soviet rule. During that time, agriculture remained the second-largest sector of the Lithuanian economy, accounting for 28 percent of GDP in 1990.[1] Livestock and dairy production were the major agricultural activities in the Soviet era, accounting for over three-fifths of total agricultural output. The country was a major supplier of livestock and dairy products, while grain and other needed inputs were delivered to the country according to central planning decisions. Lithuania had one of the most developed agricultural sectors in the former Soviet Union (FSU). The country produced 2.7 percent of the total meat and 3 percent of the milk output of the FSU, despite having only 0.3 percent of FSU agricultural land. More than a third of these products were delivered to the central funds, while Lithuania received about 1.1–1.3 million tons of feed grain in return.

Yields and the economic efficiency of the livestock sector were among the best inside the FSU, and comparable to levels in central and eastern Europe. Yet Lithuanian agriculture suffered many of the shortcomings common in the other FSU republics. The quantity of livestock products was of primary importance, which led to reduced attention to the crop sector. Quality and efficiency, both in agriculture and agro-processing, played only a secondary role, as in the rest of the FSU. The large livestock sector was based on an expensive system of subsidies and secure product markets inside the FSU.

Economic and Sectoral Reforms in Aggregate

Reforms in the food and agricultural sector started rather early, in parallel with the struggle to reestablish an independent state and a viable market economy. Lithuania initiated a transition program in food and agriculture to create a privatized and market-oriented sector. Land reform and privatization, liberalization of the macro environment, creation of a new incentive framework, and institutional and legal reform represent the major components of this program.

The Lithuanian food and agriculture sector, although it shows the first signs of recovery, is still having serious difficulties, which have been worsened by social problems in the rural areas related to the overall transition. Achievements in reforming the food and agricultural sector have been significant so far, but in some respects they lag behind reforms in other economic sectors and in the macroeconomic environment as a whole.

---

1. GDP calculated by the "old methodology."

The macroenvironment for agriculture improved relatively early in the reform period. The difficulties of adjustment from the old, distorted production system, however, were combined with the problems of coping with the pressure created by the new liberal policies; as a result, social tension increased in rural areas. The government responded to these tensions and to the initial political and economic difficulties of the agricultural transition with increased intervention and protection (the National Agricultural Program and the 1994 Law on Government Regulation of Economic Relations in Agriculture), rather than by accelerating the transition. As a result, in 1995 Lithuania introduced an agricultural support system that probably created the greatest market distortion seen among the domestic markets of the Baltic countries. The price supports provided a safeguard to a system that needed basic adjustment, and therefore prolonged the pain of adjustment, not only in agriculture, but also in the economy as a whole.

The new government that took office in late 1996 recognized that the agricultural sector's level of financial dependency on the state was no longer sustainable, and at the beginning of 1997 it began implementation of a better-targeted, more transparent, more cost-effective, and less distorting support system for farms and rural communities. These reforms have set a new direction for agricultural support policies that is more market-friendly and provides an improved framework for longer-term reforms and investments—something the sector badly needed.

The progress in farm restructuring and land privatization is significant, but is far from complete. The process of restitution of landownership and the settlement of claims was delayed in 1997 as various laws and implementation procedures were amended to facilitate acceleration of the process, but it is too early to assess if these changes will have significant results. The privatization and restructuring of agroprocessing followed a path similar to that of the other Baltic countries, providing preferential purchasing rights to raw material producers. The initial phase of privatization is over, but the objective of creating real owners with adequate capital has been only partially realized. On the whole, both agricultural and agroprocessing enterprises have major efficiency problems. With some exceptions, they are not ready to cope with the challenge of competition created by potential European Union (EU) membership.

For a small country such as Lithuania, with significant agricultural resources, the most appropriate way of preparing the sector for EU accession is to develop an agricultural system that is competitive. Such a system, both in size and structure, needs to be quite different from the system that was in place during the Soviet era. It is essential, therefore, that the policy response to rural social problems and demands of the agricultural sector for more support take an appropriate form, focusing on the enhancement of efficiency and competitiveness rather than delaying unavoidable changes and maintaining or increasing distortions.

Structure and Performance of the Sector, 1990–96

Agriculture and the National Economy

GROWTH. As in other central and eastern European countries, gross agricultural output (GAO) declined significantly in the initial transition phase, plunging more than 50 percent between 1990 and 1994 (table 4-1). The largest annual drops in output occurred between 1992 and 1994, when production contracted by 23 percent and 20 percent, respectively. These two sharp falls were a consequence of very unfavorable weather conditions, but the general decline resulted from transition adjustments that led to sharply higher real input prices, lower real output prices, declining demand in domestic and foreign markets, and disruptions caused by farm restructuring. Most of the output decline has been in meat and dairy products; up to 40 percent of these goods had been delivered to Russia in the pre-reform period in exchange for food and feed grains. Livestock production fell by more than 50 percent between 1989 and 1996, while crop production declined by less than one-third. As a result, the share of the livestock sector in gross agricultural production, which was over 62 percent in 1990, decreased to 45 percent in 1996. Even recognizing that measurement and data problems may overstate these production declines, there has been a significant adjustment in the level and structure of output.

Table 4-1. Importance of the Agricultural Sector in the National Economy, 1990–96 (percent)

Indicator	1990	1991	1992	1993	1994	1995	1996
Share in GDP	27.6	19.2	21.0				
(new methodology)			11.5	10.4	6.7	8.5	10.4
Change of GAO[a]	-9.0	-5.8	-23.4	-5.5	-20.2	6.1	10.3
Crops	-17.7	2.6	-33.5	26.0	-28.0	16.1	21.8
Livestock	-4.5	-12.0	-14.5	-26.9	-11.2	-2.7	-2.8
Structure of GAO	100.0	100.0	100.0	100.0	100.0	100.0	100.0
Crops	37.5	47.5	56.9	47.1	54.0	53.4	54.6
Livestock	62.5	52.5	43.1	52.9	46.0	46.6	45.4
Share in employment	18.0	17.5	18.7	21.9	22.5	22.9	24.0
Share in trade[b]							
Imports	6.2	5.2	11.5	4.2	11.6	13.4	13.1
Exports	16.6	30.7	19.7	12.2	19.9	18.3	17.1

a. Calculated at 1993 prices.
b. Agriculture and food industry.
Source: Lithuanian Department of Statistics.

Agricultural production showed the first signs of recovery in 1995, when, for the first time since 1989, gross agricultural production increased, by 6.1 percent over the previous year. The crop sector, to a large extent reflecting recovery from very poor 1994 growing conditions, grew significantly (16.1 percent), while the livestock sector continued to decline, but at a lower rate. Mostly as a result of favorable weather conditions, growth in agricultural output was even higher in 1996, led by a strong recovery in the crop sector and a stabilization in livestock and dairy production (figure 4-1). The growth in agricultural output for 1996 was 10.3 percent, and the sector was a major contributor to overall GDP growth for the year (table 4-1).

During the initial stage of transition (1990–93), the share of agriculture in GDP declined by about 8 percent. Since then, it has remained close to 10 percent, except in 1994, when a severe drought caused a large drop in crop output. At the same time, the total labor force employed in agriculture grew from 18 percent in 1990 to 24 percent in 1996. This indicates a large shift in the ratio of labor to GDP in the sector, and a consequent increased share of underemployed laborers in the sector and sharply declining labor productivity (table 4-1). An important factor contributing to these increases in the rural labor force was the availability of restituted land.

While Lithuania, like all central and eastern European countries (CEECs), lags behind the EU in many ways, it is neither the best nor the worst case within the group of ten CEECs that are actively seeking admittance to the EU. In 1995 Lithuania had the lowest per capita GDP of the group at current prices, but when adjusted for lower, nontradable prices using the purchasing power parity (PPP) exchange rate, per capita GDP was slightly above that of the other Baltic countries, about 75 percent of the CEEC average, and about 25 percent of the EU average (table 4-2). The share of agriculture in GDP and the share of employment in agriculture, while much higher than in the EU, were at about the same levels as the average for CEECs.

Figure 4-1. Gross Agricultural Output, 1989–96
(Index: 1989 = 100)

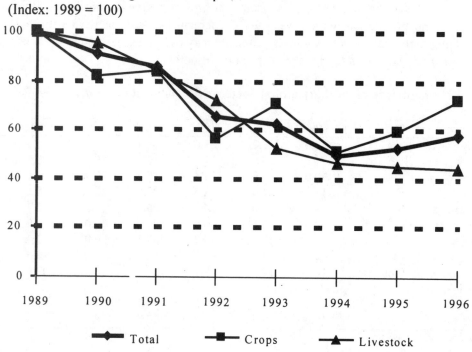

Agricultural and Food Industry Production

PRIMARY AGRICULTURE. Total planted area has declined by about 12 percent since 1991, a result of reduced fodder crop area that is directly linked to reduced livestock numbers (table 4-3.). The area in cereal has not changed significantly, and that of the remaining crops has increased only slightly. There have been significant year-to-year variations in cropping patterns, so it is difficult to see if there have been structural shifts. It is clear that potatoes and field vegetables are attracting more land, and in 1996 there was a large increase in wheat area at the expense of barley.

Grain yields per hectare have also declined significantly because of a lack of operating capital and low fertilizer and chemical use, as well as poor growing weather in 1994 (table 4-4). Only in the case of potato yields has the 1996 level exceeded that in 1991. Although data are not available for all farms, the total application of fertilizers by agricultural companies declined by more than 90 percent from 1990 to 1995, then remained stable at a relatively low level (table 4-5). By 1995, the application rate per hectare had declined to less than one-fourth of its 1990 level, but recovered slightly in 1996. Although these agricultural companies represent a declining share of land use and production, limited data for 1996 indicate that family farms use even less fertilizer per hectare than the agricultural companies.

Livestock numbers have declined by more than 50 percent since 1991, except for milking cows, which declined only about 30 percent (table 4-3). The size distribution of the cow herd, however, has changed dramatically. Many of the large dairy herds in agricultural companies did not survive, and production is now more widely dispersed in many very small farms and household plots. This is very inefficient and has led to declining milk yields (table 4-4) and a higher proportion of low-quality milk being supplied to processors. Milk yields began to recover slowly in 1995, but in 1996 they were still more than 10 percent below the 1991 level.

Table 4-2. Comparison of CEEC Applicant Countries with the EU-15, 1995

Country	Area (thousand km2)	Population, millions	GDP at current prices			GDP at purchasing power parity			Agriculture		
			Billion ECU	ECU/cap	Percentage of EU	Billion ECU (PPP rates)	ECU/cap (PPP rates)	Percentage of EU	Land (million hectares)	Percentage of total (gross value)	Percentage of employment
Lithuania	65	3.7	3.5	930	5.0	15.3	4,130	24.0	3.5	9.3	23.8
Latvia	65	2.5	3.4	1,370	8.0	7.9	3,160	18.0	2.5	9.9	18.5
Estonia	45	1.5	2.8	1,850	11.0	5.9	3,920	23.0	1.4	8.1	13.1
Baltics	175	7.7	9.7	1,260	7.3	29.1	3,779	21.9	7.4		
Percentage of EU-15	5.4	2.1	0.2	7.3		0.5	21.9		5.4		
CEE-10	1,078	105.3	234.0	2,220	13.0	582.0	5,530	32.0	60.6	8.6	22.5
Percentage of EU-15	33.0	28.0	4.0	13.0		9.0	32.0		43.9		
EU-15	3,236	371.6	6,441.5	17,260.0	100.0	6,441.5	17,260.0	100.0	138.1	2.4	5.3

Source: Agra Europe (London) Ltd., *East Europe Agriculture and Food*, No. 179 (August 1997).

Table 4-3. Areas Planted in Main Crops and Livestock Numbers, 1991–96

Item	1991	1992	1993	1994	1995	1996
Area planted	------Thousands of hectares------					
Total	2,800	2,688	2,681	2,557	2,359	2,455
Fodder crops	1,528	1,329	1,204	1,145	1,100	1,132
Cereals	1,087	1,165	1,289	1,218	1,053	1,116
Other crops	185	194	188	194	206	207
Main commercial crops						
Wheat	272	284	376	270	261	348
Barley	523	611	588	620	544	474
Potatoes	106	114	122	117	125	125
Field vegetables	21	20	25	28	26	29
Sugar beets	30	33	35	27	24	31
Livestock number, end of year	------Thousands------					
Cattle	2,197	1,701	1,384	1,152	1,065	1,054
Including milking cows	832	738	678	615	586	590
Pigs	2,180	1,360	1,196	1,260	1,270	1,128
Poultry	16,994	8,259	8,728	8,849	8,444	7,775

Source: Lithuanian Department of Statistics.

Table 4-4. Dynamics of Crop and Livestock Productivity, 1991–96

Item	1991	1992	1993	1994	1995	1996
Average yield of crops, ton per hectare						
Wheat	3.15	3.00	2.39	1.84	2.10	2.69
Barley	3.25	1.56	2.05	1.76	1.93	2.48
Potatoes	14.20	9.50	14.50	9.40	12.80	16.30
Sugar beets	27.20	19.00	24.60	17.30	28.40	25.50
Annual average productivity of livestock and poultry						
Milk, kg/cow	3,481	3,080	2,910	2,925	3,010	3,093
Eggs, pieces/hen	230	212	209	225	254	254

Source: Lithuanian Department of Statistics.

Table 4-5. Mineral Fertilizer Use by Agricultural Companies, 1990–96 (thousand tons of active ingredient)

Item	1990	1991	1992	1993	1994	1995	1996
Total application	660.7	601.4	266.6	117.4	75.1	51.7	51.1
Nitrogen	244.8	204.0	94.3	57.7	41.3	28.8	29.0
Phosphorus	153.9	144.1	61.0	23.0	13.0	10.9	10.5
Potassium	262.0	253.3	111.3	36.7	20.8	12.0	11.6
Application per hectare, kilograms	227.0	247.0	107.0	69.0	56.0	54.0	72.0

Source: Lithuanian Department of Statistics.

The indications are that levels of production in the sector are stabilizing, and for some products they are increasing (table 4-6). Potato production is 30 percent higher than in 1991, while wheat and sugar beet production are nearly the same as in 1991. Meat, milk, and egg production levels seem to have stabilized, indicating the completion of this market adjustment. Since livestock numbers declined far more than grain and fodder production, there is no longer any significant dependence on imported feed grains, as was the case during Soviet times. In normal years, domestic pasture and crop production resources need to be supplemented only with imported protein and feed supplements.

Table 4-6. Dynamics of Agricultural Output Volume
(thousand tons)

Product	1991	1992	1993	1994	1995	1996
Wheat	855	834	890	549	637	936
Barley	1,699	955	1,208	1,091	892	1,177
Potatoes	1,508	1,080	1,773	1,096	1,594	2,044
Sugar beets	811	622	855	462	692	796
Meat (carcass weight)	450	415	276	224	208	199
Beef and veal	209	226	162	116	87	83
Pig meat	194	155	90	82	93	89
Poultry	44	32	22	24	26	25
Other	3	2	2	2	2	2
Milk	2,916	2,21	2,067	1,896	1,819	1,831
Eggs (million pieces)	1,235	880	610	714	793	751

Source: Lithuanian Department of Statistics.

The largest adjustment in production for Lithuania, as in most CEECs was in meat and milk production. Although circumstances differed among the countries, the major common factors in this adjustment were significant declines in domestic and export demand for these products. Lithuania's decline in meat production was less than those recorded in Estonia and Latvia, but significantly more than in other CEECs (table 4-7). The much larger meat production declines in the Baltics relative to the CEECs are an artifact of the special role of the Baltics in Soviet meat production, which had no real economic basis and suffered a sharp loss in market demand after independence. While other CEECs began to see a slight recovery in meat production in 1995 or 1996, the three Baltic states were still experiencing declines in 1996. Milk was somewhat different, in that there was less disparity in adjustments (declines ranging from 30 to 50 percent); and among the countries in this comparison, only Lithuania and Hungary began to experience a small turnaround in milk production in 1996. This growth can only be seen as a positive development if it was stimulated by market demand rather than by government incentives. In the case of Lithuania, the government price support and subsidy incentives are the more likely reason for the increased milk production.

AGROPROCESSING. The real value of output in the manufacture of food and beverages declined by more than 50 percent between 1992 and 1994, then remained nearly constant in real terms (table 4-8). During this period, the decline in agroprocessing has been less than in the rest of industry, so the share of the food and beverage sector in total industrial production rose slightly, from 22 percent in 1992 to 27 percent in 1996. One area of concern is that employment in the food and beverage industry declined only 11 percent, while output was cut by half, indicating a large decline in labor productivity. This disparity was also evident, but to a lesser degree, in industry as a whole. Within this industry group, there is a wide dispersion in the impacts of the adjustment on products. Some products, such as fermented cheese, sugar, and alcoholic beverages, declined less then 20 percent from 1990 to 1996, while meat, soft drinks, and canned fruits and vegetables declined by 75 percent or more (table 4-9). Most products began showing the first signs of recovery in 1995, while a few were still declining in 1996.

Table 4-7. Comparison of Meat and Milk Production Changes in CEECs, 1989–95
(index: 1989 = 100)

Item	1989	1990	1991	1992	1993	1994	1995	1996
Meat								
Estonia	100.0	95.6	66.3	47.1	36.6	30.3	29.6	26.5
Latvia	100.0	93.4	89.4	74.3	58.0	41.1	37.1	22.9
Lithuania	100.0	99.2	84.1	77.7	51.6	41.9	39.0	37.1
Bulgaria	100.0	96.5	80.4	79.3	68.9	54.5	58.7	61.6
Slovak Republic	100.0	99.7	88.9	81.2	75.7	71.0	70.3	71.8
Czech Republic	100.0	99.0	98.5	90.0	85.4	78.8	77.1	77.6
Hungary	100.0	98.0	87.2	75.4	68.0	64.0	66.9	69.4
Poland	100.0	104.6	105.9	101.2	93.4	82.6	92.9	91.0
Milk								
Estonia	100.0	94.7	85.6	72.0	62.9	60.6	55.3	53.0
Latvia	100.0	95.5	87.9	74.8	58.6	50.5	48.0	47.0
Lithuania	100.0	97.5	90.1	74.7	63.9	60.5	58.0	60.2
Bulgaria	100.0	98.0	82.1	74.1	63.0	58.2	57.4	57.0
Slovak Republic	100.0	96.1	76.2	66.5	60.7	57.8	57.8	57.8
Czech Republic	100.0	98.1	84.3	76.1	70.4	65.4	63.4	62.8
Hungary	100.0	99.4	87.0	80.4	72.3	66.9	66.2	67.7
Poland	100.0	96.5	88.0	80.2	77.1	72.8	69.7	67.1

Source: OECD, *Agricultural Policies in Transition Economies: Monitoring and Evaluation* (Paris, 1996 and 1997).

Table 4-8. Dynamics of Output in the Food Industry, 1992–96

Item	1992	1993	1994	1995	1996
	Value of industrial output (current prices, millions of Lt)				
Total industry	5,076.8	13,035.1	13,773.7	17,871.1	22,391.0
Manufacture of food and beverages	1,130.0	3,387.8	3,460.6	4,781.4	6,059.0
Manufacture of tobacco products	33.5	48.1	133.1	220.5	340.3
	Real value of industrial output (1993 prices, millions of Lt)				
Total industry	19,870.6	13,035.1	7,998.7	7,434.2	7,451.5
Manufacture of food and beverages	4,422.7	3,387.8	2,009.6	1,989.0	2,016.4
Manufacture of tobacco products	131.1	48.1	77.3	91.7	113.2
	Changes in real industrial output (previous year = 100)				
Total industry		65.6	73.4	105.3	105.0
Manufacture of food and beverages		76.6	79.6	94.7	99.4
Manufacture of tobacco products		36.7	117.7	145.1	126.7
	Share in total industrial output (percent)				
Manufacture of food and beverages	22.3	26.0	25.1	26.8	27.1
Manufacture of tobacco products	0.7	0.4	1.0	1.2	1.5
	Annual average number of employees (thousands)				
Total industry	405.2	394.9	355.6	310.9	293.3
Manufacture of food and beverages	64.3	69.6	58.7	60.6	57.4
Manufacture of tobacco products	0.6	0.6	0.6	0.6	0.3
	Share in industrial employment (percent)				
Total industry	100.0	100.0	100.0	100.0	100.0
Manufacture of food and beverages	15.9	17.6	16.5	19.5	19.6
Manufacture of tobacco products	0.1	0.2	0.2	0.2	0.1

Source: Statistical Yearbook of Lithuania, 1994–95 and 1996 (Department of Statistics), and author's calculations.

CONSUMPTION. OECD estimates that at the end of the Soviet period, food prices in Lithuania averaged about one-third of world reference prices. This was the result of a combination of low administered prices and a highly undervalued exchange rate. The loss of these massive (implicit) consumer subsidies at the same time that real incomes were falling had a dramatic impact on consumption—household expenditure for food increased from 34 percent in 1990 to over 60 percent in 1993 (table 4-10). This expenditure share is declining slowly, but is still very high (56.6 percent in 1996) and contributes to the weak domestic demand for food products, especially meat and dairy products. As economic theory would suggest, the decline in real income led to a shift in consumption from higher-value meat and dairy products to lower-cost cereal products. From 1990 to 1996, meat, dairy products, eggs, and sugar consumption per capita declined by 43 percent to 56 percent, while cereal products consumption increased by 31 percent. As with production, the declines in consumption may be overstated for some products, but the influence of economic factors in the changing consumption patterns is clear. There is also a much greater variety and improved quality of food products available from domestic and foreign suppliers, which has undoubtedly increased consumer satisfaction, especially among those at the middle- and higher-income levels.

Structure of Farms and Agricultural Production

EVOLVING FARMING STRUCTURES. Before independence and until the farm restructuring, agricultural production was organized through 834 collective and 275 state farms, prior to their dissolution in 1992 (table 4-11). In the past several years, all of these farms have been reorganized and privatized, and the farming structure is evolving toward smaller, private farms (figure 4-2). The changes in farming structure are far from finished, however, although less than 20 percent of agricultural land is still cultivated by agricultural companies that are the successors to former large-scale collective or state

Table 4-9. Dynamics of Industrial Output for Major Food Commodities, 1990–96

Product groups	Units of measurement	1990	1991	1992	1993	1994	1995	1996	1996 as percentage of 1990
Meat (including I cat. offal)	Thousand metric tons	431.5	338.3	261.8	135.4	91.8	94.7	94.1	22
Sausage	Thousand metric tons	76.2	70.2	57.7	48.2	39.8	41.6	48.4	64
Fish and fish products (excluding fish preserves)	Thousand metric tons	201.6	199.7	113.2	72.2	38.9	7.4	8.0	4
Canned fruit and vegetables	Million cans	151.8	193.1	123.3	170.1	51.4	52.1	38.6[a]	25
Vegetable oil	Thousand metric tons	1.2	0.2	0.1	0.0	0.0	0.5	2.8	233
Whole milk products (converted to milk)	Thousand metric tons	831	714	401	285	297	310	313	38
Butter	Thousand metric tons	73.9	67.2	49.2	45.3	31.2	32.3	34.8	47
Fermented cheese	Thousand metric tons	26.3	24.5	17.6	19.7	18.5	16.6	21.5	82
Flour	Thousand metric tons	466.9	406.3	396.0	291.6	253.7	237.1	228.5	49
Bread and products	Thousand metric tons	332.1	319.8	295.1	279.6	240.3	212.4	188.6	43
Sugar	Thousand metric tons	158.6	150.5	87.7	90.9	51.6	105.2	136.3	86
Confectionery	Thousand metric tons	75.1	64.8	41.5	30.1	33.2	36.4	38.2	51
Vodka and liquor	Thousand dal	2,943	3,547	2,696	2,400	2,166	2,581	2,776	94
Beer	Thousand dal	15,017	14,121	14,258	11,638	13,529	10,902	11,079	74
Soft drinks	Thousand dal	10,461	8,066	4,842	2,991	1,325	1,906	1,627	16
Tobacco products	Billion units	6.7	6.4	5.3	3.4	3.9	4.9	4.5	67

Note: dal represents decaliter.
a. Preliminary data.
Source: *Statistical Yearbooks of Lithuania, 1996 and 1997* (Lithuanian Department of Statistics).

Table 4-10. Food Expenditure and Annual per Capita Consumption

Indicator	1990	1991	1992	1993	1994	1995	1996
Average share of household expenditure spent on food (%)	33.9	38.3	59.7	61.5	57.3	57.4	56.6
Meat products (in meat-equivalent units)	88.9	65.5	64.1	55.7	49.6	52.0	51.0
Milk products (in milk-equivalent units)	480	315	334	319	291	238	213
Eggs (pieces)	305	293	207	143	167	172	167
Fish and fish products	18.6	19.2	10.5	8.4	10.1	9.9	11.4
Vegetable oils	7.3	3.0	3.8	7.4	10.4	11.5	12.8
Vegetables, melons, etc.	79	83	65	69	65	65	71
Fruit and berries	33	51	30	50	45	48	52
Sugar	43.0	31.0	23.1	25.1	22.7	22.0	23.5
Cereal products (grain-equivalent units)	108	138	142	122	135	136	142
Potatoes	146	128	95	122	99	127	133

Source: Lithuanian Department of Statistics.

Table 4-11. Dynamics of Number of Agricultural Land Users and Farm Size, 1991–97
(January 1)

Item	1991	1992	1993	1994	1995	1996	1997
State and collective farms	1,212	1,219					
Average size (hectares)	2,535	2,040					
Agricultural companies			4,279	3,483	2,880	2,611	1,660
Average size (hectares)			477.0	450.0	378.0	306.3	371.6
Family farms (thousand)	2.3	5.1	71.5	111.5	134.6	165.8	196.0
Average size (hectares)	14.1	9.4	8.9	8.8	8.5	7.8	7.6
Household plots (thousand)	465.8	479.0	413.1	404.0	396.7	378.4	342.7
Average size (hectares)	0.7	1.9	2.1	2.1	2.1	2.2	2.2

Source: Lithuanian Department of Statistics.

Figure 4-2. Distribution of Agricultural Land by User Group

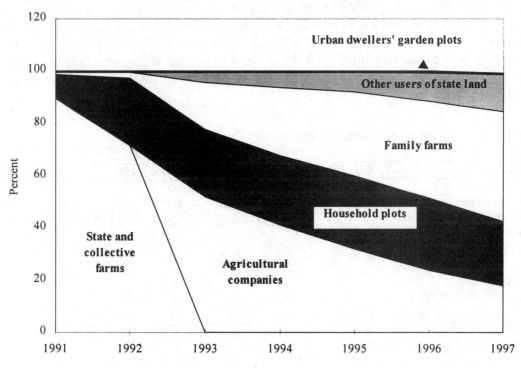

farms that were restructured to varying degrees (table 4-12). In principle, the Lithuanian government accepts the coexistence of various farming forms, although its policies favor genuine "family" farming. The current Lithuanian farming structure is characterized by three kinds of farming organizations.

Table 4-12. Distribution of Agricultural Land by Main User Group, 1991–97
(January 1, percent)

Agricultural land user	1991	1992	1993	1994	1995	1996	1997
All users	100.0	100.0	100.0	100.0	100.0	100.0	100.0
State and collective farms	89.7	71.7	0.0	0.0	0.0	0.0	0.0
Agricultural companies	0.0	0.0	51.9	41.2	32.2	23.9	18.1
Household plots	8.9	25.7	25.9	26.5	27.9	27.5	24.5
Family farms	1.0	2.2	17.9	25.9	32.1	37.2	42.1
Other users of state land	0.0	0.0	3.8	5.9	7.3	10.8	14.0
Urban-dwellers' garden plots	0.4	0.5	0.5	0.5	0.6	0.6	0.6

Source: Lithuanian Department of Statistics.

- AGRICULTURAL COMPANIES. Larger, corporate farming enterprises were created through the privatization and restructuring of the state and collective farms. In addition to primary agriculture, some of these agricultural companies are also involved in food processing and trading activities. The agricultural companies inherited the assets of the large-scale farms that were inappropriate for the smaller private farms, and are staffed by former workers of the large-scale farms who did not feel comfortable in a private farming environment. Under current law, agricultural companies, like other legal entities, are not allowed to own agricultural land. All land farmed by the companies is leased or rented, either from physical persons (often from their own shareholders) or from the state. The initial land laws of the transition instituted a system of compulsory leasing of nearby restituted private land to the agricultural companies. These compulsory leases were abolished in 1997, although the agricultural companies may still negotiate leases at market rental rates. A total of 4,279 agricultural companies were created in 1992, but their number had declined to 1,660 by 1997. Their average size was 371.6 hectares, and they used only 18 percent of total agricultural land and contributed about 25 percent to total agricultural output (tables 4-11 to 4-13). The new law on agricultural partnerships facilitates the further restructuring of these farms to increase their financial and economic viability or to dissolve them completely. It is expected that about 50 percent of current companies will be viable as joint-stock companies, and the rest will most likely disintegrate into smaller, private operations or family farms.

Table 4-13. Distribution of Agricultural Production by Type of Farm, 1990–96
(percent)

Type of farm	1990	1991	1992	1993	1994	1995	1996
Plant production							
Agricultural companies[a]	65	40	30	30	24	20	18
Family and household farms	35	60	70	70	76	80	82
Livestock production							
Agricultural companies[a]	70	62	43	42	50	44	33
Family and household farms	30	38	57	58	50	56	67
Total production							
Agricultural companies[a]	68	52	36	36	36	31	25
Family and household farms	32	48	64	64	64	69	75

a. Including state and collective farms from 1990 to 1992.
Source: Lithuanian Department of Statistics.

- FAMILY FARMS. The first family farms were established before independence under the 1989 Law on Peasant Farms, which allowed rural inhabitants to receive user rights on up to 50 hectares of land. These so-called "89er's" numbered about 5,200 families and received land amounting to about 2.8 percent of the country's total agricultural area, with an average size of 14.1 hectares. This process of land distribution continued until September 1991, when it was superseded by the new laws for land privatization through restitution. The 89er farms have not been directly affected by the later restitutions, but the settlement of claims related to the land already distributed to the 89ers further delayed the restitution process and created tensions among the rural population. As a result of land restitution and the breakup of the large-scale farms, by 1 January 1997, there were 196,000 owners of family farms, including the 89ers, with an average ownership size of 7.6 hectares. These accounted for 42 percent of total agricultural land, and together with household plots, 75 percent of production. The family farm share in agricultural land and the overall number of family farms are continuously increasing, but data on family-farm-owners who are actually farming (family-farm land-users) and the average operating (as opposed to ownership) size is not collected systematically. The best approximation of this number is the list of family farms registered for the purpose of participating in government investment programs, which includes 46,922 farms, with an average size of 11.7 hectares, as of 1 January 1997. The group of 89ers and family-farm entrepreneurs who have leased significant additional land represent the most efficient operations, while the rest are largely unconsolidated operations with lower efficiency and significant financial difficulties. Providing the incentive structure to encourage the consolidation of the large number of smaller-scale private farms will be one of the most serious challenges facing the agricultural leadership of the country.

- HOUSEHOLD PLOTS. There are more than 340,000 household plots, averaging about 2.2 hectares in size (table 4-11). These are often operated by the shareholders of agricultural companies or by rural inhabitants to provide subsistence or to supplement their income from other sources. While the number of household plots is declining, in 1997 they still accounted for 24.5 percent of agricultural land (table 4-12).

A comparison with selected CEECs also indicates that Lithuania is in an intermediate position in its farm structure at this stage of transition. More than two-thirds of family farms are below 10 hectares, which is more like the configuration in Hungary and Poland than in Estonia and Latvia (table 4-14). It is evident, however, that there has been a more radical restructuring of former state and collective farms; their average size in Lithuania is far less than in most of the other countries in this comparison. The exception is Albania, where more radical restructuring of large farms was implemented.

Table 4-14. Comparison of Farm Structure in CEECs, 1995

	Family farms		Agricultural companies, average size
Country	Percent below 10 hectares	Average size	
Albania	99.7	1.3	380
Romania	97.3	3.8	1,051
Bulgaria	88.6	4.1	1,600
Hungary	74.3	11.0	2,800
Lithuania	67.7	8.5	378
Poland	59.9	12.3	1,500
Latvia	30.9	19.9	706
Estonia	21.0	23.0	584

Source: World Bank Discussion Paper No. 268 (Washington, D.C.); data for Baltics from S. Wengren, ed., *Land Reform in the Former Soviet Union and Eastern Europe* (New York and London: Routledge, 1998).

Farm and Retail Price Developments

PRICES. Lithuania, like most transition economies, has progressed through all or most of the steps in the evolution of price formation mechanisms. Beginning with the state-determined prices and implied subsidy patterns of the pre-reform period, input subsidies were removed (1990), regulated farm and retail prices were increased (1991), prices were deregulated (1992–95), quantitative trade restrictions were replaced by tariffs (1993), and domestic market intervention policies were introduced (1992 and 1995). As of late 1997, many of the distorting components of the price support mechanism had been removed, but direct government payments to farmers remained a significant budget expenditure.

Real farm prices declined substantially, while real retail prices increased after price liberalization (table 4-15). For many products, the decline in real farm prices ended in 1994 or 1995 and began to turn around slowly. In the case of real retail prices, there were sharp increases in the early years, followed by a gradual decline. Except for chicken, meat, and eggs, however, real retail prices in 1996 were 15 to 85 percent above the December 1990 levels. Thus, for most products, the gap between farm and retail prices first increased, then stabilized or decreased. It is normal for the marketing margin between farm and retail for most food products to rise significantly during the transition, as input and product subsidies are removed and the margin must reflect the full farm-to-market processing and distribution costs. It is also encouraging that these farm-to-retail margins are beginning to decrease, indicating some improvement in processing and distribution efficiency.

Table 4-15. Lithuanian Real Producer and Retail Prices, 1990–96 Indices
(December 1990 = 100)

Product	1990 (December)	1991 (December)	1992 (Average)	1993 (Average)	1994 (Average)	1995 (Average)	1996 (Average)
Producer price							
Cattle (live weight)	100.0	57.2	47.5	46.4	28.0	24.1	25.0
Pigs (live weight)	100.0	63.3	81.8	81.6	63.3	48.4	49.2
Broilers (live weight)	100.0	66.2	54.7	65.0	79.2	62.1	56.9
Milk	100.0	30.4	63.5	46.6	25.4	28.8	27.1
Eggs	100.0	141.2	153.7	132.7	89.0	74.9	71.8
Grains							
Wheat	100.0	51.2	86.0	61.2	33.9	37.3	50.9
Barley	100.0	46.1	73.2	52.1	25.2	28.8	42.2
Potatoes	100.0	63.7	67.7	75.1	37.3	55.7	28.0
Sugar beets	100.0	124.6	47.7	33.9	22.8	22.4	20.9
Retail price							
Beef	100.0	194.1	202.5	219.9	165.8	147.9	132.7
Pork	100.0	169.5	216.7	215.3	145.0	134.7	141.8
Chicken	100.0	128.0	131.5	120.9	105.0	79.7	78.1
Milk	100.0	98.6	209.9	207.7	152.1	166.2	185.3
Eggs	100.0	146.3	129.1	94.1	71.5	62.8	65.7
Wheat bread	100.0	160.3	155.0	153.5	153.6	161.2	152.9
Rye bread	100.0	126.7	87.3	127.5	149.4	133.9	136.9
Potatoes	100.0	227.8	228.2	120.2	171.8	227.2	123.8
Sugar	100.0	193.9	281.5	232.8	137.6	127.7	115.5

Source: Calculated from Lithuanian Department of Statistics data.

An increased alignment with external reference prices reflects the impact of farm price support programs, the real appreciation of the litas, and the gradual maturation of market behavior. In general, farm prices are relatively close to U.S. or OECD reference prices, with the exception of beef, milk, eggs, and potatoes (table 4-16). Farm prices in Estonia, Latvia, and Lithuania have also been converging over the last two years, but there are still some notable differences. Assuming the data are comparable, Estonian and Lithuanian farm prices for cattle in 1996 were 10 percent lower than prices for Latvian cattle; pigs in Estonia cost 10 percent less than in the other two countries; broilers were 10 percent cheaper in Lithuania than in the other two countries; the farm price of milk in Lithuania was significantly lower than in Latvia and Estonia; wheat cost about 11 percent less in Estonia and Latvia than in Lithuania; and sugar beets in Latvia were 15 percent less costly than they were in Lithuania (table 4-17).

Retail prices across the Baltic states have converged to a greater extent than farm prices, but there are a few exceptions among the selected products evaluated (table 4-17). Items that cost less than 90 percent of the highest country price in the first half of 1997 are beef, milk, and sugar in Estonia; pork in Latvia; and wheat bread in Lithuania. The 30 percent lower sugar price in Estonia is clearly the result of Estonia's trade policies, which allow the tariff-free import of sugar at world prices, while Lithuania and Latvia have import tariffs of more than 80 percent.

Table 4-16. Comparison of Lithuanian Farm Prices and World Market Prices, 1990–96
(US$ per ton)

Item	Comparison	1990	1991	1992	1993	1994	1995	1996
Cattle, live weight	Lithuania	184	74	174	382	448	538	695
	U.S. farm	1,731	1,636	1,661	1,682	1,517	1,460	1,436
	OECD reference price for beef and veal[a] (live weight equivalent, Hungary)	728	583	633	795	880	1,090	1,084
Pigs, live weight	Lithuania	175	78	303	670	961	1,033	1,316
	U.S. farm	1,220	1,096	949	1,016	884	933	1,176
	OECD reference price for pig meat[a] (live weight equivalent, Hungary)	1,059	1,016	1,167	988	994	1,309	1,469
Poultry	Lithuania	150	70	171	476	1,031	1,137	1,312
	U.S. wholesale	1,207	1,146	1,160	1,217	1,228	1,243	1,351
	OECD reference price[a] (EC)	1,199	1,220	1,258	1,150	1,174	1,240	1,333
Milk	Lithuania	34	7	46	71	75	120	137
	Australia, average farm	179	188	202	180	205	231	225
	OECD reference price[a] (New Zealand)	122	129	144	138	147	184	192
Eggs	Lithuania	81	79	311	530	704	841	1,095
	OECD reference price[a] (EC)	1,012	1,024	928	930	968	886	1,356
Wheat	Lithuania	25	9	49	71	74	116	194
	U.S. FOB, Gulf	150	134	147	142	147	181	200
	OECD reference price[a] (EC)	142	98	133	117	115	164	199
Barley (nonmalt)	Lithuania	25	8	42	60	55	90	161
	U.S. FOB, Pacific Northwest	101	114	119	118	117	142	151
	OECD reference price[a] (EC)	109	96	104	85	81	129	167
Potatoes	Lithuania	16	7	28	54	53	110	69
	OECD reference price[a] (Germany)	106	121	88	56	135	270	91

a. Used by the OECD in calculations of PSE and for Lithuania (OECD, *Review of Agricultural Policies: Lithuania* [Paris, 1996]).

Table 4-17. Comparison of Farm and Retail Prices in Baltic States

Products	Farm price		Retail price		
				Percent of highest	
	Average 1996 (US$/ton)	Highest 1996 (percent)	Average Feb.–June 1997 (US$/kg)	Feb.–June 1997	July–Dec. 1996
Cattle (live weight)			Beef		
Estonia	717	92.0	2.36	88.4	92.3
Latvia	779	100.0	2.67	100.0	100.0
Lithuania	695	89.4	2.60	97.5	99.4
Pigs (live weight)			Pork		
Estonia	1,180	90.4	3.12	93.6	89.4
Latvia	1,305	99.9	2.95	88.6	89.3
Lithuania	1,316	100.0	3.35	100.0	100.0
Broilers (live			Chicken		
weight)	1,467	100.0	2.41	90.2	100.0
Estonia	1,312	99.3	2.61	98.0	86.4
Latvia	1,292	90.9	2.67	100.0	82.6
Lithuania					
			Milk		
Milk					
Estonia	214	100.0	0.41	87.4	100.0
Latvia	181	84.7	0.46	98.5	99.5
Lithuania	137	65.2	0.47	100.0	97.0
			Bread		
Wheat					
Estonia	174	89.6	1.00	100.0	100.0
Latvia	172	89.0	0.94	94.1	88.8
Lithuania	194	100.0	0.77	76.3	65.8
			Sugar		
Sugar beets					
Estonia	n.p.	n.p.	0.58	68.1	75.4
Latvia	40	84.1	0.83	97.5	96.3
Lithuania	47	100.0	0.85	100.0	100.0

n.p. Not produced on a commercial basis.
Source: Lithuanian Department of Statistics.

Trade in Agricultural and Food Products

TRADE. In the 1970s and 1980s, Lithuania was a net exporter of agricultural products and foodstuffs, mainly to other FSU republics. Lithuania was traditionally a significant exporter of dairy and meat products, while it was a net importer of grain, fruits, and vegetables. The positive balance of agricultural trade has been continuously eroding since 1993, and by 1996, Lithuania had become a small net importer (figure 4-3). From 1995 to 1996, net exports to Estonia and the Commonwealth of Independent States (CIS) increased by about US$50 million, but net imports from the EU increased by US$102 million (table 4-18). In 1996, food and agriculture contributed 17.1 percent to overall exports, while its share of imports amounted to 13.1 percent. Both imports and exports include a substantial quantity of goods for reexport from East to West and West to East. The main domestic products exported to Western markets are primary products designated for further processing or reexport. In Eastern markets, Lithuania still sells mainly meat and dairy products.

Figure 4-3. Agricultural Trade

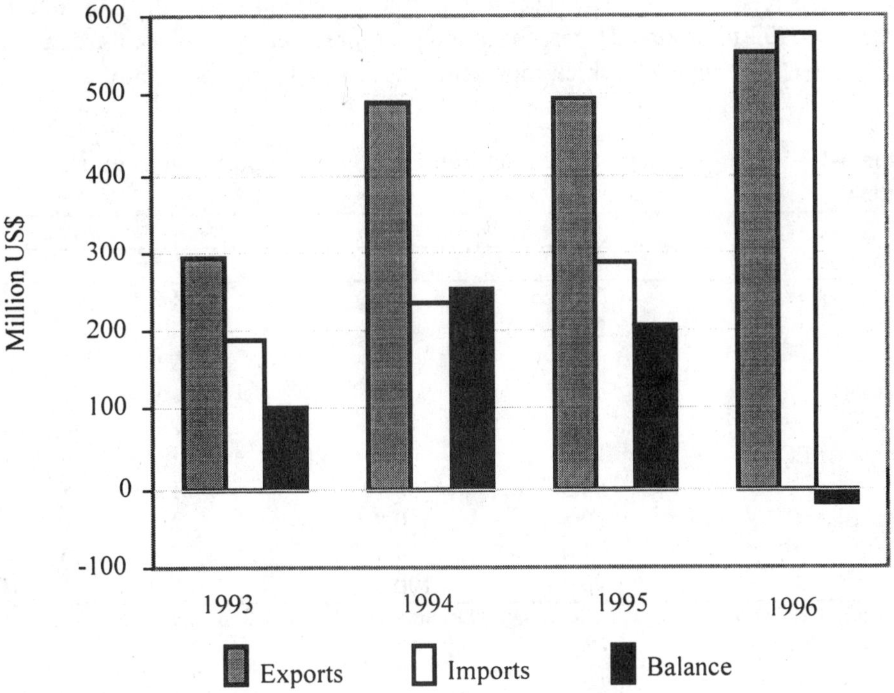

Table 4-18. Regional Pattern of Agricultural and Food Exports and Imports, 1995–96 (thousands of US$)

Country or region	Exports		Imports		Trade balance	
	1995	1996	1995	1996	1995	1996
Europe	198,129	184,365	323,255	422,178	-125,127	-237,814
EU	136,436	98,483	204,145	267,807	-67,710	-169,324
EFTA	6,866	17,404	43,851	50,418	-36,985	-33,014
Estonia	15,919	26,135	9,430	16,857	6,489	9,278
Latvia	23,856	33,653	11,165	21,811	12,691	11,842
Other CEEC[a]	15,051	8,690	54,664	65,286	-39,613	-56,596
CIS	290,204	360,181	103,674	127,016	186,530	233,165
United States	2,686	4,373	13,118	23,829	-10,432	-19,457
Other	4,939	25,274	47,571	24,843	-42,633	430
Total						
Agriculture and food	495,957	574,191	487,618	597,866	8,339	-23,675
All products	2,705,672	3,356,365	3,648,553	4,558,624	-942,881	-1,202,259

a. Albania, Bulgaria, Czech Republic, Hungary, Poland, Romania, and Slovak Republic.
Source: Lithuanian Department of Statistics.

Europe and the CIS were the destinations for 98 percent of Lithuanian exports from 1993 to 1995, and 93 percent of exports in 1996. In the past two years, there has been an increase in the share of exports going to the CIS, and a decline in the share sent to Europe (table 4-19). The EU share declined from 27 percent, where it had been for three years, to 17 percent in 1996. These shifts are related to numerous factors, including quality and marketing infrastructure, but they are also consistent with the appreciation of the litas relative to European currencies and its depreciation relative to CIS currencies. The share of exports going to Estonia and Latvia increased slightly, which is an encouraging sign for future possibilities under the Baltic Free Trade Agreement (BFTA). The principal source of imports during the last three years has been Europe, and the share from this region increased from 53 percent in 1993 to around 70 percent in 1996. The second important source has been the CIS, but this share declined from 39 percent in 1993 to around 21 percent in the past three years. A close third, and gaining in import share, are the other CEE countries, which represent close to an 11 percent share.

Table 4-19. Regional Shares of Agricultural and Food Exports and Imports (percent)

Country or region	Exports		Imports	
	1995	*1996*	*1995*	*1996*
Europe	39.9	32.1	66.3	70.6
EU	27.5	17.2	41.9	44.8
EFTA	1.4	3.0	9.0	8.4
Estonia	3.2	4.6	1.9	2.8
Latvia	4.8	5.9	2.3	3.6
Other CEEC[a]	3.0	1.5	11.2	10.9
CIS	58.5	62.7	21.3	21.2
United States	0.5	0.8	2.7	4.0
Other	1.0	4.4	9.8	4.2
Total	100.0	100.0	100.0	100.0

a. Albania, Bulgaria, Czech Republic, Hungary, Romania, and Slovak Republic.
Source: Calculated from Table 4-15.

Data for the first half of 1997 indicate that the trade deficit will likely increase in 1997. By the end of June, the trade deficit for all products was nearly 70 percent of the total deficit for 1996. For food and agricultural products, the trade deficit at the end of June was already greater than for the entire year in 1996. A positive development in late 1997 was the inspection of eleven Lithuanian dairy enterprises by EU veterinary officials, which led to approval of the enterprises for exports to the EU. This was especially encouraging in view of the denial of this approval to Polish and Estonian enterprises.

Progress on EU Accession

The free trade agreement between the EU and Lithuania, including preferential tariff rates and tariff rate quotas for food and agricultural products, became effective on 1 January 1995. Lithuania signed an association agreement with the EU in June of 1995, and later applied for full membership. The association agreement, which came into force on 1 February 1998, provides a supportive framework for the preparation necessary for full membership. Original expectations regarding improved access to EU food and agricultural markets have generally not been realized, however, primarily because of the inadequate quality of Lithuanian products. The country receives significant financial assistance through the EU/PHARE program, which will focus on pre-accession measures beginning with the 1998 Financial Memorandum. Lithuania will be eligible for additional funds for structural adjustment to bring it in line with the requirements of the EU single market. During the past five years, Lithuania received over 20 million ECU in support of the restructuring of the agricultural sector. The program provided assistance for training in agricultural policy, improvement of productivity in the livestock and crop sectors, the modernization of land information systems, an Agricultural Management Training Center, and expanded the agricultural advisory services to aid farms and to facilitate the restructuring of agroprocessing, among other things.

The country has made significant progress in preparing the sector for EU membership. According to the July 1997 evaluation of the EU Commission, however, substantial, sustained efforts are still needed to prepare the country for successful accession. In the agricultural sector, the commission evaluation for Lithuania and other applicant countries suggested a focus on the following areas:

- *Further restructuring of the overall agricultural and food sector to improve its competitive capacity and to complete the process of transition.* The acceleration of the land restitution process and the creation of a functioning land market is one of the most important tasks in this regard.
- *The strengthening of the administrative structures to ensure the necessary capacity to implement and enforce the policy instruments of the CAP.* The management and implementation of even a simplified and further reformed CAP and adapting European Union rural and structural policies would require sophisticated administrative systems, including an appropriate land registry and farm identification system. In general, Lithuanian administrative capacity needs significant further development to implement CAP programs.
- *The implementation and enforcement of veterinary and phytosanitary requirements and upgrading of testing and certification establishments to meet EU standards.* This is particularly important in regard to the inspection and control arrangements for protecting the EU external border.
- *Compliance with the* acquis communitaire *is probably the most difficult aspect of the preparation for accession.* For example, the full harmonization of legislation is needed in the areas of plant protection, pesticide residues, organic farming, seeds and propagation material, as well as plant health. Although there has been significant progress, the harmonization of Lithuanian legislation is still in the early phase of preparation.

Key Policy Issues in the Food and Agricultural Sector

Completion of the Land Restitution and Privatization Processes

DELAYED IMPLEMENTATION OF LAND RESTITUTION AND PRIVATIZATION. Lithuania started early in transforming its agricultural structure to establish farms based on private ownership and family labor. The restitution of property rights and ownership in force before 1940 was chosen as the basis for land reform. Although the country selected a manner of restitution that allowed not only in-kind compensation, but also compensation in cash and other assets, the implementation of this program has turned out to be rather difficult and time-consuming. The unfinished land reform and farm restructuring process is one of the most critical constraints on improving competitiveness and sector recovery.

The procedures selected for restitution of land parcels in original or alternative locations significantly slowed the process of assigning property rights to all agricultural land and the restructuring of the inherited large-scale farms. As of mid-1997, the restitution process had brought about transparent ownership for less than 50 percent of agricultural land, although more than 80 percent of land is now used by family-farm and household-plot operators.

The legal framework guiding the restitution and land privatization process has changed several times since independence. Although these changes have often removed obstacles that delayed completion of the land privatization process, the frequent revisions have also significantly slowed the process. At the beginning of the transition, land restitution was constrained by a host of restrictions that later had to be revised or removed. In the course of amending the original framework, however, new complications were sometimes introduced. On 16 January 1997, the process of restitution was suspended in order to enact new legislation that would provide increased opportunities for original landowners (including foreign residents) to receive land or compensation, increase the amount of land that was allowed for each original owner under restitution (agricultural land, from 80 to 150 hectares; forested land, from 25 to 150 hectares), make available more attractive compensation arrangements, and eliminate the obligatory lease to agricultural companies. The new amendments to the laws were designed to accelerate the process, but opening the process to a wider range of claimants may also cause further delays and increase the cost of restitution.

Altogether, about 500,000 claims were submitted for restitution of 3.5 million hectares of land. Of these, 89,000 claimants requested cash compensation, and 13,200 wanted forested land. By the end of 1997, about 165,000 claims were to be fully processed and 26,000 partially settled (representing about 30 percent of agricultural land). About 197,000 claims remain unsettled, which are, of course, the more difficult ones. The cash compensation is significantly constrained by the availability of financial resources. The amended restitution law has the potential to increase the number of claims by increasing the allowed size of restituted land and opening the process to heirs who are now foreign residents. According to government estimates, with the currently available resources, the completion of the restitution process will require another three to five years.

Land restitution has required an immense effort by the government. The process of surveying land, designing maps, identifying land use, and legally processing ownership documents has been extremely time-consuming and administratively and technically difficult. Administratively, land reform is being run by the National Land Survey under the Ministry of Agriculture and Forestry. Most of the administrative work is done in district agriculture boards and agrarian reform boards under the local authorities. Possibly more important than the recent legal changes, the organization and staffing of the National Land Survey has been restructured to increase the number of surveyors and streamline the administrative procedures.

SLOW DEVELOPMENT OF THE LAND MARKET. Closely related to the slow restitution process is the slow development of a real agricultural land market. The land market is constrained by the relatively low percentage of land that is actually registered and titled, the legal constraints restricting landownership to physical persons and the state, and the upper limit on individually owned land. Foreign legal persons, however, became eligible for landownership after the Association Agreement came into force. Only registered land can be legally sold or leased. There is no reliable information available on actual land sales, but according to estimates, the market is rather modest.

At the same time, there is a quite active lease market, which increased further and carried higher rents after compulsory leasing to agricultural companies was eliminated in mid-1997. The most significant land-trading activity is related to the purchase from the government of the household plots used in rural areas during the Soviet period. The current users have priority in purchasing the plots over former owners who might claim them. Of 340,000 household plots, about one-third of the owners have already purchased their plots with privatization vouchers. Another third of the users have included this land in their restitution claims. The remaining third of the cases are still unsettled.

ECONOMIC COSTS OF A POORLY FUNCTIONING LAND MARKET. One of the often-cited reasons farmers give for lack of creditworthiness is the lack of adequate collateral. In part, this problem will be solved as more landowners secure title to their land. Nevertheless, banks will continue to be reluctant to accept land as collateral unless this asset can first be acquired by a bank in foreclosure, and then sold in a reasonable period of time for a price that can be evaluated in advance. This cannot be the case unless legal entities, including banks, are permitted to own land, and the land market is sufficiently active to establish a relatively predictable market value. In addition, the currently fragmented landownership pattern in Lithuania demonstrates the clear need for consolidation of landholdings to form a more competitive production structure of viable commercial farms. Current landowners who wish to grow and become more competitive are constrained by the lack of land to purchase, as well as the lack of the long-term credit they would need to purchase it. Extensive leasing arrangements are currently a substitute for a real land market, but private investment in a farm is constrained when it depends primarily on leases of uncertain duration and cost. The development of a competitive, commercial agriculture is thus severely constrained under present conditions.

AGRO-INDUSTRY PRIVATIZATION. The privatization of industry and commerce, as in other central European countries, was one of the major initial objectives of Lithuanian economic reform. With respect to privatization in agro-industry, there is good news and bad news. The good news is that 80 percent of the enterprises are completely privatized, and these enterprises include 56 percent of the employees and nearly half of the foreign capital in the industry (table 4-20). But these firms represent only one-third of the total statutory capital in the food chain. The bad news is that nearly 36 percent of the capital in the industry is in enterprises with state ownership of 50 percent or more, although these represent only 5 percent of the firms and have only 13 percent of the employees. These are clearly the larger and more capital-intensive enterprises, and they have attracted no foreign investment. Although the definition of a food chain enterprise includes nonfood activities, it appears that in the total food chain, the government thus retains an average of 35 percent of shares, and foreign capital represents only 13 percent of statutory capital.

Table 4-20. Capital Structure of Food Chain Enterprises in Lithuania, September 1997
(percent)

State ownership	Enterprises	Employees	State capital	Private capital	Foreign capital	Total capital
Zero	79.6	55.9	0.0	48.4	48.5	31.5
1 to 9	6.2	13.6	1.5	18.2	30.8	14.1
10 to 29	6.5	11.6	7.4	15.4	13.1	12.4
30 to 49	2.6	5.4	6.7	5.8	7.0	6.2
50 to 99	2.8	9.7	72.1	12.6	0.5	31.6
100	2.2	3.8	12.4	0.0	0.0	4.3
Total	100.0	100.0	100.0	100.0	100.0	100.0

Note: Companies are classified by NACE code, based on the largest business enterprise in the company, but the data reported are for the entire company, not just the food and beverage enterprise. The total food chain is defined to include agro-service as well as wholesale and retail enterprises.
Source: Computed from Lithuanian Department of Statistics data.

FARMER PRIVATIZATION. The first phase of privatization of agro-industry, launched in 1992, achieved only limited results, mainly because of a lack of interested buyers and the complicated procedures for preparing privatization plans (see Chapter 5). A number of enterprises took the opportunity to privatize shares to employees and management, but in many cases, that still left the government with about half the shares. Then, in an effort to empower farmers in their dealings with agro-service and processing enterprises, the government launched a farmer privatization program in 1994 that included 234 of the firms involved in these activities. Shares in these firms were eventually offered to the agricultural raw material producers on very favorable terms (2.5 percent of their nominal value), and by September 1997, the process was nearly completed. Of the 234 firms involved, 13 are now bankrupt or liquidated, and government ownership in the remaining 221 firms has been reduced to an average of 14 percent (table 4-21). Nearly half of these enterprises are completely privatized, and about 80 percent have at least 95 percent of statutory capital in private hands.

Table 4-21. Degree of Privatization in Upstream and Downstream Industries, September 1997

Type of enterprise	Number	Statutory capital (million Lt)	Assets privatized (percent)
Agro-service	77	87.0	93.1
Land reclamation	45	67.8	91.7
Crop selection	9	8.2	99.1
Livestock breeding	13	1.4	90.0
Meat processing	11	86.7	80.8
Milk processing	30	261.4	77.3
Fruit and vegetable processing	7	4.5	98.8
Grain processing	21	147.3	96.7
Sugar refineries	4	98.5	90.7
Flax processing	4	13.5	75.3
Total with farmer privatization	221	776.3	86.5
Total food and beverage manufacture	421	1,789.4	59.5
Total food chain	1,527	2,274.6	65.4

Note: See note to table 4-20.
Source: Lithuanian Ministry of Agriculture and Forestry and Lithuanian Department of Statistics.

Despite these achievements, there remain many companies with a small percentage of government shares, and a significant number of large companies with controlling government shares. Moreover, there is still very little foreign investment in agro-industry, although foreign investment is a key factor in gaining access to the needed capital and experience necessary to rapidly develop a modern, competitive, and efficient upstream and downstream industry. The inability of agro-industries to produce products of the quality required by international markets, and to market them competitively, is a serious constraint for the entire rural sector.

Changing market and policy conditions caused a sharp reduction in both farm product supply and consumer demand (both domestic and external), as well as an increase of competition in the domestic market (created by the liberalization of trade policies and growing imports), so the large-scale food industry enterprises often found themselves with excess capacity, outdated technology, and underdeveloped input supply and output marketing infrastructures. The low rate of capacity utilization, combined with poor efficiency and the limitations on the ability to reduce costs created by inefficient technology, also contributed to growing product unit cost and, in some cases, bankruptcies. At the same time that successor agroprocessing industries are working far below capacity, a large number of smaller-scale, fully private, modern, and more competitive agroprocessing enterprises have been established. This trend reflects the slow pace and difficulties of restructuring within the inherited agroprocessing structures.

Strategy for Further Rationalization of Domestic Market Support and Trade Policies

AGRICULTURAL SUPPORT PROGRAMS. The evolution of the macro policy environment and the incentive framework has been one of the most critical and debated components of the transition process in the sector. The recent trend indicates a move toward supporting the development of a competitive farming sector by gradually abolishing price subsidies and supporting farm incomes through direct payments and investment support, as well as reducing the level of market protection.

The National Agricultural Program (NAP) was a fund for direct subsidies, credit programs, infrastructure investment, research, and extension support that accounted for about 70 percent of total agricultural budget expenditures from 1994 to 1995. In 1994, about half of NAP funds were used to establish soft credit funds for farmers and processors. In subsequent years, about half of NAP funds were used for the farm price subsidies introduced in 1995. The largest portion of these subsidies went to cattle and milk producers.

The minimal marginal purchase price (MMPP) was the major component of market regulation in 1995 and 1996. Price support measures implemented in 1995 included MMPPs for specified quantities of farm products, direct subsidy payments to farmers for a subset of these products, and periodic ad hoc interventions that included government stock purchases and temporary export subsidies. These programs were not well targeted, and in many cases provided conflicting incentives to private decisionmakers. Thus they contributed neither to quality improvements nor to the development of an efficient farming structure, but the measures did put additional pressure on the budget. Inasmuch as the MMPP was intended as a floor price, this program could be compared with the intervention price system in the EU. The government had no intervention system, however, and had to rely on private processing enterprises to implement this scheme. The levels of these support prices compared with farm prices indicates that MMPPs and subsidies in 1995 were high enough to distort price signals to producers in many cases, and were even more distorting at the higher 1996 levels.

RURAL SUPPORT FUND. At the beginning of 1997, the new government initiated a series of changes in these programs to integrate all support measures under the framework of the Rural Support Fund (RSF). The reform of agricultural support programs includes several measures: (1) reform of the MMPP by eliminating or reducing the levels and quotas for MMPPs and targeting direct payments to higher-quality products; (2) decreasing the amount and increasing the transparency of credit subsidies; (3) creation of a Rural Credit Guarantee Fund; and (4) introduction of investment grant programs. These programs are spelled out in a public document that includes all provisions and procedures, which indicate that support will be allocated in a much more targeted, demand-driven, and transparent fashion. The subsidized credit programs were replaced by targeted investment grants, a Rural Credit Guarantee Fund, and a copayment system for interest on short-term bank loans for fuel, fertilizer, and chemicals. Except for market regulation, implementation of all RSF programs is carried out at the district level.

The goal of these reforms is to provide a more targeted, more transparent, more cost-effective, and less distorting support system for farms and rural communities. If a farmer, rural entrepreneur, or group of entrepreneurs prepares an investment project in one of the targeted areas and is found creditworthy by a bank, he or she can compete for a grant equal to 25 percent of the investment cost. Competitions are to be held publicly in each district, and recipients of grants will be announced publicly. In addition, Lt 20 million was allocated as the government contribution to a market-driven Rural Credit Guarantee Fund. In other significant actions, the new government revoked the 12 percent increase previously announced (in July 1996) to the MMPP plus subsidy levels for products covered by the price support program for 1997.

Beginning in the second quarter of 1997, the Ministry of Agriculture and Forestry also implemented major reforms in the price support programs by reducing the number of commodities subject to MMPPs and subsidies, freezing or limiting increases in the levels of the remaining supports, and targeting higher-quality production. These changes included the complete elimination of MMPPs for barley, feed grains, lowest-grade flax straw, and lowest-grade pigs. MMPPs for higher-grade pigs, feed legumes, and buckwheat were kept at the same level as in 1996, while food wheat, rye, rapeseed, and the highest-grade flax straw increased slightly (the largest increase was 10 percent, for highest-grade flax straw). Direct subsidy payments were eliminated for the lowest grade of pigs and the lowest grade of flax straw; they were increased for highest-quality flax and rye; and they remained the same for other products. The cattle subsidy was targeted to discourage the marketing of young calves for veal. There is now no subsidy for slaughtered veal, and headage payments are only paid to farmers for heavier animals marketed in the higher-grade classes. On August 1, a direct subsidy payment of Lt 70 per ton was introduced for the 200,000-ton food-wheat quota. With the same guaranteed price (MMPP plus subsidy), the introduction of a subsidy reduces the MMPP (and thereby market price) by an equivalent amount, and thereby reduces the market distortion. On September 1, the support program for pigs was eliminated completely.

The quotas that determine the amount of the product that is eligible for MMPPs and subsidies were drastically reduced for crops. The grain quota is 33 percent lower than in 1996, and the total crop quota is 10 percent below 1996. Quotas are no longer used as an instrument in cattle and milk programs. But these quotas, unlike the quotas for grains, have been at least as large as the quantity processed by participating plants, and this change has little effect except to reduce administrative costs.

Based on increasing pressure from farm groups and supported by higher government levels, in July the Ministry of Agriculture and Forestry (MoAF) revised its price and subsidy support strategy of April 1997 and raised the support levels for milk producers. This led to an increase of 7.3 percent in MMPPs and subsidies on 1 August 1997. These levels are still well below those set by the previous government for 1997, but they will delay the overall direction of the effort by MoAF to reduce market distortions. This development underscores the need for a broadly supported, longer-term policy framework that would provide greater stability in the policy and economic environment for decisionmakers.

AGRICULTURAL BUDGET. The agricultural budget of Lithuania has been increasing since 1994, but at a rate that has caused it to remain nearly constant in real terms (table 4-22), and to increase in U.S. dollars, because of the real appreciation of the litas (figure 4-4). The total agricultural budget remained approximately 10 percent of the total state budget from 1994 to 1996; but as a share of GDP, agricultural GDP, and the value of agricultural production, the total budget and the subsidies have been declining gradually (the agricultural budget in 1996 was 1.7 percent of GDP). About one-third of the 1997

Figure 4-4. Agricultural Budget Allocation

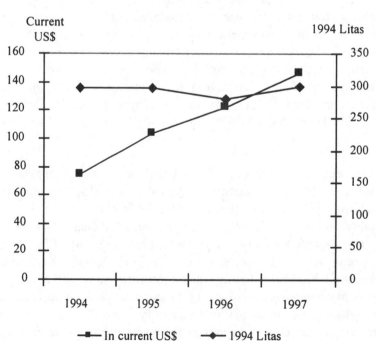

Table 4-22. Agriculture Budget Expenditure, 1994–96
(Lt thousand)

Item	1994	1995	1996
1. Financing of agricultural agencies	69,856	70,511	92,145
2. Strategic food and seed reserves	12,480	29,175	27,000
3. Capital investment	8,465	3,930	4,539
4. Compensation for agricultural land and forest	0	0	11,000
5. Ministry of Agriculture	3186	4,184	6,687
6. National agricultural program	202,900	305,500	347,541
6.1. Farm price subsidies	27,700	140,300	195,000
6.2. Net cost of intervention stocks	0	17,000	14,200
6.3. Subsidy for dairy mixes for babies	0	0	450
6.4. Credit programs	101,700	34,600	20,428
6.5. Restructuring grants to farmers in low-productivity land	0	13,800	12,354
6.6. Farm establishment and infrastructure	37,000	34,700	42,918
6.7. Subsidies for quality breeds and seeds	1,300	7,900	14,493
6.8. Liming of acid soils	0	16,000	0
6.9. Financing of breeding program	5,300	11,000	17,450
6.10. Agricultural research and extension	4,100	8,200	12,180
6.11. Development of organic production and removal of pollution	3,500	3,750	2,673
6.12. Development of cooperation and agro-service	6,400	0	10,835
6.13. Other	15,900	18,250	33,624
Total	296,887	413,300	517,976
(In 1994 Lt)	296,887	296,060	296,835

Source: Lithuanian Ministry of Agriculture and Forestry.

agricultural budget has been allocated for financing agricultural agencies to maintain strategic food and seed reserves, as well as for public investment and to cover the cash compensation of land restitution (table 4-23). The capital investment program has been significantly reduced for 1997, while there is an almost fourfold increase in the funds available for cash compensation to accelerate the restitution process. Lithuania has provided significant funds for the direct and indirect support of agricultural producers in recent years, and this accounts for about two-thirds of agricultural budget allocations.

AGGREGATE MEASURE OF SUPPORT. Although there are many conceptual problems in the application of producer subsidy equivalents (PSE) calculations in transition economies such as Lithuania, it is nevertheless a way of comparing similar countries through some aggregate measure of support. By this measure, the PSE coefficient for Lithuania was positive, at 14 percent, in 1996. Accordingly, in 1996, Lithuania had a support level about one-third of the level in the EU, slightly below the average in other CEECs, and about twice that in Estonia or Latvia (figure 4-5). Because the PSE methodology assumes that domestic price levels reflect levels of market support, the PSE has been increasing with time, partly because domestic prices are converging on world price levels, and partly because of increased direct payments (table 4-24). In support per hectare of agricultural land, Lithuania's PSE is three times the levels in Estonia and Latvia, and far below those in Hungary and Poland (table 4-25). Another indicator is the relative importance of different types of support. Here, Lithuania seems to rely more on direct payments compared with other CEECs; the proportions more closely resemble those seen in the EU and the United States. While direct payments are considered to be less distorting than market price supports, they still distort market signals to producers.

147

Table 4-23. Agriculture Budget Estimate for 1997 Compared with 1996
(Lt thousand)

Item	1996 Expenditure	1997, Projected
1. Financing of agricultural agencies	92,145	110,874
2. Strategic food and seed reserves	27,000	26,395
3. Capital investment	4,539	1,224
4. Restitution compensation for land and forest	11,000	40,000
5. Ministry of Agriculture and Forestry (MoAF)	6,687	7,379
6. Rural Support Fund (NAP in 1996)	376,605	397,000
6.1. Total at disposal of the MoAF	376,605	307,000
6.1.1. Farm Price Subsidies	195,000	210,000
Cattle	83,300	80,000
Pigs	15,800	10,600
Milk	70,700	75,700
Rye	4,600	5,700
Rapeseed	2,300	3,400
Feed legumes	3,800	4,000
Buckwheat	500	2,000
Flax	14,000	15,000
Export subsidies	0	13,600
6.1.2. Subsidies for quality breeds and seeds	14,493	16,000
6.1.3. Credit interest subsidy for fuel, fertilizer, and chemicals	20,428	10,000
6.1.4. New technology and machinery	0	4,000
6.1.5. Plant and animal breeding	17,450	18,000
6.1.6. Ecological farming	2,673	4,000
6.1.7. Expansion of production quality research system	0	2,000
6.1.8. Research, advisory service, information service	12,180	23,000
6.1.9. Rural Loan Partial Guarantee Fund	0	20,000
6.2. Total at disposal of Regional Agriculture Boards	0	90,000
6.2.1. Investment Grants Program	0	80,000
6.2.2. Disaster Assistance Program	0	10,000
6.3. Net cost of intervention stocks	14,200	0
6.4. Subsidy for dairy mixes for babies	450	0
6.5. Grants to farmers with low-productivity land [a]	12,354	*
6.6. Farm establishment and infrastructure [a]	42,918	*
6.7. Development of cooperation and agro-service [a]	10,835	*
7.0. Development of fisheries and processing	0	1,235
8.0. Other (ad hoc interventions)	33,624	0
Total	517,976	584,107
(In 1994 Lt)	296,835	298,069

a. Similar programs are carried out under the investment grants program (6.2.1).
Source: Lithuanian Ministry of Agriculture and Forestry.

Figure 4-5. Aggregate PSEs in 1996, Various Countries

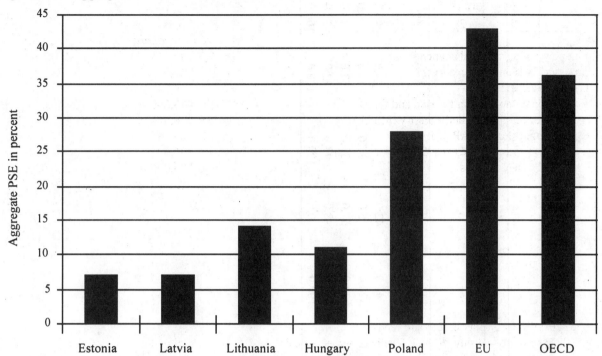

Table 4-24. Summary of Aggregate PSEs for Selected CEEC, EU, and OECD

Country/group	1993	1994	1995	1996
Estonia	-30	-6	3	7
Latvia	-38	9	8	7
Lithuania	-33	-8	6	14
Czech Republic	25	20	14	10
Hungary	23	29	16	11
Poland	15	22	21	28
Slovakia	35	31	25	19
European Union	49	49	49	43
OECD countries	42	42	40	36

Source: OECD, *Agricultural Policies in Transition: Monitoring and Evaluation 1997; Statistical annex* (Paris, 1997).

Table 4-25. Composition of Agricultural Support in Lithuania and Selected Countries, 1996

Item	Lithuania	Latvia	Estonia	OECD	EU	United States	Australia	Czech Republic	Hungary	Poland
					US$ per hectare					
PSE per hectare of agricultural land	50	13	17	161	745	63	3	76	104	291
					Percentage					
PSE	14	7	7	36	43	16	9	10	11	28
Type of support										
Market price support	69.8	44.4	85.5	60.0	51.0	47.0	42.0	-2.0	24.0	99.0
Direct payments	24.5	11.1	0.0	23.0	33.0	20.0	5.0	17.0	11.0	0.0
Other support	23.4	44.4	26.6	18.0	16.0	33.0	61.0	37.0	53.0	13.0
Feed adjustment + levies	-17.7	0.0	-12.1	-1.0	0.0	0.0	-8.0	48.0	12.0	-12.0
Total	100.0	100.0	100.0	100.0	100.0	100.0	100.0	100.0	100.0	100.0

Source: OECD, various publications.

TAX POLICY. Agriculture in Lithuania received significant tax preferences up to 1997. Recent government decisions reduced some of these indirect subsidies, but tax preferences remain significant. Agricultural companies are given a preferential profits tax rate of 10 percent, compared with a 29 percent rate for other legal entities. The income tax schedule for individual farmers provides a zero tax rate for those who receive 50 percent or more of their incomes from farming. It is unlikely that the income-share test can be enforced, since there is no universal income reporting system in Lithuania. Nevertheless, even these preferential tax rates were waived for agricultural companies and individual farmers every year until 1 January 1997, at an estimated cost of Lt 60 million annually. The waiver of income and profit tax obligations for farmers has not been extended, although farmers still benefit from preferential tax rates. A land tax was introduced in 1992 at a basic rate of 1.5 percent of land value, but it was only to take effect three years after land had been recorded in the registry. The three-year exemption is expiring on land acquired in 1994 and earlier, and collection of the land tax has begun. Those who did not farm the land themselves were required to pay the land tax immediately after registration of the land.

Since the introduction of the VAT in May 1994, and up until January 1997, there was a preferential VAT rate for domestically produced food and agricultural products (9 percent rather than the standard 18 percent on other products). In addition to the implicit subsidy for food products relative to nonfood items, this VAT preference also provided increased protection for domestically produced food products over imported products, which were taxed at the 18 percent rate. These VAT preferences were estimated to cost the budget about Lt 200 million annually in lost revenues before they were discontinued on 1 January 1997.

TRADE POLICIES. The development of trade policy proceeded from the implementation of quantitative restrictions, including export bans and licensing, toward more consistent and transparent trade regulations. External pressures to establish consistent and transparent trade policies led to elimination of nontariff barriers and a switch to the use of mostly ad valorem tariffs. Bilateral and multilateral agreements enforced this process. On 1 April 1995, a government resolution established a differentiated tariff system that includes most-favored nation, MFN (conventional); preferential (under free trade agreements); and autonomous tariffs. Tariff rates are set by government resolution and other legal acts that do not require Parliament's approval. More consistent trade policies are beginning to emerge, and they have begun to harmonize the trade regime with domestic and world market conditions and constraints. Under the 1994 EEF Arrangement with the IMF, Lithuania reduced average tariff rates on a specified basket of food products from 44 percent to 35.2 percent in October 1995, and to 27.5 percent in October 1997. Further tariff reductions did not take place after the Arrangement with the IMF was renegotiated in early 1997, and tariff levels have remained essentially unchanged since then. Import tariffs range from 20 to 30 percent for most agricultural and food products, except for butter, at 45 percent, and sugar, which was tariffed at 87 percent in 1997 (table 4-26).

The tariff rates are generally lower than those in Latvia, and substantially lower for most products than the WTO bound tariff rates of the Visograd countries (table 4-27). Latvia and Poland also still use specific tariffs that no longer exist in Lithuania. Lithuania's MFN rates are similar to the minimum access tariff rate commitments made by the Visograd countries in the Uruguay Round Agriculture Agreement for limited quantities of imports (table 4-28).

Lithuania does not have a significant or regular system of export subsidization. In 1995, there were limited export subsidies for butter, cheese, and canned milk. There was also an export subsidy for pork and ad hoc export restrictions for a few other products. In 1996 and 1997, export subsidies were paid on tenders to export beef surpluses to Russia. In general, however, export measures have been sporadic, and less important than import measures.

Table 4-26. Import Tariffs for Main Agricultural and Food Products in Lithuania, 1997
(percent)

Commodity	MFN rate	Autonomous rate
Live cattle	20	25
Live pigs	20	25
Live poultry	20	25
Beef and veal	30	30
Pig meat	30	30
Poultry meat	25	25
Milk and dairy products	20	20
Butter	45	45
Fermented and cottage cheese	30	35
Eggs	30	30
Potatoes	20	20
Grain	30	35
Wheat and rye flour	30	35
Combined feed	30	35
Sugar	87	87
Bakery products	30	35

Note: MFN, most-favored-nation.
Source: Lithuanian Ministry of Agriculture and Forestry.

Table 4-27. Comparison of MFN Tariff Rates in Selected CEECs
(percent)

Product	Czech Republic, 1995	Slovak Republic, 1995	Poland,[a] 1995	Hungary, 1995	Lithuania, 1997	Latvia, 1995
Cattle	61–115	61–115	20, max. 1,454/t	47	20	30
Beef	40	39–43	30, max. 4,740/t	112	30	30
Pork	30	24	129, max. 1,400/t	61	30	45
Poultry meat	54	54	120, max. 2,005/t	61	25	30
Sausage	20	20	140, max. 2,400/t	60	14	45
Eggs	20	20	100, min. 164/1000	30	30	30
Milk powder	50	50	160, min. 2,857/t	80	20	30
Butter	69	77.7	160, max. 3,614/t	159	45	45
Cheese	10	10	250	105	30	45
Potatoes	69	10	200	52	20	30
Wheat, durum	25	25	40	50	0	25 Ls/mt
Wheat, other	25	25	100, min. 150/t	50	30	25 Ls/mt
Other grains	25	25	80, min. 145/t	41–50	30	75 Ls/mt
Sugar	70	70	120, min. 0.53/kg	80	87	120 Ls/mt

a. Poland-specific rates are in ECU.
Note: MFN, Most-favored-nation.
Source: CEFTA countries from A. Pouliquen, "Agro-food Dynamics and Competitiveness in Central Europe: Implications for the EU Enlargement," in *Agricultural Accession of the CEECs to the European Union* (Budapest: Institute for World Economics of the Hungarian Academy of Sciences, 1997) and selected UR commitment schedules; Lithuania, from Lithuanian MoAF; Latvia, from World Bank EC4NR *Agriculture Policy Note* No. 3.

Table 4-28. Comparison of WTO Minimum Access Rates with Lithuanian MFN Rates

Product	Minimum access rates (3–5 percent of domestic consumption)				Lithuania, MFN rates, 1997
	Czech Republic, 1995	Slovak Republic, 1995	Poland,[a] 1995	Hungary, 1997	
Cattle	30	20	20	15	20
Beef	30	30	30	15–25	30
Pork	30	25–30	30	15–25	30
Poultry meat	24	30	30 or 0.3/kg	35	25
Sausage	20	20	35	25	14
Eggs	20	20	25 or min 0.03/pc	35	30
Milk powder	30–35	30–35	40	30	20
Butter	32	32	40	60	45
Cheese	10	10	35	50	30
Potatoes	50	50	50	10	20
Wheat, durum	7	7	20	10	0
Wheat, other	7	25	25	10	30
Other grains	7	25	20	3	30
Sugar	70	70	40, min 0.17/kg	80	87

a. Poland-specific rates are in ECU.
Note: MFN, Most-favored-nation.
Source: Minimum access rates from OECD; Lithuania, from Lithuanian MoAF.

Lithuania, like many other countries with fledgling customs services, has had difficulty dealing with undervaluation of imported goods. In response to this problem, the Seimas introduced a system of threshold prices in the 1994 law, but these instruments were never implemented. It is unclear how these would be set, and they would not survive negotiations with the World Trade Organization (WTO) on accession. Moreover, the implementation mechanisms would be very costly and would require additional institutional development and personnel training. There is, however, a reference price that is used to assess the sugar tariff. This means that the actual tariff is about twice as high as it would have been if it were calculated from world market prices. This is a form of protection that was extended to grain and grain products in July 1997, but will be eliminated at the time of accession to WTO.

FREE TRADE AGREEMENTS. Since independence, Lithuania has signed a series of bilateral trade agreements with neighboring countries, and also with the EU and EFTA. The Baltic Free Trade Agreement (BFTA), signed in 1994, has included free trade provisions for farm products since January 1997. Trade with CIS countries has been through a period of difficulties, although Lithuania now has trade agreements with most of these countries, and the region is a major market for meat and dairy products. The Central European Free Trade Association (CEFTA) countries have become significant trading partners, and Lithuania is actively working to join CEFTA once its membership in the WTO has been approved and bilateral free trade agreements have been signed with all CEFTA members.

WTO. Lithuania is in the final stages of negotiating its membership in WTO, having had observer status in the General Agreement on Tariffs and Trade (GATT) since 1992. Many of the major steps necessary to bring Lithuania's trade policies in line with WTO regulations have already been completed. There are, however, several important outstanding issues yet to be resolved. Membership in WTO will definitely encourage greater consistency and transparency in Lithuania's agricultural trade policies and will support the emergence of an internationally competitive sector.

URGENT POLICY ISSUES. Although the government has made significant progress in reducing market distortions, this progress has been achieved primarily by increasing direct subsidy payments that send price signals to producers that are inconsistent with market realities and continue to strain budget resources. Moreover, the continued use of MMPPs for some products in the absence of government intervention authority puts pressure on the private processing industry to pay prices that are, at times, above market-clearing levels. These problems have recently been most notable in the wheat, dairy, and sugar markets.

When world market prices for wheat fell in 1997, the MMPP (although only for a small portion of high-quality food wheat) was too high, and the government was obliged to introduce a direct payment (Lt 70 per ton) to reduce the purchase price. The cost to the budget was Lt 14 million, which had to be covered by reallocations within fixed budget resources. In the case of milk, more than 90 percent of processed milk is used for manufactured products, half of which are exported. These products must be competitive in the world market, and attempts by the government to increase the purchase price can lead to surplus products with no market. There is some evidence that the MMPP on second-grade milk has reduced the premium that processors would normally pay for higher-quality milk.

Sugar policy is by far the most distorting of all. Because of the 1995 Sugar Law that established a minimum explant price for processed sugar, competition among domestic plants is curtailed. Since this price is currently Lt 2.5 a kilogram ($625/ton), an effective tariff of over 100 percent is required to maintain competitiveness in the domestic market. As already noted, this is achieved by using a reference price in assessing the import tariff, making the tariff prohibitive. Since application of such a tariff would destroy the export potential of the domestic confectionery industry, tariff rate quotas with zero duty on sugar are permitted to allow the food industry to produce exportable products. Thus, a new sugar policy must be formulated in the near future to bring the sugar regime into compliance with WTO requirements.

Policies to Facilitate Restructuring of the Agricultural and Rural Economy

Since 1990, the share of employment in the agricultural sector has increased by a fifth (to 24 percent), while the share of agriculture in GDP has remained stagnant (at about 11 percent in normal weather years). These trends were partially the result of widespread restitution of land, and, while the statistics may overstate the case, they suggest that agricultural employment has been a safety net in the early years of the transition (albeit at income levels that are well below the economy's average). The rural population has remained fairly stable at one-third of the population, even though unemployment rates in rural areas have been rising more rapidly than in urban areas. The reduction of subsidies, opening of trade, and privatization or liquidation of food industry enterprises will very likely put further strain on rural employment and income levels. This creates important externalities in fostering integrated rural development and farm labor retraining programs that public policy may need to address.

In the Soviet era, most of the rural population was employed directly or indirectly in agriculture, and rural services were largely provided by the state and collective farms. When these farms were reconstituted during the privatization and restructuring of farming systems, rural services often suffered severely, and the existing infrastructure was not suitable for the increasing number of homestead farms.

Despite the shortcomings of the infrastructure, rural areas in Lithuania have the potential to develop a viable local economy. Extensive privatization, and the transition in general, has already resulted in a significant increase in rural trading services and small-scale production activities. Nevertheless, development of the nonagricultural rural economy still lags behind the development of agricultural activities; there remains a substantial opportunity for employment and income growth in rural service enterprises. Growth in the rural service sector has the dual benefit of creating jobs for workers displaced from agricultural employment and of creating a supporting infrastructure for a dynamic and competitive agriculture.

The role of the government in this integrated agricultural and rural development effort is not to plan or impose, but rather to provide guidance and create an enabling environment that will allow farmers and other rural entrepreneurs to exploit the opportunities that are presented to them. Such an environment includes a stable and benign policy framework as well as basic infrastructure. Some of these rural infrastructure needs are the focus of the investment grants initiative in the Rural Support Fund. One of the least developed and most needed areas of infrastructure is rural financial services. Although most discussions of financial service needs in Lithuania and elsewhere focus on credit, individuals and businesses need access to deposit and financial transaction services as well as credit.

Access to credits for the agricultural sector has been very limited and complicated, despite numerous efforts to improve it. The situation is similar for nonagricultural rural entrepreneurs. The Agriculture Bank, one of the state-owned banks, has remained the dominant source for rural credits. High transaction costs brought about by lack of information and experience, as well as the absence of sufficient and reliable collateral and land titles, are the main reason for other banks' reluctance to provide rural financing, especially for long-term investments. Moreover, under current law, banks as legal entities are not permitted to own agricultural land and cannot take landownership in foreclosure proceedings. Credit access is also very uneven among farm enterprises. Small farms and other small-scale rural entrepreneurs have scant access to outside financing, as neither the Agriculture Bank nor other banks in Lithuania have significant experience or the capacity to provide loans to small borrowers.

In the early part of transition, the government gave support to agriculture by subsidizing credits to farmers and farming enterprises, channeled through the Agriculture Bank. Interest subsidies were made available mainly for short-term credits for spring planting and the purchase of fuel. Funds were costly in terms of budget spending, but too small to have a considerable impact on the sector. Therefore, credit subsidy programs have recently been essentially phased out. When the Agricultural Support Fund under the National Agriculture Program was created in 1994, Lt 102 million was spent on "soft" credits. Government expenditures for agricultural credits decreased to only Lt 35 million in 1995 and 20 million in 1996 (table 4-22). In 1997 only Lt 10 million was allocated for interest credit subsidies for fuel, fertilizer, and chemicals (2.7 percent of the total agricultural budget), and Lt 20 million was provided for the Rural Credit Guarantee Fund (3.4 percent). Political loans that were implemented by the Agriculture Bank of Lithuania have now been separated from the commercial activities of the bank. The subsidized credit programs were replaced with targeted investment grants, the Rural Credit Guarantee Fund, and a co-payment system for interest on short-term bank loans for fuel, fertilizer, and chemicals.

While these new directions in farm credit and investment grant assistance are far less distorting than earlier capital grants and credit subsidies, government resources can only serve a limited number of farmers and rural entrepreneurs who need to be energized to stimulate rural development. By contrast, in countries where successful rural financial intermediaries have been established and have provided services to large numbers of small clients,[2] government resources have not been a constraining factor, the private companies providing the services have been very profitable, and the clients (borrowers) and their communities have been the ultimate beneficiaries. Thus, rather than operating credit programs, the government can be more effective by creating the legal and institutional mechanisms necessary to

2. R. A. Chaves and C. Gonzalez-Vega, "The Design of Successful Rural Financial Intermediaries: Evidence from Indonesia," *World Development* 24(1): 65–78.

stimulate the extension of financial services to rural entrepreneurs, large and small.

In general, the Lithuanian authorities may also need to identify impediments (legal and other) to the shedding of labor in the agricultural sector and to the creation of alternative employment and income opportunities in rural areas. The government will need to find an optimal strategy for attracting and utilizing potential pre-accession funding from the EU, with the overall objective of fostering sustainable integrated rural development as a long-term alternative to primary agricultural employment and related income support programs. Structural adjustment and infrastructure development in rural areas are very likely to be included in the pre-accession funding priorities of the EU.

Government Role in Institutional and Infrastructure Development

Lithuania has implemented significant institutional reforms to create the environment required by a market-based food and agriculture sector. Recent evaluation, however, indicates that institutional and legal frameworks in general, and in food and agriculture in particular, are not yet fully up to EU requirements. Further efforts are needed in this area, and the strengthening of government institutions for the provision of public goods comprises one of the most important tasks for the coming years.

MARKETING MECHANISMS. Wholesale markets, commodity exchanges, grades and standards systems, export promotion, market information, and the like are still in their infancy in Lithuania; there are important externalities in efficiently fostering their development. Timely information is lacking at all levels: farm, wholesale, retail, and external trade. Occasional price information is published in newspapers, but there is no system of regular market data collection, analysis, and dissemination for agricultural and food products. Nor is there a coordinated effort to disseminate external trade opportunities or technical and regulatory standards in foreign markets. The current needs of managing agricultural market policy, and EU accession particularly, require a speedy development of a modern, EU-conforming statistical information system in agriculture.

PUBLIC ADMINISTRATION. The government institutions in the agricultural sector have been reorganized more than once since independence. A Ministry of Agriculture and Forestry was created on 1 January 1997, combining two former ministries and allowing for a complete restructuring and restaffing according to the needs of a market-based agricultural sector. New functions related to EU integration and market economics were added, and at the same time there has been a significant change in the staffing of the ministry, bringing new and better-trained young staff to replace the older generation. The ministry has also been downsized, and the regional agricultural administrations have been given greater decisionmaking authority. These steps, however, are only the beginning of the changes in personnel requirements, skills, and training that will be needed to carry out administrative functions in the pre-accession and post-accession periods. The government will need to set priorities in implementing public investments in general support services (such as extension, research, and training), both as a demonstration effort and as a longer-term intervention. All this may set the stage for a redefinition of functions (and capacity upgrading) among the agriculture-related civil services.

Policy Recommendations

Completing Land Restitution and Privatization

LANDOWNERSHIP BY LEGAL ENTITIES. One key element to a smoothly functioning land market is adequate demand, which means removing the current limitations on who can own land. This does not necessarily mean that a land market needs to be completely free of government influence. It does mean, however, that regulations governing land sales should be designed to maintain proper records and ensure orderly and speedy transactions, rather than to restrict access. It means that legal entities as well as physical persons should compete in the land market.

CONTINUED IMPROVEMENTS OF LAND REGISTRATION AND TITLING. It is too early to know how well the 1997 changes in law and in implementation procedures and staffing are working to speed up the land privatization process. By government estimates, these changes will cut the completion time by half. Since the remaining cases are mostly those with disputed claims or insufficient documentation, the completion of the process is more than just a matter of having the time and technicians to do proper cadasteral work. Much of the difficulty is associated with two features of the Lithuanian restitution process. One was that too many legal heirs (including grandchildren) were given the right to claim land, and the second was that the initial right given to heirs was linked to the historical deed. As a result, there are problems associated with disputes among heirs, as well as difficulties in determining whether and how to substitute an alternative property or compensation for the ancestors if the land claimed is not available for restitution.

These problems are inherent in the process of restitution to former owners and their heirs. Restitution was a political imperative at the time of independence, and other countries that chose this basis for land privatization (principally Estonia and Latvia) have, if anything, made less progress than Lithuania. While this historical choice cannot be revisited, Lithuania has exacerbated the difficulties by adding new claimants to limited resources—earlier, grandchildren were added, and now foreign residents as well. It seems reasonable that the government should increase incentives for the claimants to accept vouchers or some other form of compensation. Any remaining government land allocated for privatization should then be sold.

LEVEL PLAYING FIELD FOR ALL FARMS. It is clear that in the process of privatization and restructuring of former state and collective farms into what are now referred to as agricultural companies, Lithuanian policy did not grant many favors to these farming entities. They are still considered to be a transitional form, and relatively few are expected to survive. It has already been mentioned that the compulsory leasing of land to these farms that was considered vital at the beginning of transition has now been eliminated. This was a kind of special privilege, but these farms have also been at a disadvantage in not being able to own land as a legal entity. The main emphasis of the government at this stage of transition should be to provide a level playing field for competitive farms to grow and flourish. Governments cannot know which size or organizational form may be best-suited for a given purpose in a developing agriculture, so it is best to let the farmer-entrepreneurs compete and find the most profitable means and organizational forms to conduct their business.

RAPID DIVESTITURE OF REMAINING GOVERNMENT SHARES. During 1997, twelve relatively large companies that were not included in the farmer privatization were prepared for privatization through the Privatization Agency. These companies have Lt 187.3 million in statutory capital; 63 percent is state-owned. This is an important step, but the procedures currently required by law are very cumbersome, time-consuming, and costly. With the current resources at the Ministry of Agriculture and Forestry, preparing several enterprises each year in keeping with these procedures would take years, but all indications are that the government wants to proceed more rapidly. Streamlined procedures need to be developed for all sectors (see Chapter 5), and applied as well to agro-industry. Where the government owns 20 percent or less of shares, it may be most efficient to sell shares on the stock exchange to quickly eliminate government ownership. If for some reason this fails, a less desirable option would be to cancel the shares or distribute them proportionately to current shareholders.

INCREASE THE TRADABILITY OF FARMER SHARES. It was noted that a major motivation of farmer privatization was to empower producers in dealings with input and processing enterprises. For this reason, the shares owned by farmers can only be sold to other producers. Farmers are not always better-off when they are shareholders in companies with whom they do business. If they actually controlled pricing decisions and decided to pay themselves higher product prices, they would merely drive their own company bankrupt, and be worse-off than before. (This did happen to a farmer-owned dairy processor in the Czech Republic.) Thus, to deprive the producer of the right to get the best possible price for his or her shares in a company is to make the producer less well-off than other shareholders in the same company. The farmer privatization should be viewed as a transition phase, not the end of the privatization process. In these companies, as in any other company, the tradability of shares is one mechanism to attract new capital by bringing new investors into the company. Essentially freezing half of the shares within a group of shareholders that have no investment capital puts that company at a disadvantage relative to companies that have no such restrictions—once again, to the disadvantage of the producers.

AVOID BAIL-OUTS. In the past, there has be a tendency to slow or prevent inevitable failures or bankruptcies. In an industry with such a large surplus capacity, this is damaging to the stronger companies that have a chance to become more efficient and competitive. If natural restructuring through liquidation and bankruptcy is allowed to occur, and to occur in a timely fashion, it will speed up the development of a competitive industry. Excess capacity in remaining firms will be reduced, and scarce capital will not be squandered on a failing enterprise.

ATTRACTING FOREIGN INVESTMENT. The measures already proposed will also have the effect of making the industry more attractive to foreign investors. There are agro-processing companies in Lithuania that have attracted significant foreign investment. Two of these are in the dairy processing business, which also has had the greatest number of bankruptcies. Their success does not owe itself to government support or special privilege, but rather to good management and ingenuity. The government, however, can make these companies less attractive by excessive regulatory or market intervention, or by prolonging the life of a failing competitor.

Rationalization of Domestic Market Support and Trade Policy

POLICY STRATEGY FOR THE FUTURE. As the current policy issues reveal, Lithuanian domestic market and trade policies need more than reform. These policies evolved in response to assorted domestic and international pressures, and it is evident that a consistent and durable policy strategy is needed. Lithuania is a small, open economy (as indicated by an openness index of 33 percent in 1996) that is a price taker on world markets and has significant levels of imports and exports of food and agricultural products. When the market institutions are adequately developed and market intermediaries are sufficiently experienced, domestic prices will reflect the border measures that are in place. Thus, domestic market policies and trade measures must be developed in a consistent framework. These measures should reflect well-defined policy objectives, which certainly need to place a high priority on building competitiveness in domestic and foreign markets.

In grains policy, the mechanisms adopted need to recognize that world prices fluctuate from year to year, and Lithuania can do nothing to influence those prices. The latest proposal for EU reform of the CAP would reduce the intervention price well below anticipated world market prices. As a prospective EU member, Lithuania should expect that the EU will have a cereal policy of that kind in effect by the year 2000. Producers and processors in Lithuania will need to be tuned to world market signals and learn how to manage risk. The government could facilitate that adjustment by replacing the current MMPP system with a risk sharing mechanism, such as a modest safety net program that would come into effect if prices fall below 70 or 80 percent of a selected average of past world market prices. This kind of mechanism would also provide a simple, self-adjusting, and stable long-term rule for minimal intervention that decisionmakers could anticipate. The disadvantage of such a safety net system is the associated budget uncertainty. Even though it would seldom be called into play, the timing and size of payments for such a safety net would be unpredictable. The best way to minimize budget exposure would be to set the safety net support percentage at a level that would seldom—if ever—be triggered. The current U.S. "loan rate" formula and the Hungarian intervention price are examples of safety net levels that are seldom triggered.

Even less distorting, and with less budget exposure, would be a partially subsidized insurance against yield and/or price risk. This is becoming a very significant approach in the United States, and it is well accepted by farmers. To develop an actuarially sound insurance product, however, requires a great deal of data that is not yet available in Lithuania. Since insurance products are very likely to be in demand commercially, whether or not they are used as a policy mechanism, it is very important to begin a process that would generate the necessary supporting data for this type of insurance in the future.

Dairy policy also needs to be market-oriented. Since a large portion of the produce is exported, competitiveness is essential. Support prices (MMPPs, or any other form) should be avoided, and any subsidies should be targeted to supplement private incentives for higher-quality milk production. A program that increases incentives for higher-quality milk and quality preservation will also contribute to competitiveness by reducing processing costs. It would, however, be preferable to avoid subsidies based on produced quantities altogether, since they provide producers with a higher production incentive than can be observed in the market. But if that type of subsidy is unavoidable, a simple and transparent rule such as a fixed direct subsidy payment per ton for highest- and first-grade milk that meets other sanitation and quality criteria would provide a better incentive structure. It would also be known well in advance, and once established, it would not be subject to two or three changes a year, as has been the case since 1995. The budget exposure could be estimated each year, based on projected price and production levels, and the payment rate could be set to keep expenditures within budgetary limits (the dairy-related subsidy budget allocation has been cut in half for 1998).

Sugar is a much more difficult issue, since it is currently highly distorted, not only in Lithuania, but in most temperate-climate countries as well. Lithuania can lead the way for other countries by introducing a forward-looking policy that recognizes the need to deregulate this industry. Given the goal to design a policy that is friendly to the dynamic Lithuanian confectionery industry, emphasis should be focused on support to farmers, rather than to processors or intermediate users of sugar. Farmers could be given a fixed payment per ton or hectare based on some portion of historical production. If this were provided to the farmer as a transferable quota right to a fixed or declining payment stream, it would allow for entry and exit, or even shifting of production among regions, as the quota is sold or transferred. Any production of sugar above or without the quota would receive only the market price, without any subsidy. The minimum explant price would have to be eliminated, with the sole market protection coming from an *ad valorem* tariff assessed to the world market price. This would hardly be a distortion-free mechanism, but such an approach would significantly reduce present distortions and would have some realistic chance of winning approval among the interested groups that influence policy decisions. The major difficulty in this approach is the cost, because no budget resources are used for sugar in the current programs. However, the consumer gains from lower prices would be sufficiently large that only a portion of these gains would be needed to compensate farmers.

Finally, policy formulations (for grain, dairy, sugar, and other agricultural products) should be designed for a period of four to five years to provide some measure of stability in the policy environment. Government and private decisionmakers would benefit from such stability. Farmers and agribusiness enterprises have plenty of risk and uncertainty to deal with on a daily basis, and they do not need the government to introduce more uncertainty through ad hoc and unpredictable policy changes.

Facilitating the Restructuring of the Agricultural and Rural Economy

The main challenge facing agriculture-related policymakers in Lithuania is to develop rural policies that provide a balance of economic opportunities and social conditions without distorting market signals. While past policies have tended to focus on support for farmers, the rural recovery in Lithuania requires a complex and comprehensive approach that would integrate agriculture into an overall rural development strategy that involves farm and nonfarm jobs and businesses. Such a strategy should include support for institutional and infrastructure development, as well as increased competitiveness of the agricultural and food industry.

RURAL FINANCIAL INSTITUTIONS. Technical assistance and public investments should be allocated to improve the institutional framework for financial transactions in rural areas that would serve both farm and nonfarm entrepreneurs, as well as individuals. This would include:

- Legislation that would permit greater use of the kinds of collateral generally available in rural areas, such as farm real estate, farm equipment, inventory, accounts receivable, warehouse receipts, and consumer goods.
- Improved public registries for collateral, especially for movable property.
- Implementation of credit bureaus to facilitate screening of credit applicants and to improve reputation-based incentives to honor credit contracts.

A pilot experiment with retail banking in rural areas should be initiated to demonstrate that retail lending to small farms and rural entrepreneurs is both feasible and profitable. A specific and detailed proposal for such a pilot project has already be developed in connection with the World Bank–supported Private Agricultural Development Program (PADP). A successful pilot project of this nature, in combination with the institutional innovations listed above, would stimulate private financial institutions to enter this market and establish enterprises or branches that provide financial services to small and micro rural entrepreneurs. By fostering financial institutions that are private, profitable, and compatible with the needs and conditions in rural areas, Lithuania can remove one of the major constraints to agricultural and rural development and provide an example that other CEECs can follow in addressing this pervasive rural credit problem.

RURAL INFRASTRUCTURE. Public investment in the improvement of roads, power and water supplies, telecommunications facilities, housing, and social services can contribute to rural economic development by allowing businesses to locate in rural areas without significant disadvantages in cost and quality of services or in communications with clients, suppliers, and professional associates. Some programs of this kind have already been initiated under the Rural Support Fund launched in 1997.

STABLE RULES OF THE GAME. The importance of a stable agricultural policy environment has already been emphasized as an important factor in reducing uncertainty for farmers and agribusiness enterprises. The same applies to other rural workers and enterprises. In addition, the growth in small-scale business activity in rural areas would be enhanced through stable rules of the game and proper incentives that reward initiative and entrepreneurship, such as secure property rights, contract sanctity protection, and tax policies that do not disadvantage small enterprises.

HUMAN CAPITAL. There is no doubt that agricultural employment will decline and labor productivity and incomes in agriculture will increase with time. However, those workers leaving agriculture will be much better off if they are pulled away from agricultural employment by higher earning opportunities elsewhere. This transition in the rural workforce will occur with less social tension if retraining programs are available to prepare farmers and farm workers to compete in growing sectors of the labor market. Experiences in United States and Europe indicate that many companies choose to locate in smaller towns rather than large cities if they can be assured of an adequate and well-trained labor pool.

INCREASED COMPETITIVENESS OF THE AGRICULTURE AND FOOD INDUSTRY. As Lithuania prepares for accession to the EU, it is essential that the agriculture and food industry become competitive in order to prosper within the Union. At the same time, the EU is gradually reducing its protectionism so that its industry can be more competitive in the global market, implying that Lithuania needs to focus on the world market. Achieving and maintaining competitiveness is primarily the task of the private sector, but the government can provide a policy environment that slows or speeds this process. The process is slowed when the government unduly protects the industry from competitive pressures, imposes excessive regulation or control (for example, administered pricing), or creates instability in policy or the macroeconomy. The government can speed up the process through investments in public goods such as improved marketing infrastructure, demonstration-type rural financial institutions, information services, and extension services. It is essential that the farm and the food processing and distribution industry be viewed together, since inefficiencies or quality deficiencies in either affect the competitiveness of the industry as a whole.

Government Assistance for Institutional and Infrastructure Development

The development of an efficient and effective public administration and the provision of public goods are a key task for the immediate future in light of EU accession. Aside from the institutional and infrastructure policy recommendations addressed in the previous section, the government has a vital role to play in providing agricultural statistics, market information, and policy analysis.

AGRICULTURAL STATISTICS. The statistics currently collected are inadequate to provide necessary information for monitoring, market information, and analysis of conditions in, and policy options for, the food and agricultural sector. The following information is missing:

- An annual statistics survey of farms is needed to provide information, by size and type of farm, on land use (owned, leased in, leased out, total operating area), farm crop production, yields, crop area, animal numbers, slaughter, births, production, productivity, input use (including labor), marketed and farm use of output, and product inventories at the end of the marketing year, as well as on cost and returns, land and assets, and financial balances. Because of the continuing change in farm structure, the best method would be to establish statistical sample-frame areas and to do a complete census within each area. Current categories of farms by type (agricultural companies, family farms, household farms) should be replaced by size categories using EU methodology. Crop and livestock inventories and livestock slaughter and replacement information should be updated quarterly. Planting intentions should be collected at appropriate times in the growing season to provide a basis for estimates of new crop production.
- A periodic survey of farm, wholesale, and retail prices in representative markets should be used to calculate national average prices at each level, at least quarterly.
- Annual balances should be produced by combining the production and inventory data above with consumption and trade data provided by other statistics sections in the Department of Statistics.

This is currently done for some products, but it needs to be extended to a wider list of products, including individual grains and some processed products such as beef, pork, chicken meat, fluid milk, butter, cheese, milk powder, and vegetable oil.

- Data should be reported in periodic publications of the Department of Statistics and provided in digital form to the units described below.

MARKET INFORMATION AND OUTLOOK UNIT. This unit would be established to provide the best available information on commodity markets to the widest possible audience as frequently as possible. This will help input suppliers, producers, processors, and other market intermediaries to make more informed decisions on production and marketing and will help the government in monitoring conditions and making informed policy decisions. This activity could be conducted in a unit set up within the Ministry of Agriculture and disseminated by various mechanisms, including the Farmer Advisory Services. It should include the following:

- Situation and outlook reports would be provided on market prices and balances, and updated based on the agricultural statistics noted above. This should done at least quarterly, but not more than monthly, and should include estimated production, disappearance, and prices for the next marketing year based on planting intentions and quarterly livestock statistics.
- Quarterly (or monthly) data should be supplemented with brief analyses of expected tendencies in the market in the current and next marketing year.

POLICY ANALYSIS UNIT. This unit would be established to provide policy options and analysis in support of policy decisionmaking and program implementation in the government and as a basis for discussion of options and impacts with representatives of producer, industry, and consumer interests. This unit should be somewhat removed from the Ministry of Agriculture to provide sufficient independence from political pressures and to increase the actual and perceived objectivity and credibility of analytical results. Both the Agribusiness Training Center and the International Agricultural Trade Agency would be possible locations, although neither currently has this mandate. The Training Center is recommended, because it has a well-developed training record, a domestic orientation, and a clientele base and physical facility that could more easily be adapted to these new tasks. However, professional staff and research facilities would have to be added to the center to carry out the new mandate. The unit should focus on the following activities:

- Data base systems and analytical tools should be developed to analyze the impacts of policy options for the food and agricultural sector and for rural economic development. A close working relationship with the Market Information and Outlook Unit described above would be necessary, both for data and analytical coordination and exchange of expertise.
- Drawing upon policy proposals, experiences, and analytical studies in Lithuania and other countries, alternative policy designs should be formulated in consultation with working groups including government and private sector representatives.
- The impacts of different policy options should be evaluated in quantitative and practical terms, including effects on farms, the food chain, consumers, trade, rural communities, government budget (taxpayers), and the national economy.
- Results of studies should be disseminated by conducting workshops and conferences, publishing briefing papers and reports, briefing government and Seimas officials, issuing press reports, and providing analytical summaries on the internet.

PUBLIC ADMINISTRATION AND REGULATION. Lithuania is already in the process of harmonizing inspection, certification, standards, and the like with EU regulations as specified in the Union's accession

White Paper and the *acquis communautaire*. This effort will also include an agenda for harmonization and strengthening of market institutions to enable them to deal with CAP measures. All of these tasks and their ultimate implementation require human capital investments, especially the training of civil servants in the national and local governments. The content of this training and its funding should certainly be a priority in the use of pre-accession funding from the EU.

5

PRIVATIZATION

Background

Lithuania's Privatization Achievements

VOUCHER PRIVATIZATION, 1991–95. Shortly after Lithuania left the former Soviet Union (FSU), the government launched a voucher privatization program that (i) restored agricultural land to former owners and provided land to former collective farm workers; (ii) moved housing from the state to private ownership; and (iii) moved the ownership of many small and medium-size enterprises from the state to private individuals. The program resulted in about 5,724 privatizations out of approximately 6,095 enterprises actually offered for sale. The total proceeds from voucher privatization were Lt 130.5 million (US$32.6 million), received by the State Privatization Fund, and Lt 18.5 million (US$4.6 million), received by municipalities.

Despite these successes, the program left a legacy of insider control, worker and management ownership, lack of good corporate governance, and poor access to capital and foreign ownership. For example, a number of companies fell into the hands of insider-controlled investment companies. There were also cases where significant firms fell into the hands of management groups and other insiders through an opaque process based on the best business plan presented.

CASH PRIVATIZATION, 1995–97. In 1995, the voucher privatization program came to an end and was succeeded by a program based on cash privatizations. A new privatization law, The Law on the Privatization of State-Owned and Municipal Property, was passed in mid-1995, and a new institution, the Lithuanian Privatization Agency, was established. Unfortunately, the law and its institutions have not been successful in promoting the privatization program. To 30 June 1997, only 140 firms (58 of these were sold by municipalities), totaling US$2.6 million in sales receipts, were privatized under the 1995 law, while total cash privatization receipts to the end of 1997 were only US$20.2 million. Table 5-1 summarizes the results of the cash privatization program from 1996 to July 1997. (No sales were made in 1995 under the program.)

CASE-BY-CASE PRIVATIZATION, 1997. In February 1997, the new Lithuanian government announced that it would privatize fourteen major Lithuanian state enterprises using the case-by-case method. Some, by a previous law, could not be privatized before the year 2000 and had to be removed

---

The "Background" section is based, in part, on B. Blaszeryk and Richard Woodward, "Privatization in Post Communist Countries" (Warsaw: The Center for Social and Economic Research, 1996, mimeo).

from the restricted list by government resolution. Table 5-2 presents details on the fourteen companies.

Table 5-1. Cash Privatization Results

	Central government	Municipalities	Total	Receipts (Lt '000)
Sales, 1996	27	20	47	3,234
Sales, 1997	218	192	410	91,323
Total	245	212	457	94,557

Source: Lithuanian Privatization Agency, July 1997.

Table 5-2. Case-by-Case Privatization, 1997

Industry group	Employees	Nominal value of state shareholding (Lt '000)	Activity
Geonafta	333	18,113.0	Oil exploration & exploitation
Lithuanian Radio & TV	593	57,317.6	Communications
Lithuanian Telekom	9,917	757,330.8	Communications
Lithuanian Oil	—	756,155.9	Distribution and sales company
Klaipeda Stevedoring (KLASCO)	2,321	116,089.9	Stevedoring services
Smelte Stevedoring	1,150	34,038.1	Stevedoring services
Western Shipyards	1,700	77,270.5	Ship repair
Lithuanian Shipping (LISCO)	2,001	37,7051.6	Seaferry transportation
Lithuanian Airlines	1,068	76,538.3	Air carrier
Air Lithuania	205	2,766.4	Air carrier
Hotel Lithuania	344	18,844.8	Hotel
Konas Aviation	54	7,760.7	Aircraft repair
Laivite	388	7,512.1	Ship building and repair
Baltija Shipbuilding Yard	1,560	11,257.2	Ship building
Total	10,791	2,318,046.9	

Source: Ministry of European Affairs, April 1997.

The Minister of European Affairs (MEA) has been charged with managing the privatization of these fourteen firms and has made progress, primarily by engaging financial (and other) advisers for Lithuanian Telekom and the Radio and TV Center, LISCO, KLASCO, Smelte Stevedoring, and units of Lithuanian Oil (Mazeikiai Oil Refinery and Lithuanian Fuel). The MEA, however, has had to work within the constraints of the 1995 law on privatization, which effectively spreads responsibility for selling state assets among a Privatization Commission, a Privatization Agency, and the "enterprise founder" (usually the relevant line ministries). It has thus been forced to coordinate three ad hoc steering committees of senior officials that have been set up to supervise the privatization work.

In parallel, the Ministry of Finance has begun the process of selling two of the three state-controlled banks. The first, the State Commercial Bank, was offered to the market twice recently, but unsuccessfully (and will be offered again). The privatization of the second, the Agricultural Bank, is moving forward with assistance from international financial advisers.

Progress continues to be slow on the privatization of some 1,100 smaller enterprises and holdings announced for privatization by the Lithuanian government in early 1997, including the disposal of a large number of minority government shareholdings in privatized enterprises.

On 1 December 1997, a new law on the privatization of state and municipal assets came into effect. The law is based on the 1995 privatization law but incorporates several major changes. A new agency, the State Property Fund (established under separate legislation), will now be responsible for privatization, having assumed the role of the enterprise founder (previously carried out by the line ministry), which was the key player under the 1995 laws. The fund is also expected to absorb the existing Privatization Agency; otherwise, the 1997 law remains similar in most key respects to the 1995 law it replaced.

Privatization Achievements in Central and Eastern Europe

In 1997, the World Bank published a comprehensive analysis[1] of the industrial restructuring that has taken place since 1992 in Bulgaria, the Czech Republic, Hungary, Poland, Romania, the Slovak Republic, and Slovenia. The study covered some 6,300 industrial firms and considered which government policies had been most effective in fostering enterprise restructuring. The results showed that privatization was by far the most important factor in restructuring and that privatized firms performed much better than those that remained state-owned. Labor productivity grew by an average of 7.3 percent yearly in privatized firms, but it declined by 0.2 percent annually in state-owned firms. The econometric analysis undertaken in the study indicated that *privatization accounted for almost all the growth in labor productivity*. The analysis also showed that privatization had increased annual total factor productivity growth by about 4 percentage points.

The study also found that privatized firms used the large productivity gains from privatization to finance needed investments. Labor productivity grew more rapidly than real wages in the privatized firms, while state-owned firms raised wages in spite of lagging productivity, which depleted their capacity to finance themselves through internal sources. The positive effects of privatization on the finances of privatized firms also had a positive effect on the banking system and made government intervention in the banking industry less necessary. In countries that had done little or no privatization, the continued weak financial situation of many state firms worsened the loan problems of banks.

A second study of 500 mid-size firms in the Czech Republic, Poland, and Hungary between 1991 and 1993 also compared the performance of privatized and state firms.[2] Not only did this study confirm that private ownership improved labor productivity and revenue, but it also found no evidence of any short-run disruption of the firms' performance immediately following ownership change. On the contrary, private ownership appears to dampen the shock of "marketization" resulting from the price liberalization and the removal of barriers to entry that characterize transitions away from central planning. All surveyed firms were forced to cut bloated payrolls, probe new markets after demand collapsed for their products, improve product quality, and reduce inefficiencies. Evidence from these firms indicates that private owners, in this regard, restructure more effectively than the state. (For details on both studies, see Annex 5-1.)

Privatization Revenues in Lithuania Compared with Central and Eastern Europe

Annual privatization revenues in Lithuania, as a percentage of GDP, have lagged those of Estonia and Latvia and are well below those of the "high performers" such as Hungary. While privatization has

---

1. Gerhard Pohl and others, *Privatization and Restructuring in Central and Eastern Europe*, World Bank Technical Paper No. 368 (Washington, D.C., 1997).

2. Roman Frydman and others, "Private Ownership and Corporate Performance: Some Lessons from Transition Economies" (unpublished manuscript, June 1997).

slowed since 1995 in most transition economies, revenues as a percentage of GDP have consistently fallen each year since 1993 in Lithuania. Annual revenues in the three years from 1993 to 1995 averaged just over 1 percent of GDP. The cash privatization program begun in 1996, however, brought in revenues that are less than one-twentieth of this amount—a 0.05 percent of GDP—and the results for 1997, up to July, are no better.

Analysis of privatization receipts in nine transition economies in central and eastern Europe confirms that countries that relied on voucher-based enterprise sales or mixed cash and voucher sales, as might be expected, lagged behind countries using traditional privatization methods—that is, case-by-case privatization or its variants. In addition, countries that registered average privatization-revenue-to-GDP ratios of less than 1 percent (Bulgaria, Lithuania, and Russia) typically suffered the most from insider-dominated enterprise sales, inadequate commercialization, and a lack of buyer demand. Figure 5.1 presents annual privatization revenues in selected eastern European countries, east-central Europe, and the Baltics from 1989 to 1996 (see Annex 5-2).

Figure 5-1. Privatization and Revenues in East-Central Europe and the Baltics

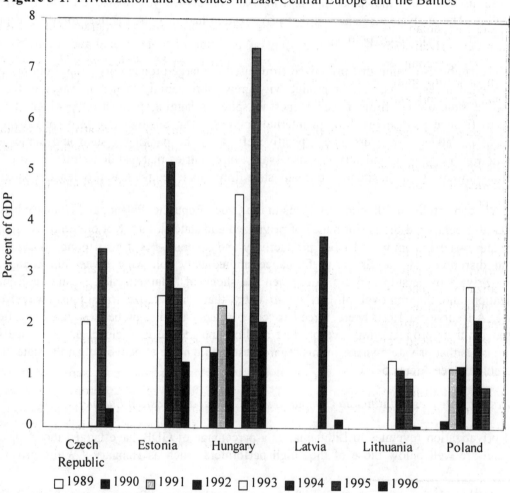

The Technical Impediments to Faster Privatization in Lithuania

Thus far it has been demonstrated that Lithuania's privatization performance has not been as successful as the records of other eastern European countries. This section attempts to identify the reasons for this. In general, the current cash privatization program, which was, until December 1997, based on legislation passed by a previous government, has major faults and weaknesses that seriously compromise the current government's ability to undertake privatizations. There are too many institutions involved. The role of the "enterprise founder" allows line or branch ministries to frustrate the privatization process. There is a serious lack of privatization knowledge (particularly pertaining to large, case-by-case privatizations) in some of the institutions responsible for the privatization process. There is a perceived reluctance to use qualified financial advisers who will be responsible for selling firms (and will be paid a commission on the sale). Valuation techniques do not reflect best practices. Transparency is often missing. There is a lack of leadership and perceived commitment to privatization. No institution is actively engaged in marketing the firms, and no institution pays a penalty if a sale is a failure. In brief, *the overall incentive structure is simply not conducive* to rapid privatization.[3]

Inadequacy of the Legal and Institutional Framework

In 1995, the Lithuanian government replaced the voucher privatization program with a cash program based on a new privatization law (The Law on Privatization of State-Owned and Municipal Property). This law and its accompanying institutional process proved to be ineffective and, by mid-1997, had resulted in only 140 small privatizations (58 were done by municipalities). The law established an institutional framework and hierarchy, including:

- The *enterprise founder*, usually the line ministry responsible for the privatization candidate
- The *Privatization Commission* (a supervisory body made up primarily of members of Seimas)
- The *Privatization Agency* (a technical, implementing institution)
- *Municipal privatization commissions* that undertake privatizations of local enterprises and property.

The enterprise founder effectively controlled the privatization process through control of the candidates put forward for sale, how they were restructured, the method used for divestment, the terms and conditions of the privatization, and by supervision of the implementation and conclusion of the sale. The Privatization Agency, on the recommendation of the enterprise founder, drafted privatization lists; noted the method, terms, and conditions of sale; looked for buyers; and suggested restructuring proposals. The Privatization Commission approved or vetoed programs put forth by the Privatization Agency and approved or disapproved transactions. (For a more detailed description, see Annex 5-3.)

Under the 1995 law, the enterprise founder had little incentive to sell enterprises, yet was responsible for choosing the companies to sell, seeing that they were valued properly, and designing the sales procedure (even though it was not responsible for the sale or its success). The privatization law did not specify the crucial matters of what should be sold or set deadlines for sales, leaving such decisions to the discretion of the founder. The Privatization Agency followed a bureaucratic process of sale but, in

---

3. It should be noted here that the Ministry of Finance has been exempted from the privatization legislation for privatizing the state banks. The Ministry of European Affairs, which has had initial success in moving forward on some of the fourteen large privatizations assigned to it, also operates a privatization process that is only partly bound by the privatization legislation.

practice, it did not value the companies or actively involve itself in marketing them or finding buyers. It appeared to consider its function fulfilled after publishing the privatization program in its *Privatization Bulletin* and managing the sales process. The Privatization Commission approved decisions but was not engaged in the sales effort, nor does it have any incentive to ensure a successful sale.

International experience has repeatedly shown that the line or branch ministries of government should *not* be responsible for privatizing companies. The line ministries have too many conflicting policy objectives and may wish to keep enterprises that the government has decided to sell. In Lithuania, the submission of firms for cash privatization was left to the judgment of the enterprise founders, who had little incentive to sell assets under their direct control. It is not surprising that, according to President Brauzaukas' annual report to Parliament in February of 1997, enterprise founders are in "open boycott" of cash privatization—they have refused to place larger enterprises on the privatization list and have delayed the sales of firms tendered for privatization.

In addition, line ministries seldom have the technical competence to manage privatizations or the highly qualified staff necessary to run a successful privatization program. It has been found to be much more effective to place privatization programs in central ministries that are close to the apex of government, free to build institutional competence, and free of the interest in keeping firms that a line ministry often shows. Best international practices suggest that a successful privatization program needs to (i) be located near the center of government (reporting to the president or prime minister); (ii) be supported at the highest ministerial and bureaucratic levels; (iii) have clearly defined aims and goals; (iv) develop institutional competence and experience to be effective; and (v) have a built-in incentive to sell (for example, the Ministry of Finances's need for enhanced and rapid revenue).

Perceived Reluctance to Use Qualified Advisers and Poor Valuation Methods

Successful privatization programs usually call upon qualified financial and other advisers to assist in valuing privatization candidates, assessing their marketability, and developing options for sale and sales plans. These advisers have the technical expertise that is needed to sell companies. More important, they have the financial incentive to do so because most of their fees come from commissions on the sale. Lithuania's privatization officials have shown reluctance to engage and use financial advisers (for unclear, but likely political, reasons). The valuation process, which is undertaken by local evaluators (effectively licensed by the Ministry of Finance), meets none of the international standards of best practice. Generally accepted valuation techniques for valuing significant companies, such as discounted cash flow analysis and "comparables" analysis (which analyzes the sale prices for comparable companies), are almost never used. Instead, the dominant valuation technique in the Lithuanian privatization process is replacement value, a method that privatization experts worldwide generally regard as improper and misleading, because it generally leads to a valuation well above the market's.

Lack of adequate financial advice and excessively high valuations have led time and again to unsuccessful privatizations or sales at less than optimum prices (see box 5-1). There have been a number of firms put up for sale by the Privatization Agency that have not sold or have sold only after repeated attempts. The inability to sell a firm or to sell it at its first offering is of particular concern. International privatization experience shows that firms that are unsuccessfully offered for sale or offered several times before a successful sale suffer commercial damage through the disruptive effect these failures have on the business of the firm, the morale of management and employees, and the confidence of the firm's bankers and other lenders.

Box 5-1. The High Cost of Not Having Professional Privatization Advice

Several years ago the government of Lithuania decided to privatize the country's biggest hotel, the Hotel Lithuania, located in the capital city, Vilnius. International financial advisers were not used, although officials envisioned a sale to a foreign buyer. A minimum price of US$10 million was set for the hotel, in spite of the very extensive renovations and refurbishing the buyer would need to do.

The first tender was unsuccessful, although the tender attracted some interest. Public criticism, however, that the minimum price was too low resulted in government cancellation of the tender before a buyer was selected.

In 1997 the new government attempted to privatize the hotel a second time in a tender supervised by the Privatization Agency. The price was again set at over US$10 million. This time no bids were received, and the tender failed. The government subsequently opened negotiations with an interested buyer, and a sale may take place at a reduced price.

The cost to the government of these two botched sales has been considerable. If the government is paying 9 percent, on average, to borrow, the interest forgone on the final sale price, of perhaps US$9 million, has been at least US$2.5 million, and this does not include the costs of organizing and running the two unsuccessful sales.

Had the government engaged internationally reputed financial advisers at the beginning of the privatization process to advise on valuation and assist in planning the first sale, the sale could have gone smoothly, and the government could have defended its minimum price. An adviser for the second sale would have advised a more realistic price. The costs of competent financial advisers would have been much less than the interest forfeited from the unsuccessful sales process. Also, the enterprise itself would not have been unnecessarily disrupted, and the image of Lithuania would have not been affected by the often widely publicized failed sales.

Lack of Perceived Commitment

Splitting the privatization process in a cumbersome and nonproductive way among three institutions means that no institution is responsible for the success of the program, nor is any one institution responsible if it fails. The program, therefore, suffers from a lack of leadership. Lithuania badly needs a privatization "champion" at the strategic policy-decision level. At the level of execution, it needs to engage highly qualified advisers who are also responsible for sales and get the bulk of their fees from successful sales; this will help ensure that privatization candidates are properly valued and packaged for sale. Both elements (unclear responsibility and poor methodology) worsened a third critical impediment to privatization in Lithuania: weak perceived commitment.

The problem of a government's perceived "commitment" to privatization is not unusual in post-communist economies. The governments face the formidable influence of the state enterprise sector—the linchpin of a reputedly powerful coalition of beneficiaries with privileged access to public resources—and, often, public hostility toward the sale of "crown jewel" firms to foreign investors. These factors have clearly been at play in Lithuania since the completion of the voucher phase of the privatization program in July 1995.

In addition, Lithuania's current cash privatization program has relied on the discretion of participating public agencies instead of uniform rules. For example, the submission of firms for cash privatization is left to the "judgment" of the enterprise founders. Experience from the rest of eastern and central Europe suggests that the problems of overlapping jurisdictions and excessive governmental discretion tend to go together. Investors, particularly foreign prospects, have been reluctant to participate in the privatization process because lack of transparency and predictability have cast broad (perhaps undeserved) doubts on the government's commitment to an economy led by the private sector. It is somewhat revealing that between 1989 and 1995, foreign direct investment as a percentage of GDP has increased in all eastern European countries except Lithuania and the Slovak Republic, where privatizations have been fostered least. The weakness of the perceived commitment hampered another important benefit of privatization: it did not prompt incumbent Lithuanian public sector managers to enhance their performance in credible anticipation of a takeover by more profit-conscious private owners (an effect that has been well documented elsewhere in eastern Europe; see Annex 5-1) (see box 5-2).

Box 5-2. Lowering the Cost of Financial Advisers

Ministers and senior government officials often express the view that financial advisers, particularly international ones, are too expensive and not justified given the smaller amounts that all but the largest SOE privatizations may bring. Governments, however, cannot run a credible case-by-case privatization program without professional financial advice. Grouping similar companies—hotels, for example—together and hiring one financial adviser to advise on the sale of all of them is a useful, cost-saving technique. Bulgaria has recently begun tendering for international financial advisers using this approach. It has grouped firms by industry and is searching for advisers for each group of firms. In addition, the extensive use of the Internet to announce tenders, and the results of tenders, lowers costs and promotes transparency.

A Potentially Lost Opportunity: The New Privatization Law of 1997

A new privatization law was recently passed by the Seimas. The law, unfortunately, carries over many of the bureaucratic and unsuccessful features of the current law, and is unlikely to lead to improvement in privatization performance. While the greater centralization of the privatization effort in a "State Property Fund" (which adopts the role of founder and may also house the Privatization Agency) could be a positive feature, the Property Fund's structure gives little confidence that it can provide the leadership, attention, and technical competence needed for a successful privatization program. The Property Fund is not attached to a strong central ministry. Its attention will not be entirely focused on privatizing firms, because its major function is managing and administering state assets, rather than selling them. As witnessed elsewhere with such institutions, the focus is likely to shift from privatizing assets to managing them. Further, the Property Fund will take some time to set up, which may create further delays in privatization. While it may inherit the staff of the Privatization Agency, the latter has little real experience in selling firms. The new law does not insist on modern best practices in privatization, but rather continues many of the unsuccessful practices of the current law (such as emphasizing the use of local valuators). But, most critical, the new proposed law fails (as its predecessor did) to enunciate what should be sold or to establish sale deadlines.

Special Challenges in Infrastructure Privatization

Privatization of infrastructure raises several special issues that differ markedly from issues of privatization in the traded goods sector. The government of Lithuania is beginning to face these issues as it seeks to enhance private sector involvement in its infrastructure sectors.

It is usually difficult to harness the many benefits of competition in infrastructure activities. In many sectors, Lithuania, like other reforming countries, may need to restructure enterprises horizontally and vertically prior to privatization to create more efficient market structures. For example, it is increasingly common for power sector enterprises to be restructured vertically by separating generation, transmission, and distribution activities, and to restructure generation and distribution horizontally to create a number of separate firms. Even in cases where competition is feasible—such as most tele-communications services—the pros and cons of temporarily restricting competition require careful evaluation. Lithuania is only beginning to grapple with these issues in the sectors slated for privatization in the near future (for example, the telecommunications and some transport subsectors), and a substantial agenda remains in the development of strategies in other sectors (such as energy and railways).

In activities where competition is not feasible, regulation is required to protect consumers from monopoly abuse, to protect investors from arbitrary government action, and to provide incentives for efficiency. In regulated industries, the details of the regulatory framework are usually much more important to potential investors than the condition of the particular assets, or even the size of the market. These issues are now being assessed in the energy and telecommunication sectors in Lithuania, but no actual solutions are yet in place. Moreover, the government is right in seeking to define the rules and institutions *before* privatization. Otherwise, potential investors will respond to the resulting uncertainty and accompanying risk—by reducing the value of their bids. Many governments, however, have found that a public commitment to privatize an infrastructure company has provided it with the needed incentive to move forward on developing and putting into place appropriate regulation as part of the privatization process leading to sale.

Lithuania recently enacted a Concessions Law that governs the scope of concessions in sectors including infrastructure and regulates the awarding of concessions. Application of the new law, however, seems to have been limited, either by the central or by the local governments. In addition, there is no clear institutional mechanism linking the provisions of that law with the public investment program, something that might prove critical, because the decision to award concessions (rather than finance investments from government resources) has considerable budgetary implications.

Also, Lithuania's Competition Law of 1992 establishes prohibitions on the abuse of a dominant market position, unfair competition, and anticompetitive agreements and mergers. It also prohibits state and local governments from adopting standards or carrying out activities that restrict competition. The law is administered by a seven-member Competition and Consumer Protection Office, which currently enjoys limited safeguards of its autonomy. A new law is in preparation that would fine-tune some of these prohibitions (and would, in principle, strengthen the autonomy of the implementing office). An important issue that warrants further attention, however, is the interaction of economywide competition rules with sector-specific rules. For example, there is potential for overlap between sector-specific rules governing access to electricity networks and economywide rules on the abuse of a dominant market position. Unless issues of this kind are clearly addressed, there may be uncertainty about the interaction of the legal regimes, as well as the responsibilities of particular regulatory authorities.

The government's desire to provide widespread access to basic infrastructure services often leads to pressures to subsidize prices to particular groups of users. In traditional, state-controlled monopolistic markets, subsidies have often been funded through cross-subsidies—some users pay higher prices to finance reduced-cost services to others. Traditional cross-subsidies, however, also involve inefficiencies, including poor targeting of beneficiaries (the middle-class often benefits much more than the poor), distortions in resource use, and the costs of forgoing competition. Rebalancing tariffs, accompanied by other measures, can allow social goals to be accomplished more effectively and at lower cost to efficiency. In Lithuania, the issue of cross-subsidies is beginning to be assessed in conjunction with the preparation for telecommunications privatization; in other sectors (such as power and rail transport), a major effort to rebalance tariffs remains to be launched.

Infrastructure industries have a critical impact on industrial competitiveness and living standards across the economy. The short-term goal of maximizing the proceeds from privatization thus needs to be weighed against the longer-term goal of providing incentives for efficient investment and operation. The ongoing telecommunications privatization will be the first experience for the Lithuanian government in balancing these goals, and if done properly, can serve as a model for future infrastructure privatizations.

In addition to the recruitment of strategic investors, a source of expertise and investment capital, there are also potential benefits in promoting widespread local ownership in infrastructure enterprises. The promise of such local participation may reduce political resistance to privatization. Well-regulated infrastructure enterprises can create a large volume of securities that are particularly attractive to institutional investors, and that can play an important role in developing local capital markets. Broad local ownership can also bolster commitments to a fair regulatory framework because it will reduce the pressure on the government to renege on regulatory undertakings. Lithuania is well-positioned to reserve some shares for public offerings during infrastructure privatization, thereby further developing its small, but growing, capital market.

Finally, while privatization in the traded goods sector is usually regarded as synonymous with the divestiture of the state's shares in enterprises, infrastructure privatization often involves choosing from a broader range of options. In many activities, for example, a common approach is to grant time-bound concessions to private operators, while retaining long-term state ownership of sector assets. Nondivestiture forms of private participation are widely used for many types of greenfield investments, but can also be used to structure private involvement in existing enterprises, such as water distribution and ports. Lithuanian municipalities have already been approached with proposals from foreign parties to manage or concession municipal infrastructure, and they will likely need assistance in considering such proposals.

Policy Recommendations

International experience shows that an effective privatization program can bring a government a range of economic benefits, including:

- *Efficiency Gains.* Privatization, done well, restructures firms and improves their performance, profitability, total factor productivity, labor productivity, and exports. Privatized firms can raise wages and increase investments using internally generated funds.
- *Improved Foreign Investment.* FSU countries that have undertaken effective privatization programs have attracted higher levels of foreign investment than countries that have not.
- *Improved Banking Sector.* The performance of the financial sector has improved in countries with successful privatization programs. Privatized firms have much better financial performance than state-owned companies, and this, coupled with the greater financial discipline that private banks exercise on their customers, has led to improved banking performance.
- *Improved Revenue Flows to Government.* An efficient, effective, and faster privatization program could bring substantial revenues to the government over the next few years, as has been the case in the other FSU countries. Hungary's privatization receipts equaled 7.4 percent of GDP in 1995 and 4.6 percent in 1993; Estonia's privatization receipts equaled 5.2 percent of GDP in 1994; and the Slovak Republic's privatization receipts were 5.8 percent of GDP in 1995.

There is no technical reason why Lithuania's privatization program should prove less successful than those of other transitional economies. Given the potential of the country's economy, its strategic location, and the quality of its workforce, a well-structured privatization program should be a promising undertaking. The analysis provided in this Policy Note shows that most policy constraints to speedy and effective privatization could be removed by public policy measures and the passage of new legislation over a relatively short period of time. International privatization experience (see Annex 5-7 for worldwide lessons) points to a number of general principles to guide that policymaking and legislation:

- The core privatization objective is to move state enterprises rapidly to effective private management (not to maximize sale revenues).
- Governments should resist restructuring firms and, when possible, should sell them quickly "as is" (restructuring happens when controlling majority ownership is transferred to competent investors).
- Large companies and infrastructure services should be a key part of the privatization program.
- Transparency, fairness, and a level playing field are of utmost importance.
- Case-by-case privatization is preferable (over mass or voucher-based programs) because it provides the largest enhancement in corporate governance, the highest returns, and the possibility of effectively addressing company- or industry-specific issues (regulation, environmental protection, and the like). (Annex 5-7 provides a more comprehensive definition of case-by-case sales.)
- Outside expertise should be sought; all best practice methods of sale should be used (IPO, trade sales, mixed sales).
- Sales to employees and insiders should be avoided, beyond those necessary to prevent union or stakeholder resistance.
- There should be proper incentives in place to ensure that those responsible for the program are rewarded (punished) because of their success (failure), not for meticulously following bureaucratic procedure.

Toward a New Privatization Strategy

In light of these principles, the institutional process for privatization in Lithuania needs to be simplified and centralized in *one* institution located at the center of government. The sole responsibility of this institution should be privatization, including the fostering of institutional competence and the imposition of government policy. The privatization process should be based on international best practices; foreign and domestic advisers, particularly financial advisers, should be used; and adequate budgets should be established to pay for them (including payment on a performance basis). Best case-by-case practices should be employed for both large and medium-size privatizations, especially in the infrastructure area. The processes should be made transparent and the most suitable sales methods—based on the advice of outside experts—should be used. Wide latitude should be provided in sales methods so that selected techniques can be applied to different enterprises of differing sizes and industries. Flexibility should also be allowed for the disposition of residual shares and small shareholdings. At the same time, the government will have to commit itself to a privatization process that meets the best international standards and can be made the flagship of the country's transition efforts.

A More Effective Framework for Privatization

OPTION ONE. Much of the above-mentioned strategy could be put in place quickly through government administrative arrangements and decisions. Privatization through the MEA was meant to be established this way. The privatization law, however, needs to be replaced, and the institutions and responsibilities of privatization detailed in the current law require major revisions. First, a new privatization law is necessary to set forth, *inter alia*:

- Explicit goals and applicability—what the goals of privatization are and what is to be privatized—are needed. Both companies in the tradable and the infrastructure areas should be considered for privatization.

- The institution that would undertake the privatization program, preferably a central ministry of privatization, must be established. The Privatization Agency and Privatization Commission would be integrated, if retained, into the privatization ministry.

- The privatization ministry would be given wide authority to use best practices (especially to engage international experts and financial advisers and to use best valuation practices) (Annex 5-4 describes the pros and cons of valuation methods and Annex 5-5 addresses some key practical issues in selecting and hiring financial advisers), to use the most suitable methods of sale, and should receive adequate funding so that it can hire needed experts.

- The proceeds of the sale would be transferred immediately to the fiscal budget, with the provision that some of the proceeds would be available to pay expenses involved in the sale in question (a standard international practice).

- The new privatization law would be specific on the (high) level of disclosure required and the need to use competitive, open tenders and sales methods to ensure transparency.

OPTION TWO. Should the government decide that it is expedient to continue its privatization program under the current law (as revised in December 1997) and with the current privatization institutions—that is, the State Property Fund and the Privatization Commission—then the government should consider the following necessary changes, *inter alia*, to assure the efficiency and effectiveness of the program:

- The government would lay out, annually, a list of state-owned companies and state holdings in companies that it wished to privatize, with a time frame for the privatization. This list would be developed in cooperation with the State Property Fund and the Privatization Commission.

- The government would indicate that best practices were to be used in these privatizations; that reputable and experienced financial and other advisers should undertake valuations, design sales options, and assist in sales; and that market-based valuations would be used in establishing prices, for example, discounted cash flow analysis and comparative companies valuations (see Annex 5-4).

- The government would indicate that public offerings, trade (third-party) sales, mixed sales, negotiated sales, and other innovative sales methods were to be used, with a view to obtaining fair prices, attracting domestic and foreign investors, and obtaining the best possible new owners for privatized firms.

- The government would provide the political and financial support to the State Property Fund and the Privatization Commission to enable them to carry out the annual privatization plan using the required advisers and techniques as outlined by the goverment.

A New Battery of Privatization Tools

The present law is restrictive in its prescription of the methods for privatization. The new legislation and privatization program should look to the best international practices for sale, some of which are listed below.

PUBLIC OFFERINGS. Public share offerings on stock markets can be used for profitable, larger, relatively well-known state enterprises. Often the share offer is an opportunity to raise additional capital for the company (through the issue of new shares), as well as to transfer ownership of the enterprise. It can also serve the objective of promoting transparency and widespread share ownership by allocating a proportion of shares to small investors. The government can offer shares on the domestic market as well as in international markets as American or Global Depository Receipts (ADRs or GDRs), given the lack of depth in Lithuania's securities markets.

TRADE (THIRD-PARTY) SALES. Trade sales use auctions or open bidding to sell the enterprise to a third party. This involves the preparation of an information memorandum by financial advisers and government officials. The memorandum is sent to potentially interested parties; nonbinding expressions of interest are received from interested bidders; and the government signs confidentiality agreements with short-listed bidders and gives them access to a confidential data room, access to management, and a draft sales agreement. Bidders then submit a binding offer (bid) and a required deposit. The government, aided by its financial advisers, then chooses the "best" offer (considerations beyond price—proposals for new investments, service standards, and the like—are normally part of the offer assessment).

MIXED SALES–TRADE SALES COMBINED WITH SHARE OFFERINGS. Of particular interest to transitional economies is the mixed sale privatization that uses a combination of trade sales to attract a major strategic investor(s) by offering a control block, and a share offering for all or most of the balance on domestic and, often, foreign markets. Such an offer has the advantage of attracting important investor(s) who will bring management and technical skills, market connections, and capital to the firm and who will pay a significant price for control, while at the same time gathering consensus for the privatization.

NEGOTIATED SALE. The negotiated sale is a special case of the more common trade sale auction. The government has already chosen the buyer, and the aim of the sale is to negotiate an agreement. The government would use a negotiated sale when there is just one buyer or a buyer possesses strategic synergies that give it a marked advantage over others. It is difficult, however, to achieve the highest price in such a sale, and the sale is less transparent than an open bidding process.

OTHER METHODS. Given the significant level of holdings, many minority, that the Lithuanian government still has in small and medium-size companies, flexible sales procedures will need to be developed using local and foreign financial advisers. Disposal of minority government holdings will require innovative techniques (such as packaging multiple share holdings in units and offering the units for sale by tender) to sell shares in companies where control has already passed to others and/or where insiders have little incentive to buy additional shares.

Facilitating Infrastructure Privatization

Experience with the new Concessions Law seems too limited. Both central and local governments in Lithuania may wish to engage advisers to determine an appropriate use for—and negotiate—any early concessions that may be undertaken. Such a decision should also be made in conjunction with the public investment programming work of the Ministry of Economy.

The interaction of economywide competition rules with sector-specific rules must be clearly defined. For example, there is potential for overlap between sector-specific rules governing access to networks and economywide rules on the abuse of a dominant market position. In addition, the roles and relationships of infrastructure regulators, sector ministries, and economywide regulatory agencies will require careful elaboration and articulation.

The government's decision to focus initial efforts on telecommunications is consistent with international practice and makes good sense. The lessons learned and expertise acquired from evaluating tradeoffs among multiple policy considerations in this sector will be useful for grappling with similar issues in other sectors. It would be advisable for the government to undertake an ex-post assessment of the experience of telecommunications privatization to identify lessons for other sectors and to establish mechanisms for sharing insights and experience among relevant sector authorities. In addition, the authorities may wish to undertake an independent assessment of regulatory capabilities and the skill mix of existing and proposed regulators to determine further staff recruitment and training needs.

The government should ensure the independence of all existing and proposed regulatory institutions. Initial steps should include the following: (i) remove the telecommunications regulatory functions from the Ministry of Communications; (ii) eliminate budgetary financing for regulatory bodies and replace it with earmarked funding; (iii) increase the autonomy of the Competition Agency; and (iv) ensure that the members of the Energy Commission are allowed to serve full terms unless professional incompetence can be demonstrated.

ANNEX 5-1. Privatization In Post-Communist Europe: Enterprise Productivity

In 1997, the World Bank published a comprehensive analysis of the industrial restructuring that has taken place since 1992 in Bulgaria, the Czech Republic, Hungary, Poland, Romania, the Slovak Republic, and Slovenia.[4] The study covered a sample of 6,368 industrial firms and examined which government policies were the most effective in fostering enterprise restructuring. The number of firms sampled in each country ranged from 700 to 1,000; the firms accounted for between 40 to 90 percent of the countries' employment in manufacturing. The results showed that privatization was by far the single most important factor in restructuring and that the privatized firms performed much better than those that remained state-owned. Table 5-3 shows the features of the study database.

Table 5-3. Features of the Database

Country	Firms	Employees (1992)	Employees as percentage of total manufacturing employment
Bulgaria	828	314,042	48
Czech Republic	706	829,312	64
Hungary	1,044	428,645	41
Poland	1,066	1,338,645	45
Romania	1,092	2,121,102	91
Slovak Republic	905	578,737	93
Slovenia	727	219,959	90
Total	6,368	5,830,442	

The measures of restructuring used in the study included profitability, the proportion of firms with a positive operating cash flow, average operating cash flow as a percentage of revenue, growth in labor productivity, growth in total factor productivity, and growth in exports. The econometric analysis focused on the two most reliable indicators of restructuring: growth in labor productivity and growth in total factor productivity.

Growth in Labor and Total Factor Productivity

Table 5-4 shows the annual percentage growth in the firms' labor productivity from 1992 to 1995 in the seven countries studied.

Labor productivity growth averaged 7.3 percent yearly in privatized firms and declined by 0.2 percent annually in state-owned firms. The econometric analysis undertaken in the study indicated that *privatization accounted for almost all the growth in labor productivity.* The analysis also showed that even a credible threat of privatization promoted restructuring. In Poland, where the government's commitment to privatization was seen as serious, firms included in the mass privatization program improved their profitability in 1994 and 1995, well before they were privatized, probably because of the signaling effect to management of the government's policy and the expectation that management would be held more accountable by new owners.

---

4. G. Pohl and others, *Privatization and Restructuring in Central and Eastern Europe*, World Bank Technical Paper No. 368 (Washington, D.C., 1997).

Table 5-4. Annual Labor Productivity Growth, 1992–95
(percent)

Country	Privatized firms	State-owned firms	All firms
Bulgaria	12.4	-1.4	-1.4
Czech Republic	8.6	-2.6	6.8
Hungary	6.0	3.2	4.8
Poland	7.5	1.4	5.4
Romania	1.0	-0.5	0.1
Slovak Republic	7.8	-4.1	5.1
Slovenia	7.2	1.8	3.6
Average	7.3	-0.2	3.6

The results of the study's analysis were similar for the productivity of all factors of production. The cumulative gains in total factor productivity for privatized firms far exceeded those of state-owned firms in the sample. The analysis showed that privatization had increased total factor productivity growth by about 4 percent a year.

OTHER FINDINGS. The study also found that privatized firms had retained most of the large productivity gains from privatization to finance needed investments. Labor productivity growth was faster than real wage gains in the privatized firms (although wages did rise rapidly), while state-owned firms raised wages faster than productivity, depleting their capacity to finance the enterprise from internal sources.

The positive effects of privatization on the privatized firms' finances also bolstered the banking system. In countries that pursued large and rapid privatization programs, privatized firms improved their profitability more quickly than expected, lessening the necessity for government intervention in, and support of, the banking system. In countries that had done little or no privatization, the continued poor financial situation of many state firms worsened the banks' loan problems.

Mid-Size Firms in the Czech Republic, Poland, and Hungary

Similar results were found in a study of 500 mid-size firms in the Czech Republic, Poland, and Hungary between 1991 and 1993 that compared the performance of privatized and state firms. This study also revealed that private ownership improves labor productivity and revenue.[5]

The simplest ordinary least-square estimations in this study generated the following equations (using averages for the period 1991 to 1993):

$$Revenue\ Growth\ =\ -15.82^* - 0.25^* \times INIPERF + 19.01^* \times PRV$$
$$(1.92)\ (0.06) \qquad\qquad (3.18)$$

$$Employment\ Growth\ =\ -7.47^* - 0.40^* \times INIPERF + 5.88^* \times PRV$$
$$(1.20)\ (0.10) \qquad\qquad (1.61)$$

$$Revenue\ per\ Employee\ =\ -5.21^* - 0.28^* \times INIPERF + 11.17^* \times PRV$$
$$(2.01)\quad (0.06) \qquad\qquad (3.21)$$

---

5. R. Frydman and others, "Private Ownership and Corporate Performance: Some Lessons from Transition Economies" (unpublished manuscript, June 1997).

$$Cost\text{-}to\text{-}Revenue\ Ratio\ =\ 30.06* -\ 0.31* \times INIPERF - 3.00 \times PRV$$
$$(4.16)\quad (0.05)\qquad\qquad (2.28)$$

where *INIPERF* is the initial value of the relevant performance indicator (for privatized firms, the initial value corresponds to the year of privatization), and *PRV* is a dummy variable, coded 1 if private, 0 otherwise. Standard errors are in parentheses, and coefficients significant at the 95 percent interval are marked with an asterisk. These equations show that private ownership significantly increases the probability that firms will have higher rates of revenue growth, higher rates of employment growth, and greater labor productivity. Additional dummy variables—indicating, among other things, whether the largest owner of the firm was an investment fund, a foreign company, management, employees, the state, and so on—generate robust findings that private owners of all institutional forms (with the exception of employees) produce significant revenue, employment, and efficiency gains. These results are found even when the level of pre-privatization performance is controlled for in the regressions.

Over the data period, all firms had been forced to reduce bloated payrolls, probe new markets after demand collapsed for their products, improve product quality, and reduce inefficiencies. Evidence from these firms indicates that private owners produce this restructuring more effectively than the state.

ANNEX 5-2. Privatization in Post-Communist Europe: Public and Private Finance

Privatization Revenues

In most transition economies, privatization has slowed since 1995. Privatization revenues as a percentage of GDP in Lithuania, which has fared worse than its Baltic neighbors over the whole period, have consistently fallen each year since 1993. Table 5-5 reflects the heavy reliance on cash sales in Estonia, Latvia, Hungary, and the Slovak Republic, as well as in the Czech Republic after 1995, all of which generated privatization revenues in excess of 3 percent of GDP at some point during the main period of enterprise sales between 1992 and 1995. Hungary and Estonia, using a modified form of the east German *Treuhandanstalt* method of enterprise sales, show the largest proportional revenue gains. The low figure for the Czech Republic in 1994 most likely indicates the end of the mass privatization program. The switch to traditional methods of enterprise sales in 1995—most notably with the sale of SPT Telecom—is responsible for the observed increase of over 3 percent in 1995. Similarly, the Slovak Republic's strong showing in 1995 primarily stems from the direct sales of a few large enterprises, including the Slovnaft Refinery and the East Slovak Ironworks.

Table 5-5 contrasts voucher-based or mixed cash and voucher sales (which, by definition, produce little revenue) with traditional methods. In addition, the countries that register average privatization-revenue-to-GDP ratios of less than 1 percent (Bulgaria, Russia, and Lithuania) typically suffered the most from insider-dominated enterprise sales, inadequate commercialization, and a lack of customer demand.

Table 5-5. Privatization Revenues in Selected Transition Economies
(percent of GDP)

Country	1989	1990	1991	1992	1993	1994	1995	1996
Bulgaria					0.42	1.51	0.86	0.31
Czech Republic					2.06	0.02	3.49	0.36
Estonia					2.58	5.19	2.72	1.29
Hungary	1.58	1.46	2.39	2.12	4.56	1.02	7.44	2.07
Latvia						3.75		0.17
Lithuania					1.34	1.14	0.98	0.05
Poland		0.16	1.17	1.23	2.78	2.13	0.81	
Russian Federation					0.07		0.29	0.09
Slovak Republic					0.52	3.01	5.79	0.08

Note: Figures for 1996 are based on revenue estimates and GDP projections from *Privatization Yearbook 1996*. Years for which figures are unavailable are left blank.

Source: World Bank, *Global Development Finance* (Washington, 1997); IMF, *International Financial Statistics*, various issues (Washington, D.C.); Privatization International, *Privatization Yearbook*, various issues (London).

Privatization and the Financial Sector

Public enterprise reform and financial sector reform are two sides of one coin. While the expansion in the range of financial services, the depth of financial intermediation, and the reliability of financial infrastructure supports and encourages public enterprise reform, public enterprise reform also stimulates improvements in the financial sector. Experience from the transition economies suggests that the privatization of public enterprises (i) increases the demand for financial services; (ii) reduces the losses that the financial sector, particularly commercial banks, must absorb, (iii) allows for more accurate monitoring of company behavior by moneylenders and other financiers; and (iv) enables financiers to punish their borrowers for poor performance more credibly than would be the case under public ownership.

In all countries, banks have reduced lending to public enterprises as a portion of total lending. Several factors may be responsible for this change, including a more prudent attitude toward lending on the part of the banking system; attractive interest rates on government paper, which induce banks to lend more to the government at the expense of its enterprises; low credit demand; and, of course, the privatization of formerly public enterprises. At the same time, table 5-6 reveals a wide range of interest rate spreads, suggesting that individual banking systems face varying levels of uncertainty. High interest rate spreads indicate one of two circumstances. They demonstrate either the level of "stress" a banking system faces, since increased spreads between borrowing and deposit rates reflect an attempt by banks to increase interest income in order to cover nonperforming loans, or the presence of an oligopolistic banking system. To the extent that the transfer of state firms to private ownership leads toward a stabilization of bad lending, narrower margins are more likely to be sustained in economies that have taken significant steps toward privatization.

Table 5-6. Interest Rate Spreads in Selected Transition Economies

Country	1989	1990	1991	1992	1993	1994	1995	1996
Bulgaria			9.86	11.69	16.90	21.44	23.03	48.80
Czech Republic					7.04	6.05	5.84	5.75
Estonia				30.50	27.30	11.58	7.21	7.62
Hungary	10.92	4.10	4.68	8.64	9.77	7.09	6.51	
Lithuania					43.20	34.94	18.66	21.57
Latvia					51.57	24.18	19.77	14.07
Poland	-36.00	12.50	1.08	1.25	1.25	-0.57	6.67	6.06
Russia							217.49	91.76
Slovak Republic					6.39	5.24	6.64	7.03

Note: Lending minus deposit rates using period averages. Years for which figures are unavailable are blank.
Source: IMF, *International Financial Statistics*, various issues (Washington, D.C.).

Indeed, there are some suggestive correlations that derive from this table. First, countries in which interest rate spreads have been held to single digits tend to be countries that have made the most substantial progress in privatization. A comparison of the figures in table 5-5—a proxy for progress in privatization—reveals that the countries that have achieved higher revenue gains from privatization have maintained lower interest rate spreads than states that have been unable to raise revenues from privatization beyond 2 percent of GDP.[6] Second, the performances of the banking systems in countries plagued by spontaneous privatization and excessive insider control—both countries that relied on voucher sales (Russia) and those that utilized cash sales (Latvia)—have been the worst in the group. Third, the *trend* in interest rate spreads may reveal more about the burden of bad enterprise loans than static values. In the Czech Republic, Estonia, Hungary, Latvia, Russia, and the Slovak Republic, the trend has been downward. In Bulgaria,

---

6. The one exception is Latvia, which raised the equivalent of 3.75 percent of GDP from public enterprise sales in 1994 (the only year for which figures are available), yet has suffered from high interest rate margins. These, however, have been cut in half in recent years.

the trend seems to be on the rise. In Lithuania, there has been a slight increase from (already high) 1995 levels. To be sure, the health of the banking system is a function of several related factors. There is, however, evidence that progress in privatization may be a necessary (although perhaps not sufficient) condition for banking reform.

ANNEX 5-3. Organizing Government for Privatization

A successful government privatization program needs to (i) be located at the center of government; (ii) be supported at the highest ministerial and bureaucratic levels; (iii) have clearly defined aims and goals; and (iv) develop institutional competence and experience.

CENTRAL LOCATION AND HIGH-LEVEL SUPPORT. Privatization programs are generally at the center of government and attached to the president's or prime minister's office; the Ministry of Finance or Ministry of Treasury; or some other powerful central ministry or department. There are a number of reasons for this:

- Privatization will inevitably meet bureaucratic opposition and political resistance because privatization changes the status quo.
- By locating the privatization group near the center of government power, government can overcome bureaucratic resistance and manage political issues effectively.
- Privatization programs are usually part of an overall program of structural adjustment or result from the government's need to raise money, and it is the central ministries and ministers of government that are responsible for the success of such initiatives and have the most incentive to make the privatization program a success.

Because privatizations affect so many parties within and outside government—line ministries, the state corporation being privatized, labor unions, national and local politicians, employees of the state enterprise, customers and suppliers, and the like— privatizations can be very contentious. It is often necessary for the most senior and powerful government ministers to intervene to resolve issues and to move the privatization forward.

International experience suggests that most successful privatization programs are operated at or near the center of government. Canada ran its most successful privatization program in association with the Department of Finance. New Zealand centered its program in the Treasury Department, as did the United Kingdom. The French used their powerful Treasury Ministry and a privatization commission. The German privatization effort under the Trehandanstalt reported to the Minister of Finance.

CLEARLY DEFINED AIMS FOR THE PRIVATIZATION PROGRAM. Privatization programs should have clearly defined goals. The government may enumerate these goals in policy statements, legislation, and decrees or as instructions to the government officials who will administer the privatization program. If these explicit aims and goals are missing from a program, confusion will develop among participants in the process about why the privatization is being undertaken and why it should be supported.

Given the wide range of interests affected by any significant privatization, government will need to trade off stakeholder and government gains and losses. To make these tradeoffs, and to prevent the privatization process from bogging down in a welter of unresolved issues, government will need to be clear on the objectives and priorities of privatization. For example,

---

This Annex is based on D. Welch and O. Fremond, *The Case-by-Case Approach to Privatization: Techniques and Examples*, World Bank Technical Paper 403 (Washington, D.C., 1998).

governments must make tradeoffs among the interests of line ministries, which may have been more concerned about how the privatization affects their policy stance and authority than the government's need to restructure the economy or raise money.

DEVELOP INSTITUTIONAL COMPETENCE AND EXPERIENCE. It is important that the government institutions responsible for the privatization program gain experience and develop competence in privatization. Privatization of state firms is a complex, difficult task, and it often requires commercial skills and experience that many government officials in developing and transitional economies do not have. The need to develop institutional competence and expertise suggests the establishment of *one single privatization body.* *Spreading the privatization effort throughout a number of institutions or ministries is a mistake* that militates against building the institutional capacity needed in privatization.

Under no circumstances should the state allow enterprises to privatize themselves. Their management in such a circumstance would experience conflicts among its own interests, the interests of the enterprise, and the interests of the government.

ANNEX 5-4. Valuation Methodology: International Best Practices

Government has a fiduciary duty toward its citizens when it privatizes. It is entrusted to sell marketable assets at or above their fair market value. Valuation is the process of estimating what buyers will pay for an enterprise, and it is the cornerstone of case-by-case privatization. As opposed to mass privatization, where the value of assets is not known with precision and is not a critical factor, in case-by-case privatization, value is of fundamental importance to both buyer and seller. Agreeing to sell below market value will favor some group of individuals over others.

Financial advisers start a valuation with a financial audit and one or more targeted methods of sale. The method of sale determines the weight and level of detail that should be applied to the various valuation methods. It is usually advantageous to select the financial adviser for the valuation ahead of the auditor so that the adviser can provide input in the preparation of the terms of reference for the audit, which normally includes an operational and legal review in addition to the financial review. At the end of this process, the financial adviser will submit a first valuation report to the government. The government is responsible for establishing the reserve price of the sales tender, or the fixed price of the public offering, but the government needs to base its decision on a set of objective data. These data are provided in a valuation report.

All valuation methods yield an estimate or range of expected market value. Some methods are particularly appropriate if the company is to be divested by an initial public offering (IPO), others if control is to be sold to a strategic investor or through a trade sale (auction). The discounted cash flow method (DCF) and comparable companies method are best practices for case-by-case privatization. The adjusted net assets method and replacement value methods should not be used, because they are not indicative of market values.

THE DISCOUNTED CASH FLOW METHOD. The DCF method is most relevant in a sale to a strategic investor who will control management of the company, and thus its cash flows. It consists of estimating the company's cash flow over a medium- to long-term horizon, taking into account variations in working capital and future capital expenditures. A discount rate is then applied to these anticipated cash flows to calculate their present value. The discount rate reflects the weighted average cost of capital of the acquisition candidate and the political risk of the country where the company's operations are based. Strategic investors concentrate their valuation efforts on the DCF method. They verify that their calculations are not significantly off market by contrasting them with market values of comparable quoted companies and with prices paid by other acquirers in recent comparable transactions, but their DCF valuation will make up a significant component of their ultimate privatization offer.

THE COMPARABLE COMPANIES METHOD. The comparable companies and comparable transaction methods are particularly appropriate when the company is privatized in whole or in part through the stock exchange. The underlying principle is that companies' market values can be determined by applying a series of empirically derived valuation multiples to their latest (or normalized) financial results. The most commonly used multiples are the multiple of turnover,

---

This Annex is based on D. Welch and O. Fremond, *The Case-by-Case Approach to Privatization: Techniques and Examples* World Bank Technical Paper 403 (Washington, D.C., 1998).

the multiples of operating income, or the multiple of net earnings, also known as the price-earnings ratio. A series of multiples are calculated and sorted to obtain a range (high, low, and arithmetic mean), which is applied to the financial results of the company being valued. In addition, for capital-intensive industries such as cement or oil and gas, a variety of operational ratios, such as the dollar per ton of capacity or the dollar per barrel of reserves in the ground, can also be used to approximate market values.

THE REPLACEMENT VALUE METHOD. The replacement value method consists of estimating the total costs of replacing a company's assets—principally the fixed assets such as plant and machinery, but also start-up costs and certain current assets, such as a transport fleet. This value is often abnormally high compared with the results obtained by the other methods described herein. Investors almost never consider the replacement value method when valuing a company because it does not give them a measure of the expected return from the proposed investment, and sellers should not use this method. It should nevertheless be calculated, and arguments should be prepared to explain why it has been discarded. Otherwise, critics of the privatization process may use this method to argue that a company is worth far more, or that it was sold for a fraction of its worth.

THE ADJUSTED NET ASSETS METHOD. The adjusted net assets method seeks to ascertain the fair market value of the shareholders' equity by estimating the market value of its assets, and then subtracting from this total the company's balance sheet and off-balance-sheet liabilities. Acquirers generally discard this method because it does not take into account the capacity of the assets to generate revenues for the firm. (The firm may well be using the assets in a suboptimal manner.) Such an approach is often the cause of unreconcilable differences between buyers and seller.

ANNEX 5-5. Hiring and Using Financial and Other Advisers for Case-By-Case Privatization

Financial advisers are investment or merchant bankers who sell and advise on the sale of firms. They sell using share flotations (IPOs), which they may underwrite; third-party trade sales; negotiated sales; or mixed sales (trade sale to a strategic buyer combined with an IPO). The government may use a single financial adviser or a consortium of financial and other advisers. If the government wants to attract both domestic and foreign buyers, it will need both a foreign-based and domestic adviser working together.

Considerations in Selecting Financial Advisers

If a small enterprise is being privatized and is unlikely to attract much international interest, accounting firms and financial consultants may suffice as financial advisers. But if the enterprise is large, or if it has an international dimension, it is preferable to award the valuation mandate to an investment or merchant bank. This is because a valuation exercise requires market awareness in addition to technical skills.

ROLE OF FINANCIAL ADVISERS. Governments need financial advisers in case-by-case privatizations to value the enterprise and to advise on timing and method of sale. Advisers will establish the price (usually a price range) that the government could receive for the enterprise, and may provide several valuations based on different sales methods (for example, whether sale is through a stock flotation or through a trade sale). The financial adviser will also advise on sales options. This advice will cover such issues as:

- Is the company salable?
- Should it be sold now or later, when markets improve?
- What sorts of sales choices are feasible, and at what cost?

Once the government has decided when and how to privatize, it will require a financial adviser (sales agent) to undertake the sale. The sales agent will help design the privatization plan and will undertake the sale, in cooperation with government officials. If a privatization moves to the sales stage through an IPO, a syndicate of investment or merchant banks will be formed to sell the shares. The government will need to appoint a firm as a lead manager for the syndicate to manage the sale process.

Other Advisers

Other professional advisers are also necessary in the privatization process. Lawyers and accountants will be required to manage due diligence activities, which involve such issues as verifying asset ownership, assessing effects of contracts the firm has made, verifying accounts, and the like. Lawyers will advise government on the legal aspects of the privatization, draft and help negotiate sales contracts, and draw up confidentiality agreements. Accountants and auditors may be needed to undertake audits prior to sale, and technical experts with special industry skill

---

This Annex is based on D. Welch and O. Fremond, *The Case-by-Case Approach to Privatization: Techniques and Examples*, World Bank Technical Paper 403 (Washington, D.C., 1998).

and knowledge may be required as well. The government may find it convenient to tender for all these advisers as a single consortium rather than hiring them separately.

SHOULD THE GOVERNMENT USE THE SAME FINANCIAL ADVISER FOR BOTH THE PRIVATIZATION FEASIBILITY STUDY AND THE SALE? Privatization literature often questions whether the same financial advisory firm that advised the government during the early stages of the privatization process should undertake the sale of the enterprise. The argument against using the same adviser is that there is a conflict of interest inherent in advising on whether and how to privatize an enterprise and the sale of that enterprise. Nevertheless, the best adviser firms are often reluctant to undertake the advisory role if they cannot participate in the sale, which is usually the more profitable assignment.

A way to manage this issue is to tender for both the initial financial advisory and the sales agent advisory, but not to restrict the winner of the first from participating in, or winning, the second. Alternatively, the authorities can bind the adviser to a two-stage assignment—a feasibility study and the sales process—giving the government an exit at the first stage if it is not content with the adviser.

ANNEX 5-6. Lessons from International Experience

Significant case-by-case privatization experience has accumulated throughout the world. A consensus is emerging about the main factors in successful privatization programs, and we can present a number of conclusions here.

STRONG POLITICAL SUPPORT AND LEADERSHIP ARE VITAL FOR SUCCESS. Government must support the privatization process from the highest levels to overcome inertia and the inevitable resistance from bureaucracy and special interest groups. Government should entrust implementation to pragmatic individuals who have no personal stake in the status quo and have access to world-class technical competence. The privatization arm of government should report to a senior minister, and it often has special status.

TRANSPARENCY, FAIRNESS, AND A LEVEL PLAYING FIELD ARE OF UTMOST IMPORTANCE. Transparency is key to a successful case-by-case privatization program. Independent, third-party experts should carry out asset valuation procedures to ensure that they are realistic, fair, and consistently applied, as are procedures for calling for bids and evaluating offers. The implementing agency should take the necessary time and effort to think out, plan, and execute the privatization process. Widespread publicity campaigns help ensure that potential investors are aware of the opportunities. In trade sales, it is important to include the contract terms as part of the bidding documents to prevent undesirable changes during post-award negotiations. The privatization award process should be transparent and clear beforehand to avoid corruption and controversies.

OUTSIDE EXPERTISE SHOULD BE SOUGHT. The need to make full use of specialized consultants is now clear. There is a growing body of specialist experience in privatization worldwide. Government can use local experts, but governments should not hesitate to resort to the services of foreign privatization experts. Investment banks, consulting firms, environmental experts, accountants, and lawyers are necessary participants in case-by-case programs. Institutional failure, the inability of the government to manage the process because of lack of qualified staff, has slowed and undermined many privatization programs.

INVESTORS WILL COME FORWARD FOR A PROPERLY PREPARED TRANSACTION. Officials are often concerned over a perceived shortage of foreign and domestic investor interest. Heavy oversubscription of share offerings in Britain, Latin America, and Africa (Nigeria, Senegal) took many by surprise. Often the level of informal savings and capital flight in developing and transition economies is underestimated. Properly designed privatizations with appropriate incentive structures can motivate domestic and international investors to buy equities.

PRIVATIZATION IN TRANCHES OR THROUGH A MIXED SALE MAY HELP MAXIMIZE GOVERNMENT RECEIPTS. Because of the lack of market depth in emerging markets, sale through several tranches may be necessary to attract the maximum number of individual and institutional investors, both at home and abroad. The use of mixed sales can help satisfy both domestic and foreign demand to the fullest extent possible and solve the issue of corporate governance through

---

This Annex is based on D. Welch and O. Fremond, *The Case-by-Case Approach to Privatization: Techniques and Examples*, World Bank Technical Paper 403 (Washington, D.C., 1998).

the introduction of a strong, controlling shareholder.

PRIVATIZATION PROGRAMS SHOULD BE PROACTIVE. Competition among governments for investors in privatized assets is fierce. Without a conscious, consistent, and aggressive policy to attract the participation of foreign investors, privatization programs may fall short on the revenue side or turn away investors who could provide market access, the latest technology, and management expertise. Privatization programs should be designed with the view that foreign investors will participate with local investors in the country's privatizations on as equal a basis as possible. It is critical to reassure investors that the state will not use its political power or any residual or "golden share" in a way that will jeopardize the company's ability to maximize profits and efficiency.

NECESSARY PRE-PRIVATIZATION RESTRUCTURING SHOULD BE SHORT-TERM AND MINIMALIST. Government should limit restructuring to balance sheet and organizational changes, which may include closures, reductions in labor, or transfers of social services. It is preferable that government undertake necessary labor restructuring prior to privatizing a state enterprise. Government should leave the implementation of technology changes, investment of capital, and major purchases to the new owners, not to government agencies or officials.

GOVERNMENTS SHOULD LIMIT THE CONDITIONS ATTACHED TO PRIVATIZATION TO A MINIMUM. Complex, elaborate undertakings will detract from the value and attractiveness of the enterprise and may undermine the deal. The government should clean up regulatory and environmental issues, price controls, subsidies, and other problem areas before the sale.

RELATED STRUCTURAL REFORMS SHOULD KEEP ABREAST WITH PRIVATIZATION. Governments should implement privatization programs in the framework of an overall package of mutually reinforcing economic reforms, such as macroeconomics stabilization, trade liberalization, financial sector reform, elimination of subsidies, a pro-competition policy, and regulatory reform. Privatization alone is unsustainable and cannot restructure the economy if other reforms are lagging.

PUBLIC INFORMATION AND PUBLICITY CAMPAIGNS PLAY A CRITICAL ROLE IN CASE-BY-CASE PROGRAMS. Most successful privatization programs placed a strong emphasis on educating the public through extensive advertising of the expected sales.

ANNEX 5-7. Case-by-Case Privatization Defined

Case-by-case privatization is often referred to as classical privatization. It moves state enterprises to the private sector, usually one at a time, through domestic and international public offerings, negotiated or trade sales, or through "mixed sales." (The latter combines a third-party sale of control to a strategic buyer with a public share offering for the remainder of the state's shares.) Case-by-case privatization allows governments to resolve the policy issues surrounding the privatization, such as regulatory, environmental, and labor issues. It encourages government to engage reputable financial advisers, to obtain market-based valuations for the firm, and to sell the firm in a transparent sales process for its market value. Case-by-case privatization transfers all or a majority of the shares—a control block—to new, private sector owners. Case-by-case privatization has a number of advantages over the mass or voucher privatization technique, because governments can structure sales to bring in needed foreign capital, technical knowledge, and market connections and can maximize financial returns.

6

PSD ENVIRONMENT: TAKING STOCK OF RECENT DEVELOPMENTS AND PERCEIVED CONSTRAINTS

The World Bank's *Lithuania Private Sector Development* report of June 1995 examined the progress and potential of private sector development (PSD) through privatization, foreign investment, and new business establishment. The study's primary goals were to explain why new domestic and foreign investment had moved only hesitantly into Lithuania and to suggest ways in which the rate of private investment could be accelerated. This Policy Note serves as a follow-up and update to the previous report, and includes the presentation and analysis of the following: (i) the anatomy of Lithuania's private sector, (ii) the perceptions of domestic enterpreneurs as to what constrains the growth of their businesses, and (iii) the perceptions of foreign investors. More important, this Note has served as a basis for the identification of key policy issues for private sector development, which are treated in detail in separate Policy Notes.

The statistical data was collected from the Lithuanian Department of Statistics, the Lithuanian Privatization Agency, and the publications of these institutions. The information on the perceptions of the private sector was gathered through two surveys, both carried out in the first half of 1997. A survey of domestic enterprises was conducted by Baltic Survey, Ltd., at the request of the World Bank, and a survey of foreign investors was conducted independently by the Lithuanian Investment Agency.

The Anatomy of Lithuania's Private Sector[1]

According to the Department of Statistics, approximately 60,000 public, semi-public, and private enterprises are currently registered in Lithuania. Only about 20,000 of these enterprises, however, were thought to be pursuing their day-to-day operations in 1997. This large discrepancy has several causes. First, because there are no requirements to report bankruptcy or liquidation, a huge number of enterprises have ceased to exist, but have not updated their registry status to reflect this change. Second, some companies that have been privatized have registered themselves as new enterprises without eliminating their former, state-owned, company names. Third, a significant number of enterprises that had stopped operating for a period of time registered themselves as new enterprises when they resumed operation. Although the number of registered enterprises overestimates the true figure, the actual number of enterprises in operation would be closer to that total if the informal sector were taken into account (see below, under "Crime, Rent-Seeking, and the Informal Sector").

---

1. In the context of this section, "private sector" excludes all financial institutions such as banks and insurance firms.

Of the 20,000 operating enterprises, some 12,400 have taken part in a statistical survey that was conducted by the Lithuanian Department of Statistics at the end of 1996. Although the number of enterprises corresponds only to about one-sixth of those registered, the Department of Statistics has found, by double-checking with the tax authority, that those 12,400 account for almost 90 percent of the sector's total sales.

Tables 6-1 and 6-2 present the economic and financial findings of the survey. Of the 12,400 enterprises included, about 11,000 (89 percent) were classified as "private," which is defined here as enterprises with less than 50 percent state ownership. Extrapolating that proportion to the total population of firms, we can assume that approximately 17,800 (89 percent of 20,000) operating enterprises are privately held. Since the total accumulated number of privatized enterprises is 5,880 (according to the Privatization Agency), an estimated 12,000 private enterprises have been established since independence that are still in operation.

Table 6-1. Breakdown of Nonfinancial State-Owned and Private Enterprises Surveyed by Sector, as of 1 January 1997

Activity	*Number of companies*				*Number of employees*			
	Total	*State sector*	*Private sector*	*Percent of private sector*	*Total*	*State sector*	*Private sector*	*Percent of private sector*
Agriculture, hunting, and forestry	245	69	176	71.8	20,214	16,445	3,769	18.6
Fishing	56	2	54	96.4	882	17	865	98.1
Mining and quarrying	41	8	33	80.5	2,982	582	2,400	80.5
Manufacturing	2,527	241	2,286	90.5	233,844	36,771	197,073	84.3
Electricity, gas, and water supply	131	109	22	16.8	40,836	40,460	376	0.9
Construction	1,174	62	1,112	94.7	73,161	9,005	64,156	87.7
Wholesale and retail trade	4,980	311	4,669	93.8	95,044	7,860	87,184	91.7
Hotels and restaurants	597	54	543	91.0	11,322	2,716	8,606	76.0
Transport, storage, and communications	1,025	86	939	91.6	81,432	61,380	20,052	24.6
Real estate, rental, and business activities	1,080	200	880	81.5	22,875	12,683	10,192	44.6
Education	60	28	32	53.3	1,583	1,231	352	22.2
Health and social work	89	18	71	79.8	4,647	2,275	2,372	51.0
Other community, social, and personal service activities	386	150	236	61.1	13,923	9,166	4,757	34.2
Total	12,391	1,338	11,053	89.2	602,745	200,591	402,154	66.7

Source: Lithuanian Department of Statistics.

Only 11 percent (1,338) of the surveyed enterprises have been identified as having more than 50 percent state ownership. At the same time, state enterprises, on average, are much larger than private concerns, because the former hold more than half of the assets and employ one-third of the (surveyed) workforce. The private sector of the (surveyed) businesses accounted for 70 percent of total annual sales and 52 percent of annual net profits. This indication of lower profitability in the private sector is not in

Table 6-2. Breakdown of Nonfinancial State-Owned and Private Enterprise Sales, Profit, and Assets, by Sector, as of 1 January 1997

Activity	Total sales (Lt million)			Profit after tax (Lt million)			Total assets (Lt million)			Average in private sector(%)
	Total	State sector	Private sector	Total	State sector	Private sector	Total	State sector	Private sector	
Agriculture, hunting, and forestry	599	424	175	4	24	(20)	577	391	186	30.7
Fishing	30	1	29	(2)	0	(2)	54	1	53	97.8
Mining and quarrying	203	39	164	31	9	22	298	70	228	76.1
Manufacturing	13,129	3,189	9,939	436	105	331	12,538	3,167	9,370	75.4
Electricity, gas, and water supply	4,292	4,271	21	267	268	(0)	9,723	9,696	27	0.4
Construction	2,789	263	2,526	86	7	80	4,462	2,259	2,202	77.4
Wholesale and retail trade	15,010	822	14,188	320	(16)	336	6,264	544	5,720	92.9
Hotels and restaurants	298	73	226	1	(0)	1	452	128	324	73.7
Transport, storage, and communications	3,755	2,563	1,192	364	321	43	7,007	5,783	1,224	20.3
Real estate, rental, and business activities	568	225	343	25	8	17	1,038	501	537	59.8
Education	22	16	7	2	1	1	21	17	5	30.7
Health and social work	118	64	54	7	5	2	178	100	78	40.1
Other community, social, and personal service activities	258	166	92	6	7	(1)	453	354	98	28.7
Total	41,073	12,117	28,956	1,546	738	808	43,065	23,012	20,053	56.4

Source: Lithuanian Department of Statistics.

agreement with information from other sources, and may be the result of accounting differences (or statistical error).

The number of enterprises, employment, total sales, profit after tax, and assets are also broken down by industry sector in tables 6-1 and 6-2. In sectoral distribution, the private sector vastly dominates the Lithuanian economy, with the notable exception of infrastructure (electricity, gas, water, transport, and communications). While leaving room for further improvement, this dominance is remarkable in an economy that fully embraced a state-driven, central planning model less than a decade ago.

Privatization, especially voucher privatization, boosted the size of Lithuania's private sector in the early stages of transition. Out of the 8,063 eligible enterprises in 1991, 5,724 were privatized during the first stage, which was completed in 1995. According to the Lithuanian Privatization Agency, total privatized capital has risen to Lt 3.4 billion (US$850 million), or approximately 30 percent of all state-owned property. The assets of 156 companies were privatized during the second stage, which started in August 1996; 93 of these enterprises were privatized in the first half of 1997. Table 6-3 shows the residual shares retained by the government in enterprises sold through share subscription.

On 17 February 1997, with the purpose of accelerating Lithuania's second stage of privatization, the Lithuanian government approved a new list of companies to be privatized in 1997. The list of over 800 companies includes 14 major enterprises—among them are Lithuanian Telecom, Lithuanian Oil, the Lithuanian Radio and Television Centre, Lithuanian Airlines, Western Ship Repair Yards, and Hotel Lietuva.

Table 6-3. Residual Shares Retained by the Government in Enterprises Sold Through Share Subscription (Number of enterprises by sector)

Percentage and year	Industry	Transport	Construction	Trade	Household economy	Public services	Other	Total
< 10 percent state-owned								
1994	45	9	39	32	2	10	17	154
1997	133	21	102	103	5	27	72	463
10–20 percent state-owned								
1994	161	45	152	209	8	70	102	747
1997	244	56	208	278	12	82	157	1,037
20–30 percent state-owned								
1994	72	22	83	87	6	16	62	348
1997	76	13	48	63	1	12	46	259
30–40 percent state-owned								
1994	80	10	71	25	3	21	39	249
1997	50	6	17	19	5	3	14	114
40–50 percent state-owned								
1994	91	12	80	23	8	13	109	336
1997	73	4	37	16	9	9	32	180
> 50 percent state-owned								
1994	108	12	65	66	16	27	27	321
1997	53	16	19	44	32	9	40	213
Total								
1994	596	124	521	491	50	186	388	2,356
1997	629	116	431	523	64	142	361	2,266

Source: Lithuanian Privatization Agency.

Privatization was not the only, or even the most important, factor in private sector expansion in Lithuania. As table 6-4 shows, over 8,000 newly created, privately owned enterprises have entered the economy, and the entry of such enterprises proceeded at an accelerating pace during the first four years following independence (with a slowdown in 1995). These firms entered virtually all sectors of the economy, but their greatest representation is clearly in manufacturing, retail and wholesale trade, and business services.

The figures described above probably underestimate the true size of Lithuania's private sector. According to a study done by the Economic Research Center of Lithuania—"Preliminary Estimation of Monetary Flows in Lithuania (Hidden Economy)," March 1996—the "underground" or informal economy accounted for as much as 36 percent of GDP in 1994 and 41 percent in 1995. Similar estimates by the Department of Statistics indicate that the private informal economy may have produced value added amounting to 23 and 18 percent of the formal economy's GDP in 1995 and 1996, respectively.

Table 6-4. Private Enterprise Establishments by Economic Activity and Year of Creation (percent)

Sector	Total	1990	1991	1992	1993	1994	1995	1996
Agriculture	48	12	14	5	5	8	5	2
Fishery	16	1	4	—	6	1	3	—
Construction	258	65	50	46	43	36	18	107
Mining	8	—	—	2	4	2	—	3
Financial intermediary	48	—	7	22	5	13	2	8
Hotels	16	3	3	3	3	3	—	6
Construction and installations	113	30	25	12	13	20	13	15
Insurance	8	3	3	3	3	3	—	6
Manufacturing	1,711	642	364	264	173	205	62	257
Repairs	258	63	45	55	42	32	21	33
Individual services	379	69	79	69	67	74	23	68
Business-related services	509	68	107	107	107	91	29	99
Social services	242	29	18	100	37	40	18	44
Real estate	65	2	7	30	10	10	7	26
Restaurants	274	46	31	55	67	55	21	78
Retail trade	2,640	322	330	475	573	747	195	437
Wholesale trade	944	59	154	212	262	190	69	158
Transport	468	62	109	64	96	109	29	159
Other	65	8	11	19	13	11	2	3
Total	8,072	1,485	1,364	1,542	1,526	1,647	517	1,500

The largest share of underreported income belongs to small companies (with less than ten employees) engaged in retail trade. In employment, 180,000 workers (or 14 percent of the private sector labor force) were identified as "illegal workers" in 1995.

Constraints to PSD in Lithuania: The Perceptions of Domestic Entrepreneurs

Based on a previous enterprise survey conducted in November 1994, an updated survey (with some revisions in the questionnaire, sample, and size) was conducted by Baltic Surveys, Ltd., at the request of the World Bank in June 1997.[2] This section presents the results of this last survey and compares them with the data from the previous survey in order to identify incipient trends.

The new survey expanded the sample's coverage from only two locations (Vilnius and Kaunas) in 1994 to a total of five Lithuanian cities, adding Klaipeda, Siauliai, and Panevezys. Out of the sampling of 150 private enterprises that were randomly selected from the register of Lithuanian enterprises, the 131 that responded are the basis of the analysis in this section. Table 6-5 presents the breakdown of the sample of enterprises by location, number of employees, and operations.

---

2. The samples of the two surveys (1994 and 1997) were similar in the size of the enterprises, sector of activity, and structure of ownership. In both the 1994 and the 1997 surveys, over half of the enterprises were established as new, and two out of five had been privatized. Therefore, the data of the two waves of the surveys are broadly comparable.

Table 6-5. Characteristics of Companies in the 1997 Enterprise Survey

	Number of enterprises surveyed	Percent
Location		
Vilnius	50	38
Kaunas	23	23
Klaipeda	18	18
Siauliai	20	15
Panevezys	20	15
Total	131	100
Form of company		
Newly established	75	57
Privatized	52	40
Other	4	3
Total	131	100
Number of employees		
Up to 10	36	27
11–100	57	44
101 and more	38	29
Sector		
Industry	70	53
Retail/service	61	47
Total	131	100

Main Constraints

Table 6-6 shows the perceptions of the enterprises surveyed regarding the main constraints to operations and growth in order of importance. In the following paragraphs, the constraints are analyzed and discussed.

Table 6-6. Main Constraints to Company Operation and Growth

Rank (June 1997)	Rank (November 1994)	Constraint
1	1	High level of taxes
2	5	Access to finance
3	2	Cost of finance
4	6	Weak demand
5	4	Inflation or price instability
6	3	Government regulation
7	7	Judicial system
8	8	Political or policy uncertainty
9	10	Technology and production
10	9	Lack of qualified labor

According to both surveys, the high level of taxes was by far the main constraint to operations and growth. However, as can be deduced from the part of the survey that deals specifically with government-related action and regulation, the problem is really taxation in a broader sense. Tax regulation and tax administration are considered almost as problematic as the level of the taxes. During direct interviews with Lithuanian businessmen, it became clear that contradictions and frequent changes in taxation rules and regulations, and arbitrariness and unpredictability in interpretation and implementation, are more bothersome than the level of taxes, which are not high by international standards. (The taxation issue, particularly tax administration, is the subject of a separate Policy Note.)

Access to finance and the cost of finance ranked second and third, respectively, among the constraints to private sector development in the 1997 survey. The problem of the cost of finance does not seem to have decreased much in importance since the previous survey, despite the considerable decrease in interest rates since 1994. At the same time, the problem of access to finance seems to have worsened since 1994, when it ranked much lower on the list of problems. It should also be noted (see table 6-7) that large companies seemed to have more problems with finance than small and medium-size enterprises (SMEs). It may be that SMEs have accepted that external financing is more or less out of reach for the time being. It probably also indicates that larger enterprises, particularly those endeavoring to increase exports, feel a mounting need to modernize their production facilities. (The Policy Note on the Lithuanian banking sector deals with impediments to increasing credit availability from banks.)

Table 6-7. Main Constraints by Size and Sector of Enterprises, June 1997

Constraint	Overall score	Size of company			Sector	
		Small	Medium	Large	Industry	Commerce
High level of taxes	4.38	4.42	4.28	4.50	4.36	4.41
Access to finance	3.58	3.27	3.56	3.91	3.37	3.88
Cost of finance	3.55	2.96	3.64	3.86	3.48	3.64
Weak demand	3.54	3.39	3.38	3.93	3.67	3.38
Inflation or price instability	3.42	3.60	3.08	3.80	3.30	3.55
Regulation	3.30	3.16	3.25	3.47	3.13	3.51
Functioning of judicial system	3.00	2.85	2.92	3.24	3.00	3.00
Political or policy uncertainty	2.53	2.72	2.42	2.57	2.48	2.60
Technology and production	2.48	2.21	2.49	2.68	2.68	2.20
Lack of qualified labor	2.30	2.40	2.38	2.10	2.31	2.30
Access to services	2.26	2.09	2.27	2.38	2.38	2.10
Procuring inputs	1.91	1.74	1.93	2.00	2.00	1.78
Infrastructure problems	1.72	1.63	1.83	1.62	1.68	1.76

Note: On a scale from 1 to 5, 1 = no constraint and 5 = severe constraint.

Fourth on the list of constraints in 1997 was weak demand. It was considered almost as serious as the finance constraints and has become more serious than in 1994, when it ranked only sixth on the list. The problem is partly a reflection of the continued low domestic purchasing power and increasing competition from imports. Exports, which still make up a relatively small part of total sales, also pose a problem for most Lithuanian enterprises. Among the surveyed enterprises, exports accounted for an average of 24 percent of the sales of large enterprises, 16 percent of the sales of medium-size firms, and 14 percent of the sales of small enterprises. The share of exports has actually been decreasing for small and medium-size enterprises over the last year. The notion of weak demand is likely to be linked to a low level of competitiveness; weak marketing skills; and, above all, weak management. (Mechanisms to improve management performance are discussed in the Policy Note on corporate governance.)

Inflation and price instability are considered a relatively serious problem, although less so than the problems mentioned above. It was considered less severe in 1997 than in 1994, which, of course, is a result of the considerable reduction in inflation over this period. Inflation, however, has still been considerably higher than in Lithuania's trading partners in the West. Combined with the nominal exchange rate fixed by the Currency Board, this has led to a real effective appreciation of the lita against the currencies of those countries. Anxiety in regard to the fate of the lita after the abandonment of the Currency Board is also possibly embedded in the concerns regarding inflation and price stability.

Government regulation (and bureaucracy in general) is still considered a problem, although the situation has improved, judging from the lesser worries of entrepreneurs about these matters in 1997 compared with 1994. Taxation issues, however, loom far above other worries about government interference, as discussed below.

The judicial system is seventh on the list, and the last of the constraints that can be classified as "serious" according to the 1997 survey. Its relatively low ranking, however, conceals a general lack of confidence in the judicial system; the disillusion of those who have tried to use the system; and, ultimately, the resignation of those who assume the courts away. Of the enterprises surveyed, one-third—the majority of them large enterprises—had gone to court an average of just over four times to get justice in the last three years. Of those who won their cases, less than 60 percent managed to get their judgments enforced. And of those who went to court, only about half said they were likely to go to court a second time. It is interesting to note that for every case solved in court, approximately one case was solved before going to court. (The judicial system is the subject of a separate Policy Note.)

Government Regulation

The survey also attempted to determine the areas of government regulation (and which agencies of government) caused the greatest problems in the activities of enterprises. As shown in table 6-8, taxation (the level of taxes, tax regulation, and tax administration) clearly caused the most trouble. Tax administration has become much more troublesome in 1997 than it was in 1994. Labor regulations, ownership rights, licensing requirements, import regulation, and customs procedures were next in line in the 1997 survey, but the difficulties in these areas were considered only moderate. In particular, import regulation and customs procedures were considered much less of a problem in 1997 than they were three years ago. Export regulation, price controls, and restrictions relating to labor were not considered problems in 1997 or 1994.

Table 6-8. Government Regulation–Related Constraints

Constraint	1997	1994	Change
1. High level of taxes	4.30	4.60	(0.30)
2. Tax-related regulations	4.25	4.35	(0.10)
3. Tax administration/collection	3.64	3.17	0.47
4. Government labor regulations	2.59	1.89	0.70
5. Annual licensing requirements	2.20	2.09	0.11
6. Regulations on land ownership, sale, or mortgage	2.20	2.53	(0.33)
7. Import regulations/customs procedures for imports	2.11	2.94	(0.83)
8. Regulations on changes in ownership and capital of my firm	2.09	2.17	(0.08)
9. Regulations on foreign investment	1.90	2.08	(0.18)
10. Export regulations	1.84	2.08	(0.24)
11. Price controls of inputs	1.74	1.48	0.26
12. Labor union restrictions	1.33	1.14	0.19

Note: On a scale from 1 to 5, 1 = no constraint and 5 = severe constraint.

Predictably, the Ministry of Finance, which is responsible for taxation, is considered to be the most problematic agency of government. It is perhaps surprising that the government in general and Seimas are next on the list of troublesome "agencies." Enterprises seem to have little difficulty with labor inspection, the Social Insurance Agency (SODRA), and local governments (table 6-9).

Table 6-9. Government Agencies Causing the Greatest Difficulties, June 1997 (percentage of answers)

| Agency | All respondents | Size of company (employees) | | | Sector | |
		Up to 10	11–100	101+	Industry	Retail/service
Ministry of Finance, tax inspection	21	19	23	18	17	25
Government	15	14	14	18	19	11
Parliament	11	5.6	14	11	4.3	18
Customs	9.2	11	7	11	11	6.6
State social insurance (SODRA)	4.6	0	7	5.3	2.9	6.6
Labor inspection	5.3	5.6	7	2.6	7.1	3.3
Local government	3.1	5.6	1.8	2.6	0	6.6

Finance-Related Constraints

The part of the 1997 survey that takes a closer look at the finance-related constraints (table 6-10) indicates that the level of interest rates was the most severe constraint, although less of a problem than in 1994. Other constraints appear to have been much less troublesome. Lack of access to supplier credit, lack of access to nonbank investors, and other requirements of banks were rated as only modest constraints. The collateral requirements of banks were rated more serious, but not nearly as significant as the level of interest rates.

Table 6-10. Finance-Related Constraints

Constraint	1997	1994	Change
1. Level of interest rates	4	4.58	(0.58)
2. Collateral requirements of bank/financial institution	3.21	3.25	(0.04)
3. Requirement to produce financial documents	2.4	2.02	0.38
4. Lack of access to supplier credit	2.29	2.68	(0.39)
5. Lack of access to specialized export finance	2.19	2.06	0.13
6. Lack of access to nonbank investors/partners	2.1	1.87	0.23
7. Lack of connections with bank/financial institutions	1.92	1.61	0.31
8. Other requirements of lending institutions	1.8	1.59	0.21
9. Requirements to have a deposit or track record	1.3	1.1	0.20

Note: On a scale from 1 to 5, 1 = no constraint and 5 = severe constraint.

Survey results also show that internal funds are still clearly the main source of financing, both for capital investments and for working capital. Bank financing is second, but not far ahead of local moneylenders and family and friends. Only 34 percent of the respondents said they had received financing from banks, and even in the case of large enterprises, such funding was secured by no more than 50 percent of firms.

The 1997 survey also explored the attitudes of enterprises toward attracting new equity investors. While 73 percent of the surveyed enterprises said they were interested in attracting outside investors, only 21 percent were interested in being listed on the Lithuanian Stock Exchange (4 percent were already listed). The reasons given for the lack of interest in a listing seem to indicate a lack of knowledge of the functioning of the stock exchange and a lack of confidence in being able to access this source of funds. (The securities market is the subject of a separate Policy Note.)

One of the main prerequisites for access to external financing is the ability and willingness to provide timely and reliable financial information to prospective investors of both loan and equity funds. Reliable financial information, in turn, is dependent upon the use of internationally accepted accounting standards and audits. The survey looked at the extent to which enterprises use internationally accepted standards in accounting and audits and the degree of interest within enterprises in learning more about, and using, such standards. The survey shows that only 15 percent of the enterprises use international standards in their accounting, and that only 21 percent have their accounts audited. At the same time, a large portion of enterprises are interested in learning more about, and using, international standards in their accounting and having their accounts audited in accordance with those standards. Legislation and regulation for accounting and auditing are deficient, however, and appropriate training in these areas is scarce. (The Policy Note on corporate governance mentioned above deals with the problems of accounting and auditing in Lithuania.)

Crime, Rent-Seeking, and the Informal Sector

The 1994 and 1997 surveys also looked at the extent of crime and corruption that enterprises are encountering and the extent of the informal sector, or "grey economy."

Racketeering does not seem to be as great a problem as it was in the past. Only 8 percent of the enterprises surveyed in 1997 (down from 15 percent in 1994) said they were paying for "protection." Those levels are probably less accurate than the general trend, because the security considerations of respondents might be at play. Very few large enterprises admitted to having to make such payments. There was little difference among industrial, service, and retail enterprises in this area.

Rent-seeking in government, however, is still quite common according to the survey. Over 40 percent of the respondents claim they have to pay informal fees to government officials to get things done. And the amounts are not insignificant in the Lithuanian context; the average of bribes paid to government officials in a year for all enterprises was Lt 3,800 (US$950), and the average for large enterprises alone was Lt 6,400 (US$1,600). Nevertheless, there has been a significant improvement since 1994, when 54 percent of enterprises said they had to bribe officials with an average of Lt 13,000 (US$3,250) a year to see their business done.

On the question about how much of the enterprise sector the respondents thought was represented by the informal sector, the answers were 28 percent of production, 43 percent of retail trade, and 41 percent of the service sector. These figures may seem high, and they are, almost by definition, merely rough estimates. The results, however, coincide with those of a more scientific study made by an economic research organization in Vilnius in 1996. This study concluded that the size of the informal sector was around 40 percent of the enterprise sector at that time.

When asked about the percentage of their own activities that were not recorded for tax purposes, the enterprises conceded to 11 percent in nonrecorded sales. In this case, it would be natural for enterprises to "underestimate" such sales. None of the enterprises surveyed operated totally outside the official economy. The reported nonrecorded sales varied from 20 percent in small enterprises to only 1 percent in enterprises classified as large, and from 10 percent in manufacturing enterprises to 14 percent in retail trade and service industries.

Entrepreneurs were also asked about problems with unfair competition—that is, from competitors who break rules or regulations. Of the respondents, 71 percent said they did suffer from such unfair competition. The figure was higher (75 percent) in retail trade and service industries than in manufacturing industry (67 percent), and, surprisingly, the percentage rose with the size of the enterprise. Most problems were caused by competitors not paying social security taxes, followed by avoidance of payment of VAT and other taxes; avoidance of import duties; violations of health and safety regulations; and violations of copyright, patent, or trademark laws. All of these problems seem to have increased between 1994 and 1997 (see table 6-11).

Table 6-11. Problems Related to Unfair or Illegal Practices of Competitors, June 1997

Practice	All respondents	Size of company (employees)			Sector	
		Up to 10	11–100	101+	Industry	Retail/service
1. They avoid sales tax and other taxes	3.99	3.95	4.13	3.83	3.90	4.09
2. They do not pay duties or observe trade regulations	3.60	3.55	3.67	3.53	3.52	36.8
3. They sell imports below international prices	3.63	3.95	3.64	3.40	3.77	3.48
4. They unfairly sell below my prices	4.04	3.86	4.05	4.17	4.09	4.00
5. They avoid labor taxes/regulations (e.g., social security)	4.11	3.90	4.17	4.17	4.16	40.5
6. They violate copyright, patent, or trademark laws	2.90	3.21	3.14	2.40	3.00	2.78
7. They collude to limit my access to credit, supplies, land, equipment, or customers	2.90	3.21	2.76	2.87	2.93	2.85
8. They don't obey health and safety regulations	3.34	3.11	3.33	3.50	3.25	3.45

Constraints to PSD in Lithuania: The Perceptions of Foreign Investors[3]

Foreign Investment in Lithuania

The flow of foreign direct investment (FDI) into Lithuania has been relatively insignificant thus far, and it has been much less (on a per capita basis) than foreign investment in its Baltic neighbors and in most other east European countries, but it picked up significantly in 1997. The total amount of FDI through 1996 was Lt 2.3 billion (US$580 million), and it is estimated to have exceeded US$1 billion in 1997. The largest investors in Lithuania (as of 1 October 1997) were the United States (25 percent of total FDI), Sweden (11), Germany (10.5), the United Kingdom (7), Luxembourg (5.4), and Finland (5.3). Figures 6-1 and 6-2 show the cumulative foreign investment flow to Lithuania from 1991 to 1997, as well as the total investments by country for the period 1991–96.[4]

Overall Assessment of the FDI Environment

According to the previously mentioned 1994 survey, the three main factors that attracted foreign investment in Lithuania were found to be (i) the proximity to both European and FSU markets, (ii) a skilled labor force, (iii) successful macrostabilization, and (iv) relatively rapid privatization. A survey

---

3. The source for this section is "Country Information 97.2," by the Lithuanian Investment Agency.

4. The ranking differs to some extent from the one above, because the graph is based on data as of the end of 1996.

conducted by the Lithuanian Investment Agency (LIA) in early 1997 ranked (i) low-cost and high-quality labor, (ii) professional services, and (iii) market access eastward as the three main attractions for foreign investments. Although the geographical location was then considered a significant advantage, it was not a major reason to invest, because many investors had included Lithuania as part of a global or regional marketing strategy.

Figure 6-1. Cumulative Foreign Investment in Lithuania, 1991–97

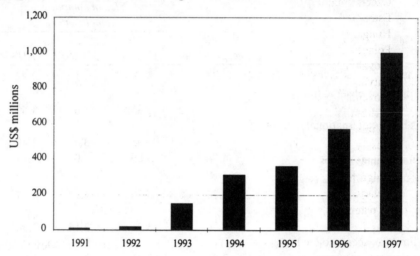

Figure 6-2. Cumulative Foreign Investment in Lithuania by Country, 1991–96

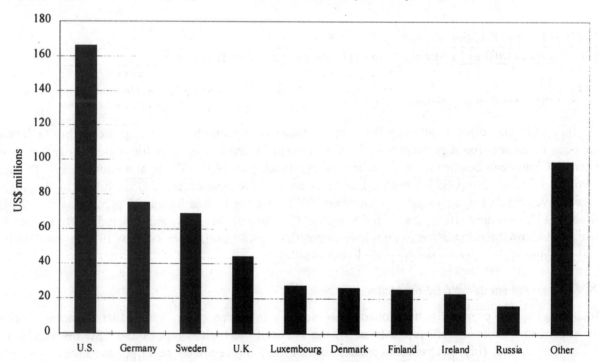

Also in the LIA survey, 83 percent of the respondents expressed interest in investing more in Lithuania. The survey also ranked east European and FSU countries by the attractiveness of their investment climate. Table 6-12 shows that Lithuania ranked in the middle of the group, considerably below Estonia and also below Latvia.

Table 6-12. Investment Climate in Central and Eastern Europe

	Country	Score
1.	Czech Republic	1.90
2.	Estonia	2.22
3.	Hungary	2.29
4.	Poland	2.43
5.	Slovakia	2.66
6.	Latvia	2.77
7.	Slovenia	3.00
8.	**Lithuania**	**3.10**
9.	Ukraine	3.14
10.	Russia	3.38
11.	Rumania	3.63
12.	Bulgaria	4.04
13.	Belarus	4.54

Note: On a scale of 1 to 5, 1 = most favorable and 5 = least favorable.

A separate survey made by the European Bank for Reconstruction and Development (EBRD) that polled foreign investors regarding the investment climate in the three Baltic capitals ranks Tallin and Riga ahead of Vilnius. The respective advantages of the three cities identified in the survey are listed in table 6-13.

Table 6-13. Baltic Cities' Advantages for FDI

Tallin	Riga	Vilnius
• Openness	• Largest market	• Relations with Russia
• Economic stability	• Better growth prospects as a "Eurocity"	• Ethnic stability
• Speed of economic development	• Availability of business partners	• Lowest labor costs
• Low costs	• Closeness to Russia	• Lowest manufacturing costs
• Linguistic skills		
• Proximity to Nordic countries		
• Knowledge of the West		

Main Constraints to Foreign Investment

In the 1994 survey, the foreign investors interviewed uniformly perceived three main constraints to foreign investment: (i) a generally negative attitude toward FDI and pervasive FDI discrimination (mentioned by 80 percent of firms interviewed); (ii) frequently changing and often vague and nontransparent legislation, a problem exacerbated by red tape and corruption; and (iii) slower overall progress with market reforms and liberalization and key institutional reforms compared with neighbors and other FDI competitors.

Fortunately, in LIA's 1997 survey, negative attitudes toward discrimination against FDI were not raised as major constraints by the foreign investors interviewed. The major obstacles were identified as related to regulatory issues, such as the legal, tax, and customs systems in the form of deficient, unclear, and frequently changing laws, and regulations and their unpredictable and nontransparent interpretation and enforcement. Inefficient customs services were perceived as most cumbersome, with the duty drawback system as a leading obstacle (see table 6-14).

Table 6-14. The Major Constraints to FDI as Seen by Foreign Investors

Constraint	Score
Customs procedures	4.27
The banking system	3.86
Tax collection procedures	3.70
Import conditions	3.60
The legal system	3.56
Tax system (laws)	3.48
Level of technology	3.45
The securities market	3.30
Foreign investment incentives	3.00
Export conditions	2.97
International trade agreements	2.91
Ease of implementing new technology	2.80
Manufacturing costs	2.21

Note: On a scale of 1 to 5, 1 = no constraint and 5 = very severe constraint.

It is interesting to compare these results with those from this project's 1997 survey of domestic enterprises. Regulatory issues and the taxation system were identified as serious obstacles by both foreign and domestic investors. The customs services issue, which is ranked as the number one obstacle for foreign investors, was ranked only number seven by domestic enterpreneurs, and with a considerable improvement since 1994.

Regarding rent-seeking, the results of the survey show that many foreign investors perceive the civil service as corrupt. When asked what should be done in Lithuania first in order to attract more foreign investments, "reduction of crime and corruption by broad administrative reform" was the answer of most of the investors. Legal reform, legal stability, education of government and public on benefits of FDI, improvement of the tax system, and promotion of information on Lithuania were the other major recommendations made by the foreign investor community.

7

PSD ENVIRONMENT: TAX ADMINISTRATION

Although the focus of this chapter is tax administration, its problems cannot be separated from those arising from the tax law. Over the past few years, the Lithuanian government has demonstated a recognition that taxpayers in general, and foreign investors in particular, prefer certainty, stability, and impartiality to tax incentives, as evidenced by the phasing out of tax holidays and the broadening of the VAT tax base. This pattern follows the practice of both OECD countries and a number of eastern European countries that have made efforts to increase the simplicity and neutrality of their tax systems by withdrawing tax concessions to selected groups of taxpayers. Such concessions inevitably create borderline cases, inhibit the administration and consistent interpretation of the tax system, and are considered unfair by the taxpayers who are not entitled to such concessions.

Many of the difficulties in administering individual and corporate income taxes in Lithuania follow from the past proliferation of special rates for selected groups or activities that were designed to confer preferential treatment. For example, farmers, small traders, recipients of dividend income and capital gains, and enterprises reinvesting their profits all receive special treatment. In addition, the absence of clear criteria make it difficult to interpret the law on such questions as what constitutes a legitimate deduction from taxable profits. The widening of the individual and corporate income tax base that has occurred in virtually all OECD countries and a number of others has enabled income tax rates to be lowered considerably without loss of revenue, but this has not yet taken place in Lithuania, where the erosion of the individual and corporate income tax base has led to administrative complexity, distortions of economic decisions, and low tax compliance.

This chapter, apart from a summary of the Lithuanian tax system and its comparison with the systems of other countries, is confined to suggesting possible improvements in the *administration* of business taxes.[1] Broadly speaking, these suggestions take two forms: the first is the implementation of measures that will lead to greater compliance and cooperation by taxpayers; the second is to improve the efficiency of the tax inspectorate and its revenue collection techniques.

The Lithuanian Tax System and Tax Administration

Tax Structures

As in virtually all countries, over 95 percent of total tax revenues in Lithuania are derived from the taxes

---

1. In Lithuania, business taxes also comprise VAT and excise taxes. Although designed to fall on consumers, these taxes are collected by businesses.

listed in table 7-1. Other taxes, as well as some of the small excise taxes on products such as chocolates, are frequently referred to as nuisance taxes because they complicate tax administration and add to taxpayers' compliance costs without bringing in much revenue. It would be reasonable to consider the abolition of such taxes. Compared with most OECD countries, Lithuania relies more heavily on indirect taxes (especially VAT), is about equally dependant on payroll taxes, and is much less reliant on income taxes on individuals, which is the main source of revenue among most OECD countries.

Table 7-1. Structure of Lithuanian and Average OECD Tax Receipts
(percentage of total tax receipts)

Tax	Lithuania			OECD average, 1995[a]
	1994	*1995*	*1996*	*1995[a]*
Taxes on income and profits	32.7	29.7	29.8	35.3
Taxes on individuals	22.3	22.2	23.2	27.0
Taxes on companies	10.4	7.5	6.5	8.0
Payroll or social security taxes	27.9	26.7	28.7	25.1
Taxes on goods and services	35.1	39.3	39.2	30.8
VAT and sales taxes	21.6	25.9	25.3	17.6
Excises and other specific taxes on goods and services[b]	13.5	13.4	13.9	13.1
Property taxes	0.7	2.0	2.0	5.4
Total of above taxes	96.4	97.7	99.7	96.6

   a. Firm OECD figures for 1996 are not yet available. Subtotals of income and consumption taxes do not completely round up.
   b. In Lithuania this includes road tax and foreign trade taxes.
   Source: IMF tables for Lithuania and *OECD Revenue Statistics*, 1965–96 (Paris, 1997).

Tax Levels

Table 7-2 provides an international comparison of total tax revenues and revenues from major taxes as a percentage of GDP. It shows that, apart from Turkey, Lithuania is much less heavily taxed than any OECD country, and that this discrepancy is almost entirely the result of the relatively light burden of income taxes (less than half the OECD average). As explained in more detail below, the low revenue capacity of individual and corporate income taxes is largely the result of the numerous concessions built into the system and the avoidance of payroll taxes by many citizens. Taxpayers who are not favored by the tax law or who cannot avoid payment of the payroll tax resent the unfairness of the tax system and seek to evade the taxes if they can, through such measures as hiding secondary employment.

   With the exception of excises, Lithuania's relative tax collection position is unlikely to improve in the medium term. Although income tax revenues are expected to rise (through the increase in the share of total factor payments to labor, the broadening of the tax net to include self-employed and agricultural workers, and administrative improvements), several currently proposed measures will lower total tax collection. These measures include (i) lowering the VAT rate to 16 percent; (ii) reducing the income tax of natural persons from 33 percent to 29 percent; (iii) exempting purchases of modern technologies from taxation; (iv) increasing the nontaxable income ceiling; (v) abolishing a tax on profits retained for investment (already done); (vi) introducing a tax amnesty (already done); (vii) putting a ceiling on compulsory health contributions; (viii) making further tax concessions for small and medium-size enterprises; (ix) providing further tax preferences for enterprises supporting charity, culture, sports, and the like; and (x) allowing up to 2 percent of the personal income tax to be paid to charity and other recognized activities rather than to the state.

Table 7-2. Comparative Levels of Tax Revenue in Selected OECD Countries (1995) and Lithuania (1996 and 1997)
(percentage of GDP)

Country/economy	Total	Income and profits	Social security/payroll	Goods and services	Property and other
Canada	36.1	16.0	6.1	9.5	4.5
Mexico	18.8	5.8	3.7	9.0	0.3
United States	27.6	12.3	7.0	5.0	3.3
Australia	29.9	16.2	2.0	8.9	2.8
Japan	27.8	10.5	9.8	4.3	3.3
New Zealand	37.0	22.2	0.3	12.5	2.0
Czech Republic	47.3	11.7	19.0	15.9	0.7
Denmark	51.6	31.1	1.9	16.5	2.0
France	44.1	7.8	20.2	12.0	4.1
Germany	39.3	11.5	15.4	11.3	1.1
Hungary	41.0	9.3	14.2	16.5	1.0
Ireland	37.5	15.1	6.0	14.7	1.7
Italy	41.7	14.5	13.1	11.8	2.3
Netherlands	45.9	12.3	19.3	11.9	2.1
Norway	41.2	14.3	9.9	15.8	1.1
Poland	43.2	13.3	13.4	15.4	1.2
Portugal	33.0	8.6	8.7	14.7	1.0
Spain	35.8	9.9	13.8	10.0	2.1
Sweden	51.0	21.6	14.6	13.2	1.6
Switzerland	33.9	13.4	12.4	5.5	2.5
Turkey	22.2	6.6	3.5	8.3	3.9
United Kingdom	34.1	12.1	6.1	12.0	3.8
Lithuania (1996)	22.7	6.7	6.5	7.8	1.7
Lithuania (1997, projected)	25.9	5.1	9.3	10.1	1.4
OECD average (unweighted)	38.3	13.6	10.5	12.1	2.1

Source: OECD Revenue Statistics, 1965–95 (Paris, 1996); and International Monetary Fund staff estimates for Lithuania.

Tax Rates

Table 7-3 provides the nominal rates of central government individual and corporate tax as well as VAT for a selected list of countries. It should be noted that local income tax rates are not included, although in some countries (but not in Lithuania) these taxes are much more important than the taxes imposed by the central government (for example, in Nordic countries and Switzerland). Lithuania's nominal rates of corporate income tax and VAT are not very different from those of other countries. Only Lithuania, however, exempts tax on reinvested profits, which reduces the already declining revenues from the corporate income tax, provides possibilities for tax avoidance, and unnecessarily complicates tax administration.[2]

---

2. It is difficult to compare rates of social security tax, but in most OECD countries, employees pay from 5 to 20 percent of their income (which is withheld along with their income tax). In only a few OECD countries (France, Italy, Spain, and Sweden) is the employers' payroll tax as high as in Lithuania. It is also difficult to compare rates of excise tax, but the Lithuanian rates, particularly on tobacco, are much lower than those of OECD countries.

Table 7-3. Nominal Rates of Personal and Corporate Income Tax and VAT at the Federal/Central Level

| Country | 1995 | | | 1996, |
| | Personal income tax | | Basic rate of corporate | Standard rate of VAT as percentage |
	Top rate	Number of rates	income tax[c,d]	of tax-exclusive price
Australia	47	4	33	n.e.
Austria	50	5	34	20
Belgium[a,b]	55	7	39	21
Canada[a,b]	31.3	4	29	7(6)[e]
Denmark[a,b]	34.5	4	34	25
Finland[a,b]	39	6	25	22
France	56.8	6	33	20.6
Germany	53	n.a.	30 (45)	15
Greece	40	13	40 (35)	18
Iceland[a]	38.15	2	33	24.5
Ireland	48	2	50	21
Italy[b]	51	7	36	19
Japan[a,b]	50	5	38	3
Luxembourg	50	17	33	15
Netherlands	60	3	35	17.5
New Zealand	33	2	33	12.5
Norway[a,b]	13.7	2	19	23
Portugal[a,b]	40	n.a.	36	17
Spain[a,b]	56	16	35	16
Sweden[a]	25	1	28	25
Switzerland[a,b]	11.5	13	4 to 10 progressive	6.5
Turkey[a,b]	55	7	25	15
United Kingdom	40	3	33	17.5
United States[a,b]	39.6	5	35	n.e.
Latvia	25	1	25	18
Estonia	26	1	26	18
LITHUANIA	33	1[f]	29 (0)	18

n.a. Not applicable.

n.e. Nonexistent.

a. Countries with subcentral government personal income taxes.

b. Countries with subcentral government corporation income taxes.

c. Some countries have special rates for firms with lower profits and for particular sectors.

d. Parenthetical figures represent special rates for *retained* as distinct from *distributed* profits.

e. Also sales taxes at subcentral levels of government.

f. Special rates for different sources of income also apply, including rates from 10 to 35 percent for secondary work.

A Summary of the Main Lithuanian Taxes

THE INDIVIDUAL INCOME TAX. Most OECD countries find it fair and administratively convenient to aggregate various kinds of income (global taxation) and apply the same progressive rate scale to all of them. In Lithuania, individual dividend income and capital gains are not subject to income tax, which apart from the regressivity involved, creates administrative problems, because taxpayers may attempt to disguise taxable income as tax-free capital gains. In addition, tax administration is handicapped by the complexity of the Lithuanian individual income tax, which, unlike those of the other Baltic countries, does not follow the typical OECD pattern of global taxation, but instead provides different rates for secondary employment, as well as reduced rates for selected kinds of income, as explained below.

Income from employment is taxed in two ways. Income from an individual's main employment by a company, institution, or organization in Lithuania or by a branch or representative office of a Lithuanian company, institution, or organization in a foreign country is taxed at a rate of 33 percent. Income from an individual's secondary employment is taxed at three different rates, ranging between 10 and 35 percent (income less than half the basic nontaxable minimum, BNM, is taxed at 10 percent; income between half and the full BNM is taxed at 20 percent; and income over the BNM is taxed at 35 percent). Personal income tax is deducted at the source by the employer. Income from an individual's employment by a foreign company, institution, or organization is taxed at a rate of 20 percent. The BNM does not apply to such income. Payment of this portion of personal income tax is the responsibility of the individual taxpayer.

Income derived from other sources is taxed as follows: (i) income from royalties is taxed at 13 percent; (ii) income from the sale of mushrooms, berries, medicinal herbs, and other forestry products is taxed at 5 percent; (iii) income from the sale of property is taxed at 10 percent; and (iv) income from the rental of property and income from other sources is taxed at 20 percent.

The income of partnerships and personal companies without the rights of legal persons is taxed at 24 percent, which is reduced to zero on income that is reinvested.

It is difficult to see the rationale for all these distinctions, which certainly complicate tax administration. It is particularly unclear why a distinction is made between an individual's main and secondary employment, with a progressive schedule applying only to the latter, and why partnerships are taxed at 24 percent while companies are taxed at 29 percent. It has already been noted that the share of receipts from the individual income tax is unusually low (table 7-1). This is partly the result of the numerous concessions described above, and partly the product of evasion by the self-employed, and partly an outcome of the government policy to move to indirect taxation on grounds of economic efficiency and ease of collection. In addition, the lack of progressivity of the individual income tax may cause resentment among taxpayers on equity grounds. Such resentment provides a strong motive for noncompliance.

THE CORPORATE INCOME TAX. The standard rate is 29 percent, but as with the individual income tax, there are a number of concessions that complicate the administration of the tax on enterprises and facilitate tax avoidance. Some of the more important concessions are: (i) agricultural enterprises are taxed at 10 percent; (ii) companies in priority sectors, determined by the government, are taxed at a rate between 5 percent and 29 percent; (iii) manufacturing companies and organizations that employ handicapped workers qualify for a reduction in the corporate income tax of between 25 percent and 100 percent, depending on the proportion of handicapped workers in their workforce; (iv) under the Law on Small Enterprises, the corporate income tax applied to certain companies with no more than 50 employees and total gross annual income of less than Lt 500,000 is reduced by 50 percent.

In addition, there is no withholding on income from dividends and interest, although a 10 percent withholding tax is levied on payments by residents to nonresidents for marketing, consultancy, and mediation services and on the rights to use trademarks, licenses, and company names.

All enterprises can apply straight line depreciation of fixed assets for tax purposes; the depreciation period depends on the nature of the asset. With the phasing-out of tax holidays for foreign enterprises and the planned introduction of a three-year carry-forward of losses, Lithuania is moving nearer to the practice of other countries. At the same time, Lithuania is unique in having a zero tax rate for reinvested profits.

In 1995, 72 percent, and in 1996, 87 percent of corporate tax receipts were obtained from joint-stock and private companies, while 22 percent of corporate tax receipts in 1995 and 6 percent in 1996 were from state public and municipal enterprises and companies.[3] Minimal corporate tax revenue is obtained from other sources, such as banks, agricultural partnerships, and branches of enterprises. While disaggregated data are scarce, it seems probable that many small enterprises, especially the self-employed and the agricultural sector, are escaping tax altogether.

SOCIAL SECURITY CONTRIBUTIONS OR PAYROLL TAXES. Contributions are paid to the State Social Insurance Fund and comprise a 30 percent tax on a company's monthly wage bill, payable by the employer, and a 1 percent tax on an employee's wage, payable by the employee. As already noted, the 30 percent employer contribution is very high, and the 1 percent employee contribution is low, in comparison with most OECD countries.

THE VAT. The VAT was introduced in May 1994 and modernized in February 1997. It applies to most goods and services at the rate of 18 percent. It is similar to VAT systems in most countries and largely meets the requirements of the European Union (EU). It should be observed, however, that a proposal to reduce VAT to 15 percent would bring it down to the minimum rate permitted by the EU and would be contrary to the EU aim of reducing VAT rate differentials among EU member countries. Also, between 1990 and 1996, at least fifteen OECD countries[4] *increased* their standard VAT rate by 1 to 3.5 percentage points. It was thought to be one of the less painful ways of reducing their budget deficits.

EXCISE TAXES. Although recently increased, the duties on gasoline products, alcoholic drinks (other than wine), and cigarettes, in particular, are very low by OECD standards and would have to be increased if Lithuania joined the EU. One constraint on such an increase in excise tax rates is the danger of cross-border smuggling. At the same time, there are a number of small excises in Lithuania on products that are not generally taxed in this way, such as chocolate, jewelry, and coffee. These taxes would eventually have to be eliminated under the EU Rates Directive of 19 October 1992 (92/77/CEC) if Lithuania joined.

Table 7-4. Breakdown of Excise Tax Revenues
(percent)

Item	1994	1995	1996
Alcoholic drinks	57.1	46.0	43.9
Tobacco products	7.0	5.7	9.5
Petroleum products	18.3	44.1	45.2
Electricity	9.9	1.0	0.2
Other goods	7.7	3.2	1.2

Source: Table 1.17 of *Government Finance of the Republic of Lithuania 1997* (Vilnius, 1997).

TAX ON REAL ESTATE AND LAND. Lithuania has a real estate tax of 1 percent on the regionally adjusted replacement value of real estate, payable by enterprises, and a separate tax, currently reduced to 1.5 percent, for most taxpayers (from the statutory 6 percent) of the value of the land, which is applicable to physical persons owning land and to physical and legal persons renting state land.

---

3. Table 1.14 of *Government Finance of the Republic of Lithuania 1997* (Vilnius, 1997).

4. Belgium, Denmark, Finland, France, Germany, Ireland, Italy, Luxembourg, New Zealand, Norway, Portugal, Spain, Sweden, Turkey, and the United Kingdom.

OTHER TAXES. There is a "road tax" that is based on revenue from goods sold and services provided. Rates vary from 0.1 percent to 0.5 percent, depending on the activity of the company. Such taxes do not exist in most countries. There is also a tax on pollution and on the value of extracted natural resources.

Tax Administration

Lithuania's tax administration is divided into fifty-six offices; the vast majority deal with fewer than 2,000 taxpayers. Apart from directions from the head office to local offices, there appears to be little contact or coordination among those fifty-six offices, although each follows rough central guidelines. There is also little contact or information exchange among the tax administration, the customs administration, and the social security administration. Nevertheless, the same tax inspector is responsible for the collection of the personal and corporate income tax and the VAT from each enterprise. This is a useful method of enabling cross-checking of tax declarations and reducing taxpayer compliance costs, and is an enhancement that is often lacking in the tax administration of OECD countries.

The administration of Lithuania's tax system is summarized below, first, as seen by tax officials in a small local tax office and in the largest (Vilnius) district; and second, in relation to the unanimous dissatisfaction, although expressed to varying degrees, of the private sector, including bankers, tax lawyers, and tax accountants, as well as managers of large and small enterprises.

THE POINT OF VIEW OF TAX OFFICIALS. The small tax office of the district of Salcininku R. is atypical in that it includes only one large firm of contractors; otherwise, it is responsible only for small to medium-size firms. Nevertheless, it illustrates how the administration of the corporate income tax system operates at this level. Although sophisticated audit selection techniques were unavailable because the office is still in the early days of computerization, the choice of firms for priority audit is not random. The aim is to audit all enterprises in full every three years, so about 30 percent of the enterprises are audited each year. The criteria for selection are to concentrate on the following: firms that have not been audited for a long time, larger firms from which little tax has been collected or that claimed to realize no profit, and firms in the alcohol and oil sectors. Around 90 percent of the declarations are found to require (generally small) adjustments upward. In cases where the enterprise challenges this ruling, virtually all cases are settled at the local level, and the final settlement is usually at the amount of taxable profit determined by the local office. During the past year, only two appeals (by the same firm) have been made to the central tax office. It is unclear whether taxpayers systematically underdeclare their taxable profits, knowing that whatever they declare, the tax authorities will adjust them upward, or whether they do not appeal against local rulings for the reasons indicated below. Nor is it clear whether these settlements at the local level result in too much, too little, or about the right amount of tax being paid. The tax authorities note that while they use their discretion in imposing maximum or minimum fines for administrative offenses, the law obliges them to impose heavy penalties (25 percent of turnover) when informal laborers or unsealed bottles of alcoholic drinks are found.

The central tax office (and the largest local office, Vilnius) appears well aware of the deficiencies that exist in the country's tax administration (discussed below). To some extent, officials are prevented from making the improvements they would like, and know how to make, by lack of resources and the considerable extra work created by frequent changes in the tax law (following the move away from the former Soviet form of tax system).

Among improvements recently made—or contemplated—by the tax administration are the following: (a) plans for the implementation of minimum or presumptive taxation on hard-to-tax small traders; (b) preparation of a staff manual documenting changes in the tax law and interpretations thereof to reduce inconsistent rulings; (c) the reduction of the fifty-six tax collection centers to approximately ten, one for each Lithuanian district; and (d) sending more local tax inspectors to training courses in tax administration (such as those organized by OECD). Although changes in tax law and interpretations are sometimes published in local newspapers, there is no systematic source of information. There is also little dialogue with the private sector on tax matters of common interest.

THE POINT OF VIEW OF LITHUANIAN ENTERPRISES. Chapter 6 of this report presents the results of two extensive surveys of Lithuanian enterprises (carried out in October 1994 and July 1997) designed to identify what they perceive as the main constraints to their future operation and growth. In both surveys, of thirteen suggested factors, "high level of taxes" was considered by far the most important among all kinds of enterprises (small, medium, and large, in both industry and commerce). While both surveys indicate intense dissatisfaction in the Lithuanian private sector with the tax system, because of the wide scope of the survey, the dissatisfaction registered most clearly at a general level, primarily under the vague statement that the main constraint was the high level of taxes. It should be recalled, however, that enterprises in all countries complain about high taxes, and that Lithuanian taxes are among the lowest in Europe. It thus seems reasonable to interpret this general complaint on the level of taxes as shorthand for related factors, such as unnecessarily complicated tax laws, high compliance costs, and poor tax administration that results in unfair competition from tax dodgers. The degree of seriousness conferred by Lithuanian entrepeneurs on these factors is presented in table 7-5.[5]

Table 7-5. Tax-Related Constraints: The Incumbent Private Sector's Views

Constraint	1994	1997	Change
High level of taxes	4.6	4.3	-0.3
Tax-related regulations	4.35	4.25	-0.1
Tax administration/collections	3.17	3.64	0.47
Competitors avoid payroll taxes	3.26	4.11	0.85
Competitors avoid other taxes	3.8	3.99	0.19
Competitors avoid import duties	3.53	3.6	0.07

Note: Importance of a constraint is ranked on a scale of 1 to 5, where 1 = no constraints and 5 = very serious constraints.
Source: Annex.

Direct interviews carried out in the context of this report with selected domestic tax accountants, lawyers, bankers, and traders in July 1977 revealed more specific reasons for dissatisfaction with the Lithuanian tax systems than could be gleaned from the more general results of the 1994 and 1997 surveys. The following is a summary list of these reasons:

- The tax inspectors with whom enterprises or their representatives must deal at the local level are perceived as untrained, unhelpful, and unaware of standard accounting procedures.
- The tendency of local inspectors is to search for technical mistakes that would enable them to increase their assessment of tax declared and impose penalties—frequently severe—even for minor offenses (for example, representing 25 percent of a firm's total turnover, enough to drive it out of business).
- Rulings are frequently inconsistent among inspectors, especially with regard to what constitutes allowable deductions from taxable profits.
- Little faith is placed in appeal procedures, because the central tax office that receives the appeal is

---

5. Of the 131 enterprises surveyed in 1997, 93 made the unfair competition point.

staffed entirely by tax inspectors, who are perceived to support the local tax rulings. If a case is considered sufficiently important to take to court, it is alleged that judges have insufficient technical knowledge of the issues involved and would tend to support the tax inspector's ruling. Meanwhile, apart from the costs and delays involved, the taxpayer is obliged to pay tax claimed by the tax inspector until the matter is finally resolved.

- Large firms with standard accounting procedures believe their declarations are challenged by the tax administration largely because of the latter's inability to collect tax from small firms that keep no records. Such tax disparities distort competition.
- Contract prices invariably provide the basis of tax assessments, even if the supplier could prove his customer has failed to make full, or even partial, payment of that price.
- It is never clear why a particular tax official goes for the maximum or minimum in the penalty range, and when questioned, replies are slow or nonexistent.
- Uncertainty over tax liability is increased by the absence of any precedents that might influence the tax administration.
- Although bribery is said to occur, it is not believed that corruption is widespread. But it is claimed that serious deterioration could occur in the absence of reform.

Key Potential Long-Term Improvements to Business Tax Administration

Politicians, senior officials, and the private sector, if not entirely in agreement on how the present tax administration should be modified, all accept that Lithuania's tax administration requires urgent reform. How to embark on such reform raises questions of priorities and feasibility. This section makes some suggestions on how progress might be made and draws heavily on the experience of EU and other OECD countries that have faced analogous problems during the last decade.

Although they may overlap and reinforce each other, there are two broad areas that would benefit from more effective tax administration. The first is generally known as the voluntary tax compliance strategy. The aim is to persuade all but the most delinquent citizens that it is in the interests of the taxpayers themselves, and the community as a whole, to pay the taxes that are legally due. The second area is the improvement of the efficiency of the tax inspectorate. Both elements are addressed below.

Winning the Taxpayers over: A Voluntary Compliance Strategy

The aim of the strategy is to persuade the taxpaying community that tax officials are providing the service of collecting taxes in an impartial manner and are not trying to overtax or discriminate among taxpayers. The success of this strategy depends on whether tax officials normally feel sufficiently confident of the accuracy of taxpayers' declarations that they can dispense with full verification. This allows officials to devote their limited resources to investigating areas where they consider tax is unlikely to be paid—in full or in part. The other side of the coin is that voluntary compliance occurs when taxpayers customarily file the information required by the tax authorities in an accurate and timely manner and make correct tax payments when due, without intervention by the tax authorities. The following paragraphs outline some of the measures that, together, constitute a voluntary compliance approach and that have been introduced over the past ten years in a number of OECD countries. They have been considered successful, in that tax compliance has improved and tax revenues have increased *without changes in the tax law*.

THE ESTABLISHMENT OF AN INDEPENDENT TAX APPEALS TRIBUNAL. This is perhaps the most important way of improving relations between the tax administration and taxpayers. When there are disagreements on tax assessments, after attempts have been made to resolve them at the local level, there may or may not be further discussion in the central tax office. In either event, the taxpayer in OECD countries, unlike those in Lithuania, has recourse to the judgment of an independent tribunal that generally does not include representatives of the tax authorities. Instead, members of professional bodies (accountants, lawyers, judges, and the like) are appointed to the body by the government as tax experts. The Nordic countries (and Switzerland) present another example of unbiased tax appeal committees: they involve local elected laymen, assisted by the tax authority and/or juridical experts. Similarly, in the United Kingdom, most appeals that cannot be settled by agreement are heard by a local body of appointed laymen, although taxpayers can elect to have their cases heard by an alternative, national quasi-judicial body of tax specialists. Details of tax appeal procedures in OECD countries are presented in table 7-6, in the Annex. In Lithuania, however, the tax authorities act as judges in their own cause, which naturally provokes suspicion among taxpayers, who, in addition, often have to wait about six months for a ruling (although theoretically it should be only one month). A draft of a new law on tax administration is said to include the establishment of some kind of tax appeal tribunal.

Both in Lithuania and in OECD countries, a very small proportion of cases (primarily those in which large amounts are in dispute) reach the law courts, but for different reasons. Taxpayers (and tax authorities) in OECD countries rarely need to take their cases to court; the first and second levels of appeal usually suffice to provide a fair settlement. In Lithuania, taxpayers are obliged by law to immediately pay half of the court costs and all the costs of the external appeal committee. Only after payment has been made can they sue for reimbursement, and, as already noted, they have limited confidence in the ability or impartiality of the courts, whose decision normally involves a delay of an additional year.

Although the biased composition of both tax appeal committees and the de facto lack of recourse through the court system reinforce the discretionary power of the tax authority, it actually hampers tax collection and discourages private sector development. By removing independent avenues for reversing overtaxing, and thus enhancing the power of individual tax inspectors, the current appeal system makes taxpayers more inclined to accept (and, indeed, to seek) informal settlements with the tax inspector. At the same time, potential investors (especially from abroad) unfamiliar with the workings of the system are deterred by the prospects of unpredictable, arbitrary taxation.

Fortunately, Lithuania may have a base that could, in principle, be used to construct better tax appeal mechanisms. The Auditing and Accounting Institute, set up under the control of the Ministry of Finance, has made considerable progress toward a draft law that follows international practice in auditing. A considerable number of auditors has also been licensed by the institute. Although little progress has been made in advancing accounting practice, the institute, along with some of the larger accounting and legal firms already established in the country, could provide the mechanism for setting up independent tax tribunals.

SYSTEMATIC DISSEMINATION OF INFORMATION TO HELP TAXPAYERS. This is another way of obtaining the good will of the taxpayer. Without such long-term measures as the adoption of officially accepted accounting standards and greater coordination among tax officials (discussed below), it is difficult to remove the taxpayers' main concerns of uncertainty and inconsistency regarding their tax liability. But even under the present regime, the tax administration could still become more taxpayer-friendly—for example, by providing systematic information to taxpayers on their rights and obligations, on changes in the tax law or in administrative interpretations, and through the provision of explanatory booklets on all the main taxes. At present, this is done sporadically in local newspapers, by organizing seminars, and by publishing booklets on taxation, but use of television and leaflets addressed personally to the taxpayer would be more effective.[6]   In this context, many countries have recently introduced taxpayers' charters to inform them of their rights. Among the rights of the taxpayer in a modern tax administration are: (i) the right to be informed, assisted, and heard in a courteous fashion; (ii) the right to certainty; and (iii) the right to privacy, confidentiality, and secrecy. (See box 7-1, the United Kingdom's "tax charter," a flagship example of taxpayers' rights protection. Also, table 7-9 in the Annex presents an OECD review of taxpayers' rights in selected countries.)

The appointment of an independent ombudsman to safeguard such rights at the request of taxpayers, or on his own initiative, is another measure that a number of OECD governments have recently put into effect. Many tax administrations explain that the contributions of taxpayers are spent largely on objectives that taxpayers would approve—social welfare, education, health, and pensions—and that when some taxpayers evade their legal responsibility, a greater burden is placed on the honest taxpayer. Tax administrations also organize seminars with groups of lawyers, accountants, and the like to consider ways of simplifying or otherwise improving the tax administration and reducing taxpayers' compliance costs (for it is likely that the higher these costs, the lower the tax compliance). All the measures outlined in this paragraph tend to be performed by a specialized unit in the central tax office that is staffed by well-trained tax inspectors.

SIMPLIFICATION AND REDUCTION OF FORMS. This is another aid to taxpayers that also improves the efficiency of tax collection. The complexity of Lithuania's tax law requires taxpayers to fill in many forms, which may be unclear or ambiguous. A number of tax administrations have—often in consultation with academic specialists in designing forms, tax lawyers, and accountants—simplified and reduced the number of forms to be completed. This process would be facilitated if there were greater coordination among the tax, customs, and social security administrations, as discussed below.

SYMPATHETIC ATTITUDES TOWARD POTENTIALLY COMPLIANT TAXPAYERS.   This is an essential part of a voluntary compliance strategy. Taxpayers usually have been divided into three categories: (a) the minority that is determined to pay no tax or as little tax as possible; (b) the majority, which is willing to pay the tax they consider due under the law; and (c) taxpayers who simply do not understand the tax law. With the first category of taxpayers, tax administrations are obliged to provide coercive measures in the form of heavy penalties. Policies of providing as much help as possible to *potentially* compliant taxpayers, however, have frequently been adopted in recent years in OECD countries. Examples included waiving fines for late declarations or minor errors in tax calculations and allowing overpayments made too late to be refunded (in all cases, of course, provided these errors were not made frequently). Helping taxpayers to fill in their forms when they clearly do not understand what they have to do and cannot afford to pay an accountant is another example of this taxpayer-friendly strategy, as is allowing payment by installments in the case of hardship.

It is also part of the voluntary compliance strategy to instruct tax inspectors to collect the tax legally due, not the maximum tax they may be able to collect. It follows that inspectors should inform the taxpayer of any available tax relief that the taxpayer has failed to claim in his declaration through ignorance, provided that the taxpayer has been found to be honest and is not habitually careless.

---

6. Tax information should also be available on the telephone, in person, and over the Internet, and forms should be reproducible by electronic means.

Box 7-1. Voluntary Compliance at Work: The United Kingdom Tax Charter

In 1994, the tax authorities of the United Kingdom de facto institutionalized a system of voluntary compliance for tax administration by publishing a "Tax Charter." The following is the core of that charter as published and widely distributed to the public.

Filing your Tax Return, you are entitled to expect the Inland Revenue:
* To be fair:
   * by settling your tax affairs impartially
   * by expecting you to pay only what is due under the law
   * by treating everyone with equal fairness.
* To help you:
   * to get your tax affairs right
   * to understand your rights and obligations
   * by providing clear leaflets and forms
   * by giving you information and assistance at our inquiry offices
   * by being courteous at all times.
* To provide an efficient service:
   * by settling your tax affairs promptly and accurately
   * by keeping your tax affairs strictly confidential
   * by using the information you give us only as allowed by the law
   * by keeping to a minimum your costs of complying with the law
   * by keeping our costs down.
* To be accountable for what we do:
   * by settling standards for ourselves and publishing how well we live up to them.

If you are not satisfied:
   * we will tell you exactly how to complain
   * you can ask for your tax affairs to be looked at again
   * you can appeal to an independent tribunal
   * your MP can refer your complaint to the Ombudsman.

In return, we need you:
   * to be honest
   * to give us accurate information
   * to pay your tax on time.

DISTRIBUTION OF LEGAL COSTS. The usual practice is to award costs to the taxpayer if he wins his appeal, but not if he loses it. This could be regarded as part of the voluntary compliance strategy. In some countries, however, the taxpayer is not awarded costs even if he wins (Spain and Sweden), or his legal fees are not reimbursed (Japan and Portugal), and in still others, the awarding of costs is left to the discretion of the courts or tribunals (Canada, France, Ireland, and Turkey).

A more difficult concession is the provision of *advance rulings*. In most countries where inspectors are prepared to advise taxpayers of the tax consequences of their proposed transactions, it is a condition that the ruling is not legally binding. The transaction may, in practice, differ from that originally described, or the area involved may lack clarity according to legal precedents. In relatively straightforward cases, however, the tax inspector may be able to inform the taxpayer of his probable tax liability, a free service that is likely to be met with gratitude. Table 7-10, in the Annex, reports on the availability of advance rulings in selected OECD countries.

AMNESTIES. Amnesties are rarely granted; if they are, it is usually when there is a large backlog of cases and a pending change of law. Amnesties are not popular with either tax collectors or honest taxpayers, who consider them unfair, and they usually bring in less revenue than the government had hoped. Of the eleven OECD countries where amnesties are reported, only three were described as successful.[7] Governments generally agree that amnesties should be employed very rarely, and only Italy and Portugal have used them more than once in recent years. Many countries prefer not to apply them at all.

Enhancing the Efficiency of the Tax Inspectorate

RECRUITING, TRAINING, AND RETAINING QUALIFIED STAFF. Staffing is a problem that faces all tax administrations in view of the higher salaries generally available to tax experts in the private sector. To meet this challenge requires not only paying tax inspectors market-competitive salaries, commensurate with the skills required of them, but also providing them with comfortable working conditions, varied work, prospects for promotion, and enough responsibility to be motivated in their work.

The bonus system practiced in some countries, including Lithuania until January 1997, is not recommended. In Lithuania, a proportion of tax revenues was collected for the purpose of supplementing tax officials' salaries. These bonuses represented a high proportion of the tax official's regular salary, and may also have resulted in inequalities of remuneration among inspectors doing the same kind of work with similar efficiency. Bonuses also gave rise to the suspicion in the private sector that the tax inspector was overcharging tax in order to increase his bonus. While the removal of the collection bonus system is a step in the right direction, tax inspectors claim to have been insufficiently compensated for their loss of income.

Some countries have tried to solve the problem of remuneration by privatizing tax administrations under a revenue board or revenue authority, so that tax collectors were not subject to the constraints of civil service pay.[8] This radical approach has not been found necessary in most OECD countries, however, and it would be recommended only if the central tax administration determined that further extensive training of tax officials would result in their massive desertion to the private sector.

THERE IS NO LEGALLY ENFORCED ACCOUNTING OR AUDITING STANDARD IN LITHUANIA. Although the Auditing and Accounting Institute bodies have developed "usually accepted auditing practices," over time these practices have no legally binding power, and agreed accounting standards seem an even more remote possibility. Beyond other important consequences for the economy as a whole (for example, limiting banks' ability to accurately determine the creditworthiness of firms), the lack of officially accepted accounting standards has two main effects on the efficiency of tax administration. First, it effectively converts tax "audits" into tax "assessments." Tax inspectors are de facto entitled to judge how profitable a certain business is, and hence how much tax it should pay, independent of books and records. Second, it strengthens the discretionary power of the inspector, already strong because of the biased system of appeal. This, in turn, results in an enhanced willingness of the taxpayer to agree to informal settlements, which the experience of other countries in similar situations suggests may reduce overall tax collections.

A MINIMUM TAX. A number of countries that, like Lithuania, have a complicated system of reduced rates, exemptions, and tax holidays that erode the corporate income tax base collect a minimum

---

7. Reported in OECD, *Taxpayers' Rights and Obligations: A Survey of the Legal Situation in OECD Countries* (Paris, 1990), *op. cit.* (table 27, page 90).
8. Canada, Singapore, Spain, and a number of African and Latin American countries.

tax. Such a tax may be a low percentage of gross profits, a small annual percentage of net worth of assets, or a minimum amount of turnover. It is usually payable instead of the ordinary income taxes if the amount is greater than the latter once the tax reliefs have been taken into account (as in Canada and the United States, for example). A variant of the minimum tax is the "gross tax," payable as a small percentage of gross income, which is payable *in addition* to the standard income taxes (as in Denmark and Norway). Lithuania does not impose any kind of minimum tax, thereby eroding the income and corporate tax base, reducing horizontal equity between taxpayers, and causing resentment among enterprises not subject to favorable tax treatment. The complicated system of tax reliefs, combined with the lack of a minimum tax, has the effect of reducing revenue yields, while making the taxes more unpopular through their perceived unfairness.

PRESUMPTIVE TAXATION. Based on such observable indicators as fixed capital stock, turnover, and number of employees, presumptive taxation is applied in many countries, including France and Italy, to the very numerous small enterprise owners such as farmers, shopkeepers, and artisans who are incapable of keeping records of their profits and expenditures. The Lithuanian tax administration has the information necessary to apply presumptive taxation. For example, to track down these small enterprises, registration numbers (such as those for motor vehicles or real estate) might be of use in the absence of more long-term measures, such as those envisaged below.

LACK OF STAFF MANUALS. Tax administrations normally have official internal staff manuals to clarify both the internal organization of the various tax departments and the legal and administrative decisions relevant to the assessment of future cases. Lithuania's tax administration lacks such manuals (although it is understood that there is an intention to compile one), which increases the possibility of arbitrary differences among the assessments made by different tax officials, or across different tax districts.

LACK OF COMMON CONTROL. In Lithuania (and in many other countries), the lack of common control of tax, customs, and social security with a common tax identification number for all three levies, together with the apparent decentralization of the fifty-six tax collection offices, has a number of disadvantages for both the tax administration and taxpayers. First, it facilitates the task of the would-be tax-evader, who can provide different information to the tax, customs, and social security administrations and the numerous tax offices. Second, it hampers consistent rulings, both within and between the levies, which are separately administered, especially for enterprises operating under the control of several tax offices. Third, it renders a common penalty policy more difficult. Fourth, it increases the administrative costs of the tax authorities and the compliance costs of business because it precludes the streamlining that would otherwise be possible. Finally, it increases the number of necessary forms and audit inspections. Integration of collection by the tax, customs, and social security administrations has evidently been a long-term goal. In the meantime, there would seem to be administrative advantages to the tax administration in reducing the number of tax offices and establishing a more centralized system of control (for example, a regional structure based on the five largest cities, with heads of regional offices responsible for all tax inspectors in their area and reporting to a director at the central tax administration).[9]

AUDIT SELECTION TECHNIQUES. This has been a growth area in many OECD countries in recent years, and their application has been responsible for vast increases in revenues collected. But until a fair number of the tax officials are equipped and familiar with computers, there are limits to the utilization of

---

9. This recommendation was also made on page 43 of the IMF report, by E. Sunley and others, *Lithuania: A Program for the Reform of the Structure and Administration of the Tax System* (Washington, D.C., 1994).

these techniques. Nevertheless, it does seem possible to improve on the Lithuanian practice of auditing nearly all taxpayers' transactions. This activity absorbs a great deal of tax administration resources (as well as increasing taxpayers' costs). As noted earlier, it would appear rational to reduce the extent of audits, both across taxpayers and within tax declarations. This would free resources for concentration on areas identified prior to the audit. Identification of appropriate areas for investigation will vary from tax to tax, and extensive training through technical assistance is a prerequisite of an effective audit selection system. Once in force, many firms will rarely be audited, and then only for certain kinds of transactions. The central tax office plans to develop a program for audit selection and has arranged for a Swedish company to help them in this effort.

REDUCTION OF TAX COLLECTION LAGS. Such a reduction will improve revenue collections. Delays in collecting tax mean that the government will lose revenue in real terms through inflation and loss of interest. Except in rare cases, tax is not now collected at the time of the tax inspection, but afterward, and much of the work of local tax offices is directed against late filers and late payers. Ideally, filing tax declarations and making payments should be carried out simultaneously, and it is recommended that the tax authorities move toward such a system as soon as the tax law can be amended and arrangements for immediate payment negotiated with banks. This is a problem faced by many tax administrations and is, of course, especially important when inflation is high.

A "STICK" APPROACH. Both the threat and the reality of punishment for noncompliance must accompany the taxpayer-friendly voluntary compliance strategy to deal with taxpayers who refuse to cooperate, whether they are deliberately evading tax or are habitually careless. Maximum fines or imprisonment in sufficiently serious cases is the obvious treatment. One method is to prosecute the worst tax offenders and to publicize some of the heavier penalties imposed by the law courts as a deterrent to other would-be tax evaders. Publishing the names of habitual tax offenders is also done in some countries, including Lithuania. Rigorous punishment should also be applied to taxpayers and tax inspectors involved in informal settlements that enable them to share a portion of the tax due the government.

Nearly all countries withhold tax on wages and salaries, but income tax revenue is also secured by applying the withholding technique to other sources of income such as dividends, interest, royalties, directors fees, pensions, and capital gains. (Table 7-11, in the Annex, describes practices of OECD countries in this area.) If, as earlier recommended, the Lithuanian income tax base were extended, it would be rational to rely more heavily on the withholding taxes.

Finally, it should be noted that the Lithuanian government has already announced its intention to implement a number of the suggestions listed in this section as part of its "Action Program for 1997–2000." These measures include: (i) abolition of the bonus system (now accomplished); (ii) distinguishing between persistent nonpayment and nonpayment by mistake, and reducing fines in the latter case and increasing penalties for fraudulent or careless declarations; (iii) provision of broader rights for taxpayers; and (iv) keeping tax laws unchanged as long as possible, and changing them when necessary, but only after providing preliminary information.

Policy Recommendations

Until quite recently, most OECD tax administrations had similar problems to those now faced in Lithuania: bad relations between tax authorities and the private sector and a perception that the tax system was inefficient and unfair (mainly because of high nominal rates and complicated exemptions, which encouraged widespread tax evasion by some businesses and laid a heavy burden on others).

Unfortunately, unlike most OECD and eastern European countries, Lithuanian income tax laws retain too many rates and concessions, which hamper improved tax administration. There is a project to unify tax rates for all types of income. In addition, reform of tax administration is an urgent matter if a rapid deterioration in tax compliance, which would be difficult to reverse, is to be avoided. Lithuania has enough accumulated technical experience to provide, in a relatively short period of time, a more efficient, transparent, and fair tax administration, and one that could gather larger revenues for the fiscal budget. For that purpose, the overall priority should be greater cooperation with the private sector in the context of a full involuntary compliance strategy. This should be combined with technical improvements in the collection process.

Lithuania should immediately establish independent tax appeal tribunals. While other policies are implemented, giving taxpayers a credible means of recourse would rapidly transform the relationship between taxpayers and the tax inspectors and would reduce the attraction of informal settlements.

In the medium term, the Lithuanian tax authorities should move to a voluntary compliance system. Implementing such a system will require a battery of policies, including the adoption of a tax-related ombudsman, regular reports on how the taxes collected are actually used, and greater assistance provided to bona fide taxpayers.

To improve efficiency within the tax administration, a centralized and unique tax identification number should be used for all taxes, customs duties, and social security contributions, and the current universal auditing system should be abandoned and replaced by a selective auditing mechanism. Delays between assessment and collection of tax should be minimized. To improve equity among taxpayers and to reduce inconsistencies, a minimum tax for both corporate and unincorporated businesses should be introduced, along with guidelines for presumptive taxation of hard-to-tax groups. Tax collection offices should be reduced in number and centralized, and an internal staff manual containing current tax laws and their interpretations by the court and the central tax office should be issued and kept up to date. Finally, a legally enforced system of accounting and auditing standards (following international practices, after necessary adaptation to Lithuania's circumstances) should be put in place.

There is already integration of the collection of income tax, profit tax, and VAT within the tax administration, which evidently facilitates consistent assessments and efficient revenue collection, as well as reducing taxpayer compliance costs. In the longer run and for the same reasons, the authorities should consider the integration of the tax and customs administration (both of which are responsible for consumption taxes), as well as the joint control of VAT and income and profit taxes, with that of social security contributions.

ANNEX
Data Tables

Table 7-6. General Appeals Procedures for Selected Countries

Country	Right of appeal against measurement	Appeal must first be made to administrative authority	If yes, taxpayer can appeal against judgment in a higher body of court	Appeal generally resolved at administrative level
Australia	Yes	Yes	Yes	Yes
Austria	Yes	Yes	Yes	Yes
Belgium	Yes	Yes	Yes	Yes
Canada	Yes	Yes	Yes	Yes
Denmark	Yes	Yes	Yes	Yes
Finland	Yes	Yes	Yes	Yes
France	Yes	Yes	Yes	Yes
Germany	Yes	Usually	Yes	Yes
Greece	Yes	Yes	Yes	Yes
Ireland	Yes, except preliminary tax notice in self-assessment cases	Yes	Yes, if dispute cannot be settled by administrative authority	Yes
Italy	Yes	Generally, no	Yes	No
Japan	Yes	Yes	Yes	Yes
Netherlands	Yes	Yes	Yes	Yes
New Zealand	Yes	Usually	Yes	Yes
Norway	Yes (some restrictions)	No	Yes	Yes
Portugal	Yes	Sometimes	Yes	No
Spain	Yes	No	Yes	No
Sweden	Yes	Yes	Yes	At first administrative level
Switzerland	Yes	Yes	Yes	Yes
Turkey	Yes	Yes	Yes	Yes
United Kingdom	Yes	Yes	Yes	Yes
United States	Yes	No, but taxpayers' ability to recover costs is harmed by failure to appeal administratively	Yes	Yes

Table 7-7. Decisions Subject to Appeal and Time Limits, Selected Countries

		Time limits for appeals by taxpayers	
Country	Decisions subject to appeal[a]	Administrative appeals[a]	Appeals on court decisions[b]
Australia	All assessment and administrative decisions	60 days[c]	60 days[c]
Austria	All assessment and administrative decisions of substance	1 month	None (except criminal proceedings); court decisions in tax matters are only issued by the Supreme Court of Public Law (except criminal cases)
Belgium	All assessment and administrative decisions	30 April after end of assessment year	40 days
Canada	All assessments	90 days	90 days
Denmark	All assessments	4 weeks	8 weeks (Tax Board) 6 months (National Tax Tribunal)
Finland	All assessments	14 days	5 years from year assessment
Germany	All decisions on a tax claim/refund	1 month	1 month
Greece	All assessments	Normally 20 days	Normally 60 days
Ireland	All decisions on a tax claim/refund	30 days	10 days (General Court) 21 days (High Court)
Italy	All assessments and administrative decisions	60 days	60 days (90 days for appeals before Court of Appeal)
Japan	All administrative decisions	2 months	3 months
Netherlands	Decisions taken in response to objections against assessments or pursuant to any other provision of legislation. It is not possible to appeal against a provisional assessment.	2 months[d]	2 months[d] = (Courts of Appeal) 2 months (Supreme Court)
New Zealand	All assessments	2 months	30 days (High Court) 3 months (Court of Appeal) 21 days (Privy Council)

230

Table 7-7. Decisions Subject to Appeal and Time Limits, Selected Countries (continued)

		Time limits for appeals by taxpayers	
Country	Decisions subject to appeal[a]	Administrative appeals[a]	Appeals on court decisions[b]
Norway	All assessments	3 weeks[d]	6 months
Portugal	All assessments	30 days to 1 year	90 days
Spain	All assessments and administrative decisions	15 days	2 months
Sweden	All decisions on tax claims/refunds	28 February after end of fiscal year	2 months
Turkey	All decisions of the tax administration	Possible within 5 years	2 months
United Kingdom	All assessments and certain administrative decisions	30 days	Varies according to what stage, or what court, the proceedings have reached
United States	All assessments and administrative decisions	Generally 30 days written notice from examiner. If the taxpayer does not file a protest with the appeals office, the government issues a notice of deficiency allowing the taxpayer 90 or 150 days in which to file in Tax Court. A taxpayer may choose to pay the tax, file a claim, and appeal a denial of the claim to U.S. District Court or to U.S. Claims Court within two years after the claim is denied.	90 days after Tax Court decision; generally 30 days from U.S. District Court or U.S. Claims Court judgment, decree, or order. For appeal to U.S. Supreme Court, 90 days from the date of entry of judgment appealed.

a. Usually after assessment is issued.
b. Usually after initial decisions.
c. Refers to first appeal procedure (see table 7-6). In most countries, the discretionary powers of the tax authorities are not subject to appeal.
d. Some discretion to extend.

231

Table 7-8. Specific Appeals Procedures, Selected Countries

Country	Bodies that can hear appeals	Members of tax court board[a]	Taxpayer representation — Tax court/board[b]	Taxpayer representation — Regular courts	Hearings made public — Tax court/tribunal[c]	Hearings made public — Regular courts
Australia	Specialist tribunal Supreme/ Federal Court	Governor-general-appointed member with tax experience	Tax agent or lawyer	[Lawyer]	No	No
Austria	Tax official, specialist tribunal, Supreme Court	5 members, appointed by the administration	70% represented by tax accountant	[Lawyer]	No	Generally no (applies to Supreme Administration Court decisions)
Belgium	Administrative authorities and courts	Government-appointed judges	Taxpayer	Lawyer	No	No
Canada	Tax Court/Federal Court/ Appellate Court/ Supreme Court	Government-appointed	Taxpayer	Lawyer	Yes	Yes
Denmark	Assessment Committee, Tax Board, National Tax Tribunal, courts	Primarily appointed laymen	Taxpayer or lawyer	Lawyer	Yes (when they are essential)	Yes
Finland	Appeals board, Provincial Court, Supreme Adminstration Court	Elected laymen; tribunal; government-appointed judges, court	Taxpayer	—	No	—
France	Administrative Tribunal, Juridical Tribunal (tribunaux de Grande Instance et Cour de Cassation)	—	Taxpayer	Lawyer	Yes	Yes
Germany	Finance courts	3 professional judges, 2 laymen Judges appointed by government for life	Tax authorities' lawyer; Taxpayer or lawyer		Yes	Yes
Greece	Administrative Courts, Specialist Tribunals		Taxpayer or lawyer (second instance = lawyer)		Yes	Yes
Ireland	Appeal commissioners, court	Government-appointed experts and judges	Accountant, lawyer	[Lawyer]	No	Yes
Italy	Tax Commission, Appeal Court	Government-appointed experts and judges	Lawyer/accountant and taxpayer	Lawyer	Yes	Yes

Table 7-8. Specific Appeals Procedures, Selected Countries (continued)

Country	Bodies that can hear appeals	Members of tax court board[a]	Taxpayer representation		Hearings made public	
			Tax court/board[b]	Regular courts	Tax court/tribunal[c]	Regular courts
Japan	Tax Office, tribunal, and court	Tax official: tax office Government-appointed experts: tribunal Government-appointed judges: courts	Taxpayer or adviser: tax office tribunal (no tax court)	Lawyer	No	
Netherlands	General Court of Appeals (tax division). Fiscal criminal offenses are heard in the first instance by the Law Court and in appeal by the criminal division of the General Courts of Appeal. Cassation proceedings are heard by the Supreme Court.	Government-appointed judges	No obligation to be represented. Representation by legal or tax counselor in nevertheless the general rule. In criminal preceedings, representation by legal counsel is obligatory.		No, however, court decisions may be published anonymously unless the taxpayer objects on the grounds of possible infringement on his privacy. Criminal court cases are public unless the judge decides otherwise.	Yes
New Zealand	Tribunal, High Court	Government-appointed judges	Generally taxpayer, lawyer	[No]	Yes	
Norway	Elected tax boards/ regular court	Elected laymen[d]	Taxpayer	Lawyer	No	Yes
Portugal	Tax courts, authorities, and special commissions on certain issues	Judges, civil servants	Taxpayer	Lawyer	No	Yes
Spain	Administrative tribunals and ordinary courts	Public officials	Representation from tax advisers	Lawyer	No	Yes
Sweden	Administrative courts	Government-appointed judges and laymen	Taxpayer	Lawyer	No	Yes
Switzerland	Tax Board, Administrative Court, Supreme Court	Elected judges, elected laymen, civil servants	Taxpayer, adviser, lawyer	No	No	

233

Table 7-8. Specific Appeals Procedures, Selected Countries (continued)

Country	Bodies that can hear appeals	Members of tax court board[a]	Taxpayer representation		Hearings made public	
			Tax court/board[b]	Regular courts	Tax court/tribunal[c]	Regular courts
Turkey	First tax administrations or compromise commissions, then tax courts	Appointed by the Ministry of Justice	Taxpayer, lawyer, or accountant	No	No	
United Kingdom	Appeal commissioners and Court	General commissioner, government-appointed laymen, special commissioner, government-appointed tax experts.	Taxpayer/accountant	Lawyer	No	Yes
United States	Appeals Division (administrative function), U.S. Tax Court, U.S. District Court or U.S. Claims Court, U.S. Court of Appeals, U.S. Supreme Court	Courts or bodies within judicial branch are presided over by judges.	In Tax Court, taxpayers or person admitted to practice before the court (generally lawyers). In adminstrative appeal, taxpayer or person admitted to practice before the IRS (lawyers and others).	Taxpayer or lawyer	Yes (but administrative appeals process is not public).	Yes (but administrative appeals process is not public).

a. These refer to tax courts and not regular courts.
b. Parentheses show that taxpayer must employ a lawyer.
c. Brackets indicate that the hearings are in private, although the results are published without identifying the taxpayer.
d. Signifies that laymen-jurors may be appointed in the regular court proceedings.
Source: This Annex table is reproduced from OECD "Taxpayer's Rights and Obligations: A Survey of the Legal Situation in OECD Countries" (Paris, 1990).

Table 7-9. General Review of Taxpayers' Rights, Selected Countries

Country	Time and type of review
Australia	Taxpayers' rights were considered in conjunction with the change to self-assessment in the late 1980s. The right to privacy of personal information was reviewed as part of enhancements to the integrity of the tax file number as an identification system. The resulting Privacy Act was part of a package of bills dealing with tax file number arrangements.
Austria	None (the present Fiscal Code, which governs powers of tax authorities as well as taxpayers' rights, dates back to 1961 and has been subject to several amendments).
Belgium	(See table 7-6) A series of measures as implemented in 1985.
Canada	"Declaration of Taxpayers' Rights" published and distributed in spring 1985.
Denmark	Two committees have been set up on the question of protection of the individual in relation to tax legislation. The work of these committees has led to legislative changes increasing the security of taxpayers.
Finland	None.
France	A number of amendments were passed in 1986 and 1987 to improve taxpayers' rights (such as the introduction of advanced rulings and clarification of provisions and penalties).
Germany	The amended version of the Fiscal Code in 1977.
Greece	None.
Ireland	The report "Tax Administration," mentioned in table 7-6, also deals with the taxpayers' right of appeal.
Italy	None (a Bureau of Public Relations was created in the 1980s).
Japan	None.
Netherlands	The Government Information (Public Access) Act protects taxpayers' rights through legislation.
New Zealand	A White Paper was released in 1985 and a "Bill of Rights" covering the rights of all persons in New Zealand has been drafted. It is not known when the bill will be enacted.
Norway	The Assessment Act adopted in 1980 became effective in 1984.
Portugal	The legislation enacted under tax reform, in force as from 1989, has improved taxpayers' rights.
Spain	New legislation on taxpayers' rights and duties during tax audit procedures was adopted in 1986.
Sweden	A committee is presently reviewing the powers to secure tax payments, taking taxpayers' interests into consideration. Finally, the government is preparing proposals to "soften" regulations in the field of taxation (for example, an advanced ruling and distribution of legal costs).
Switzerland	None.
Turkey	None, but in 1982, independent Tax Courts were set up, and in 1986 "Compromise Commissions" were established (last major review in 1961).
United Kingdom	Taxpayers' rights were also covered by the Keith Report. On the basis of the report, Inland Revenue and Customs and Excise jointly published a "Taxpayers' Charter" in July 1986, setting out the principles that govern the authorities' handling of taxpayers' affairs.
United States	The "Taxpayer's Bill of Rights" was enacted in 1988.

Source: See table 7-8.

Table 7-10. Availability of Advance Rulings, Selected Countries

Country	Advance rulings		If used, general form		Comment	Taxpayer bears cost
	Not used	Used	Legally binding[a]	Not binding		
Australia		X		X	Must establish new interpretation covering number of taxpayers	No
Austria	X					
Belgium	X					
Canada		X		X (binding as a matter of department policy)	Seriously contemplated, specific transactions only	Yes
Denmark		X	X			Yes
Finland		X	X		In exceptionally important cases only	Yes
France	X	X				
Germany		X	X		Limited purpose only	No
Greece		X	X		According to interpretations of the law	No
Ireland	X (except for relieves for Industrial Development Authority or other state agency projects)					
Italy		X	X			No
Japan	X					
Netherlands		X	Yes		Limited use in matters involving corporation tax	No
New Zealand		X		X	Applies to specific transactions only	Yes
Norway		X		X	Opinion usually followed	No
Portugal		X	X		Can be appealed	No
Spain		X		X	Legally binding only in cases of investment of foreign capital in Spain	No
Sweden		X	X		If referred to by the taxpayer	Yes
Switzerland	X					
Turkey	X					
United Kingdom		X	X (if all information disclosed)		Limited use, mainly in corporate area	No
United States		X	X[b]			Yes. A fee of $50–$3,000, depending on the subject matter, is charged. The nominal fee is $2,500.

a. Normally binding on the tax administration only if the facts are not misrepresented.
b. Binding on the tax authority only.
Source: See table 7-8.

Table 7-11. Withholding Tax Systems, Selected Countries

		Source of income subject withholding tax[a]		
Country	Wages and salaries	Dividends	Interest	Other
Australia	Yes	No (except for that part of dividends paid to nonresidents, which do not carry an imputation credit, and to persons who do not quote a tax file number to an investment body after 1 July 1991)	No (except for nonresidents and persons who do not quote a tax file number to an investment body after 1 July 1991)	The prescribed payments systems (e.g,. work in building, construction, architectural, engineering, and cleaning industries); royalties and national resource payments to nonresidents
Austria	Yes	Yes	No (with certain exceptions)[b]	Certain items of income by nonresidents (such as income derived by nonresident artists and athletes, royalties paid to nonresidents)
Belgium	Yes	Yes	Yes	Forms of income received by nonresidents
Canada	Yes	No (except to nonresidents)	No (except to nonresidents)	Most source payments to nonresidents
Denmark	Yes	Yes	No	No
Finland	Yes	Yes	Yes (except to nonresidents)	Pension payments; royalties paid to nonresidents
France	No	No	A number of income types paid to nonresidents	
Greece	Yes	Yes	Yes	A number of income types paid to foreign businesses and organizations not permanently established; tax on director fees
Germany	Yes	Yes	No	Nonresident artists and athletes; royalties, patents, know-how; and the like to nonresidents; directors' fees
Ireland	Yes	No (except to nonresidents if tax credit is given)	Yes, subject to specified exceptions	Loans by companies to participants; annuities, if these are allowable to the taxpayer as a reduction; royalties; rents paid to nonresidents; professional fees; certain capital gains payments made to subcontractors
Japan	Yes	Yes	Yes	Royalties, fees to lawyers, entertainers, and the like

Table 7-11. Withholding Tax Systems, Selected Countries (continued)

Country	Wages and salaries	Dividends	Interest	Other
		Source of income to which withholding tax is applied[a]		
Netherlands	Yes	Yes	No	No
New Zealand	Yes	No (except to nonresidents and dividends received by a resident company from a foreign source)	No (except nonresidents)	Commissions, company directors' fees, agricultural work, contributors to newspapers, resident and nonresident entertainers; payments to nonresidents, contractors, and of dividends, interest, royalties, and the like to nonresidents
Norway	Yes	No (except to nonresidents)	No	Nonresident entertainers and artists
Portugal	Yes	Yes		
Spain	Yes	Yes		
Sweden	Yes (including pensions and sickness benefits)	No (except to nonresidents)	No	Nonresident entertainers and artists
Switzerland	No	Yes	Yes (with certain exceptions)	Nonresident artists, athletes, members of boards of directors; lottery winnings and insurance payments.
Turkey	Yes	Generally, no	Yes	Rental income, agricultural sales, and professional fees; exemptions from corporation tax are subject to withholding tax.
United Kingdom	Yes	No (except for non-residents if tax credits are given)	Yes (with certain exceptions)	Royalties; nonresident entertainers and athletes; subcontractors in the construction industry.
United States	Yes	Generally no (except for nonresident aliens and foreign corporations). If the payee fails to furnish his taxpayer identification number (TIN) to the payer, the payment is subject to tax.	In general, no	Prizes, awards, and the like; certain payments to foreigners, such as royalties; income of foreign partners and gains on dispositions of U.S. real property interests.

a. In general, withholding is operated by the payer of the income. In some cases, the tax withheld represents the final tax liability; in most instances, however, it is seen as a prepayment of an annual tax liability.

b. Since 1989, interest income has been, with certain exceptions, covered.

Source: See table 7-8.

8

PSD ENVIRONMENT:
THE COMMERCIAL JUDICIAL SYSTEM

This chapter focuses on the judicial system, particularly the commercial judicial system, in the context of its impact on private sector development. Because the problems of the judicial system stem partly from issues related to legislation and the legislative process, these are also discussed.

Overall, the transition from a Soviet-style judicial system toward a more modern, market-driven system has been remarkably swift and efficient. Nevertheless, the Lithuanian judicial system cannot yet fully support the needs of a diversified and privately oriented economy. While the quantity of court services, with some exceptions, is not a problem, quality is, especially in PSD-sensitive areas such as bankruptcy proceedings and disputes relating to commercial contracts and business relationships.

There are several reasons for the poor quality of court services: a shortage of experienced and trained judges and other court personnel; a lack of court support structures; poor court procedures, inefficient pricing of court services; and the absence of alternative dispute resolution mechanisms. Contributing to the difficulties is an underdeveloped legislative process that has resulted in an inconsistent and somewhat confusing legal framework.

The difficulties of the judicial system have thus far frustrated a move toward greater independence and the eventual emergence of the judiciary as a full-fledged, self-contained branch of the Lithuanian government. Instead, the judiciary has been brought under even tighter control of the executive branch in a probably misguided effort to improve the quality of judicial services. The weaknesses of the judicial system are reflected in the lack of confidence the private business sector and the public at large show in its services.

A number of measures have been, and continue to be, taken to enable the judicial system to catch up with and match the demands of a fast-growing and diversifying private sector. The court system was extensively reformed in 1994–95, and the next reform wave is currently being planned. The production of this Policy Note is thus timely. It provides a brief assessment of the judicial system in Lithuania, with particular attention to the main constraints to PSD, and offers a set of broad policy recommendations for consideration by the Lithuanian government.

Lithuania's Judicial System: A Descriptive Analysis

The Legal Framework

The first permanent Constitution of the Lithuanian state was adopted in 1922. It was based on the traditional separation of powers into the legislative, executive, and judicial branches. Another important principle expressed in this Constitution was the independence of courts and judges. Commercial legislation did not consist of an integrated civil code, but of a number of separate laws that differed somewhat throughout the country. The legislation was based on continental European civil law and German legal tradition.

In the Soviet Union, the Lithuanian judiciary functioned largely as an enforcement arm of the government—in effect, of the Communist Party. Many areas of law, such as constitutional and commercial law, were virtually ignored, and the judiciary did not protect citizens from the state or realize the guarantees explicitly provided in the Soviet Constitution. Judges were reasonably well educated, trained, and paid, and public respect for the judiciary was in some ways greater in Soviet times than it is now, but it clearly played a subservient role within the government structure.

After the restoration of independence in 1990, Lithuania quickly readopted a Western-style legal system, largely a modernized version of the system in place before the Soviet annexation. A new Constitution was enacted by referendum in 1992. The commercial judicial system is also based on the Law on Courts adopted in 1994 and the Soviet Civil Code, with substantial revisions and supplementation by special laws, such as the Law on Bankruptcy, the Law on Enterprises, the Law on Commercial Banks, and the Law on Trading of Securities.

The Court System

The Lithuanian Constitution and the Law on Courts establish a four-level court system: the Supreme Court, the Court of Appeals, district courts, and local courts. Most countries in western and eastern Europe have three-level court systems. The Lithuanian Constitution—in line with those of many other eastern European countries—also established the Constitutional Court and allowed for specialized courts for administrative, labor, family, and other purposes. Unlike most western European countries, Lithuania does not have separate courts for administrative cases. The only specialized court, the Commercial Court, an offspring of the Soviet-era court for adjudicating commercial cases, was recently abolished.

A Law on Commercial Arbitration was adopted in April 1996. The law provides for private dispute resolution by an arbitral tribunal, either organized by a permanent arbitral institution or by the parties themselves. The Vilnius International Commercial Arbitration was established in July 1996 as a private, nonprofit arbitral institution.

The main functions of the courts are the following:

- Local courts are tribunals of first instance for all cases that are not assigned to some other court by law. Local court judges conduct pretrial investigations of cases as provided by law. A minimum of two judges serve on each of these courts. There are fifty-four local courts.
- The district courts are courts of first instance for civil and criminal cases specifically assigned by law to their jurisdiction. The designation of a district court as the court of first instance depends on the amount at issue and the nature of the charge. District courts also hear appeals from local court decisions. There are five district courts.

- The Court of Appeals is composed of a civil and a criminal division. The court hears appeals of decisions of the district courts in cases where the district court has acted as the court of first instance. Cases where a district court acted as a court of appeal are appealed directly to the Supreme Court.

- The Supreme Court includes a civil division, a criminal division, and a Senate of Judges. The Supreme Court is an appellate court for cases from the Court of Appeals and for cases from district courts when these courts have acted as courts of appeal. The Supreme Court will strive to ensure uniform practice in the application of laws. The Senate of Judges, consisting of the Supreme Court chairman, the division chairmen, and other members of the Supreme Court, shall, at the request of the Supreme Court chairman, confirm rulings of the Supreme Court and cassation rulings of the Court of Appeals, if such confirmation is important for the formation of uniform legal practice. The Senate will also rule on decisions by Lithuanian courts that violate the European Convention on Human Rights and Protection of Major Liberties according to the European Court on Human Rights. Its decisions on the applicability of laws are binding upon lower courts. The minister of justice, the prosecutor general, the chairman of the Court of Appeals, and the chairmen of district courts have the right to participate in meetings of the Senate of Judges and to propose issues concerning the application of laws for Senate consideration. There has been some controversy in Lithuania regarding the Senate—a body uncommon in other legal systems—in relation to its role as a "supercassation" instance and the apparent conflict of interest of Supreme Court judges confirming their own rulings.

- The Commercial Court, which derived from the Soviet body and handled disputes between state-owned enterprises, adjudicates disputes between legal persons arising out of economic and commercial activities. If one of the parties is a physical person or a foreign entity, cases are usually solved in ordinary court. Commercial disputes between persons are always solved in ordinary courts. The Commercial Court has the status of a local court, and appeals against the court's decisions are made to a district court. The future of this court is uncertain. Draft legislation is currently under review, which may result in the Commercial Court being merged with the district courts or local courts.

- The Constitutional Court, at the request of the president, members of Seimas, the government, or the judiciary, reviews the constitutionality of laws and other legal acts, as well as that of actions by the president of the republic and the Council of Ministers. The court also reviews alleged violations of presidential and parliamentary election laws, determines whether the president's health is limiting his ability to continue in office, and rules on the constitutionality of actions by members of the Seimas (parliament) against whom impeachment proceedings have been instituted. The Constitutional Court has earned a great deal of respect within the Lithuanian legal and governmental system, and its authority to issue the final word on subjects within its jurisdiction is unquestioned.

Status of Judicial Services

A major reform of the court system commenced with the enactment of the Law on Courts in 1994. Since 1995, the number of positions for judges and other court personnel has more than doubled, and judges' salaries were increased considerably. Although a number of positions in the lower courts remain unfilled because of budget constraints, on 1 January 1997, the number of judges had increased from less than 200 at the beginning of 1995 to around 500 (317 in the local courts, 8 in the Commercial Court, 122 in the district courts, 24 in the Court of Appeals, and 18 in the Supreme Court), about 135 judges for each one million inhabitants. This is much below the ratio in Germany (224 judges for each 1 million inhabitants), Hungary (200), Slovenia (250), and Spain (244), for example. It is about the same as the number in Italy (130 for every one million people) and above the relative number of judges in Belgium (88), France (90), and Venezuela (68).[1]

Although the relative number of judges is low compared with some countries, quantity is not a major problem in Lithuania. The problem is quality, which is one of the main weaknesses of the Lithuanian judiciary. The rapid increase in the number of judges since 1995 has created an acute shortage of experienced, well-trained judges. The government is recognizing the seriousness of the problem and is taking a number of palliative measures. (This subject is analyzed in the section "Policy Issues," below.)

A factor counterbalancing the lack of skilled judges has been the relatively low number of cases filed. Based on information received from the Ministry of Justice for the first six months of the year, around 100,000 civil cases will be filed in 1997. As a comparison, in Slovenia, with about half the population of Lithuania, more than 250,000 civil cases were filed in 1990.[2] In Finland, where the number of cases filed has been decreasing since the 1980s, 240,000 civil cases were filed in 1996; in relation to the population, this number is 1.8 times greater than in Lithuania.[3] In Poland, 540,000 civil cases were filed in 1995; in relative terms, this is only half of the figure in Lithuania.[4] According to the statistics prepared by the Ministry of Justice, the clearance rate—that is, cases disposed of as a percentage of cases received within a certain period of time—is high in Lithuania. It reached 94 percent for civil cases in the first half of 1997, which compares favorably with Belgium's 50 percent and Japan's 80 percent in 1993.[5] In Finland, where concerted efforts to increase the effectiveness of the courts have been made, the clearance rate was 105 percent in 1996. In the Lithuanian Supreme Court, the clearance rate was actually close to 100 percent, and the backlog of pending cases had been reduced to eighteen at the end of June 1997. For all courts taken together, the backlog of pending cases is at a reasonable level, although it has been slowly rising. From the beginning of 1997 to the end of the first half of the year, the backlog of civil cases increased from 17,600 to 19,700, which, in both absolute and relative terms, is much less than the 56,000 cases pending in Finland at the end of 1996, for example.

The waiting time for resolution of civil cases is currently relatively short, usually 3–6 months. The exception is bankruptcy cases, which take 1–2 years to resolve. As a comparison, in the beginning of the 1990s, it took an average of 1.8 years to get a commercial case resolved in Portugal, 2 years in Hungary, 3–5 years in Slovenia, and over 6 years in Egypt.[6] At the other end of the spectrum are the Nordic countries. In Finland, for example, most civil cases are resolved in 2–3 months, and even the relatively few complicated cases require, on the average, no more than 6–7 months.

Although judicial services have improved appreciably, particularly since the reform in 1994–95, and Lithuania compares rather favorably in the statistics presented above, the confidence in the commercial judicial system is low, as is the perceived public standing of judges. This lack of confidence, together with some other factors, such as the structure of court fees, are most likely the reasons that so few commercial cases are filed compared with many other countries. Lithuania was not included in an

1. Waleed Malik and others, "Judicial Sector Benchmarks: Examples from Developing Countries" (Washington, D.C.: World Bank, Latin America and the Caribbean PREM, 1994), processed.

2. Cheryl W. Gray, "Evolving Legal Frameworks for Private Sector Development in Central and Eastern Europe," World Bank Discussion Paper 209 (Washington, D.C., 1993).

3. *Annual Report 1996*, Ministry of Justice of Finland.

4. *Statistical Yearbook 1996*, Poland.

5. W. Malik, "Judicial Sector Benchmarks."

6. W. Malik, "Judicial Sector Benchmarks."

international survey of user confidence in commercial justice systems made in 1993. On a scale of zero to ten, the Scandinavian countries ranked high, with Norway at the top (confidence factor, 8.2). Hungary (4.4) and Poland (3.2) were at the lower end, while Russia trailed at 1.0.[7] Based on interviews in Lithuania, its confidence factor is likely to be close to that of Poland. These matters will be discussed further below.

Independence of the Judiciary

In accordance with the law, the judiciary is an independent branch of the Lithuanian government. This independence is guaranteed under Article 109 of the Constitution and Articles 46–55 of the Law on Courts. To realize this independence, the Constitution prohibits any interference with the work of the judiciary or attempt to influence judges by any citizen or office of government. Nevertheless, both by law and in practice, the executive branch, through the Ministry of Justice (MoJ), is heavily involved in the administration of the judicial branch, with the exception of the Supreme Court, which enjoys a large measure of independence. This is no different from most other transition countries in eastern Europe. Similarly, in many western European countries, the judiciaries are in many respects dependent by law on the government. In practice, however, the judiciaries in these countries enjoy a large measure of independence based on tradition; in many of them, greater independence for the judicial branch is being introduced or contemplated.

In Lithuania, the independence of the judiciary is, in practice, limited in several ways. First, the budget of the judiciary is part of the budget of the MoJ. The judiciary has limited authority over its own revenues, expenses, and resources; it is heard, and can make proposals, but the MoJ, the president, or Seimas will determine the number and remuneration of judges, resources for other court staff and expenses, and investments. While not uncommon, this pattern is not best international practice. In Denmark, where a proposal for a comprehensive reform of the court system has been submitted to the Parliament, three alternatives for the allocation of funds to the judicial branch were considered; one was total financial independence; the second was a shift of responsibility from the working government (Council of Ministers) to Parliament; and the third, which was chosen by the committee, was the common western European practice of the judiciary remaining dependent on the government for its finances. To strengthen the independence of the judiciary, however, the committee has proposed the establishment of an independent body within the judiciary to prepare budget proposals for the judiciary and to appropriate funds within the approved budget.[8] Similar systems exist in many other countries as well. In Chile, where a major reform of the judiciary was realized at the beginning of the decade, the Administrative Corporation, a technical advisory body for the judiciary, governed by a council of judges, was established to *inter alia* prepare budgets and to administer, invest, and control the funds assigned to the judiciary by the national budget law.[9]

The second limitation of the independence of the judiciary is that appointments, promotions, and dismissals of judges for all courts except the Supreme Court are decided by the president of the republic at the proposal of the minister of justice. (Supreme Court judges are appointed by the Seimas at the proposal of the president.) The Council of Judges, consisting of nine judges, including the chairmen of the Supreme and Appeals Courts, makes recommendations to the minister and the president regarding

---

7. W. Malik, "Judicial Sector Benchmarks."

8. "Domstolsudvalgets Betaenkning Nr. 1319" (Proposal of the Courts' Committee), Denmark, 1996.

9. World Bank, *Judicial Reform in Latin America and the Caribbean*, Malcolm Rowat, Waleed H. Malik, and Maria Dakolias, eds., World Bank Technical Paper No. 280 (Washington, D.C., 1995).

candidates. (In the case of Supreme Court candidates, the Supreme Court makes recommendations to the president.) In many countries, including the Netherlands, Sweden, and the United Kingdom, the government is also legally entitled to decide on appointments, promotions, and dismissals. But in practice, decisions follow the recommendations of courts or bodies of judges established for this purpose. In Denmark, the reform referred to above includes steps to strengthen the influence of the judiciary. Currently the Minister of Justice (formally, the queen) decides about appointments, promotions, and dismissals at the suggestion of the respective courts. Although the minister almost always follows the recommendations of the courts, the reform committee has nevertheless proposed a separate body— consisting of judges from the various courts, a lawyer, and representatives of the public—to prepare and submit such proposals.[10] In Finland, judges are appointed and dismissed by the president of the republic at the suggestion of the appropriate courts.

Key Medium- and Long-Term Policy Issues Facing the Lithuanian Judicial System

Legislation and Legislative Process

Because the current Lithuanian civil and commercial legislation was based mainly on Soviet law, there was initially a need to renew the legislation and to pass new laws after independence was regained. There was also tremendous pressure to get things done in the shortest possible time. In addition, there was little tradition or experience left in handling the legislative process, and technical assistance was offered from a large number of countries with different legal traditions, but there were no systematic efforts or guidelines to guide the selection of the foreign jurisdictions that would serve as models in given areas of law. Consequently, Lithuanian commercial legislation has become something of a patchwork, with a lack of conformity and consistency. Laws have been changed frequently, sometimes with retroactive effect. New laws have been enacted ad hoc to solve specific problems, sometimes in areas already covered by other legislation and without proper harmonization with related legislation. For instance, legislation governing the activities of enterprises is reportedly included in some two dozen different laws. And, although the Law on Commercial Banks includes most of what is needed to regulate banking, there are still a number of more general laws, such as the Law on Enterprises, which include provisions affecting banks, often ill-suited for their special circumstances. In addition, the Seimas has enacted laws that pertain to specific banks, instead of amending the laws that apply to all banks.

The legislative process, from the development of a concept for a law to solve a specific problem to the implementation of that law, is not yet fully developed in Lithuania. In the Nordic countries, for example, the process starts with the appointment of an expert committee to develop and propose a concept for the legislative solution to the problem at hand. Such a committee typically consists of experts in the fields to be covered by the law, both from the private and the public sectors. The task of the committee is to compare the circumstances and relevant legislation in the country with those of other countries, to discuss possible alternative solutions and concepts, and to make a proposal for the concept best-suited for the purpose. The proposal usually includes an outline of the needed legislation or amendments to existing legislation and detailed explanations of what the various elements of the proposed legislation are intended to achieve—that is, an *ex ante* interpretation of the law. This process is often missing or deficient in Lithuania, or takes place during actual drafting of the law. Committees are not always formed, and when they are formed, usually include civil servants and scientists, but seldom representatives of the "consumers" of the law. Comprehensive analyses and international comparisons are not regularly or systematically undertaken.

---

10. "Domstolsudvalgets Betaenkning."

The most common next step in the legislative process is the submission of the committee report to all interested parties for comment. In the Nordic countries, this includes comprehensive distribution to the private sector. In Lithuania, comments are solicited from ministries, government agencies, and usually from academics, but comments are not sufficiently and systematically collected from the private sector or civil society.

The drafting of the text of a law or the checking of the draft text, as well as the harmonization of the new law with existing legislation, is the responsibility of a specialized unit within the Ministry of Justice in many other countries, including Finland. In Lithuania, this function is performed mainly by the legal department of the Seimas, but not in a systematic and consistent way, which is why gaps, duplications, and contradictions in legislation are common. This is largely the result of an extreme shortage of staff in this department.

Also, laws in some countries—in the Nordic countries, for example—are always accompanied by governmental decrees that are generally prepared and enacted in tandem with the law. Such decrees contain detailed instructions about the implementation of the law and facts and figures that require periodic adjustment, and are therefore not included in the text of the law. The decrees are essential elements of the legislation and intended to assist in the implementation and interpretation of the law. In Lithuania, such decrees are usually prepared only after the law has been passed, often with considerable delay, and sometimes they are never issued. For instance, the Law on Prevention of Money Laundering, which came into effect on 1 January 1998, needs to be accompanied by detailed instructions about *inter alia* suspicious transactions and the like. No such instructions have been issued. This understandably causes difficulties in implementation and interpretation and is a major reason for inconsistent court decisions in an environment made difficult enough by the myriad of new laws and the relatively recent adoption of legal principles and concepts that are totally different from those prevailing during Soviet times.

Finally, laws sometimes emerge from the review process in the Seimas with numerous, sometimes considerable, changes that were not contemplated during their preparation. If important changes are made to a draft law in the reading of the law in the Seimas, such a law should go back to the drafting board for a review of text to determine consistency and workability of the concept. This procedure is not always consistently applied, which is one more factor behind the current difficulties in the implementation of laws.

The Limited Independence of the Judiciary

By law, the Lithuanian judiciary is guaranteed a relatively large measure of independence and immunity from pressure by the other branches of government. In theory, this independence is much like the independence enjoyed by the judiciaries in many Western countries. In these countries, however, the legal tradition has usually developed in the direction of extending a larger measure of independence to the judiciaries than the law requires. And, despite this, many countries are in the process of strengthening the independence offered by law. In Lithuania, as in many other transition countries, the absence of Western legal tradition and the lack of experience and training, both within the government and in the judiciary, has resulted in the Ministry of Justice more or less "running the show" in an administrative sense. In the early days of independence, this may have been a practical approach in the absence of a better alternative. Nevertheless, unless control is handed over to the judiciary itself as soon as possible, the development of the judicial branch into an independent and efficient branch of government will be hampered, and ultimately delayed. Some developing countries, among them many Latin American countries, have opted for a relatively large measure of independence for the judiciary in an effort to overcome some of the difficulties associated with a high degree of dependence on other branches of government.

In the description of the judicial system presented earlier, the two major factors affecting the independence of the Lithuanian judiciary—budgetary dependence and the rules for appointing, promoting, and dismissing judges—were discussed. They manifest themselves in the actual extent to which the government solicits and takes into account opinions and proposals from the judiciary regarding the need for monetary, human, and technical resources, as well as appointments, promotions, and dismissals of judges. Perceptions in this matter vary considerably. Those directly involved on both sides, government and judges, do not seem to perceive the influence of the government as a major problem, while outside observers cite this influence as one of the main handicaps of the country's judicial system.

The role of the government in the administration of the courts is formally established in the Law on Courts, which stipulates that, with the exception of the Supreme Court, the operation of the courts shall be guaranteed, and the improvement of qualifications of judges and the "material-technical supply" of the courts shall be overseen by the minister of justice. At the same time, it stipulates that the chairmen of the courts and the divisions "shall administer justice and conduct the operation of the court." In practice, the chairmen have little staff to assist them in these tasks, and the Ministry of Justice is therefore involved in court administration and in the operation of the court system. For instance, the ministry has been in charge of arranging and administering examinations for judges and other court personnel, supplying equipment and material, and maintaining buildings and equipment. The ministry also arranges for the inspection and audit of the business and financial activities of the courts, again with the exception of the Supreme Court, which is audited by a commission formed by the Seimas. The right of the government to inspect these activities of the court is common in other countries as well. In the Lithuanian case, however, the government is partly inspecting itself.

The general trend—in many Latin American countries and in some eastern European countries, for example—in the administration of the judiciary is to establish mechanisms for self-administration of the court system, with the executive branch involved only in the general allocation of resources to the judiciary and the audit of its operational and financial activities. In Lithuania, in contrast, draft amendments to the Law on Courts[11] significantly increase the involvement of the Ministry of Justice in determining resources for the courts; in the appointment, promotion, and dismissal of judges; in the administration of the court system; and even in case management. For instance, according to the draft proposal, the right to appoint a majority of the members (judges) to the commission that administers and supervises the examination of candidates for judgeships would shift from the judiciary to the ministry, and the Council of Judges, which currently recommends candidates for judgeships, would only have an

---

11. According to the Ministry of Justice, the amended Law on Courts has recently been passed by the Seimas. The president of the republic has not signed the law and is likely to send it back to the Seimas with some suggestions for changes. These changes, according to the ministry, would make the judiciary less dependent on the ministry. The most important factor in this regard would be that the Courts Department will be established as "a separate, independent department with its own budget." The department would, however, not come under the jurisdiction of the judiciary. The prime minister would appoint the director of the department, and the department would, in most cases, make its proposals (for example, candidates for judgeships) to the Ministry of Justice. The department would be staffed with judges on one-year assignments from their judgeships. It is unclear how much independence the draft law actually grants the Courts Department. In practice, its independence is likely to depend to a large extent on how much independence the Ministry of Justice and the government are going to be willing to grant to it. And the judiciary would, in any case, be heavily influenced from the outside, whether by the Ministry of Justice or the Courts Department. If the important posts in the department are occupied by judges, this could, of course, lead to increased influence by the judiciary on its own affairs, but only if it has a decisive say in nominating candidates for these posts.

advisory function in the future. The selection of candidates would be transferred to a special Courts Department in the Ministry of Justice, which would take over the current and new tasks of the ministry relating to the judiciary. According to a concept paper prepared in connection with the draft amendments, the ministry, through a purpose-built Training Department, would be heavily involved, not only in the training of judges and other court staff, but also in university studies by instituting "state examinations" as final examinations for law degrees and by introducing other compulsory certification requirements also to be supervised by this department, instead of by the universities themselves. Such "reforms" would seem to return legal education almost to Soviet-style patronage. The heavy involvement by the Ministry of Justice is allegedly a matter of necessity, and the plan is that tasks and responsibilities will be transferred to the judiciary as soon as it is capable of taking them over. Experience from most countries, however, shows that such transfers of responsibility are rendered unlikely or very difficult by entrenchment and politics.

Shortage of Qualified Judges and Other Court Personnel

The shortage of skilled and well-educated judges (especially in market-driven commercial practice) and other court personnel is undoubtedly one of the main problems of the judicial system and a reason for the lack of public confidence.

The problem in regard to judges became even more acute when, as a result of the past court reform, the number of judges more than doubled in a relatively short time. There were simply not enough qualified lawyers in Lithuania. Consequently, qualifications for judges were lowered to make it possible to fill the positions. For judges in local courts, no prior experience is required. A person twenty-five years of age or older with a law degree can be appointed a "candidate to local court judge" and get practical training (but not independently solve cases) as a judge at a reduced salary for one year. It is then possible for the candidate to become an ordinary judge after the probation period by passing a local court judges' examination. Persons with five years of practice as judges, prosecutors, or practicing lawyers can be appointed local court judges without any probation period. Despite these relatively lax requirements, the output of new lawyers has not been sufficient to fill the gap. Vilnius University, which is the main institution for higher legal education, graduates only eighty to one-hundred masters of law each year, and a large portion of these graduates is quickly absorbed by the private sector. Despite the significant increase in judges' salaries as a result of the reform, making them about twice those of civil servants at equivalent levels, their income still does not match salaries in the private sector. Nevertheless, relative salaries in the profession are only a partial explanation of the shortage of qualified judges. The difference in salary levels between judges and the private sector is smaller in Lithuania than in many Western countries. The problem in Lithuania, as in eastern Europe generally, is not just compensation, but also the rapidly increasing demand for legal expertise and assistance, particularly in areas such as international commercial law, which together with the low output of new lawyers and the increase in demand from the judiciary, has caused difficulties, particularly for the latter.

With the exception of the Supreme Court and the Court of Appeals, judges do not specialize in a particular field. The judges of the Commercial Court do not specialize in particular areas of commercial law. The lack of specialization causes difficulties in complicated commercial cases, particularly in bankruptcy cases. The new draft of the Law on Courts allows specialization in local courts at the discretion of the chairman, but limits the specialization to three years[12] in any one field, which is a short time, and partially defeats the purpose of specialization. In many countries, judges are specializing, and

---

12. The limitation of specialization in any one field to three years has, according to the Ministry of Justice, been deleted from the final draft of the law.

their choices are often directed toward the particular needs of the country. In the United States, for instance, there are special bankruptcy judges; Venezuela has commercial and labor judges; and Panama has family and maritime judges. Hungary has a special Labor Court, and judges in general courts tend to specialize as well (in commercial cases, for example).

Lithuania's university education for lawyers suffers from a lack of resources and modern teaching methods and equipment. Teaching is heavily concentrated on theory. Case-solving and discussion groups are uncommon, and practical training is not offered. Salaries of university teachers are very low, and the law faculty of Vilnius University thus has difficulty attracting talented lawyers as teachers. Most of the teachers have other jobs as their main source of income. While the development of private university education may eventually fill the gap, there are few other programs of legal education in addition to Vilnius University. A semi-private university in Kaunas has recently started a master of law program, partially staffed by teachers from the United States. The program, however, does not require a legal degree for admission, and graduates may thus not qualify for judgeships (the first graduation is scheduled for 1998). Also, the Police Academy is being turned into an institution to teach law in order to provide legally trained staff for public administration. The teaching will be at the college level. Neither of these two institutions, however, are likely to alleviate the shortage of judges, at least in the short run.

There is also a serious shortage of skilled court secretaries, bailiffs, and other court personnel. There is no formal education or training that qualifies students for such positions. The status and salaries of court personnel are low. Courts have little staff for general and court administration—there is only a little more than one support person (assistants, court secretaries, and court office staff) for each judge in Lithuanian courts. In comparison, the ratio is 6:1 in Portugal, 5:1 in Quebec (Canada), and 4:1 in Belgium.[13]

The Ministry of Justice has recognized the need to give high priority to increased and improved education and training of both judges and other court staff. A concrete result of efforts in this regard is the establishment of the Lithuanian Judicial Training Center (the Center), which was established in March 1997. The Center is an independent, not-for-profit institution established to provide legal training to Lithuanian judges and other court personnel on a systematic and continuing basis. Other goals of the Center are to continuously analyze the status of the court system and current practices; to maintain relevant research and reference material; and to publish, both on paper and electronically, information necessary for judges.[14] The Center started operations with three full-time staff and part-time consultants. The first training course was arranged in September of 1997. So far, a dozen courses have been offered and many more are planned, including courses on labor law, economic crimes, and copyright law. The program will include courses for other court staff starting in 1998. The courses, which are free of charge, have been well attended and considerably oversubscribed.

Modern judicial systems put strong emphasis on developing specialized legal skills and management capacity. Some countries, such as France and Spain, have excellent schools to train future judges, and new judges are selected solely from graduates of those schools. In other countries, such as

13. W. Malik, "Judicial Sector Benchmarks."

14. The founders of the Center are the Ministry of Justice, the Supreme Court, the Lithuanian Judges' Association, the Open Society Fund of Lithuania, United Nations Development Program (UNDP), and the American Bar Association/CEELI. Donors to the Center, in addition to the founders, are United States Agency for International Development (USAID), EU Phare, and the government of Finland.

the United States, the emphasis is on training newly appointed judges and developing specialized administrative capacity among other court staff. Both systems attempt to develop a strong sense of ethical responsibility that discourages corruption and emphasize the importance of continuing education to keep judges informed about legal developments and to provide them with opportunities to exchange lessons learned from experience. This is the direction in which Lithuania's incipient (and potentially promising) efforts should be channeled.

Inadequate Court Procedures

Case management and the administration of court proceedings suffer from the above-mentioned lack of skilled personnel, but they are also hampered by the lack of computerization, and even more critical, from poor design and practice. Case management is handled manually by court or division chairmen and is mainly restricted to the distribution of cases among judges. The Ministry of Justice maintains computerized records of laws and decrees that are available electronically to the courts, but electronic equipment in the courts is usually limited to one station in each court, rather than one for each judge. Court hearings are manually recorded, but because of the absence of parallel electronic recording and the lack of education and training of hearing secretaries, the records are often deficient and incorrect. Often, no more than a summary of testimony is transcribed by hearing secretaries. The records of proceedings in lower courts are thus often of little or no use in the upper courts, and procedures, in case of appeal, must largely start from scratch. The problem of appellate proceedings being bogged down with factual inquiries, basically *de novo*, have plagued the Lithuanian court system since independence.

Court proceedings are public, unless otherwise specified by law, and records of proceedings and decisions are to be published. In practice, only parts of the records and decisions are published, and there is no comprehensive database for court decisions. The principles of the validity of jurisprudence are somewhat unclear, and access to jurisprudence is lacking, with the exception of decisions and opinions published by the Supreme Court. The reason for uncertainty regarding the binding effect of jurisprudence is said to be its neglect in the Constitution. Even the binding effect of decisions and opinions published by the Supreme Court is being questioned.

Also, according to the law, the burden of proof in commercial disputes lies on both parties—both parties must present evidence in support of their respective claims. In practice, the burden of proof is said to lie mainly on the plaintiff. Defendants are able to delay proceedings considerably on technical and other grounds. The rules and practices with regard to appeals are not always observed. For example, the enforcement of time limits for appeals is lax. Cases are sometimes heard in the court of appeal, despite expiration of the time limit. Another problem is that judges tend to issue their formal opinions long after the initial decision has been made, and after the appeals process has been set in motion. This is contrary to rules and international practice because it may interfere with—and contradict—the findings of the higher court.

The enforcement of court decisions presents problems as well. There are too few bailiffs, particularly qualified bailiffs. There are currently 290 bailiffs, or a little more than one bailiff for every two judges. This compares with a bailiff-to-judge ration of 1:1.3 in Finland. Moreover, unclear laws and regulations further complicate enforcement. For instance, temporary restraining orders are difficult to obtain, which allows assets to be hidden or squandered before they can be seized. The problems of improperly influencing judges and others involved in an action, as well as outright corruption, are also present, although apparently they are not a very serious problem. Court orders and decisions are difficult to deliver, in part because of a deficient law on enterprise registers that has resulted in an incomplete and unreliable enterprise register.

Inefficient Pricing of Court Services

The pricing of court services, in practice, restricts access to the court system. The court fee for getting a case heard in the first instance is generally 5 percent of the amount of the claim. The fee has to be paid at the outset, and is not reimbursable once it has been paid. The fee for appealing a court decision is half of the fee in the first instance, and again, half of this fee in the court of cassation. For tax and other administrative disputes, however, no fees are charged, and in bankruptcy cases only a nominal fee is required.[15] The system of charging relatively high up-front fees, partly to ensure partial or total cost coverage, and partly to reduce incidences of frivolous charges, is not uncommon. For example, courts in Poland require a deposit of 12 percent of the disputed amount by the party bringing the claim to court in commercial cases. This deposit is supposed to be returned in part or in whole following a decision in the case, but it nevertheless imposes a significant financial burden on the plaintiff, particularly since commercial cases often take about two years to be resolved in Poland.[16]

Although Lithuanian courts usually order a losing defendant to reimburse all or part of the court fee to the plaintiff, the obligation to pay the fee in advance and the uncertainty about reimbursement when winning a case is said to significantly deter enterprises, particularly small enterprises, from seeking justice in court. Many Western countries, such as Canada, France, and the United Kingdom, have resorted to relatively low flat or fixed fees rather than percentage-based fees. The court fee in the United Kingdom, for example, is only about $300, irrespective of the amount of the claim.[17] In Finland court fees are $100–200, depending on the court.

Plaintiffs in Lithuania usually cannot get relief from paying court fees. Moreover, Lithuanian legislation does not provide for the possibility of free legal aid. Although lawyers' fees are lower than in western Europe and the United States, they are nevertheless significant in the Lithuanian context, and further restrict the possibilities for enterprises to seek justice in court.

Lack of Alternative Dispute-Resolution Mechanisms

The development of alternative dispute-resolution mechanisms in Lithuania is not currently motivated by the need to ease case loads or shorten the time required for decisions; as noted above, these are not major problems. What is needed are mechanisms that can offer cheaper ways of resolving commercial disputes than the avenues available through the ordinary court system. Many enterprises, particularly small businesses, cannot afford the fees. Also, alternative dispute-resolution mechanisms can involve specialists in the subjects of disputes, an option that is not available in the courts.

There are no provisions in the Law on Courts for court-associated dispute-resolution mechanisms. Settlements mandated by judges or equivalent settlements out of court are not excluded by the law, but in the absence of related mechanisms, procedures, and tradition, cases are usually not settled out of court. Bankruptcy law—both the old and the new, which became effective on 1 October 1997— provides for extrajudicial bankruptcy proceedings. In a portion of bankruptcy cases currently in court (mainly concerning state enterprises), extrajudicial proceedings are being applied. But so far, such proceedings have not been much more effective than proceedings in court, largely for the same reasons:

---

15. Before the reform of the court system, court fee revenues exceeded the costs of operating the court system. The significant increase in the number of judges and in the salaries of judges has reversed this relation, but fees still cover a considerable portion of costs.

16. C. Gray, "Evolving Legal Frameworks."

17. W. Malik, "Judicial Sector Benchmarks."

lack of detailed procedural rules and experienced bankruptcy administrators and judges.

The Seimas adopted the Law on Commercial Arbitration in April 1996. The law recognizes, and is based, on the New York Convention of 1958 "On Recognition and Enforcement of Foreign Arbitral Awards." The law provides for private arbitration of commercial disputes, either in the form of institutional arbitration (that is, arbitration facilitated and organized by a permanentarbitral institution) or in the form of ad hoc arbitration, which is organized without the assistance of such an arbitral institution. There is now one such permanent arbitral institution, the Vilnius International Commercial Arbitration, which was founded by the Lithuanian Lawyers Association in May 1996. The Ministry of Justice has approved a list of recommended arbitration chairmen, but both the chairman and the other members of the arbitral tribunal may be chosen from outside the list. Arbitral awards may not be appealed.

The arbitration mechanism is not yet functioning, and only one case has been brought to arbitration in Lithuania so far. The legislation has some significant flaws, and it is reported that the set-up of the arbital institution is flawed as well. Experts have expressed doubts about the enforceability of arbitral awards outside Lithuania. There is also uncertainty and lack of knowledge about the arbitration process, and few people have experience with arbitration. Lawyers are not yet including provisions for arbitration in commercial contracts in Lithuania.

The success of alternative dispute-resolution mechanisms—both court-associated and private—in the United States has inspired many countries to introduce and try out such mechanisms. Common court-associated mechanisms, which in many countries have been incorporated into codes of procedure, are mediation, early neutral evaluation, settlement conferences, and arbitration. Examples of private dispute-resolution mechanisms that have been introduced, in addition to arbitration, are negotiation and mediation. Alternative dispute-resolution mechanisms are actively encouraged by both courts and private organizations, such as Chambers of Commerce. In Poland and Slovenia, for example, private arbitration is directly connected with the Chambers of Commerce, which provide organized forums—arbitral institutions—for arbitration. In Latvia, where private arbitration is regulated by out-dated legislation and new legislation is only now being drafted, the Riga International Arbitration Court nevertheless received ninety-four requests for arbitration in the first nine months of 1997, a considerable increase over the twenty-five requests received during all of 1996. Assessments of the quality and effectiveness of arbitration in the Riga International Arbitration Court vary, but many users consider arbitration to be a cheaper and quicker way to get decisions than going to court. In Finland, a system of adjudicating routine cases by nonlegal staff, without hearing by a judge, has recently been introduced, and by now is the mechanism used for a large portion of civil cases.

Policy Recommendations

The Framework and Principles for Judicial Reform

WHAT IS BEING DONE? The Ministry of Justice has prepared a draft, "Guidelines for the Reform of the System of Legal Institutions," as a continuation of the reform of the judicial system, originally approved by the Seimas in December 1993. According to the draft, the Ministry of Justice and the Ministry of Interior shall be reformed to be better able to perform their functions as "governing institutions" of the system for law and order. The Ministry of Justice would, *inter alia*, establish a division within the ministry to analyze "judicial practice" (case law) and to make recommendations concerning the improvement of such practice. The ministry would also be charged with developing judicial training programs for judges and other court personnel and legal studies in universities. The suggested reforms also include the development of a system for adjudicating administrative cases, either by using the current court system or by setting up specialized administrative courts; the further reform of the general court system and court procedures, particularly the merging of the Commercial Court with the general court system; reform of the prosecutor institution and the police; and the recognition and development of regulations for the Lithuanian bar.

A draft of amendments to the Law on Courts has also been prepared, with the aim of improving the functioning and administration of the courts. The suggested amendments would transfer a number of tasks and responsibilities, including those involving appointments, promotions and dismissals of judges, judge examinations and training of judges, and the interpretation and application of laws from the courts and the judges to the Ministry of Justice. At the same time, it moves many such tasks and responsibilities from the minister of justice to the Court Department of the ministry. The amendments also lessen the importance of jurisprudence, lower requirements for appointments of judges to local courts, and require local court judges to be reappointed twice instead of once before confirmation of appointment until retirement. These amendments, while designed to improve the functioning of the judicial system, considerably decrease the independence of the judiciary. Such a reform would be contrary to the trend in the European Union, where the courts and the judges are given progressively more independence and responsibility in running the judicial system. The rejection or lessening of the importance of jurisprudence would be in sharp contrast to the system in other European countries. In addition, a recent report of the United Nation's Human Rights Commission cited the review process for local court judges after five years of service in preparation for permanent appointment as one of Lithuania's outstanding human rights issues.

A significantly amended Law on Enterprise Bankruptcy came into effect on 1 October 1997. The law is an improvement over the old version, although it fails to correct some problems, but rules and procedures for implementing the law and for the training of judges and bankruptcy administrators and trustees are needed for the law to have the desired effect of speeding up and improving bankruptcy procedures. The Civil Code is being thoroughly revised too, with the principal aim of completing, systematizing, and consolidating commercial legislation. Finally, as mentioned earlier, the Judicial Training Center was established and has started operations. The Center could, if properly supported and funded, have a major impact on improving the knowledge and expertise of judges and other court staff.

WHAT CAN AND SHOULD BE DONE? International experience suggests that commercial judicial reform should (a) have a long-term approach, with a clearly defined set of actions for both the short and the medium term; (b) be broad in scope and address judicial sector issues as a whole, and at the same time, contain targeted intervention in areas in urgent need of improvement; (c) build on the strong points or reinforce ongoing activities of the sector; (d) have a mechanism that constantly evaluates progress and makes necessary adjustments; and (e) be broadly participatory and involve all stakeholders in the system (judges, lawyers, court staff, users, and so forth).

Experience in other countries also shows that successful judicial reforms have made the judiciary more independent. Important components in such reforms have been simplified and updated legal procedures and laws; improved administration of justice; improved legal education and training; expanded access to justice; and the provision of alternative mechanisms for dispute resolution. Basic vehicles for reforms of the administration of justice have been improved training; enhanced and automated case management; computerization; and alternative or innovative solutions. In Singapore, where these vehicles were the main elements in a major overhaul of the administration of justice in 1988–93, the number of cases awaiting trial in the Supreme Court was reduced by more than 90 percent, the time to reach decisions in lower courts fell from 11–22 months to 4–6 months, and the world ranking of Singapore's commercial judicial system improved from eleventh to first.

The policy recommendations presented below, while based on observations about deficiencies and needs in Lithuania, largely coincide with measures that have proven successful elsewhere.

Improving the Legislative Process

Many elements of an appropriate and smoothly functioning legislative process are essentially in place in Lithuania. The enormous pressure on lawmakers of the great need for new and amended laws during the transition of the legal system caused shortcuts to be taken in the process and reduced the quality of the end product in order to create a new legal framework in the shortest possible time. Whatever its faults, the basic legal framework is now in place and in need of a thorough review. International experience suggests that a meaningful and standardized legislative process, such as the one outlined below, although including many time-consuming phases, is in practice more expedient and, above all, will result in better and more easily applicable legislation.

It is thus suggested that the government cause the following adjustments to be made to the legislative process. First, the process of drafting and enacting a law should be standardized. Any new law or amendment to an existing law should essentially go through the same procedure. Although the initiative in preparing new laws usually lies with the ministry with jurisdiction in the subject area of the law, as is the case in Lithuania, there should be unified "quality control" along the way by a specialized unit. This quality control should include the assurance of the legal correctness of the language and the practical applicability of the law, as well as its conformity with (and, if necessary, the initiation of changes in) other legislation. In case of changes to the law during the review process, this quality control process must be repeated, including a control phase after the law has been passed by Parliament. This quality control, or at least its major steps, is usually assigned to a law preparation unit in the Ministry of Justice. The government should consider implementing such a system in Lithuania, at least over the medium to long term. Since this apparently requires a considerable increase in resources and changes in procedures of the Ministry of Justice, an alternative or a transitionary arrangement could be that the legal department of Seimas take over part or all of this process. Although this department already performs some of these tasks, however, its capacity is already insufficient, and the need for additional resources would be considerable. A third, perhaps most practical, alternative would be to divide the responsibility between the Ministry of Justice and the legal department of the Seimas. The latter would take over responsibility when the law is submitted for review to the Seimas. Any of these alternatives requires additional resources, the preparation and approval by the relevant authority of clear and concise procedures for this quality control process, and the unequivocal assignment of the necessary authority to the chosen unit(s). Such an arrangement, if properly realized, is likely to result in a considerable payoff over time in the form of more consistent, more easily implementable legislation, as has been the case in many other countries. Possibilities for comprehensive technical assistance for this effort should be explored.

In parallel, the practice of appointing a committee to make a proposal for a law or an amendment to a law should be made standard for any law or amendment of significance. Time limits for the committees to prepare proposals have often been much too short, and should be set realistically, based on the complexity of the task. The members of the committee should be experts in the subject from government, academia, civil society, and the private sector, including future "consumers" of the new law. The task of the committee should be to work out a proposal for the concept of the law, using international comparisons to explain in detail what the law is intended to accomplish and how it should work and to propose an outline of the law or a first draft of the text. The proposal should be submitted to the coordinating and law preparation unit recommended above for the drafting or finalizing of the law's text, drafting of necessary decree(s) to accompany the law, and drafting of amendments to any other laws and decrees that need to be harmonized with the law in question. The unit should send proposals of any significance—including drafts of laws, decrees, and amendments—for comprehensive review, with deadlines for comments, to ministries and government agencies, but also to other interested parties, mainly in the private sector. A comprehensive and transparent review process should eliminate the occasional appearance of several parallel drafts of the same law, which has caused considerable confusion and delay.

In case the reading in the Seimas results in major changes to the law, or to the whole concept of the law, the proposal needs to be returned to the coordinating and law preparation unit, which will determine the need for resubmission—if necessary, all the way to the start of the process.

Increase the Independence of the Judiciary

Although the ultimate goal of the government is an independent judicial system, it currently appears to be moving in the opposite direction. It has deemed it necessary to participate in and supervise the administration of the judiciary more closely to achieve improvements in the functioning of the system. As mentioned before, increasing rather than limiting independence has usually been the best way to realize that improvement.

There are, in principle, several alternative approaches to achieving greater independence for the judiciary. A basic element in the functioning of the judiciary, and thereby in its independence, is the allocation of resources for its activities—that is, who controls the budget. Today, the budget of the judiciary is part of the budget of the Ministry of Justice and is controlled by the ministry. Very few judiciaries have full control over their own revenues and expenses, but many (Denmark, Chile, and Hungary) have a large say in the planning and determination of the budget.

Although the country models of judicial independence have differences, they are usually based on separate administrative bodies within the judiciary, governed by a board staffed mainly by judges and charged with budgetary and administrative tasks. It is thus recommended that the Lithuanian government consider proposing to the Seimas the establishment of a Court Administration Agency (CAA) to assist the courts on issues concerning budgets and administration, along the lines of the Chilean model. Appropriations to the judiciary would remain in the sphere of the Ministry of Justice, but the budget of the judiciary should be separated from the budget of the ministry, and the judiciary should be given a large measure of independence, both in regard to its budget and its administration. According to the Ministry of Justice, the Courts Department (referred to in footnote 11) will be vested with many of the tasks proposed for the CAA and is a more realistic alternative at this stage. However, as pointed out above, since the Courts Department comes within the jurisdiction of the government rather than the judiciary, the latter is unlikely to be able to exert much influence over this department. An alternative realization of a CAA would be to make a plan for the gradual shift of the Courts Department to the jurisdiction of the judiciary. In case this alternative is realized, the judiciary should be given more influence over the department at the outset—for example, by being given the right to nominate or appoint the director and at least part of the professional staff.

The CAA should be governed by a board with representation from, but not control by, the Ministry of Justice. The Supreme Court Senate or Council of Judges could serve as such a board. One of the first tasks of the CAA would be to carry out studies of the gradual transfer of administrative tasks from the courts and the Ministry of Justice to the agency. Examples of functions to be transferred to the CAA would be preparation of budgets; administering, investing, and controlling the use of funds assigned to the judiciary; administering, acquiring, fitting, and maintaining buildings and furnishings for the courts; providing technical advice concerning the design and analysis of statistical information and the development and application of computer systems; and organizing and supervising training and examinations for judicial personnel. The CAA could also gradually take over functions relating to court procedures, such as case management, and the production, maintenance, printing, and distribution of court records, decisions, and jurisprudence. This reform, if realized, would be a major effort, and should therefore be realized in stages.

In addition, to be truly independent, the judiciary should have a major say in the appointment, promotion, and dismissal of judges in all courts. In no case should the judiciary's role in this regard be reduced from the role currently granted by the Law on Courts. The possibilities for nominations and appointments on political or other nonprofessional grounds should be eliminated as much as possible. This has been achieved in western Europe, for example, by excluding the executive branch from the process (France) or by a long tradition of decisionmakers adhering to proposals or recommendations made by judicial bodies (Nordic countries). The government should consider proposing reductions in the role of the Ministry of Justice in judicial appointments. As a minimum, it should consider proposing to the Seimas that the Supreme Court or the Council of Judges be given the authority to designate and propose candidates for appointments and promotions, as well as to propose dismissals from all judicial positions. To maintain outside control of the judiciary, the Seimas (in the case of the Supreme Court) and the Ministry of Justice (in the case of other courts) should continue to arrange for the inspection and audit of the business operations (but not the decisions) and the financial activities of the courts.

Training Judges and Other Court Personnel

The Lithuanian Judicial Training Center is off to a good start and enjoys broad support from the government, the judiciary, and international donors. The Center should be supported and further developed to become a major and long-term provider of training for judicial personnel. The action plan of the Center is meaningful and correctly geared toward covering the most pressing needs for training. Nevertheless, even when operating at full capacity, the present and planned resources of the Center allow it to fill only a relatively small part of the large gap in knowledge and experience among judges and other court personnel. Although any expansion of its activities must be gradual because of the constraints in human resources and funding, the government should give high priority to continued strong support for the Center and to securing regular and increasing budgetary funding for its activities. Although the Ministry of Justice and other interested parties should continue to be involved in the supervision of the Center and contribute financially, the main responsibility should, in line with the suggested general increase in the independence and self-sufficiency of the judiciary, be transferred to the judiciary, preferably to the Supreme Court and the Judges Association.

Understandably, the Center has limited its initial activities to training of judges and other court staff. As noted above, the successful implementation of the new laws on commercial arbitration and bankruptcy requires a cadre of skilled and efficient arbitrators and bankruptcy administrators. In view of the considerable difficulties in getting bankruptcy cases through court, there is a special need for training and practice in bankruptcy procedures for both judges and administrators. Unless something is done to address this deficiency, the mere existence of the new laws will have little effect. Although the focus of the Center should no doubt continue to be on the training for judges, the government, in consultation with the Supreme Court and the board of the Center, should consider including the above-mentioned professions among the targets of its training program over the medium term. Court lawyers and other private lawyers could also benefit from, and would probably be interested in, taking part in training arranged by the Center. Participants from the private sector and from governmental units beyond the judiciary should pay fees for participation, and could thus contribute to the funding of the Center. Because the Center has only recently started operations and has limited resources, an alternative solution could be to arrange separate training for arbitrators, and particularly for bankruptcy administrators. Training for the latter could possibly be arranged in conjunction with the recently established work-out unit, Turto Bankas.[18]

The Law on Courts contains provisions for appointing "candidates to local court judges." Persons who do not qualify for local judgeships because of their insufficient age or inadequate experience can serve as assistant judges for a year, and then be confirmed as ordinary judges. This way of moving young lawyers into the court system and alleviating the shortage of judges is expanded in the draft amendments to the law. This is an effort in the right direction, but the draft also includes less desirable features. The major undesirable element is the provision that the entire process, from designating candidates to confirming final appointments, would be almost completely the responsibility of the Ministry of Justice. The government should consider sharing the responsibility for this system of traineeships with the judiciary. The CAA, if established, could administer this process.

Judges in the local and district courts are not specialized and are hearing both criminal and civil cases, although there are separate panels for civil and criminal cases in district courts. The draft amendments to the Law on Courts encourage specialization, but at the same time limit periods of work in special fields to three years. The government should, in consultation with the Supreme Court, introduce requirements for specialization in various areas of commercial law. There is a particular need for specialization in bankruptcy procedures, but also in other areas, such as contract law, intellectual property legislation, and financial legislation.[19]

State-sponsored university education for lawyers and other legal professionals needs reform. More and better-educated lawyers are needed, and there is no education available for other legal professionals such as prosecutors, bailiffs, and court secretaries. Lack of funds is clearly the main hindrance to hiring more qualified teachers and improving teaching facilities and methods. One concept being considered (mentioned earlier) is to improve the quality of legal graduates by instituting final examinations arranged and supervised by the Ministry of Justice. Such a system is unlikely to produce the desired results and would infringe significantly on academic freedom. An alternative strategy to improve the quality of graduates—practiced, for example, in the Nordic countries—is to require a period of training (usually 6–12 months) in court for graduation. In addition, the government, in consultation with Vilnius University and possibly with other universities and colleges as well, should consider instituting lower-level (bachelor) legal examinations for those interested in careers as prosecutors, bailiffs, court secretaries, and the like. Although possibilities for establishing significant, fully private universities may be remote, the government should nevertheless remove any disincentives to the establishment of such universities and actively promote their creation.

A crucial aspect of improving judges' skills is a viable code of ethics. The Judges Association has issued a one-page list of ethics rules, but a comprehensive code is missing. The government should instruct the Judges Association to prepare such a code, and the association should also be made responsible for enforcing ethics, which should apply to all judges. The Ministry of Justice should interfere only if enforcement is not effective.

---

18. The work-out unit (Turto Bankas), established as part of the governments' plan to restructure the state banks, is in the process of taking over the assets of the defunct Innovation Bank. Turto Bankas is, in effect, acting as a liquidator of the bank. The knowledge being accumulated within the unit could be utilized by assigning the task of administering and liquidating bankrupt banks.

19. According to the Ministry of Justice, the limitation to three years on specialization in a particular field has been removed from the final text of the Law on Courts, which reportedly also includes the discontinuation of the Commercial Court.

Improving Court Procedures

Although cases pass through the courts relatively quickly in Lithuania in comparison with many other countries, there are a number of measures that could be taken to improve the quality of court services and decisions, and thus to increase public confidence in the judicial system. This, in turn, would likely result in an increase in cases brought to court. Many of the measures suggested above are likely to result in improvements in court procedures. More consistent and clear legislation facilitates reaching correct and just decisions; better educated, trained, and motivated judges and other court personnel improve procedures, decisions, and enforcement; and the CAA, if established, could spearhead efforts toward improved court procedures.

There are several additional measures that would improve the flow and administration of cases. First, court functions, including case assignments and case management, should be computerized. In Argentina, computerization of case assignments enabled courts to avoid "judge shopping" (that is, the possibility of choosing a judge of your liking to hear your case) and rationalized judges' work. In Singapore, automated case management contributed to the improvement of the country's judicial system, which has become one of the top-ranking systems in the world. Second, the tape recording of court proceedings and automated production of court transcripts should be introduced to facilitate proceedings in higher courts, in case of appeal, as well as in the lower courts. Third, court decisions should be stored electronically, published, and made easily accessible to judges and the public. Fourth, the right of the Supreme Court to publish decisions and interpretations should not be decreased, as proposed in the draft amendments to the Law on Courts, but rather expanded to explicitly include publication and interpretation of decisions of lower courts. Fifth, rules regarding court procedures should be tightened and strictly enforced. For instance, hearing cases in appellate court, despite expiration of time limits, should be avoided. And the practice of issuing opinions by judges after appeals have been made should be discontinued. Sixth, fines for dilatory tactics should be introduced and enforced. Finally, the enterprise register has become an unreliable source of information to the courts and other users because of a deficient law; as a result, the register contains insufficient and unreliable information. The government should review the law, the rules, and the functioning of the register with the aim of implementing a major overhaul.

Better Access to the Court System Through More Efficient Pricing

The cost of bringing commercial cases to court—mainly court fees and lawyers' fees—is a particularly effective deterrent to small and medium-size enterprises that would seek justice in court. Court fees are high in comparison with fees in the courts in western Europe, for example, and the practice of charging the fees up-front is particularly cumbersome (and sometimes unfair) for many prospective plaintiffs. Consequently, the government should review the court fees for commercial cases with a view to facilitating access to courts. One alternative is to institute a system of relatively low, flat fees. This would have the drawback of reducing income from fees (unless the number of cases increases dramatically) at a time when government finances are strained. As an alternative, court fees could be made payable "in installments," with an affordable first installment due at case registration (the registering of ill-founded cases could be prevented by other means, such as giving judges a larger measure of discretion to refuse cases), and with the last installment payable upon release of the judgment. There should also be an upper limit for the amount of the fee. The rule that losers pay the cost should be made standard practice.

The government should also consider setting up a legal assistance program for commercial users. The program, which could be administered by the CAA, should provide for the possibility of covering both court fees and lawyers charges, in whole or in part. To avoid an excessive burden on the budget, the program could be made restrictive, and available only to those most in need of such aid. Another way of helping those who cannot afford to bring disputes to court—a method practiced in the United States—is to form legal aid "clinics" run by the bar association and universities. Vilnius University is planning to arrange such clinics as part of the program for advanced students. The government should consider supporting this effort as part of a legal aid program.

Fostering Alternative Dispute-Resolution Mechanisms

Despite the apparent lack of need for alternative dispute-resolution mechanisms, the government should nevertheless provide a framework conducive to such mechanisms, both court-associated and private, and actively promote their use. This would diversify the possibilities for the resolution of commercial conflicts; provide cheaper, and often faster, alternatives to court procedures; and help avoid an increase in the backlog of cases. Such an increase is likely to occur in the next few years with the growth and diversification of the private sector and the increased propensity to seek justice in court that will accompany growing confidence in the judicial system.

The government should thus consider proposing additions to the Law on Courts to provide for some court-associated mechanisms. Several such mechanisms are possible. First, mediation and early neutral evaluation could be developed. In both of these practices, the parties to a pending suit, either through mutual agreement or at the instigation of the judge, try to settle the case out of court with the help of a third party. In mediation, the third party—the mediator—only facilitates the mediation effort, while in the early neutral evaluation, the third party, usually an attorney with expertise in the kind of case involved, makes an early evaluation of the case to help the parties to come to a settlement. A second mechanism includes the pretrial conference and settlement conference. In these cases, the judge hearing the case or a designated "settlement judge" tries to mediate a settlement out of court, either before (pretrial conference) or during (settlement conference) trial. All these mechanisms are appropriate; if legally sanctioned, they could be effective in Lithuania, and could lessen the time and the cost of relatively minor or clear-cut cases, and thereby allow the courts to concentrate on the more complicated cases and help clear backlogs.

Despite the existence of a legal framework for private dispute resolution since mid-1996, private arbitration has not gotten off the ground. To get things started, a productive approach would probably be to concentrate on institutional arbitration as the more organized, and therefore less unfamiliar, method of dispute resolution. The government should make an evaluation of the arbitration law to remove alleged flaws, and should, together with the Lithuanian Lawyers Association (LLA), which is the founder of the Vilinius International Commercial Arbitration (VICA), make an assessment of the workability of VICA as an arbitral institution. The rules and regulations of VICA should, if necessary, be changed to make the arbitration process workable and the awards enforceable. LLA should explore the possibilities of establishing an arbitration-promotion partnership with the Lithuanian Chamber of Commerce, a model that has been successfully applied in Poland and Slovenia, for example. The government, together with the judiciary, should also launch an information campaign to encourage the use of private arbitration. Such a campaign should also promote the inclusion of arbitration clauses in commercial contracts.

A campaign to promote alternative dispute resolution mechanisms should, if it is to have a chance to be successful, be preceded by training of judges, arbitrators, and mediators. Judges should be encouraged to promote alternative dispute resolution. As mentioned above, the Judicial Training Center should include training in alternative dispute-resolution mechanisms in its program and should be allowed to include—for a fee—private arbitrators as participants in such training.

9

PSD ENVIRONMENT: CORPORATE GOVERNANCE

This chapter reviews the status of the main determinants of corporate governance in Lithuania—that is, the ways of enforcing accountability on the management of enterprises by those who invest in them. It attempts to consolidate the aspects of corporate governance indirectly treated in the other Policy Notes (in this volume, see the chapters treating securities markets, banking, and privatization), to add some new aspects, and to analyze the information in a systematic way. Corporate governance is examined, mainly from the viewpoint of the investors, and elements and structures of corporate governance in other areas, primarily Japan, the United States, and the western Europe, are considered in order to extract practical lessons and policy recommendations for Lithuania.

Corporate Governance—In the International and Lithuanian Contexts

In recent years, policy reform efforts, initiated partly as a result of constraints to private sector development (PSD) identified in the World Bank's 1995 *Lithuania—Private Sector Development Report*, have substantially improved Lithuania's business environment. Nevertheless, lack of adequate corporate governance—that is, positive influence by shareholders, banks, and other interested outside parties on management to improve performance—is one of the most serious remaining constraints to an efficiency-led increase in long-term growth. The economywide enhancements to efficiency that were expected to result from Lithuania's early and, in some respects, successful (voucher-based) privatization have not fully materialized. It is unlikely that they will come to pass unless remaining impediments to better corporate governance are removed; measures to increase transparency and to develop channels of influence by providers of finance are introduced and enforced; and a framework for the emergence of new, strong categories of investors, such as pension funds and investment funds, is created.

The most effective systems of corporate governance have arguably been developed in countries such as Germany, Japan, and the United States. There are, however, important differences among them. While corporate governance in the United States and the United Kingdom is based substantially on legal protection of investors, in much of Continental Europe and Japan there is more reliance on large investors and banks.[1] In much of the rest of the world, legal protection of investors is considerably weaker, and ownership is usually heavily concentrated in families and among a few large outside investors and banks.

The system of corporate governance in Lithuania is still underdeveloped; the legal protection of shareholders and creditors is slight, although some improvements have been realized or are planned; and the enforcement of rules and regulations intended to protect investors is generally weak (for example,

---

1. A. Shleifer and R. W. Vishny, "A Survey of Corporate Governance," NBER Working Paper 5554 (Cambridge, Mass.: National Bureau of Economic Research, April 1966).

requirements for disclosure of information to investors by enterprises quoted on the stock exchange are insufficient and inadequately enforced). In addition, during the first stage of privatization, a majority of the ownership of a large portion of the privatized enterprises was transferred to incumbent managers and workers. The second stage of privatization has started on a cash basis, but many enterprises, particularly many of the largest, remain state-controlled. These forms of concentrated ownership, as one would expect, have not led to good corporate governance. Most state-controlled enterprises are poorly run and managers have little or no incentive to improve performance, especially in the large, infrastructure-related enterprises that operate in nontradable markets. Also, many of the large enterprises that have a significant or majority insider stake (such as the agro-industries) have restrictions on transfer of shares. Because such enterprises are generally internally financed, there are often no outside agents with the power to control insider abuse, poor management, or moral hazard behavior. And finally, the capital market in Lithuania is still in its infancy. There is an almost total lack of domestic institutional investors, such as investment funds, pension funds, and insurance companies, in the markets.

According to the survey of private enterprises presented earlier in the volume, Lithuanian business managers and employees hold, on average, two-thirds of the shares in privatized companies and about half of the shares in newly established enterprises. In privatized companies, there has been a notable shift from employee ownership to management ownership after privatization. Although not directly brought out by the survey, enterprises dominated by management and employees are generally thought to have been inefficiently run, and restructurings and reorganizations have been uncommon. Misappropriation of company resources in favor of management and other actions to the detriment of nonmanagement shareholders have also been frequent. Such misappropriation or outright fraud have, for example, been major reasons for the demise and ultimate bankruptcy of most failed banks. Most of these observations can also be made for enterprises with less or no management or employee ownership. Because of both deficiencies in company legislation and bad or fraudulent practices, outside shareholders have had little influence on the way companies are run and managed. According to the above-mentioned enterprise survey, only one-quarter of managers interviewed were of the opinion that shareholders were the main decisionmakers in the major issues in their enterprises.

Key Constraints to Better Corporate Governance in Lithuania

Weak Legal Protection of Investors

There are several main weaknesses in Lithuania's legal framework that make effective corporate governance by investors, irrespective of their size, difficult, and sometimes impossible. First, while in principle company legislation in Lithuania provides a reasonable framework for corporate governance by shareholders, many rights and protective rules explicitly or implicitly afforded to shareholders in most industrial countries are missing. The duties of managers to serve the interests of shareholders first are not defined in the Company Law. The law sets forth a general obligation of management to act in accordance with the law and the bylaws and decisions made by management bodies, but there are few explicit obligations or restrictions—such as restrictions on self-dealing by management and excessive compensation, a requirement to consult with the board of directors or shareholders before making important decisions, and the like. The requirement to refer decisions to sell, transfer, lease, or mortgage fixed assets exceeding 5 percent of the enterprise's authorized capital to a shareholders' meeting is reportedly not often met. Mechanisms that enable shareholders to interfere in management decisions, impose the will of shareholders on management, or change management through proxy solicitation and procedures and rules for takeovers are not included in Lithuanian legislation. Individual and minority shareholders, in particular, are generally referred to the courts to repeal decisions of the management and the board of directors. (The deficiencies in company legislation in shareholder protection, and recommendations for improvement, are included in the chapter on the securities market.)

Second, listing on the Lithuanian Stock Exchange does not yet require enterprises to disclose sufficient information, and disclosure requirements are frequently not observed or are followed with considerable delay. Although the basic legal and institutional framework for securities trading is in place in Lithuania, disclosure rules, of both financial and nonfinancial information, and the critical enforcement of compliance need to be substantially improved. With the exception of a handful of enterprises—mainly those quoted on the official list (currently only 5 out of around 250 firms listed and traded on the exchange)—the information provided for public consumption is often scanty and unreliable. Information is provided late, if at all, and with long intervals, often as much as a year (at least quarterly disclosure is required in all major stock markets in Europe). The Securities Commission has issued a detailed list of so-called special events (incidents that are likely to affect the price of the enterprise's shares) that must be reported to the commission, the stock exchange, and the media within five days of their occurrence. This obligation is persistently disregarded despite numerous sanctions by the commission (in 1996, for example, the commission imposed sanctions on management in the form of fines, mainly for violations of disclosure requirements, about 100 times; one of the major banks, which in June was warned about violations of provisioning rules, did not provide information about the incident until November). Also, the five-day limit for reporting special events seems too long—it is certainly overly generous compared with most stock markets in Europe, where such events must be reported immediately.

Third, although the Law on the Principles of Accounting requires accounting practices for enterprises to be in accordance with international standards, Lithuania lacks a system of accounting and auditing based on such standards (the banking sector is an exception; audits based on international standards were introduced in 1995, and accounting based on international accounting standards became mandatory as of 1 January 1997). Accounting regulations are scant and very general, but their very vagueness leaves room for accounting and financial statements that are close to international standards. In practice, however, few enterprises in Lithuania, other than banks, present financial information in accordance with such standards. The main demand—and in the case of most enterprises, the only external demand—for financial information comes from the tax authorities. Accounting practices have thus largely been formed by the requirements of the taxmen, and therefore differ in many respects from international accounting rules. These requirements are not eliminated by audits, because accounts are not always audited. When they are, with a few exceptions, it is not in accordance with international auditing standards. The accounting law is currently being thoroughly revised. As it currently stands, the draft of the new law is, in principle, based on international standards and European directives and includes some improvements. According to accounting professionals, however, it still has many flaws and includes a large number of detailed provisions and standard charts of accounts that would make it rigid, unworkable, and cause it to deviate from international and European Union (EU) standards. The draft attempts to conform accounting to the demands of taxation, when, as mentioned, taxation should conform to accounting. The draft includes provisions that cover areas treated in other laws and may possibly conflict with those laws. The important international accounting standard (IAS) principles of "substance over form" and "true and fair" view are difficult to implement in accordance with the draft law. There has been no discussion of the concepts involved, and the draft was prepared without consulting local accounting and auditing professionals. Even if a new and better law is passed, the main problem will still be implementation and enforcement. There is currently no law on auditing, but such a measure is under preparation. Company legislation and stock exchange regulations, however, do include provisions regarding auditing, but these are insufficient and not generally enforced. Most enterprises, including a large number of the 645 enterprises listed on the B list of the stock exchange, are not audited by licensed auditors. Only a handful, including those listed on the official list of the stock exchange, are audited in accordance with international auditing standards; many enterprises are not audited at all.[2]

Until recently, the government, through the Accounting Methodology Department of the Ministry of Finance, has been the only regulatory authority in the areas of accounting and auditing. As has been the case in most other countries in similar situations, the authorities have had difficulty keeping up with the rapidly developing and changing demands of the private sector. While the government retains the ultimate authority in these areas, the Lithuanian Auditing and Accounting Institute (LAAI) was set up in 1996 as a semi-autonomous body to develop accounting and auditing standards and practices and to license auditors. LAAI, although it has had a good start, is still in its infancy and has very limited resources to carry out its tasks. In practice, LAAI has mainly been involved in tasks relating to auditing (training and licensing auditors and preparing auditing standards). What it will accomplish in the area of accounting standards is unclear. The members of the LAAI board are mainly civil servants, and only one of its seven members—an auditor—is from the private sector. LAAI receives no funding from government other than the value of the premises put at its disposal at no charge. It is financing its activities through licensing fees, by arranging training for auditors and accountants, and by charging for publications.

The effect of weak accounting and auditing standards on corporate governance is compounded by the absence of credit-rating agencies and other institutions that provide general and specific market information. In addition, the quality of the economic information provided by independent news media, both printed and electronic, is allegedly not high, a likely consequence of the lack of a tradition and demand for such reporting.

Fourth, the Lithuanian judicial system—the subject of a separate Policy Note—is still in an early stage of development and has some distance to go before it will become a smoothly functioning, independent branch of government. The Law on Courts provides for the establishment of commercial courts to solve commercial disputes. Only one such court—the Vilnius Commercial Court—has actually been established. This court has very limited resources and capacity, and the judges in this and other courts have little training and experience in solving complicated commercial cases. Few cases against managers or board members of commercial enterprises have been brought to court by shareholders. In a few instances, charges of fraud or other criminal acts have been raised against managers and board members, and in some of these cases managers have actually been prosecuted. Shareholders, however, have gained little or nothing from such prosecutions. Lack of confidence in commercial courts, and in the court system as a whole, and lack of knowledge about the judicial system and its workings are likely the reasons that Lithuanian shareholders and other investors are not yet trying to exercise their corporate

---

2. There is currently considerable debate in Lithuania regarding the desired degree of self-regulation in the fields of both accounting and auditing. Government representatives are inclined to maintain, or even expand—at least for the time being—the state's role in regulating and supervising accounting, while the private sector prefers the gradual transfer of regulation to a private, or at least independent, body such as the Lithuanian Auditing and Accounting Institute. Of the two other Baltic countries, Latvia has recently chosen to transfer most of the regulatory and supervisory functions for accounting and auditing to the private sector. The Latvian Association of Certified Auditors is in the process of preparing new Latvian accounting and auditing standards based on international accounting standards, international standards on audit, and EU directives. In Estonia, in contrast, these regulatory and supervisory functions are vested in a governmental agency, the Estonian Accounting Board. This agency, however, enjoys a large measure of independence, and the private sector is represented on its board.

governance rights through the court system.[3]

Fifth, the size-specific legal protection afforded minority shareholders in many developed societies is still partly missing in Lithuania (in addition to protection for shareholders as a whole). For example, mandatory systems of cumulative voting, qualified majority, and supermajority requirements in major decisions; extensive disclosure requirements; and explicit obligations for managers to run companies in the interest of all shareholders, not just majority shareholders or insiders, are lacking in the country's legislation. Moreover, although Lithuanian company law requires a two-thirds majority for some basic decisions (for example, approval of annual accounts, increase of share capital, and liquidation or reorganization), other areas are not covered. Managers, especially owner-managers, are known to have jawboned small shareholders, particularly employees, into supporting them or selling their shares to management. Evidence of the latter can be observed in the changes in ownership patterns chronicled in the enterprise survey mentioned above: employee ownership in privatized enterprises decreased by half from 1991 to 1997, with a corresponding increase in ownership by management.

Finally, in Lithuania, the legal framework has been debtor-biased—favoring shareholders over creditors and weakening creditors' ability to exercise "outside" pressure on nonperforming managers—until very recently. (The Lithuanian situation in this regard is discussed in the Policy Note on the Lithuanian banking sector and is therefore only briefly touched upon here.) The Law on Bankruptcy has been extensively amended and now gives creditors first priority to the full extent of their collateral (previously, several categories of creditors were prioritized ahead of collateral-holders), but it does not clearly address recovery through disposal of collateral outside the bankruptcy process, a common practice in western Europe and the United States. New and amended collateral laws and laws on the registration of liens have also recently been adopted, but are not yet fully implemented. As a result, banks, the only large private creditors in Lithuania, have not yet assumed a significant role in corporate governance. Banks, and the banking sector as a whole, are still small, even in relation to the Lithuanian economy. Lending to the corporate sector remains insignificant—total lending by banks is about 12 percent of 1996 GDP—although a few of the stronger banks have begun increasing their lending volumes and improving credit analysis capabilities significantly. Despite existing shortcomings, the use of banks as large creditors may still be one of the quickest and most realistic ways of improving corporate governance in Lithuania. Their power comes, in part, from control rights through default and debt covenants in loan agreements, and in part because they typically lend short term, so borrowers must return at short intervals for more funds.

Absence of Large Investors

The most direct form of outside control of enterprises is concentrated nonmanagement ownership. This can take the form of majority ownership by one shareholder or a substantial minority ownership stake by one or several investors. Experience around the world shows that large shareholders play an active role in corporate governance and that their presence is associated with better performance.[4] The other side of

---

3. In March 1995, Lithuania became the first Baltic country to establish a (well-functioning) Seimas Ombudsman's Office, based on the Swedish model, which hears citizens' complaints about abuse of official position or bureaucracy by officials of the central government, the municipalities, and the army. This includes complaints against officials in the Ministry of Finance and Tax Inspectorate for abuse in taxation matters. In 1996, close to 1,300 complaints were filed with the Seimas ombudsman. Of these complaints, close to 1,000 cases were investigated or rejected. In time, the ombudsman could become a means for shareholders to exercise their rights when the system proves to be ineffective.

4. Shleifer and Vishny, "A Survey of Corporate Governance."

the coin, however, is that large shareholders represent their own interests, which may not coincide with those of the enterprise or other shareholders. The risk of such a divergence of interests increases with the availability of classes of shares that give one class superior voting rights over other classes—for example, if control rights exceed cash flow rights. Large shareholders may expropriate enterprises at the expense of other shareholders, management, or employees. On balance, however, the positive influences of large shareholders dominate, especially in developed economies; there is little evidence of serious abuse or expropriation in countries such as Germany, Sweden, and the United States.[5]

There are few large shareholders in Lithuania other than the government and management insiders, neither of which has been known for inducing good corporate governance. There is also a total dearth of institutional investors. The voucher-based investment funds that played a large role in the initial privatization effort have all but disappeared, partly as a result of the amended legislation on investment funds that requires the funds to reorganize. Pension reform is under way, but the emergence of institutional investors under the new compulsory or voluntary pension schemes that have been envisioned is still years away.

Similarly, the market for life and property insurance is still very small in Lithuania. Insurance companies are thus small, and play almost no role as investors in the securities market. (As a comparison, in Finland, where the securities market is more developed than in Lithuania, but still far behind the markets of countries such as the Germany, the United Kingdom, and the United States, investments by insurance companies in the securities market totaled US$30 billion at the end of 1996, which was about 25 percent of the market's capitalization.) The insurance sector is dominated by one state-owned insurance company (Joint-Stock Company Lithuanian Insurance), a legacy of Soviet times, with about three-quarters of the market. It is inefficiently run and has required government support. Its main business is the insurance of apartment buildings and single-family homes, which by law must be insured for fire. Liability insurance for cars is not mandatory, and a very small percentage of cars have even rudimentary insurance. The introduction of mandatory liability insurance is under discussion.

The banking sector—although more developed and larger than the insurance sector—is still relatively small and weak. Banks are not significant investors in the securities market, mainly because of the restriction on investments in shares (a bank is allowed to invest a total of 10 percent of its equity in shares of nonfinancial enterprises).

Finally, foreign investment in Lithuania is still modest (despite a marked upward trend since the change in government at the end of 1996), and the impact of foreign shareholders on corporate governance has been small. A recent survey of foreign investors in Lithuania conducted by the Lithuanian Investment Agency (recently renamed the Lithuanian Economic Development Agency, after a merger with the Lithuanian Export Promotion Agency) indicates that, although the general attitude toward foreign investment has improved and discrimination against foreign investors has decreased, there are still many obstacles in the way of foreign investment, and Lithuania still ranks behind Estonia and Latvia in attractiveness for foreign investment. The most severe constraints in the perceptions of foreign investors, according to the survey, were related to legislation and regulation (frequently changing, vague, and nontransparent laws and regulations, exacerbated by heavy bureaucracy), the tax system (unclear and frequently changing rules, low predictability, confiscatory administration), the customs system, and restrictions on landownership.

The entrance of large investors into the market is further complicated by the absence of hostile

---

5. Shleifer and Vishny, "A Survey of Corporate Governance."

takeovers in Lithuania (a problem common in other east European countries as well). This is an unknown phenomenon for a variety of reasons, but mainly because of the structure and stage of development of the corporate sector, the lack of provisions for such activities in the legislation, and the underdeveloped securities market. Corporate takeovers, mainly hostile takeovers, even the possibility of a hostile takeover, can serve as a powerful corporate governance mechanism. In a hostile takeover, one or a few corporate bidders generally make an offer to the dispersed shareholders of the target enterprise, and if the offer is accepted, they acquire control of the enterprise. The targets often have shown poor performance; the management is replaced and measures to improve performance are introduced. In the United States and the United Kingdom, where large shareholders are less common, takeovers have been viewed as a critical corporate governance mechanism. Nevertheless, the history of takeovers, particularly in the United States, is checkered, and their effectiveness in corporate governance is questioned by many. In other countries, hostile takeovers are rare, partly because of political opposition. Also, takeovers require a liquid capital market, one that can give access to large amounts of capital on short notice.

Inadequate Legal Framework for Board-Management Interaction

An important part of the owners' governance-related rights and responsibilities in the operation of an enterprise is usually exercised through its board(s). Some countries (such as Germany and the Netherlands) have a two-tiered structure, with a supervisory board and a board of directors. In most countries (including Japan, the United Kingdom, the United States, and the countries of Scandinavia), enterprises operate with a single-board system. In countries with tiered systems, the supervisory boards usually have nonexecutive (outsider) members, and the board of directors is mainly composed of executive (insider) members. In theory, the supervisory board serves as the shareholders' "prolonged arm" for corporate governance and as a link to provide two-way communication between shareholders and management. In practice, there is some question of whether supervisory boards, which usually meet only a few times a year, have been effective in enforcing accountability of management. As a result, some countries (such as Finland) have been moving away from a two-tier structure toward a single-board mechanism. Single-board systems vary in the proportions of executive and nonexecutive directors, but tend to be dominated by insiders, which also raises questions about their effectiveness in corporate governance. There are many proponents of a single-board system with exclusively—or at least majority—outside directors as the preferred system for effective corporate governance. (For example, Denmark, Norway, and Sweden have adopted single-board systems, with only nonexecutive directors.) Such a system—to be effective—requires that the size of the board be limited, that the board members are appropriately qualified, that the positions of chairman of the board and the chief executive officer be kept separate, and that the board meet frequently enough and have sufficient power to enforce accountability.

Lithuania's Company Law provides for a choice between a tiered system; a single-board system; and, in the case of private companies, no board at all. Supervisory boards, if established, may only have nonexecutive directors, while boards of directors may include both executive and nonexecutive directors. If an enterprise chooses a single-board system, the rules governing the composition and powers of the board follow those of the supervisory board. In practice, Lithuanian enterprises use both two-tiered and single-board systems. Recently, however, there has been a trend toward only one board. In both cases, the boards have often been formally or informally dominated by insiders or a few large management shareholders. Supervisory boards in Lithuania have not been very effective instruments for enforcing discipline on management as a rule, and the real decisionmakers have been the management boards. Knowledge and information about the enterprise is not always shared with the supervisory board or is deficient or inaccurate. For example, the supervisory boards of many of the failed Lithuanian banks could do little to stop expropriation, and were, directly or indirectly, dominated by management and a few owners (often having only small direct shareholdings). Also, members of enterprise boards can, by law, be reimbursed only out of net profits, which increases the uncertainly and lessens their incentive to participate in companies that require major restructuring.

Much of management's domination of supervisory boards and shareholders' meetings is an outgrowth of the Company Law. Although it obligates management to act in accordance with law and the bylaws and board decisions of an enterprise, it does not impose "duty of loyalty" toward the company or the shareholders, and while it requires management to compensate the company for losses that are "their fault," it does not specify penalties for breach of this duty. The only penalties imposed on managers, other than penalties decided by courts in a civil or criminal suit, are imposed by the Securities Commission for breach of the disclosure rules mentioned above. The general threat of sanctions has not prevented managers from acting in their own interest to the detriment of shareholders, particularly since the risk of such behavior is quite low, both because of the deficiencies in the legislation and because sanctions have been difficult to impose in practice. A much-discussed complement to these "sticks" embodied in the law is the "carrot" of incentive contracts; that is, agreements between the enterprise and managers on performance-based remuneration and other benefits that could align the interests of managers with those of investors. Effective incentive contracts, however, are not easy to establish; the evidence of correlation between incentives and performance is not always clear, and high-powered incentive contracts may create enormous opportunities for self-dealing by managers if poorly negotiated. In addition, long-term contracts are needed to avoid actions by managers that may be beneficial to investors in the short run, but detrimental in the long run. All of these factors would be difficult to control given Lithuania's legal, judicial, and accounting frameworks. Incentives in the form of stock options and warrants remain unknown in the country. The Company Law speaks vaguely of such instruments (in somewhat contradictory language, it also requires payment for all shares issued), but there are no instructions regarding how such instruments should be structured and treated. For all these reasons, incentive contracts are rare in Lithuanian enterprises and are confined mainly to cash bonuses.

High Degree of State Ownership

Some 30 percent of Lithuania's GDP is still produced by state-owned or state-controlled assets. Energy, telecommunications, infrastructure, and part of manufacturing industry are still in state hands. While the country is moving toward full privatization—fourteen large enterprises are on a special list for case-by-case privatization and close to 800 small and medium-size enterprises (many with minority state holdings) are scheduled for sale—the first such large privatization has yet to take place, and there is limited knowledge or experience in this field. The privatization of the large number of minority holdings (in such varied activities as production of pumps and compressors, retail trade in fruits and vegetables, dental surgery, and public baths) is progressing slowly, and not very efficiently; much of this activity is the byproduct of the earlier voucher-based disinvestment effort. (The privatization process is the subject of a separate Policy Note.) Experience with majority state ownership—a record of inefficient, outdated, and often loss-making enterprises—shows that the government has not been exerting effective corporate governance. Of some 2,000 enterprises with state ownership (ranging from 1 to 100 percent), the government is represented in the boards of about 200. The State Fund of Securities administers approximately 1,200 minority holdings (an average of 11 percent ownership) of the state, but the government is not represented on their boards. The priority of the State Fund is not to influence decisionmaking in these enterprises, but to prepare information and plans for their sale. Since establishment of the fund in 1993, however, only some 100 shareholdings have been sold. Its staff of ten has concentrated primarily on collecting information rather than actively participating in corporate strategies—with an average of 120 companies for each staff member, it would be impossible for the fund to closely track management performance on a continuous basis. Assorted ministries also administer majority shareholdings of the state as "founders." The most important ministry in this regard is the

Ministry of National Economy, which is the founder of 250 enterprises, among them all the large, infrastructure-related enterprises. The ministry is represented on the boards of the approximately 100 enterprises in which the state holds a majority of the shares. Representation is at the ministerial or vice-ministerial level in a handful of the most important enterprises, and usually involves more than one person representing the state (for example, representation from the Ministry of Finance as well). Representation in other enterprises is provided from the level of department director to division deputy head. The ministry has a special department to manage those holdings, and a total of approximately thirty people act as board members and take part in shareholder meetings.

Policy Recommendations

Several important measures to enhance corporate governance are presented in policy recommendations in other Policy Notes (the chapters that discuss the securities market, judicial system, banking sector, and so forth); they are mentioned, but not repeated, here. Only recommendations directly related to corporate governance and not discussed elsewhere are listed below.

Improving the Legal Protection of Investors

MANAGEMENT DUTIES AND SHAREHOLDERS' RIGHTS. The Policy Note on the securities market recommends changes to company legislation to clearly delineate the obligations and responsibilities of managers of publicly held enterprises and to improve the rights of shareholders, particularly minority shareholders. Such changes to company law should be extended to all enterprises. Although nonlisted enterprises are usually smaller and more closely held, and therefore easier to control for shareholders, minority shareholders in such enterprises need protection as much as minority shareholders in publicly held companies do, particularly in view of the absence of the protection afforded by listing and trading privileges on the stock exchange.

Company law in many countries (such as the Nordic nations) goes beyond requiring the management and board of directors not act or make decisions in breach of laws and company bylaws and regulations. It imposes the positive obligation on managers and directors not to take actions that will, or are likely to, benefit selected shareholders or other persons at the expense of the other shareholders or the company. Such legislation usually does not detail penalties for violations of these obligations, but it does require managers and directors to provide compensation for the damage caused by their willful misconduct or negligence. The law in these countries can thus be said to be biased in favor of shareholders, and it places a high degree of responsibility on management and boards of directors to act prudently and in favor of the company and its shareholders. Moreover, provisions governing procedures for filing suits against managers and directors, special rights for minorities to file such suits despite majority decisions to the contrary, and special procedures for court proceedings and arbitration in disputes between shareholders and management and directors are also usually part of company law. Because of the dearth of legal tradition and jurisprudence in this field in Lithuania, legislation should give shareholders greater and more specific protection against the consequences of misconduct by managers and directors than is the case in the developed countries. Accordingly, the duty of loyalty should be clearly spelled out, and penalties, in the form of maximum fines and imprisonment, should be defined in the Company Law (as is proposed in the draft of a new accounting law; see below).

ACCOUNTING AND AUDITING. Drafts of a substantially amended accounting law, the Law on the Annual Financial Statements, and of an audit law, the Law of the Republic of Lithuania on Audit Procedures, have been prepared. These draft laws should be reviewed by experts, especially accounting and auditing professionals. The laws should be in agreement with and clearly spell out the requirement that international standards and EU directives serve as the basis for Lithuanian accounting and auditing standards.

As explained earlier, taxation has largely driven both accounting and the preparation of financial statements. In contrast, in most of Europe and in North America, accounts and financial statements are prepared on the basis of standards designed to give a true and fair view of the financial position and results of the enterprise. Such financial statements, usually with certain adjustments, form the basis for taxation. Thus, Lithuanian accounting standards should also be made applicable to accounting and the preparation of financial statements for tax purposes, and they should be made binding for tax collectors.

In addition, the draft accounting law goes into considerable detail (189 pages, including tables), and includes standard forms of financial statements and standard charts of accounts. Such forms and charts should be specimens rather than standard to allow for adaptation to the differing needs of enterprises. They should be issued by the relevant ministry or by a regulatory body rather than included in the law.

The draft accounting law suggests the creation of a "Commission for Accounting and Audit Standards" run by the Ministry of Finance. It is recommended that the Lithuanian Auditing and Accounting Institute (LAAI) be designated as regulatory body for this law. While the ultimate regulatory authority—the power to approve Lithuanian accounting standards and major changes to such standards and accounting principles—should, at least for the time being, rest with the Ministry of Finance, the gradual shift toward self-regulation of accounting and auditing by the private sector is likely to benefit both the government and the private sector through better and more transparent financial statements and disclosure of financial and related information. This has been the experience in many countries (for example, in Finland and Sweden) where bodies appointed by the appropriate ministry, but consisting mainly of experts from the private sector, issue accounting standards and regulations, interpretations of accounting laws and regulations, and opinions relating to accounting at the request of individual enterprises or organizations. Similarly, auditing regulation has—in the Nordic countries, the United Kingdom, and the United States, for example—been assigned to professional organizations of chartered accountants or licensed auditors.

The designation of LAAI as the regulatory body will require considerable strengthening of its organization and funding. This is not an easy task, in view of the limited availability of individuals with relevant education and sufficient experience. Nevertheless, it is preferable to trying to build up such capacity and experience within the civil service. The Ministry of Finance is currently the only "founder" of LAAI. Licensed auditors should be given a greater say within the LAAI, and in the medium term—if necessary, by amending relevant legislation—they should be admitted as founders of LAAI. This would be particularly appropriate if auditing firms, which already pay a large part of the costs, paid an annual fee to the LAAI as proposed in the draft auditing law.[6] The Board of LAAI should also be reconstituted to include a majority of representatives from the private sector, mainly licensed auditors and experienced accountants. LAAI has formed, and is forming, committees of participants, mainly from the private sector to work on issues such as accounting standards, auditing standards, ethics for auditors, and education and training. The LAAI badly needs more staff and larger premises to be able to cope with its increasing responsibilities, even if one excludes the suggested additional tasks. At the same time, LAAI

6. A problem in this regard is that there are presently three competing organizations representing auditors, and, to some extent, accountants. The government and LAAI could contribute to the formation of one nationwide federation by forming a "roof-organization" for licensed auditors registered with LAAI. Auditors could belong to this organization as individuals or through one of the existing associations.

has recently been assigned to take care of training and licensing of enterprise evaluators (who participate in the evaluation of enterprises slated for privatization), which is not the area of its expertise and has little to do with its main tasks. Despite increasing revenues from the private sector, partial funding from the state would be necessary for LAAI to effectively perform the role assigned by the government and to manage the burden of increasing activities and new tasks, partly as a result of the above proposals. The possibility of donor financing for the build-up and training of LAAI's organization should be explored. Over the medium to long term, LAAI could become largely, or even entirely, self-financing. In sum, the government should strengthen the organization of LAAI, reconstitute its board, and provide the necessary additional funding as detailed above.

In western Europe, it is customary that all companies be audited in accordance with "good auditing standards," effectively international standards. In addition, many countries (such as Denmark, Finland, and Norway) require large and medium-size enterprises (in Finland, for example, these are defined as enterprises with annual sales in excess of $30 million, or more than 300 employees) and all enterprises quoted on stock exchanges to be audited by highly qualified, specially licensed auditors. The Lithuanian draft auditing law requires enterprises with sales exceeding Lt 0.5 million, total assets exceeding Lt 0.25 million, or twenty employees or more to be audited by a licensed auditor. The provision does not ensure that the audits are of an international standard. Audits based on international standards on audit (ISA), or Lithuanian standards based on ISA, should be made mandatory for all enterprises traded on the stock exchange and for large (in the Lithuanian context) enterprises, irrespective of whether they are traded or not.

Finally, although it does not necessarily require legislative action, an essential prerequisite for an improvement in the standard of accounting and auditing is the availability of appropriate education and training for accountants and auditors. LAAI is arranging training for both auditors and accountants and expects to increase such activities in the future. LAAI has had, and still has, EU-Phare funded assistance in this effort. While LAAI's efforts in this area are important and should be supported by the government and donors, it cannot be expected to take on this rather formidable task on its own. Private efforts should also be encouraged and supported. One initial and temporary form of such support could be to arrange, under the auspices of LAAI, training for trainers, both from LAAI and the private sector, to be funded (but not delivered) by the state. In the medium term, the possibilities for establishing a training center along the lines of the Lithuanian Judicial Training Center should be explored (see Policy Note on the commercial judicial system), possibly within LAAI or as a combination of LAAI and private efforts. In many countries in western Europe, arranging for the training of auditors and accountants is mainly a private activity, carried out by professional organizations, by chambers of commerce, and through commercial courses arranged by business schools. Privately funded and arranged training, however, cannot be expected to become significant in Lithuania in the near future. The government should thus support and competitively allocate funding for both the efforts of LAAI and the private sector to arrange appropriate education and training for accountants and auditors.

Improving Corporate Governance Through Large Investors

With the exception of the state and management insiders, there are very few large investors in Lithuania. The Policy Note on the securities market suggests policy measures to build domestic institutional investment capacity by enabling and facilitating the emergence of investment and pension funds. (Pension reform is also discussed in detail in a separate Policy Note.) A third category of potential institutional investor—insurance companies—already exists in Lithuania, but the insurance sector is insignificant and state-dominated, and insurance companies are small and their activities in the securities markets, and therefore their impact on corporate governance, is negligible. The government should review the status, legislation, and regulation of the insurance sector—both life and property insurance—and identify policy options that would promote the development of an insurance industry led by the private sector that could eventually become an active participant in the domestic capital market. Further, the government should consider privatizing all its stakes in insurance companies.

Improving Corporate Governance Through Banks

Although Lithuanian banks are still too small to have a significant impact on corporate governance, banks, as large creditors, in addition to foreign direct investors, may still be Lithuania's best hope in corporate governance in the short run. In addition to amendments to the legal framework to remove impediments to increasing the volume of (quality) loans, several other measures should be taken to facilitate (safe) lending. The Policy Note on the banking sector suggests measures to implement laws relating to collateral and the registration of collateral, to enable lending in foreign currencies, and to promote syndicated lending. The privatization of all state banks would, almost by definition, improve corporate governance. Representation by banks on the governing bodies of client enterprises would be a direct way to exert influence. In Japan and, in particular, in Germany, where creditors have strong rights, banks are frequently represented on the boards of enterprises. In Lithuania, there are no legal hurdles to board membership by bank representatives, but in practice such cases are rare. The severe restrictions on shareholdings by banks mentioned earlier (10 percent of equity) preclude bank representation on enterprise boards as shareholders. Nevertheless, bank representation on boards could have considerable disciplinary effects on enterprise management and contribute to better portfolio quality of banks, particularly in enterprises dominated by insiders. The government could, in consultation with Bank of Lithuania, consider proposing changes to the banking regulatory environment to encourage banks to include good representation clauses in case of large lending contracts.

Improving Corporate Governance Through Board-Management Interaction

The Lithuanian system of one or two external boards (or possibly no board, in the case of private companies) is outdated and apparently is not working well. The boards of directors are often dominated by insiders and leave little opportunity for supervisory boards to have a strategic influence on the way enterprises are run. This is also one of the reasons that most countries have, or are now moving to, one-board systems, with all or majority outside membership. (This, of course, does not exclude enterprises from having internal management boards, which can be prescribed by their own bylaws.) In most countries, board members' fees are considered normal business expenses rather than being paid out of profits, as in Lithuania. The government should consider proposing changes to the Company Law to introduce a governance system with one external board with at least a majority of nonexecutive members, with only nonexecutive members eligible to be chairman, and with board members' fees paid as normal business expenses (not exclusively out of net profits). To give minority shareholders a larger measure of influence, the introduction of cumulative voting in enterprise elections should be considered.

The Company Law should include both "sticks" and "carrots" to prompt management to perform their duties in the best interests of the enterprise and the shareholders. Measures to clarify the obligations of management and penalties for noncompliance have been suggested in the Policy Note on the securities market, and their importance is reemphasized here, for both publicly held and privately held firms. Management incentives are more difficult to legislate or regulate. The Company Law should be reviewed, however, and, if necessary, it should be amended to enable a full range of management incentives, such as stock options, warrants, and the like.

Reducing the Government's Role in Corporate Governance

As recommended in the Policy Notes on privatization and the banking sector, state enterprises, including banks, should, with few exceptions, be entirely privatized and the government should immediately rid itself of minority holdings. None of the corporate governance structures discussed above will be effective unless enterprises are allowed to operate in an environment where government interference is predictable and restricted to the necessary minimum and enterprises are forced to function subject to market forces, without the promise of government bailouts if they fail. The recently established Seimas' Ombudsman Office could play an increasing role in this area if its supporting law were amended to allow the filing of complaints against public enterprise managers (as part of the civil service), filing by foreign individual and institutional investors operating in Lithuania, and a broader range of penalties for failure to disclose information to the ombudsman.

10

PENSION REFORM

Lithuania's pension program is a reformed pay-as-you-go (Paygo) public pension system, introduced by the Seimas in 1994. Pension benefits are among the lowest in eastern and central Europe—the targeted benefit for a full-career worker is about 40 percent of the final year of wages, and the actual average benefit is about 36 percent of average wages. The relative modesty of the benefit package enables the payroll contribution rate of employers to be set at 22.5 percent. Even after taking into account a portion of the 1 percent contribution paid by workers and an additional 1 percent in employer contributions that have been effectively diverted from other programs to help pay for pensions, the resulting effective rate of about 24 percent is one of the lower rates in the region. This reduces incentives for tax payment avoidance and migration of the workforce to the informal economy. Moreover, the inclusion of a flat benefit component in the benefit package and the wage ceiling used in the benefit computation for the earnings-related benefit component make the program highly redistributional, particularly for very high wage earners.

As is the case in most countries in the region, Lithuania's population is aging. Lengthening life expectancy, combined with lower birth rates over the past decades and liberal early retirement under the old Soviet regime, has resulted in an increasingly small population of working persons relative to the population of retirees. The aging of the population is inevitable, and two issues must be addressed now to prevent a financial crisis in the pension program in about the year 2010. First, benefits paid to current retirees must not be allowed to grow beyond the capacity of the wage base to support them. Second, the retirement age must be increased to restore long-term demographic equilibrium. These issues were addressed by the government's structural reform program with the support of the World Bank's 1996 Structural Adjustment Loan (SAL). In that program, authorities agreed to implement policies to limit the rate of growth in pension benefits to available resources and to accelerate the rate of increase in the retirement age.[1]

The 1994 pension law, coupled with the ongoing reforms, has made significant progress toward restoring the medium- to long-term financial health of the Lithuania's public pension system. The most recent projections forecast that the system will face relatively small deficits over the next three years, and it should be financially sustainable over the medium to long term, provided that retirement age increases

---

1. Under the 1994 reform, the retirement age is scheduled to increase from 55.0 to 60.0 at the rate of four months annually for women and from 60.0 to 62.5 at the rate of two months annually for men, with the ultimate age attained by the year 2009. Under the SAL-supported reforms, the government will *accelerate* these increases at the rate of six months yearly for both women and men and will increase the retirement age for women further, to 62.0.

are accelerated and are eventually extended to age 65.0 for both women and men.[2] Absent these changes, however, the pension system could suffer persistent deficits, on the order of 5 percent or more of taxable payroll, by the year 2030. Accordingly, there is a continuing need for prudence in setting benefit levels.

This Policy Note starts with two premises. The first is that, assuming that the government follows through with the amendments to the 1994 law under its structural adjustment program as discussed above, the existing pension system is financially viable. The second is that the 1994 reform, itself the product of a World Bank–supported project, embodies a clear set of social values concerning redistribution and the appropriate size of a mandatory pension system. Accordingly, this Policy Note addresses the question not of how to "fix" a fundamentally flawed pension system, but of how to improve it over the medium to long term. From this perspective, the key issues before the government include (a) improving public perception of the current pension program and reducing adverse labor force incentives by making the features of the current program more transparent to workers and retirees and (b) using the pension program to promote the development of capital markets, thus fostering economic growth. Of the two, the most compelling justification for further reform of the pension program is the second. Because the 1994 reform continued the pattern of financing pension benefits on a Paygo basis, rather than moving the system toward partial funding,[3] Lithuania's current pension system does not contribute to the accumulation of investment capital, and therefore remains largely neutral with respect to the challenge of promoting higher levels of economic growth. While estimates vary, real, long-term economic growth may be suffering by as much as 0.5 to 1.0 percent annually as a result.[4]

A working group under Lithuanian government auspices has drafted a framework law for voluntary private pensions. The law is well drafted and provides a solid framework for most contingencies. Unfortunately, its enactment has not yet been made a priority.

This Policy Note makes the following recommendations:

- *Modifications to the current program*: (a) increase incentives for long-career and older workers to participate in the Paygo system; (b) monitor compliance, particularly among the self-employed; (c) raise the retirement age at the rate currently envisaged by the SAL-supported reforms, but to an *ultimate* age of 65.0 for both women and men; (d) shift 11.0 percentage points of the 22.5 percent payroll contribution rate to employees, with a mandatory and commensurate "gross-up" in wages to leave workers with the same level of post-tax income, and create and

---

2. These forecasts are subject to some caveats: (a) genuine uncertainty regarding long-term trends in the wage base, compliance, and mortality (risks inherent in the nature of Paygo financing) and (b) some of the economic growth assumptions used in the government's projections may be overly optimistic. In addition, the last forecasts were done in early 1997 and do not reflect events since then. It has been suggested that those forecasts are based on unrealistically low real wage and labor force participation assumptions. Given that Lithuania's system is largely wage-indexed, changing the real wage assumption is not likely to have major effects on the results. Increased labor force participation would improve short-term financing, but at the price of larger long-term liabilities. In any event, it would be desirable for Lithuania to have a more flexible model available to test economic and demographic scenarios, and steps have been taken to develop and make available such a model.

3. By this it is meant that the accumulated payroll contributions in investment accounts are then invested in securities and other financial instruments, in contrast with the present practice of using current contributions to pay for the benefits of retirees.

4. For a discussion of this issue in the context of the Chilean pension reform, see R. Holzmann, "Pension Reform, Financial Market Development, and Economic Growth: Preliminary Evidence from Chile," *International Monetary Fund Staff Papers* 44, No. 2: 149–78 (June 1997).

distribute annual statements to workers; and (e) facilitate at least the growth of voluntary private pension savings (see below) by making enactment of the government's well-drafted framework law a priority. In doing so, the governement should clarify regulatory responsibilities and put the necessary resources in place as soon as possible.

*   *Funded accounts*: two options for introducing funded accounts in Lithuania merit consideration. The first option involves the encouragement of purely voluntary, tax-advantaged private pension plans by the government; the first step, as noted, would be enactment of the draft law on Private (Nonstate) Pensions. This option takes advantage of the modest size of the current public program. Even when allowing for a 5 percent contribution to voluntary private pension accounts, for example, the resulting total private and public pension contribution of 27.5 percent would still be lower than the contribution rates to the public systems alone in many countries of the former Soviet Union. The capital flows generated as a result of this option, however, would not be substantial. The second option involves offering a voluntary opt-out for existing workers, but making the opt-out mandatory for new workforce entrants. This option would generate substantially larger flows into the capital markets, and is thus recommended. The opt-out would permit workers to divert some portion of their payroll contribution to private pension accounts, with a commensurate reduction in their accrual of benefits under the earnings-related benefit component. For all future workforce entrants, the opt-out should be mandatory, and phased in over time, subject to the constraint that the transition would not be financed solely with debt, except in the very short term.[5] One strategy might be to permit only individuals more than ten years away from retirement to participate in the opt-out and to limit its initial size to 2.5 percent of payroll in 1998 and 1999, and 5.0 percent for the period 2000–2005. It should then be allowed to grow linearly to 10.0 percent by 2010, essentially replacing the supplementary portion of the pension benefit package. Such a scheme has the advantage of pacing the growth of the opt-out to forecast medium-term surpluses in the public pension system, while still providing for the accumulation of substantial amounts of investment capital. This scheme would cost the fiscal budget about 0.3 percent of GDP initially, rising to between 2.0 and 3.0 percent of GDP by 2015. It could be funded by some combination of (a) an increase in the level of the VAT, (b) a modest increase in the contribution rate, and (c) the indexation of the earnings-related benefit by price inflation, rather than wage growth, or by some combination of the two.

Descriptive Assessment of Lithuania's Pension Program

Background

The 1994 reform represented a commendable act of political will on the part of the Lithuanian government. It eliminated the Soviet legacy of early or arbitrary retirement privileges, began the process of raising the retirement age for current program participants, and made much progress toward reestablishing the medium- to long-term financial viability of the pension system.

Under the ongoing SAL-supported reforms, the government is enhancing the 1994 reform by (a) accelerating the rate of increase of the retirement age, (b) severing the direct link between the years-of-service flat benefit component and the so-called minimum subsistence level (MSL), (c) adjusting the

---

5. The transition costs associated with moving toward a partially funded pension system should largely be paid through reductions in other government spending or increases in taxes. Funding the transition exclusively through increases in government borrowing would only work to offset the gains in aggregate savings generated by funded accounts.

indexing of the earnings-related benefit component to limit expenses within the envelope of available resources, (d) modifying eligibility conditions and the benefit structure to provide incentives to workers who make contributions throughout their working lives, and (e) agreeing to effect transfers from the state's budget for noncontributory periods.

Pension Benefits

The benefit package provided under the 1994 reform combines redistribution and individual return in roughly equal measure. The benefit package has two components. The first is a years-of-service flat benefit—the "basic pension"—which effects substantial redistribution from the comparatively well-off to the less-well-off in support of the objective of providing income adequacy among the aged (see figure 10-1). The second is an earnings-related benefit—the "supplementary pension"—which reflects the principle of individual equity; that is, that benefits received in retirement ought to be proportional to contributions paid during a worker's productive years.

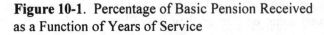

Figure 10-1. Percentage of Basic Pension Received as a Function of Years of Service

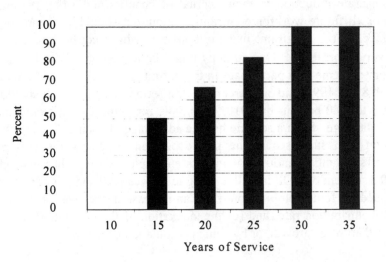

Benefit levels are modest. The total targeted replacement rate (defined as the average benefit divided by the average wage) for a full-career, average wage earner is about 40 percent. Because one-half of the benefit package (the basic pension) is not wage-indexed and benefits for disability and survivor pensions are lower than old-age pension benefits, the overall "system" replacement rate is about 36 percent, which is very low on both an absolute and comparative basis.[6]

The basic pension benefit is currently set at 110 percent of the MSL. Workers with thirty or more years of service are awarded a full benefit. Workers with between fifteen and thirty years of service are awarded a partial benefit equal to their years of service divided by the full service period of thirty years (that is, a worker with fifteen years of service will receive half the full benefit). Workers with less than fifteen years of service are not eligible for the basic pension and receive no benefit. For a full-career worker, the basic pension currently contributes about 20 percent of the average wage to the total pension benefit.

---

6. For example, replacement rates in Poland and Hungary are 60 percent or higher, and replacement rates in Russia are roughly comparable, even though most workers retire at a substantially younger age.

The MSL is purportedly recomputed quarterly based on the rate of price inflation (see figure 10-2). In February 1997, however, the government adjusted the MSL, and thus the basic pension, by about twice the increase in the cost of living index because it anticipated a greater inflationary effect from increases in VAT than has actually occurred—or is likely to occur. In principle, the government has agreed to sever this link between the basic pension and the MSL in favor of some other adjustment measures in order to constrain increases in benefit payments to the available fiscal envelope. Indeed, under the policies established by the SAL-supported reforms, the basic pension should be allowed to erode in real terms. The extent to which this will happen, however, is subject to intense political pressure and is difficult to predict. For instance, actions by the government during the first half of 1997 have undermined the core message that the longer-term financial sustainability of the public pension program depends upon the preservation of tight fiscal discipline in the short run. Real benefit levels increased by about 8 percent during the first eight months of 1997 as a direct result of February's increase in the amount of the basic pension and the government-established minimum wage.

Figure 10-2. Comparison of Cumulative Growth in Average Old-Age Pensions and Average Prices, 1997

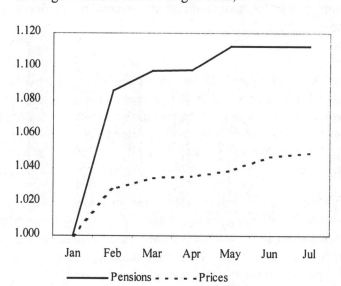

The supplementary pension benefit is based on a worker's average lifetime earnings relative to the average wage. Earnings are adjusted for inflation through of the German coefficient system, which is simply a technique for adjusting earnings for wage growth and expressing them relative to average wages. Under this system, a record is kept of a worker's wages, expressed relative to the average wage, for each year of employment. (For example, in a given year, someone who earns 200 percent of the average wage is credited with a point value of 2.0.) At retirement—and subject to a legislated award ceiling of 5.0 points in any one year—a worker's twenty-five highest points are averaged to compute the average lifetime earnings relative to the average wage.

Benefits are computed by multiplying the worker's average lifetime relative earnings (points) by the average wage in the period prior to retirement, with credit given at the rate of 0.5 percent for each year of service. Thus, an average wage earner who worked for forty years will receive a benefit of exactly 20 percent in replacement rate value from the supplementary pension. The value of the supplementary pension is indexed after retirement on the basis of the rate of wage inflation, although the

SAL-supported reforms empower the Social Insurance Council to index benefits at a lower rate to limit expenses within the envelope of available resources, subject to the constraint that the rate of indexation cannot be less than either wage or price growth, whichever is lower.

Two factors—the inclusion of a flat benefit component in the pension benefit package and the existence of a ceiling on wages used in the benefit computation for the supplementary pension—make the program very redistributional, particularly among the small number of persons earning more than five times average earnings. (Approximately 1 percent of workers earn more than five times average wages, and the total contributions collected on the basis of wages in excess of this ceiling is about 2 percent of total program revenue.) The overall level of redistribution provided under the program is roughly comparable to that of the Swiss and U.S. systems.

Coverage

All citizens in Lithuania, including farmers, sole proprietors, and the self-employed, are covered by the basic pension, although only citizens with fifteen or more years of service credit are eligible to receive benefits.[7] Only persons employed under labor contracts are covered by the supplementary pension.

Retirement Age

Prior to the introduction of the 1994 reform, the retirement age was 55.0 for women and 60.0 for men. As originally drafted, the 1994 reform provided for the retirement age to increase to 65.0 for both women (at the rate of four months annually) and men (at the rate of two months annually), but the law was later modified. It now specifies that the retirement age will increase to only 60.0 for women and to 62.5 for men, although the *rates* of increase have not changed. The ultimate retirement age will be reached in the year 2009 for both women and men.

Under the government's current reform effort, the increase in the retirement age is to be accelerated to six months annually, attaining the target age of 62.0 for women and 62.5 for men (both in the year 2010),[8] and the retirement age for women is to be raised by an additional six months in order to equalize the ages for women and men at 62.5. It appears unlikely, however, that scheduled changes to the retirement age will be enacted until the late spring or early summer of 1998, if at all. This is problematic, because the long-term fiscal sustainability of the pension program hinges not only on these changes, but also on further increases in the retirement age to 65.0 for both women and men (see figures 10-3 and 10-4).

Payroll Contributions

The payroll contribution rate in Lithuania is 22.5 percent and is paid by employers. An additional 1 percent of payroll is paid by workers, and in 1995 and 1996, about 1 percent of payroll was diverted from other activities to help finance pensions. The effective rate for pensions, therefore, is roughly 24 percent. Although not as low as in Latvia and Estonia, where the pension contribution rates are closer to 20 percent, Lithuania's pension rate is among the lowest in the region (compared with Hungary or Poland, for example), although promised benefits are commensurately lower as well. Unlike its neighbor, Latvia,

---

7. Coverage refers to benefit eligibility, not to benefit entitlement.

8. This assumes that the changes are made effective in 1998.

which requires that part of the social levy be paid by employees (9 percent of a total of 37 percent),[9] only 1 percentage point of this levy is paid by workers in Lithuania; the remainder is paid by employers.

Figure 10-3. Comparison of Retirement Ages (Males)

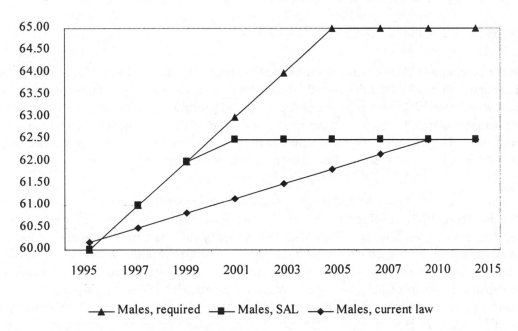

Figure 10-4. Comparison of Retirement Ages (Females)

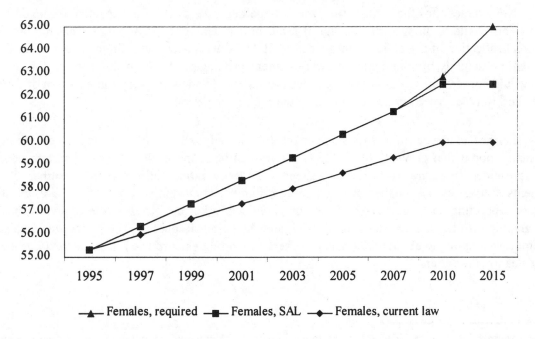

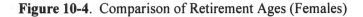

9. A pending change to Latvia's Social Insurance Law will reduce the total levy to 33 percent and will increase the employee portion of the social insurance levy to 50 percent of the total contribution, effective 1 January 2002.

Farmers, sole proprietors, and the self-employed (who are covered only by the basic pension) pay a flat monthly fee that is equal to one-half of the basic pension benefit. Payment of contributions for soldiers in obligatory service and for parents on leave to provide care for a child under the age of three is paid from the state budget.

Demographics

Lithuania's population follows a demographic pattern similar to those of many countries in eastern and central Europe, and much of the developed world: the population is aging. Lengthening life expectancy, combined with lower birth rates over the past decades, has resulted in a steadily shrinking population of working persons relative to the population of retirees. The aging of Lithuania's population is inevitable and irreversible. It is already a major contributor to the country's pension financing difficulties and will become the predominant issue facing the pension system in the foreseeable future.

This pattern of aging in Lithuania's population is evident in the old-age dependency ratios presented in figure 10-5. Defined as the number of persons over the retirement age divided by the number of persons of working age, the old-age dependency ratio is currently about 0.33 (or about 3.0 persons of working age for each person over the retirement age). It will rise to about 0.44 (or about 2.3 persons of working age for each person over the retirement age) by the year 2030. Lithuania's current old-age dependency ratio of 0.33 is roughly average for countries in the region, and it is substantially better than that of countries such as Bulgaria and Hungary. In the long run, the population of aged persons in Lithuania as a percentage of the total population will be roughly comparable to that of most other countries in the region.[10]

Nevertheless, for the next decade, the old-age dependency ratio is expected to remain relatively stable. This would be an encouraging sign if it meant that demographic pressure is easing, but instead it is a direct reflection of the policies introduced in 1994, which raised the retirement age for both women and men, particularly by eliminating early retirement privileges. Without this reform, the dependency ratios would not remain stable over the next decade, but would show the very same pattern of degradation in the short run that is seen in the remainder of the projection period.

Further evidence of the postponement (albeit only slight) of the impact of the aging of Lithuania's population provided by the 1994 reform can be found in the pattern of system dependency ratios presented in figure 10-5. The system dependency ratio, defined as the number of pension recipients divided by the number of program contributors, is currently about 0.56 (there are about 1.8 workers supporting each retiree). This is comparable to other countries in the region with a similar demographic profile, such as Slovakia, Poland, and the Czech Republic. The system dependency ratio will improve slightly, to about 0.50 (or 2.0 workers supporting each retiree) over the next decade, before rising steadily thereafter.

---

10. For example, by the year 2030, approximately 26 percent of Lithuania's population will be over age sixty-five. Estimates for other countries in the region include 23 percent (Poland), 25 percent (Russia), 26 percent (Latvia), and 29 percent (Slovenia and Croatia). The weighted average for all of eastern Europe and the former Soviet Union is somewhat lower—22 percent—because of historically high fertility rates in the countries of central Asia.

Figure 10-5. Dependency Ratio

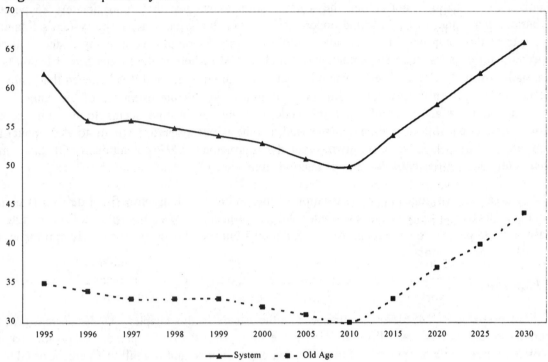

Note: "System" refers to total pensioners per 100 workers. "Old age" refers to persons older than retirement age per 100 persons of working age.

The conclusion to be drawn from these observations is that like many countries in the region, Lithuania is—and will continue to be—burdened by problems of an aging population. As a population ages, fewer workers are available to support the payment of pension benefits to the aged. This will impose significant constraints on the ability of the pension system to satisfactorily balance issues of adequacy and individual equity as long as the system is financed on a Paygo basis. Put another way, as long as current pension contributions are used to pay current benefits, Lithuania will continue to be challenged to provide an adequate level of pension income without forcing substantial intragenerational redistribution (from the relatively well-off to the less-well-off) or intergenerational redistribution (from the young to the aged) of income.

Labor Force Trends and Compliance

Labor force trends will create pressure on the wage base in the short run as the Lithuanian economy continues its transition toward a market-driven allocation of labor resources. According to projections prepared by the Ministry of Social Security and Labor (MSSL), the percentage of self-employed in the labor force is expected to increase from almost zero as recently as four years ago to about 20 percent by the year 2000. While the self-employed will accrue a correspondingly lower pension benefit at retirement, the trend in employment away from large companies to smaller enterprises and self-employment will reduce average payroll contributions over the short run because the self-employed are eligible only for the basic pension and pay a flat monthly fee, rather than the full pension levy.[11]

---

11. The monthly fee is equal to half the amount of the basic pension. For the average wage earner, moving to self-employment status results in a drop of about 45 percent in the total payroll contribution.

These same patterns have implications for payroll tax payment compliance as well. While Lithuania's track record is not among the worst—estimates suggest that approximately 85 percent of contributions that ought to be collected under the law are actually collected—the system's financing is suffering from the compliance ills characteristic of the region. Compliance in many eastern and central European countries is less than 80 percent, and compliance elsewhere in the former Soviet Union is often substantially lower.[12]   Some covered economic activity is unreported, and it is believed that many firms report money wages only up to the statutory minimum. No reliable estimates of the extent of such evasion in Lithuania are available, but the underreporting of income seems to be quite common. Moreover, collection of contributions on reported income is not assured. Arrears totaled about Lt 615 million as of July 1997, or about two months of projected 1997 collections. Of this amount, approximately one-third is considered to be uncollectible.

A great deal of hope for the alleviation of the problem of long-term fiscal deficits is placed in improved collection of payroll taxes—under MSSL projections, for example, collection rates will increase from 85 percent to 90 percent by the year 2000—but such hopes may be overly optimistic, given current labor market trends.

Cash Flow Projections

Projections prepared by MSSL are summarized in the Annex to this chapter. Under current law, these projections predict annual cash flow deficits in the range of 1.0 to 1.25 percent of taxable payroll— between 5.0 percent and 6.5 percent of total pension expenditures, and roughly 0.3 percent of GDP—for the next three years. This compares favorably with other countries in the region; about half of these countries have incurred deficits in excess of 2.0 percent of GDP in recent years. Nevertheless, the State Social Insurance Fund's reserves at the end of 1996 were close to depletion, and arrears had developed in payments to medicine vendors and for some short-term benefits.

In the medium term, the aging of the population will work to Lithuania's advantage, because a large portion of the workforce will enter their most productive years. Deficits are projected to decline to zero between 2000 and 2005, and to actually grow into small surpluses. When these cohorts begin to retire in about the year 2010, however, the surpluses will disappear, and the projections predict persistent annual deficits, on the order of 5 percent or more of taxable payroll (between 1 and 2 percent of GDP) by the year 2030.

These long-term deficits are primarily the result of the demographic imbalance created by a relatively large caseload inherited from the old regime coupled with an insufficiently fast increase in retirement ages. If the retirement age is gradually increased to 65.0 for both women and men at the proposed rate of six months annually, these same simulations illustrate that equilibrium will be reestablished, and Lithuania will avoid what would otherwise be persistent long-term deficits in the financing of its pension system (see figure 10-6).

The following conclusions can be drawn from this analysis. First, continued increases in the retirement age are necessary for the long-term financial stability of the pension program. Without such increases, the aging of Lithuania's population will force the government to take radical action to restore fiscal balance to the pension system, starting in about the year 2010. Such actions could include (a) substantial reductions in benefit levels, leaving many aged in poverty or further eroding the principle of individual equity (that benefits ought to be proportional to contributions); (b) an increase in the

---

12. Compliance among the central Asian republics is generally well below 50 percent.

contribution rate of as much as 5 percent; or (c) a perpetual transfer of funds from the state's general budget to the pension system equal to more than 1.0 percent of GDP annually. Second, even with such increases, the financial stability of the system will remain subject to uncertainty regarding, *inter alia*, long-term trends in the wage base, tax payment compliance, and mortality trends that are difficult to forecast, even in mature economies, but are inherent elements of Paygo financing. In short, given changes in retirement age policy, Lithuania's pension program can be financially sustainable over the medium to long term.

Figure 10-6. Net Cash Flow of Pension System as Percentage of Wage Base under Current Law and SAL-Supported Reforms

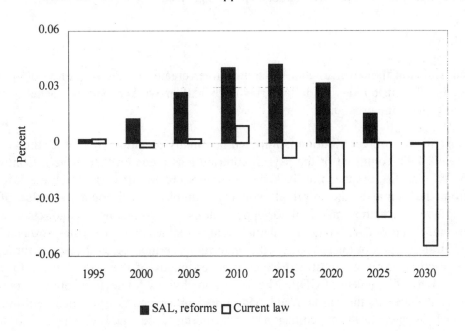

In addition, Lithuania has developed a well-drafted law for private (nonstate) pensions. The draft law provides for regulating both pension "programs" (schemes, plans) as the underlying contract and for pension "funds" as the fiscal intermediaries. Pension programs can be either employer-sponsored or created by workers on their own. Funds can either be open funds to which employers and individuals might subscribe, or closed funds maintained by individual employers. Appropriate safeguards are provided for all the contingencies, although the allocation of regulatory responsibility is muddled, and the government may not be willing to provide the right levels of management direction and resources to assure that the correct regulatory conditions are met.

Key Remaining Issues in Pension Reform

The 1994 reform made substantial progress toward restoring Lithuania's pension program to financial viability, and it did so in the face of considerable demographic and political pressure, and without resorting to draconian cuts in benefits, imprudent increases in payroll contribution rates, or ill-advised long-term dependency of the pension fund on the state budget. The rapid elimination of early retirement privileges, in particular, is an example yet to be followed by many other countries in the region. The relative modesty of the benefit package enables the payroll contribution rate in Lithuania to be one of lower in the region and has the advantage of reducing incentives for tax avoidance and migration to the informal economy. With necessary adjustments in retirement age policy, Lithuania's current pension program would arguably be a model of successful Paygo pension reform. The program represents a reasoned and prudent effort to balance a number of conflicting objectives, including the core issues of income adequacy and individual equity (which, from an incentive perspective, always present a tradeoff).

Within this context, the question becomes not how to fix the Lithuanian program, but how to improve it. The key issues in addressing this question are (a) the challenge of introducing greater transparency in the features of the current program in order to improve its public acceptance and reduce adverse labor force incentives and (b) the policy alternative of using the pension program to promote the development of capital markets and accelerate economic growth.[13]

Labor Incentives

The first issue is that of the adverse labor force incentives created by the lack of an obvious connection between the payroll contributions made by firms on behalf of workers and the benefits these workers ultimately receive from the program.

Because the payroll contribution is imposed nominally on employers rather than employees, the employees are not fully cognizant of the payroll contributions made on their behalf. Combined with the murkiness of the benefit formula, this lack of awareness creates incentives for the migration of the workforce from the formal to the informal economy. Employees discount the value of the pension benefit in their labor negotiations and look for opportunities to negotiate labor contracts outside the net of the social insurance program. Although Lithuania's total social levy—31 percent—is one of the lowest in eastern and central Europe, for many workers the opportunity to increase cash income through evasion is nonetheless attractive. This is confirmed by existing estimates of the size of the informal economy, which range as high as 40 percent of GDP. The lack of an obvious connection between contributions and benefits also contributes to the chronic and widespread underreporting of income within the formal economy, which is the result of collusion between employees and employers to avoid paying contributions on the total wage package. There are no reliable estimates that can be used to calibrate the extent of such behavior, but it is widely believed that many firms report money wages only up to the statutory minimum.

Moreover, the current program creates disincentives for workers to remain in the workforce beyond the statutory retirement age. Full-career workers receive no additional credit for added years of service under the years-of-service basic pension. For workers who remain in the workforce beyond the statutory retirement age, the actuarial adjustments for delayed retirement may be too low. The current system also may encourage workers to characterize themselves as self-employed; in so doing, they can obtain the minimum basic pension after only fifteen years of work, and then supplement that minimum pension with the proceeds from private savings, which likely will have a higher rate of return than

---

13. Debate on precisely how redistributional the mandatory pension program ought to be and on the best mechanisms to effect such changes is necessary and important. No clear consensus exists, however, on either the degree or means of redistribution in public pension schemes. Accordingly, this Policy Note has taken as settled the basic structure and underlying distributional policies of the 1994 reform, which are partly the product of Bank-supported assistance.

continued participation in the basic pension or voluntary subscription to the earnings-related supplementary Paygo pension.

Capital Market Development

The third pension policy issue faced by Lithuanian authorities in the medium term relates to the alternative of trying to use the pension program to promote the development of capital markets, and thus to enhance economic growth. There are a number of arguments that can be made for introducing some form of private pension account within the context of the public pension program. First, over the long run, aggregate savings may be increased. In Chile, for example, assets held by private pension funds totaled 35 percent of GDP by 1991, ten years after the old Paygo system was replaced with a scheme of fully privatized, individual savings plans.[14] Second, the formation of funded pension plans— particularly if coincident with, or subsequent to, privatization—increases the efficient allocation of capital within the economy and can accelerate economic growth. This is the lesson of Chile, where the gross annual real rate of return on private pension fund capital during the first ten years of the reform exceeded 13 percent, and the net yield to workers, after fees, exceeded 9 percent. In addition, the placement of large blocks of shares of Lithuanian companies in the portfolios of professional investors may lead to increased market liquidity and improved corporate governance.[15] Third, funded accounts may offer Lithuania a more efficient mechanism for financing retirement income, given expected trends in the country's system dependency ratio. Put another way, the rate of return available from Lithuania's Paygo public pension program, which is determined by the pattern of real wage growth and demographics, may be bettered substantially by the rate of return available in the private capital markets. Finally, funded accounts eliminate the labor force and demographic risks resident in the financing of purely Paygo regimes. (Admittedly, this gain comes at the expense of exposure to other risks, but these new risks can, to some degree, be mitigated through legal and regulatory oversight and investment diversification, particularly if pension funds are allowed to invest assets in the financial markets of other countries.)

Because the 1994 reform continued the pattern of financing pension benefits on a Paygo basis rather than moving the system toward partial funding, Lithuania's pension system currently provides none of the above-mentioned benefits. The current system does not contribute to (a) increasing national savings, (b) improving the allocation of investment capital and corporate governance, or (c) reducing labor force disincentives. *While estimates vary, real economic growth may be suffering by as much as 0.5 to 1.0 percent annually as a result.*[16] For these reasons, Lithuania needs to stage an explicit debate

14. Other factors were at work during this period, so it is difficult to arrive at a precise estimate of the contribution of private pensions to higher levels of aggregate savings. The point remains, however, that funded private pensions are superior to Paygo systems in promoting national savings.

15. See R. Holzmann, "On the Economic Benefits and Fiscal Requirements of Moving from Unfunded to Funded Pensions," American Institute for Contemporary German Studies, The John Hopkins University, Research Report Number 4, Economic Studies Program (Baltimore, Md., 1997); also to be published in a special issue of *European Economy*, Commission of the European Union, forthcoming.

16. For a discussion of this issue in the context of the Chilean experience, see R. Holzmann, "Pension Reform, Financial Market Development, and Economic Growth: Preliminary Evidence from Chile." Holzmann estimates that in the long-run, the Chilean pension reform improved total factor productivity by 0.5 to 1.3 percent, increased capital formation by 0.2 to 0.6 percent, and enhanced labor market performance by 0.0 to 1.1 percent, leading to a total long-term growth effect of between 0.7 and 3.0 percent, assuming a labor share of 0.7. Holzmann notes, however, that such gains arose only in the context of a comprehensive and consistent program of macroeconomic reform, and that the impact of the reform on savings was achieved indirectly through increases in public savings (by reducing the large stock of debt implicit under the former Paygo system) and increases in savings from higher levels of economic growth.

on the question of whether to convert all or some of its earnings-related benefit (the supplementary pension) to a funded, second pillar of private pension accounts. This discussion is currently under way in neighboring countries (Latvia and Poland), and the system has been implemented in a number of countries worldwide.

In addition, it should be noted that the current combination of a modest and redistributional replacement rate schedule, if combined with accelerated increases in retirement ages, eventually to age 65 for both genders, creates, at least in principle, space for voluntary private retirement schemes. Even after allowing for a 5 percent contribution to voluntary private pension accounts, for example, the resulting total private and public pension contribution of 27.5 percent would still be lower than the contribution rates to public systems in many countries of the former Soviet Union. The enactment of a framework law for such schemes awaits final government sign-off, a clear allocation of regulatory responsibility within government, completion of a satisfactory draft, and a consensus among key actors. At this point, it is difficult to gauge the public demand for voluntary tax-advantaged retirement savings, or to envision how quickly the financial intermediaries can respond (or will be interested in responding).

Continuity

Balancing continuity with the advantages of further reforms also merits consideration, although this is more an issue of implementation than economic policy. Arguments are firmly voiced by those responsible for administering Lithuania's pension program that (a) substantial resources have been invested to educate the public about the current program, and any further reforms will only serve to increase confusion and decrease the transparency of the pension system to the general public; (b) to effect changes to the program now would undermine the credibility of the government; and (c) implementation of reforms involving funded accounts will be met with skepticism, given massive public mistrust of financial markets and the banking sector. To some degree, all of these arguments have merit and deserve to be factored into any decision to make additional changes to the current program.

Policy Recommendations

Overall Strategy and Principles

The basis for the discussion of recommended changes in Lithuania's pension program is the premise that the program, as established by the 1994 reform, is generally financially viable over the medium to long term. Nonetheless, several of the SAL-supported reforms have not yet been implemented, including (a) the acceleration of the rate of retirement to six months yearly for both women and men (up from four months annually for women and two months annually for men); (b) the severance of the direct link between the years-of-service flat benefit component and the MSL; and (c) a change in the indexing of the supplementary pension benefit to reflect the envelope of resources available to pay for higher benefits.

Unless the government implements these remaining reforms and continues to raise the retirement age further, to 65.0 for women and men from the 62.5 under the current structural reform program, Lithuania's pension program will face deficits in the medium to long term (possibly starting between 2010 and 2015) that will necessitate an ever-increasing contribution rate or an increasing shift toward (and perpetual reliance upon) general budgetary financing.[17]   This is illustrated in figure 10-7, which shows the relative rates of growth in real old-age pension expenditures under current law and under the SAL-supported changes, which provide for an acceleration in the rate of increase in the retirement age. *In less than two decades, under current law, the cumulative growth in real benefits over 1995 expenditures is more than twice the growth under SAL-supported reforms.*

Figure 10-7. Rate of Growth in Real Old-Age Pension Expenditures under Current Law and under SAL-Supported Acceleration of Increases in the Retirement Age

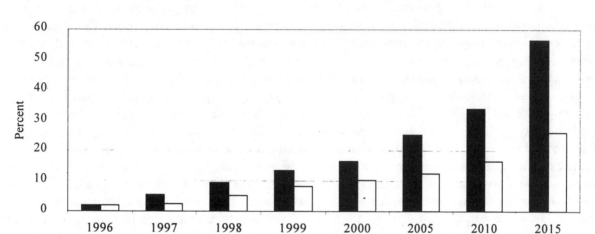

In addition to the criteria of financial sustainability, potential reforms should also consider the following:

- Transparency of the program and the degree to which understanding of the program minimizes labor force distortions.
- Economic growth and the degree to which the boundaries between the public and private sectors can be repositioned to facilitate investment and increase overall economic efficiency.

Modifications to the Current Program

Some narrowly focused modifications to the current program are discussed below. With one exception, they are part of the structural adjustment program, although they have not been developed as provisions to accelerate the retirement age increase or to contain expenditures within existing revenues. One measure, increasing the retirement age to 65.0 in the long run, is not part of the structural adjustment program, as such.

---

17. Unfortunately, one recently proposed amendment to the public pension law—a change that effectively increases benefits for roughly one-half of all of Lithuania's old-age pension recipients—is moving the pension system in exactly the opposite direction. This amendment, which increases the credit given for wages earned prior to 1 January 1994 under the supplementary pension program, is estimated to increase the cost of old-age pension benefits by about 5 percent yearly (worth Lt 85 million in 1998) over the next decade, after which the costs should decrease. Depending upon how rapidly the government implements the remaining provisions of the amendment, its cost could rise to as much as 7 to 8 percent of total old-age pension expenditures.

INCREASE INCENTIVES FOR PARTICIPATION IN THE PAYGO PENSION. Under current law, accruals under the basic pension are stopped after 30 years of work. In addition, the roughly 4 percent per annum adjustment factor for delayed retirement after the statutory retirement age is insufficient as the statutory retirement age increases. Incentives to comply after thirty years of work and to delay retirement would be enhanced through these relatively minor changes in the law. In principle, the government has agreed to making such changes in the current law under the structural adjustment program, but clear legislation along these lines has not been developed.

FOCUS COMPLIANCE EFFORTS ON THE SELF-EMPLOYED. The self-employed and, to a lesser extent, farmers present a difficult policy choice under current law. Quite reasonably, Lithuania decided not to compel participation in the supplemental-earnings-related pension for the self-employed (including farmers) on the grounds that the costs of administration (for example, measuring "earnings" in the agricultural sector) and compliance with respect to these groups are too high relative to likely results. In addition, the urban self-employed represent a natural constituency for voluntary private pensions. But by exempting the self-employed from the earnings-related supplementary Paygo pension, the self-employed may escape their fair share of the financing of the redistributiive burden of the two-tier nature of the overall scheme (that is, a proportional contribution that finances a redistributive benefit formula). At the extreme, a self-employed person could rationally participate for only fifteen years under the basic pension, avoid if possible further mandatory contributions to the basic pension, and concentrate his or her savings in private savings vehicles that earn a greater return than continued participation in the basic pension. In any event, the self-employed would not voluntarily choose to participate in the earnings-related supplementary pension so long as its rate of return is, as is likely, inferior to what can be obtained in private savings. Accordingly, higher-income people under conventional labor contracts are likely to bear a disproportionate burden of the current system's redistributional structure, and such individuals have an incentive to characterize themselves as self-employed.

Under the current structure, the issues of the self-employed can be addressed only through better compliance. One step would be closer collaboration with the general tax service in monitoring the self-employed, who represent the greatest problem for tax compliance generally. Along these lines, there should be careful monitoring of any tax-favored private pensions so that any self-employed participants must show that they are in full compliance with respect to their contributions for the basic pension. The distributional advantage that the wealthier self-employed enjoy under the current system could be addressed only by forcing their participation in the Paygo supplementary pension, or gradually shifting the supplementatry pension to one based on capitalization, with its higher rate of return (see below).[18]

CONTINUE TO INCREASE THE RETIREMENT AGE TO 65.0 FOR BOTH WOMEN AND MEN. As shown in the Annex, under the government's projections, the current system will remain financially sustainable until about the year 2010, when the system will begin to exhibit progressive and debilitating annual deficits, primarily as a result of demographic forces, on the order of 5 percent or more of taxable payroll (between 1 and 2 percent of GDP) by the year 2030. A continuing increase in the retirement age

---

18. Because roughly half of the benefit provided under the current formula is based on a flat amount for each year of service rather than on relative earnings or contributions paid, the overall pension scheme is highly redistributional. In theory, it might be possible to secure the income adequacy objective and the consequent redistribution through other means such as "volkspension" (typically, a function of age and residency only) or required participation in the basic pension, even by those not in the labor force (as in Switzerland). These structural options, however, have uncertain effects on labor incentives, and their financing may impose just as many compliance and incentive issues as a wage tax.

to age 65.0 for both men and women is necessary for the long-term financial viability of the pension program.[19]   Without action to effect further increases in the retirement age, not only is the system likely to become financially unsustainable in about fifteen years, but the cost of restoring balance to the system once it becomes financially insolvent will grow enormously.

SHIFT 11.0 PERCENTAGE POINTS OF THE 22.5 PERCENT PAYROLL CONTRIBUTION RATE TO EMPLOYEES, WITH A MANDATORY AND COMMENSURATE INCREASE IN WAGES TO LEAVE WORKERS WITH THE SAME LEVEL OF POST-TAX INCOME.[20]   As noted earlier, this has recently been done successfully in Latvia, and the formal splitting of the contribution between employers and employees is relatively common in developed countries, including, for example, the United States and Canada. The merits of explicitly imposing some portion of the payroll tax directly on employees appear to be generally understood in Lithuania. Such a move has obvious merit in improving labor force incentives—tightening the connection between contributions and benefits and making clear the implications of noncompliance— without affecting the take-home pay of workers.[21] To reinforce the effectiveness of this shift, workers should be provided periodic benefit statements showing how additional contributions have—and will— affect future benefit levels.[22]

ENACT A PRIVATE (NONSTATE) PENSION LAW AND DEVELOP A PLAN TO IMPLEMENT IT.   The working group on the private (non-state) pension law has crafted a well-drafted law that comprehensively and logically deals with all the necessary issues for a good framework law on private pensions. It makes the necessary distinctions between the underlying economic contract (pension "program") and the fiscal intermediaries ("funds"). It provides for both individual and employer-based schemes with a high degree of institutional and other protections. The law should be enacted as soon as possible, although in so doing, the regulatory responsibilities for the respective agencies should be clarified. In addition, the government should devote management time and sufficient resources to assure that its regulatory responsibilities will be met. Given the relative modesty of Lithuania's mandatory pension system, failure to make voluntary retirement savings readily available poses the risk that political pressures will build to expand the size of the mandatory Paygo regime.

---

19. A retirement age of 65.0 (or higher) for both women and men is common to many countries, particularly countries with aging populations, including, for example, Belgium, Canada, Denmark, Finland, Germany, Japan, the Netherlands, Norway, Sweden, and the United States.

20. Given that this Policy Note addresses only the pension component of social programs funded by the payroll tax, the recommendation presented here addresses only that portion of the payroll tax attributable to pensions. Nonetheless, the principle applies to the full social levy as well.

21. This can be accomplished by effecting the change all at once, at the end of a tax year, by keeping a record of contributions paid on behalf of workers and stipulating that gross pay be increased by the amount an employee would have paid had he or she borne the cost of some portion of the contribution, with an adjustment made for inflation.

22. In addition to making workers more aware of the connection between contributions and benefits, another step might be to recharacterize the earnings-related supplementary pension along the lines of a so-called "notional defined contribution" system, such as that being implemented in Sweden and Latvia. The advantages of this notional account formula over the German coefficient system now being used to express rights in the Lithuanian supplementary Paygo pension are not so great, by themselves, to justify the public communication and other administrative burdens that such a change would entail. The notional account formula, however, could facilitate conversion of the earnings-related pension to a funded scheme ("privatization"), and in that context, it may be an appropriate change that could have the additional benefit of increasing the perception of a link between contributions and benefits.

OTHER PROGRAMMATIC ISSUES.   Any proposal to increase the size of the basic pension or to provide for a minimum pension that, in effect, overrides the current benefit structure is not recommended. The degree of redistribution provided under the current system is already very high—comparable to that of the U.S. and Swiss systems, which are highly redistributional—and such changes could not be accomplished without either increasing costs substantially or effecting additional redistribution, and thus further discouraging compliance.

Funded Accounts

The merits of funded systems appear to be generally understood in Lithuania. Two options merit consideration.   The first involves the encouragement by the government of purely voluntary, tax-advantaged private pension plans. This takes advantage of the modest size of the current public program. Even when allowing for a 5 percent contribution to voluntary private pension accounts, for example, the resulting total private and public pension contribution of 27.5 percent would still be lower than the contribution rates to the public systems alone in many countries of the former Soviet Union. In addition, the establishment of a purely voluntary system is unlikely to face much political opposition. As noted earlier, a solid framework law for a voluntary private pension has been drafted, although it awaits final government clearance. As also noted, failure to enact and promote the use of this law runs the risk that, instead, pressures will build to expand the mandatory Paygo pension system.

Despite the attractiveness of the voluntary approach, however, some form of mandatory funded system should also be considered; the capital flows generated by this option, however, would not be substantial. The second option, and the one recommended here, is to provide for an opt-out that permits workers to divert an increasing fraction of their supplementary pension contribution to private pension accounts, with a commensurate reduction in their accrual of benefits under the supplementary pension. The opt-out should be voluntary for current workers but should be made mandatory for all new workforce entrants.   As noted earlier, this opt-out arrangement, in effect, already exists for the self-employed. Unless the opt-out arrangement is formally extended to other workers, there likely will be continued efforts among wealthier individuals to characterize themselves as much as possible as self-employed.

A variant on this sort of proposal appears to be already under consideration. The variant provides for a voluntary opt-out of contributions on wages in excess of a preset wage ceiling for high-wage-earners. Although such a proposal has some logical basis, it suffers from a number of limitations. First, only a very small percentage of the workforce will be eligible to participate, unless the ceiling is very low.[23]   Second, it will result in only modest capital flows into the private capital markets.[24]   Third, and most important, high-wage-earners could probably be induced to participate in tax-deferred, voluntary private pension schemes even without such a program, so the scheme being proposed may not result in additional net savings, while it will certainly reduce short-term revenue to an already financially constrained program.

A better approach is to make the opt-out available to *all current workers* on a voluntary basis, and to make the opt-out mandatory for new workforce entrants. Under this proposal, current workers

---

23. If the ceiling is set at five-times average wages, roughly 1 percent of contributors will be eligible to participate. Even if the ceiling is set at three-times average wages, eligibility will only increase to about 3.5 percent of contributors.

24. Contributions on wages above the ceiling of five-times average wages represent only about 2 percent of total revenue; contributions on wages above the ceiling of three-times average wages represent about 5 percent of total revenue.

would be given the right to divert some of their payroll contribution to private pension accounts, and their accrual of benefits under the supplementary pension would be reduced in keeping with this amount. This would give workers the right to explicitly trade the certainty of some portion of their supplementary pension for the potential of higher returns from an investment in the capital markets. For new workforce entrants, participation should be mandatory, because the risks of a mandatory funded pillar are lower for persons further from retirement.

Purely Voluntary, Tax-Advantaged	Voluntary Opt-Out for Current Workers
Private Pensions	(Mandatory for New Workforce Entrants)
• Preserve the existing structure of the supplementary pension.	• Replaces, over the long term, the supplementary pension.
• Modest capital flows and modest impact on the capital markets.	• Substantial capital flows and substantial impact on the capital markets.
• Politically noncontroversial, but a perk to the relatively well-off.	• Potentially controversial, but far less so than fully mandatory alternatives.

Unless the vocabulary of the Paygo supplementary pension is changed from that of a *defined benefit* pension scheme to that of a *defined contribution* scheme, however, the mechanism for reducing the value of the supplementary pension to reflect participation in the opt-out could become quite complicated and would probably not be transparent to most workers.[25] For this reason, if Lithuania wishes to provide for a partial opt-out to funded accounts within the structure of the public pension program, it is recommended that Lithuania consider shifting to the use of the "notional account" formula (now used in Sweden and Latvia) in defining rights in the remaining supplementary Paygo pension. If the notional account approach is used (instead of the current supplementary benefit formula based on the German coefficient system), workers can simply choose to have some portion of their "notional" contribution invested in actual securities through the pension fund,[26] with a commensurate reduction in the amount of the contribution credited to their account on a notional basis. This would give workers the right to explicitly forego the notional rate of return (determined, optimally, by the rate of growth in aggregate wages) for whatever return is generated by their investments. This is a major advantage of the notional account structure, because it employs the vocabulary of a *defined contribution* pension scheme, making the transition to funded accounts much more transparent and greatly simplifying the accounting and other administrative requirements of moving toward a partially funded system. In addition, in combination with shifting half of the contribution rate to employees and periodic reporting to workers on what extra contributions "buy" in future benefit levels, the consequences of noncompliance under such a scheme become very clear.

Any move toward a funded system, however, raises a handful of policy questions:

---

25. The reason for this is that the supplementary pension is calculated on a worker's average earnings (as computed under the German coefficient system) and the worker's length of service. Adjusting this benefit formula to reflect that some percentage—for example, 5 percent—of the total payroll contribution rate has been diverted into a funded account would require relatively complicated adjustments to ensure that the decrements to the supplementary pension benefit are fair.

26. The same funds created under the forthcoming Voluntary Private Pension Law could be used.

- Who should be eligible?
- How can the needs of the disabled and survivors be protected?
- For what portion of the contribution rate should workers be allowed to opt-out?
- How can the transition be financed?

Given that any efficiencies inherent in funded schemes will manifest over relatively long time horizons, eligibility should be restricted to persons ten years or more from retirement. The relatively high level of transaction costs associated with private pension schemes calls for a relatively long break-even period, and the risks of market volatility are greatest in the short term, rather than the long run.

The needs of survivors and the disabled can be protected by providing them with some form of benefit top-up to ensure adequate income in retirement for those unable to accumulate sufficient balances in their investment accounts. This issue merits additional study in order to tailor the top-up to the characteristics and needs of Lithuania's survivors and disabled and to ensure that the costs are sustainable with the current payroll contribution rate, but the general concept would be to provide a minimum benefit floor, financed on a Paygo basis.

Under this proposal, funded accounts would largely or completely replace the supplementary pension over the long term, although the transition to funded accounts will have to be gradual. One example of a gradual transition would be to enable current workers to divert 2.5 percent of their contributions (out of the 11 percent employee contribution) to funded accounts in the initial years; 5.0 percent for a ten-year period thereafter, and 10 or 11 percent when the transition is complete. (As noted above, for new workforce entrants, participation would be mandatory.) The supplementary pension would essentially be replaced over the long run, as illustrated in the Annex. The capital accumulation resulting from even this gradual a transition will be substantial—as much as 60 percent of GDP, or about five times the current market capitalization of the Lithuanian stock market, by the year 2025. This scheme also has the advantage of pacing the growth of the "opt-out" to forecast

Table 10-1. Comparison of Value Added Tax Rates

(percent)

Country/area	Rate	Notes
Baltic		
Estonia	18	Exemptions for medicines, education, some services, among others.
Latvia	18	Limited exemptions.
Lithuania	18	Limited exemptions.
Other		
Bulgaria	18	
Czech Republic	24	Rate ranges from 23 to 24%. Rate of 5% for most services and foodstuffs.
Hungary	25	Rate of 12% on basic food products and utilities.
Poland	22	Rate of 7% on foodstuffs and other items.
Romania	18	Various exemptions for bread, fuel sources, and utilities, *inter alia*.
Russia	20	Rate of 10% on foodstuffs. Other exemptions.
Slovak Republic	25	Rate of 6% on foodstuffs and most services.
Slovenia	20	Slovenia levies a sales tax, not a VAT. Rates vary by category.
Ukraine	20	Exemptions for fuel supplies.

Source: Coopers and Lybrand, *Business and Investment Guides*, 1997; Deloitte-Touche-Tohmatsu International, *Taxation in Eastern Europe*, 1995.

medium-term surpluses in the public pension system, while providing for the accumulation of substantial amounts of investment capital. If the rates of return earned on the funded accounts are high, the government should also consider adjusting the level of the basic pension downward, with a commensurate reduction in the contribution rate.

Finally, the proposed partial opt-out scheme would cost the fiscal budget about 0.3 percent of GDP initially, rising to between 2.0 and 3.0 percent of GDP by 2015. It could be funded by some combination of (a) an increase in the level of the VAT, (b) a modest increase in the contribution rate, and (c) the indexation of the earnings-related benefit by price inflation, rather than wage growth (or by some combination of the two).

It is worth noting that Lithuania's VAT rate of 18 percent is comparable to those of its Baltic trading partners, but significantly lower—by 4 percentage points—than the VAT rate in Poland and a number of other countries in the region, as is illustrated by the VAT rates for a selection of countries from the former Soviet Union presented in table 10-1.

ANNEX
Data Tables

Table 10-2. Summary of Assumptions Used in Projections Model
(percent)

Year	Growth rate, real wages	Growth rate, real basic pension	Nonparticipants, percent of population	Unemployment, percent of labor force	Self-employment, percent of labor force	Unpaying persons, percent of labor force	Collection rate, percent owed
1995			22	6.1	3	18	85
1996		6.10	20	7.1	8	17	86
1997	3.0	1.15	18	8.1	10	18	87
1998	3.0	2.27	18	8.2	12	17	88
1999	3.0	2.22	18	7.0	14	16	89
2000	2.0	2.22	18	6.8	16	16	90
2005	1.0	0.64	18	6.6	20	15	90
2010	1.0	0.62	18	6.4	20	15	90
2015	1.0	0.60	18	6.2	20	15	90
2020	1.0	0.59	18	6.0	20	15	90
2025	1.0	0.57	18	5.5	20	15	90
2030	1.0	0.55	18	5.0	20	15	90

Note: All projections reported in real (constant currency) terms.
Source: Ministry of Social Security and Labor (with input and discussion from the World Bank).

Table 10-3. Current Law Projections
(real 1995 Lts and thousands of persons)

Year	Number of contributors	Taxable payroll	Payroll contributions			Total number of pension recipients					Working pensioners
			Self-employed	All other	Total	Old age	Disabled	Survivor	Early	Total	
1995	1,330	6,416	19	1,911	1,930	657	139	28	2	826	110
1996	1,504	6,922	66	1,845	1,911	667	151	29	1	848	113
1997	1,514	6,954	87	1,876	1,963	667	153	30	1	851	110
1998	1,543	7,105	109	1,938	2,047	668	154	30	1	853	107
1999	1,599	7,397	133	2,041	2,174	669	156	30	1	856	105
2000	1,616	7,403	161	2,065	2,226	671	158	30	1	860	102
2005	1,692	7,672	216	2,140	2,356	674	164	32	1	871	93
2010	1,750	8,325	231	2,323	2,554	673	171	33	1	878	83
2015	1,756	8,796	237	2,454	2,691	748	170	34	1	953	90
2020	1,761	9,293	243	2,593	2,836	824	169	35	0	1,028	98
2025	1,767	9,824	249	2,741	2,990	894	168	36	0	1,098	101
2030	1,772	10,385	254	2,897	3,151	965	168	37	0	1,170	105

Year	Pensions paid to nonworking pensioners			Pensions paid working pensioners	Pensions paid earlies/ hazard	Total pensions	Sick pay, maternity	Employment fund	Other benefits	Total, nonpensions	Total, all benefits
	Old age	Disabled	Survivor								
1995	1,027	201	68	153	3.1	1,452	142	53	274	469	1,921
1996	1,047	221	72	167	2.2	1,509	153	62	274	489	1,998
1997	1,085	231	75	165	2.3	1,558	154	71	282	507	2,065
1998	1,125	240	78	164	2.4	1,609	157	72	290	519	2,128
1999	1,166	250	81	164	2.6	1,664	163	61	299	523	2,187
2000	1,198	258	84	163	2.7	1,706	164	60	305	529	2,235
2005	1,287	282	91	154	2.8	1,817	169	58	308	535	2,352
2010	1,376	308	100	141	1.9	1,927	184	56	311	551	2,478
2015	1,606	322	109	158	1.9	2,197	194	54	314	562	2,759
2020	1,855	338	118	176	1.9	2,489	205	53	318	576	3,065
2025	2,122	353	128	188	0.3	2,791	217	48	321	586	3,377
2030	2,412	369	139	201	0	3,121	229	44	324	597	3,718

Table 10-3. Current Law Projections (continued)

Year	Contribution rate (%)	Cost rates (percent) Pensions	Nonpensions	Total	Contribution rate less cost rate (%)	Yearly net cash flow	Net cash flow, % of payroll	GDP (1,000,000s)	Contributions, percent of GDP	Benefits percent of GDP	Net cash flow, percent of GDP
1995	31	22.6	7.3	29.9	1.1	8.9	0.1	30,034	6.4	6.4	0.03
1996	31	21.8	7.1	28.9	2.1	(87.2)	-1.3	31,115	6.1	6.4	-0.28
1997	31	22.4	7.3	29.7	1.3	(102.3)	-1.5	32,235	6.1	6.4	-0.32
1998	31	22.7	7.3	30.0	1.0	(81.4)	-1.1	33,589	6.1	6.3	-0.24
1999	31	22.5	7.1	29.6	1.4	(12.6)	-0.2	35,201	6.2	6.2	-0.04
2000	31	23.0	7.1	30.2	0.8	(8.7)	-0.1	37,032	6.0	6.0	-0.02
2005	31	23.7	7.0	30.7	0.3	4.2	0.1	39,328	6.0	6.0	0.01
2010	31	23.1	6.6	29.8	1.2	76.1	0.9	42,081	6.1	5.9	0.18
2015	31	25.0	6.4	31.4	-0.4	(67.9)	-0.8	44,816	6.0	6.2	-0.15
2020	31	26.8	6.2	33.0	-2.0	(228.9)	-2.5	47,505	6.0	6.5	-0.48
2025	31	28.4	6.0	34.4	-3.4	(387.3)	-3.9	50,118	6.0	6.7	-0.77
2030	31	30.1	5.7	35.8	-4.8	(567.0)	-5.5	52,624	6.0	7.1	-1.08

Source: Ministry of Social Security and Labor (programmatic projections); World Bank (GDP growth rates to 2050); independent estimates (GDP growth, 2006–2030).

299

Figure 10-8. Comparison of Contributions and Total Benefits
(real 1995 Lt millions)

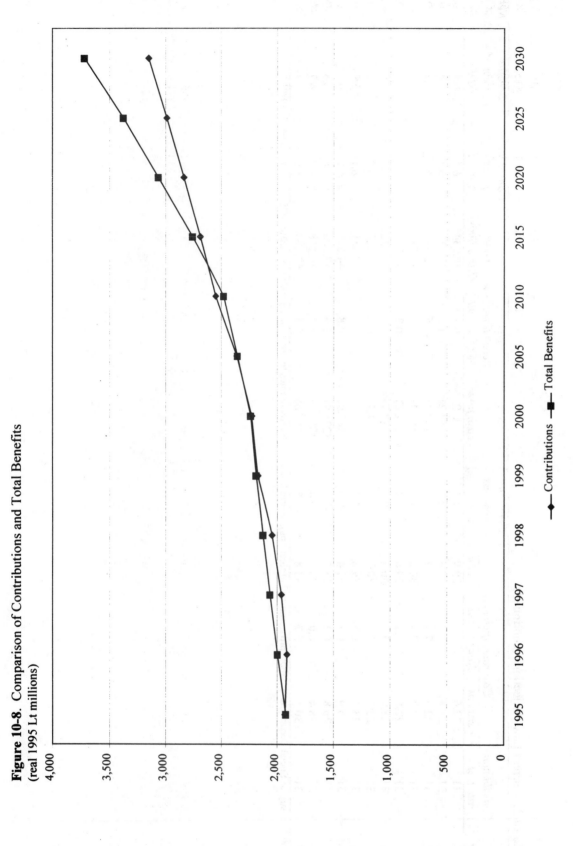

Table 10-4. Projections Given SAL Conditionalities and Increases in the Retirement Age to 65 for Both Genders (real 1995 Lts and thousands of persons)

Year	Number of contributors	Taxable payroll	Payroll contributions Self-employed	Payroll contributions All other	Payroll contributions Total	Total number of pension recipients Old age	Disabled	Survivor	Early	Total	Working pensioners
1995	1,330	6,416	19	1,911	1,930	657	139	28	2	826	110
1996	1,504	6,922	66	1,845	1,911	667	151	29	1	848	113
1997	1,523	6,993	88	1,886	1,974	643	155	30	1	829	103
1998	1,557	7,158	111	1,953	2,064	635	157	30	1	823	98
1999	1,616	7,463	136	2,059	2,195	629	159	30	1	819	93
2000	1,637	7,478	165	2,086	2,251	623	161	30	1	815	88
2005	1,732	7,813	225	2,180	2,405	586	171	32	1	790	69
2010	1,806	8,558	242	2,388	2,630	573	178	33	1	785	65
2015	1,848	9,208	254	2,569	2,823	587	182	34	1	804	63
2020	1,867	9,785	263	2,730	2,993	641	183	35	0	859	67
2025	1,869	10,327	269	2,881	3,150	718	182	36	0	936	72
2030	1,871	10,898	274	3,041	3,315	796	180	37	0	1,013	76

Year	Pensions paid to nonworking pensioners Old age	Disabled	Survivor	Pensions paid working pensioners.	Pensions paid earlies/ hazard	Total pensions	Sick pay, maternity	Employment fund	Other benefits	Total, nonpensions	Total, all benefits
1995	1,027	201	68	153	3.1	1,452	142	53	274	469	1,921
1996	1,047	221	72	167	2.2	1,509	153	62	274	489	1,998
1997	1,053	234	75	153	2.3	1,517	155	71	282	508	2,025
1998	1,081	244	78	149	2.4	1,554	158	72	290	520	2,074
1999	1,111	255	81	145	2.6	1,595	165	61	299	525	2,120
2000	1,132	264	84	141	2.7	1,624	165	60	305	530	2,154
2005	1,155	293	91	113	2.8	1,655	173	58	308	539	2,194
2010	1,197	322	100	110	1.9	1,731	189	56	311	556	2,287
2015	1,296	346	109	110	1.9	1,863	203	54	314	571	2,434
2020	1,487	365	118	120	1.9	2,092	216	53	318	587	2,679
2025	1,750	381	128	133	0.3	2,392	228	48	321	597	2,989
2030	2,035	397	139	146	0	2,717	241	44	324	609	3,226

Table 10-4. Projections Given SAL Conditionalities and Increases in the Retirement Age to 65 for Both Genders (continued)

Year	Contribution rate (%)	Cost rates (percent)			Contribution rate less cost rate (%)	Yearly net cash flow	Net cash flow, % of payroll	GDP (1,000,000s)	Contributions, percent of GDP	Benefits percent of GDP	Net cash flow, percent of GDP
		Pensions	Nonpensions	Total							
1995	31	22.6	7.3	29.9	1.1	8.9	0.1	30,034	6.4	6.4	0.03
1996	31	21.8	7.1	28.9	2.1	(87.2)	-1.3	31,115	6.1	6.4	-0.28
1997	31	21.7	7.3	29.0	2.0	(51.3)	-0.7	32,235	6.1	6.3	-0.16
1998	31	21.7	7.3	29.0	2.0	(10.4)	-0.1	33,589	6.1	6.2	-0.03
1999	31	21.4	7.0	28.4	2.6	75.4	1.0	35,201	6.2	6.0	0.21
2000	31	21.7	7.1	28.8	2.2	97.3	1.3	37,032	6.1	5.8	0.26
2005	31	21.2	6.9	28.1	2.9	211.2	2.7	39,328	6.1	5.6	0.54
2010	31	20.2	6.5	26.7	4.3	343.1	4.0	42,081	6.2	5.4	0.82
2015	31	20.2	6.2	26.4	4.6	389.1	4.2	44,816	6.3	5.4	0.87
2020	31	21.4	6.0	27.4	3.6	314.1	3.2	47,505	6.3	5.6	0.66
2025	31	23.2	5.8	28.9	2.1	160.7	1.6	50,118	6.3	6.0	0.32
2030	31	24.9	5.6	30.5	0.5	(11.0)	-0.1	52,624	6.3	6.3	-0.02

Source: Ministry of Social Security and Labor (programmatic projections); World Bank (GDP growth rates to 2050); independent estimates (GDP growth, 2006–2030).

Figure 10-9. Comparison of Contributions and Total Benefits under SAL Conditionalities/Increase in Retirement Ages to 65 for Both Genders (real 1995 Lt millions)

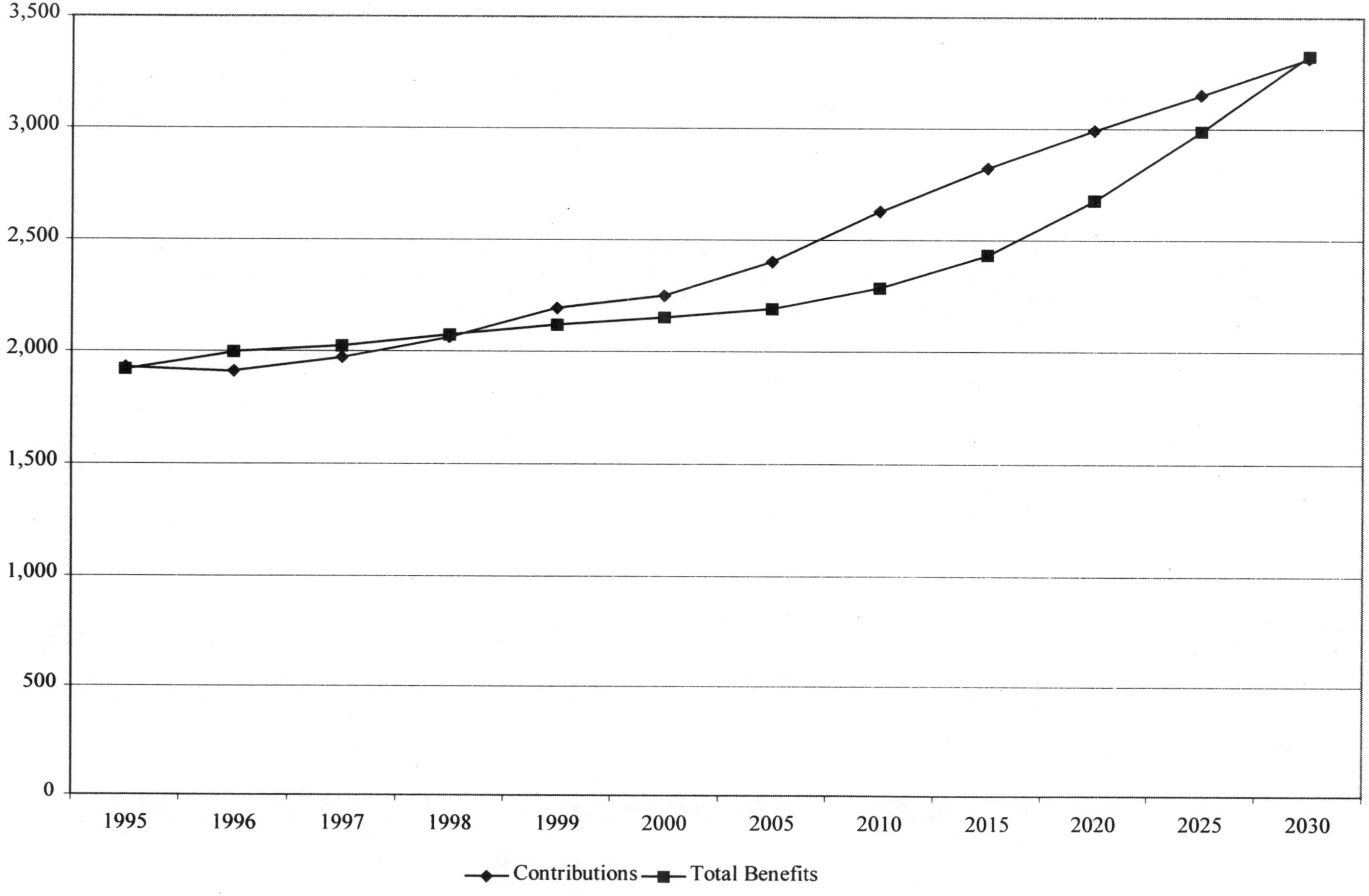

◆ Contributions — ■ Total Benefits

Table 10-5. Comparison of Wage Taxes in the Baltic Countries
(percent)

Country	Income tax	Social taxes	Total
Estonia	26	33	59
Latvia	25	37	62
Lithuania	33	31	64

Source: Coopers & Lybrand, *Business and Investment Guides, 1997* for the Baltic countries, Russia, and central and eastern Europe.

Table 10-6. Projections for Second-Pillar Accumulation
(real 1995 Lt millions)

Year	Opt-out percentage allowed	Yearly contribution	Second-pillar stock	GDP	Second-pillar as percentage of GDP
1995	0.0	0	0	30,034	0
1996	0.0	0	0	31,115	0
1997	0.0	0	0	32,235	0
1998	2.5	117	117	33,589	0
1999	2.5	129	250	35,201	1
2000	5.0	276	536	37,032	1
2005	5.0	353	2,391	39,328	6
2010	10.0	848	6,389	42,081	15
2015	10.0	911	12,565	44,816	28
2020	10.0	965	20,393	47,505	43
2025	10.0	1,016	30,201	50,118	60
2030	10.0	1,069	42,416	52,624	81

Note: Projections provide for a voluntary "opt-out" whereby workers may divert some portion of their payroll contribution from the public pillar to private accounts, subject to a corresponding reduction in the amount of their benefits accruing under current law. Projections assume that everyone eligible for the opt-out chooses the opt-out; thus the second pillar accumulations shown represent ceilings on the possible accumulation. Accumulations assume a 4 percent real rate of return.

Figure 10-10. Assets Invested in Second-Pillar Accounts Expressed as a Percentage of GDP
(assuming 4 percent real rate of return)

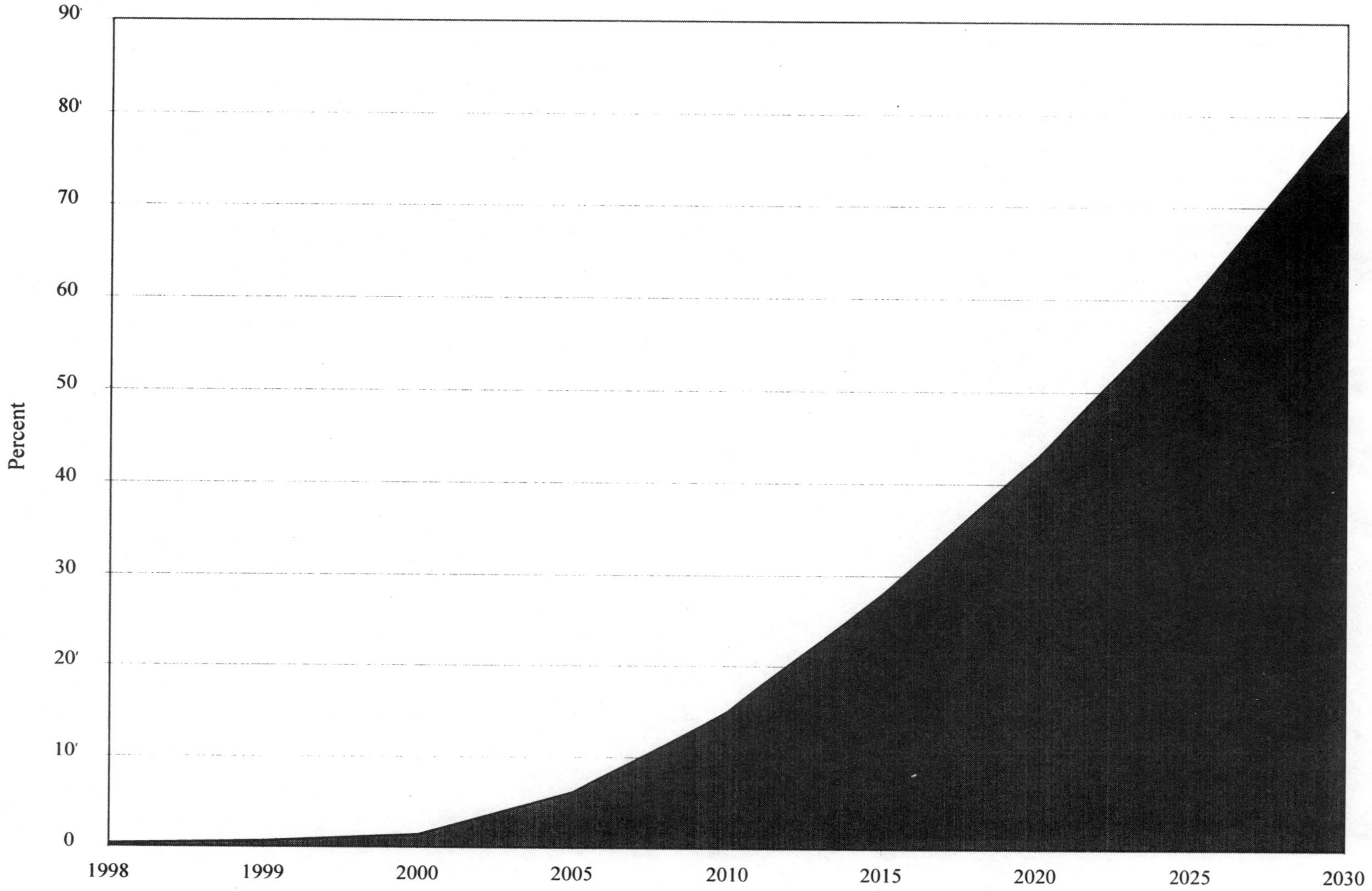

11

THE SECURITIES MARKET

This chapter focuses on the role of securities markets in supporting privatization and pension reform. It suggests that Lithuania has the basis of a suitable securities market policy, as well as the required legal framework and operational capacity, but that there are areas that need further development to ensure that the securities market contributes as it should to the success of privatization and pension reform.

The principal *policy* nexus between privatization and pension reform and the securities market is corporate governance. The securities market imposes incentives and disciplines on managers of publicly traded companies through its information disclosure and price-setting mechanisms and through the actions of institutional investors and other substantial minority shareholders, who lead the market in the effective exercise of the shareholder rights accorded them under securities law. Lithuania has the basis of a securities market capable of imposing such incentives and disciplines, but important gaps remain. These can be filled by (i) developing the aspects of the legal and regulatory system that can improve the quality and timeliness of information disclosed to the market, provide more comprehensive checks and balances on the exercise of management prerogatives, and strengthen the rights of minority shareholders and (ii) building the capacity of domestic institutional investors to analyze and judge the quality of management performance.

The principal *operational* nexus between privatization and pension reform and the securities market is the securities market's absorptive capacity. If the expected increase in supply of securities and investment arising from privatization and pension reform is to be absorbed by the securities market without disruption or distortion, the operational capacity of the market must be high. Lithuania has achieved a great deal in a short time in creating its securities market, but to handle the increased supply of securities and investment expected from privatization and pension reform, two things are necessary. First, the uncertainties in the law pertaining to the application of the securities law to shares issued under cash privatization and to the concept of nominee shareholding as it is applied to custodian services for foreign institutional investors must be remedied. Second, the planning and implementation of privatization and pension reform need to be coordinated with development of the securities market to ensure that the securities market is able to fulfill the role expected of it.

The Structure of the Present Lithuanian Securities Market

This section describes the main structural features of the Lithuanian securities market. (Data on the market can be found in the Annex to this chapter.)

Legacy of Mass Privatization

The present structure of the Lithuanian securities market has been greatly influenced by mass privatization. Like other countries that undertook mass privatization, Lithuania has rapidly created a large number of public companies, but most are very small. There are 1,500 Lithuanian public companies, but only the top 100 had annual revenues of more than US$10 million in 1997. Without mass privatization, companies with annual revenues of less than US$10 million would ordinarily remain in private hands, owned by individuals or families. But the political imperatives of rapid transformation from a socialist to a capitalist market economy in Russia and much of eastern Europe led to privatization programs that were intended to spread ownership of former state enterprises widely and equitably among the population. As a result, many companies that would not usually qualify for public company status on financial or economic grounds were created as public companies rather than as private or closely held enterprises.

As a corollary, mass privatization created a large number of small shareholders in a short time. There are approximately 1.5 million shareholders in Lithuania—40 percent of the total population—and each owns, on average, less than 0.2 percent of the shares of the companies in which they have a stake. In comparison, in the United States, which is considered to have a high rate of share ownership, less than 20 percent of the population owns shares. In the United Kingdom and Australia, which are notable for the scale of their privatization programs over the last decade, the figure is approximately 15 percent.

In addition, because the companies created under mass privatization were so recently and rapidly created, very few have a proven profit history or reliable audited accounts. For 1997, only 54 of the 607 companies listed on the National Stock Exchange of Lithuania (NSEL) prepared accounts according to international standards and had them audited by an auditing firm working at the international standard. In comparison, any company listed on a stock exchange in the United States or western Europe must have a three-to-five-year record of audited financial accounts and any public company, whether listed or not, must have its accounts audited annually.

Lithuania implemented a voucher-based mass privatization similar to the programs in the Czech Republic and Russia.[1] One part of such voucher-based schemes was the creation of investment funds that were used to accumulate vouchers and convert them into a portfolio of significant holdings of securities in privatized companies. These voucher investment funds were intended to provide the same benefits offered by the more common kind of cash investment fund in the West: higher returns and better risk management for investors and more influence over the management of the privatized companies through the accumulation of significant holdings by the investment companies. Most of these funds have failed to operate successfully, however, because they lacked revenue, cash reserves, and management skill. A significant number have collapsed because of fraud. Lithuania has shared this unhappy experience with the Czech Republic and Russia.[2] The Lithuanian government is now attempting to address the problem through liquidation and consolidation of the voucher investment funds into a small number of potentially

---

1. See Ira Lieberman and Raj Desai, eds., *Between State and Market: Mass Privatization in Transition Economies* (Washington, D.C.: World Bank, 1997), especially the chapter "Investment Funds in Mass Privatization" by Pistor and Spicer; and Stijn Claessens, Simeon Djankov, and Gerhard Pohl, *Ownership and Corporate Governance—Evidence from the Czech Republic*, Policy Research Working Paper 1737 (Washington, D.C: World Bank, April 1997).

2. At its peak, Russia had 500 registered voucher investment funds. The number is now just over 300, and it is estimated that only 25 to 30 of these have an active portfolio with long-term prospects. In the Czech Republic the numbers were 620 funds initially, 250 now, and 30 that are viable.

viable investment holding companies.

Overall, the legacy of privatization in Lithuania is the large number of domestic companies with publicly issued shares and a large number of domestic shareholders, although there are few domestic investors. This at first appears somewhat paradoxical, but it is a typical outcome of voucher-based privatization. The large number of domestic shareholders was created through the mass issuance of vouchers, but these are shareholders who are not investors: they did not invest their own savings to obtain securities. In addition, following voucher privatization, relatively little domestic savings has been directed to securities investment other than by banks managing their reserves. For example, according to an NSEL survey at the end of 1996, about US$220 million of domestic savings was invested in the securities market as a whole (equities and treasury bills). Of this total, almost 60 percent was in treasury bills (TBs) held by banks, leaving about US$140 million invested in equities from domestic sources in 1996. According to the survey, most of this was accounted for by existing insiders, such as company managers, as they accumulated additional shares to consolidate their control over the companies they manage. Other domestic investors are few in number. The main reason for this lack of activity appears to be that the reliable information required as the basis for investment decisions is not readily available and the securities market is not widely trusted as an investment mechanism. Nevertheless, activities on NSEL are picking up, partly because of domestic investors. At the end of 1997, holdings of shares by domestic investors had increased to US$240 million, an increase of US$100 million, of which about US$70 million was new money and US$30 million was an increase in value.

Institutional Arrangements

STOCK EXCHANGE. The NSEL was created by government resolution on 3 September 1992. It is the only organized securities market in Lithuania and trades both private and government securities. It is organized as a nonprofit company. The major shareholder is the state through the Ministry of Finance, which holds 44.6 percent of NSEL's capital, with the balance of the shares divided into small holdings as described in table 11-1 of the Annex. The exchange has membership, listing, and trading rules, and supervisory arrangements to enforce these rules. The rules must be approved by the Securities Commission and are regularly amended to keep them in line with market developments.[3]

The trading system of the exchange is a computer-based, order-driven, and, until recently, single-price market with one price fixing each day. In April 1998 the exchange moved to continuous trading for the official list and around 50 securities on the current list. The system was provided to the NSEL by the French government in 1993. It was modified in 1996 to facilitate greater order clearance at the fixed price, and further modified in 1997–98 to enable continuous trading.

SECURITIES DEPOSITORY. The Central Securities Depository (CSDL) was created by government resolution on 20 May 1993, and began operation on 31 March 1994. It is the only securities depository in Lithuania and keeps accounts for both private and government securities. The depository is a nonprofit company; the major shareholder is the state through the Bank of Lithuania (60 percent) and the Ministry of Finance (32 percent). The remaining 8 percent is held by the NSEL.

The depository issues rules and procedures related to admission to participant status, accounting for securities, registration of securities, payment in settlement of securities transactions, and other relevant topics. It also provides standardized computer software that permits participants to integrate the

---

3. Resident foreign technical assistance is available to the exchange to assist with this work.

central system with their office management systems.[4] The depository operates a dematerialized transfer and settlement system, which allows account balances for both securities and cash to be maintained and enables book-entry settlement of trading in registered securities of all public companies. Securities transfer is effected by the depository itself; cash transfer is done by the Payments Center of the Bank of Lithuania on instructions from the depository.

Size and Liquidity

At the end of 1997, the NSEL listed 668 securities issues of 607 corporate issuers. There are two trading lists: (i) the *Official List*, which was created in April 1997 and contains the securities of seven issuers that meet capital, accounting, and legal requirements (at least Lt 5 million in authorized capital; annual financial reports prepared according to international accounting standards and audited by an international auditor; securities fully paid up, of equal rank and without restriction on transfer); and (ii) the *Current List*, which is divided into group A (48 issues) and group B (615 issues), according to established criteria. Group A includes securities of issuers that have shown a profit in their annual financial statement for the preceding year; have been on the current list for at least one month; have traded at least once; and have had bid and offer prices quoted at least three times during the previous month. Group B includes the remainder.

Six characteristics of the market stand out. First, *it is small*. Market capitalization at the end of 1997 was US$2,200 million, or 23 percent of GDP. It is notable that a large part (more than one-third at the end of 1997) of the shares are still held by the state. The average of market capitalization to GDP ratio for securities markets in the International Finance Corporation's (IFC) emerging market index is 25 percent, and for most it is more than 40 percent. Second, *it is illiquid*. There were approximately 71,000 trades during the 1997 calendar year: 70,500 share transactions for a turnover value of US$240 million and 500 TB transactions for a turnover value of US$126 million. The turnover ratio (turnover value/market capitalization) for shares in Lithuania was 9.5 in 1997, almost twice as much as in 1996, but still well below the 30 percent average turnover ratio in the IFC index. Third, *it is narrow*. The top five companies accounted for a quarter of turnover by value, and the top ten companies accounted for 60 percent. The average market concentration in the IFC index is 30 percent for the top ten companies. Fourth, *the share of foreign investment is increasing*. In 1996 and 1997, holdings by foreign investors increased manyfold, to about half of total holdings. Investment by residents has been increasing, but at a slower pace. By country of origin, the United States, at the end of 1997, had the largest share, 38 percent, of foreign investments in the stock market, followed by Estonia, 16 percent, the United Kingdom, 13 percent, and Sweden, 5 percent. Fifth, *intermediation is highly concentrated*. In 1997 the top three brokerage firms accounted for 54 percent of the secondary market turnover, sharing it about equally among themselves. Many of the remaining brokers conduct a negligible number of trades and are not viable. At the end of 1996, there were sixty-three licensed brokers, but in early 1997, ten went out of business. Finally, *nonbrokerage intermediation is very limited*. Corporate finance activity is small, as is the average transaction size. There were 109 new issues in 1997, with an average size of Lt 8 million, or US$2 million. Issues of this size are not really viable as public offerings, because the regulatory and administrative costs make the price of capital too high. There is currently no securities market asset management activity, but the five biggest brokerage firms have plans to establish investment companies under the Investment Company Law when certain impediments are removed (see the "Key Issues" section, below).

---

4. Foreign technical assistance is also available to the depository to assist with this work.

Regulation

LAWS. The most fundamental aspects of the legal foundation of Lithuania's securities market are found in the Civil Code, which defines the nature of legal persons, including companies, and the nature of securities and how title to securities is created and transferred. Building on the Civil Code, the Securities Law and Companies Law more specifically define the processes, rights, and obligations of the parties engaged in forming and managing companies and issuing and trading securities.[5]

Overall, Lithuania has established a reasonable legal foundation for the development of the securities market, but there are some gaps and uncertainties that impede market development. These relate to the quality and timeliness of information, the powers and responsibilities of managers, the rights of minority shareholders, and the concept of nominee ownership. They are discussed in the "Key Issues" section, below.

SECURITIES COMMISSION. The Securities Commission was first established under the Ministry of Finance through a number of temporary laws. In 1996, Chapter 7 of the Securities Law allowed the commission to be permanently established as an independent authority reporting to the Seimas. The commission is charged with responsibility for regulating all aspects of the public trading of securities, including licensing stock exchanges, securities depositories, and intermediaries and approving prospectuses and periodic reports by public companies. The commission consists of a chairman and four members appointed by the Seimas for staggered terms of up to five years. It has an active training program to improve the knowledge and skills of its staff and members, as well as resident foreign technical assistance available to assist in its work.

Key Outstanding Policy Issues

There are a number of key securities market issues related to supporting privatization and pension reform. The issues can be grouped under two headings: corporate governance and absorptive capacity.

Corporate Governance

One of the underlying policy objectives of privatization and pension reform is improvement in the standard of corporate governance. (Corporate governance is discussed in more detail in Chapter 9 of this volume.) Briefly stated, the objective is to expose company management to the disciplines and incentives of the market economy so that the assets of companies will be used in the most productive way, and thus make the maximum contribution to economic growth.

The securities market is an important—perhaps the most important—mechanism for the transmission of such disciplines and incentives. When a company is actually financed through the securities market, the performance of the company's management comes under public scrutiny, and good performance is rewarded, while poor performance is penalized. This behavior is first seen in the secondary market price of the company's securities. Companies that are performing well see their price rise on the securities market, and companies performing poorly will be subject to falling prices. These rising and falling prices provide a direct incentive for managers to maximize the company's return on

---

5. The relevant laws are: Law on Public Trading of Securities, issued on 16 January 1996; Company Law, issued on 5 July 1994, as amended 22 August 1996; Law on Investment Companies, issued on 5 July 1995; Law on Enterprises, issued on 8 May 1990, as amended 23 January 1996; and General Accounting Rules for Securities and their Circulation, issued by the Securities Commission on 5 August 1993.

investment in order to reduce the marginal cost of capital, because a higher secondary market price translates into a lower primary market cost of capital in any subsequent securities issue of the company.

But more important, the rising and falling secondary market price provides an incentive to prospective investors to monitor management performance and take action accordingly. The simplest available action in the case of a falling price is to sell the securities. This in itself has an effect on managers. If enough investors decide to sell because the company's prospects are poor, their actions will contribute to a further fall in the price, which should potentially motivate managers to change their plans for the company. For substantial shareholders, there may also be more direct avenues of influence over managers available, such as solicitation of proxies to allow passage of resolutions at general meetings of shareholders. Such resolutions can involve the election or removal of board members, the issuance of special shares or options to directors, the provision of other benefits to directors, and other matters that directly affect the balance of responsibilities between directors and shareholders. And finally, a substantial shareholder or other party may use the securities market to make a takeover bid for a company. The potential for such takeovers is a check on management conduct, because it implies that poorly performing managers may be ousted by new owners who are better able to manage the company's assets. In all these ways, the securities market can be a mechanism for encouraging higher standards of corporate governance.

The effective operation of these disciplines and incentives depends on the following:

- Timely information about the financial performance and profit potential of companies must be available so that investors can assess company value. An efficient price-setting mechanism in the securities market is needed so that investors' assessments can be signaled through buy and sell decisions and translated into publicly observed price movements.
- Well-balanced rights, powers, and obligations—such as those between majority owners and managers on the one hand, and minority shareholders on the other—must be established by law.
- Avenues of action against poorly performing management, such as proxy solicitation and company takeover processes, must be available.
- There must be a pool of investors who are able to exercise their rights and protect their interests if they run counter to those of management.

Each of these is discussed below in relation to Lithuania.

INFORMATION AND PRICING

Financial Information. Public disclosure of accurate and timely financial information is a cornerstone of securities market efficiency and is directly linked to improved corporate governance. Unless such information is available to the securities market, the market will trade blind—that is, it will be speculative and not based on an assessment of fundamentals—and entrenched managers and majority owners will have an enhanced ability to misuse the assets of public companies.

The Lithuanian authorities recognize this danger, and they have made a start in improving the quality and timeliness of the financial information disclosed to the securities market. But in practice, financial disclosure of a high standard is still very limited. Only 54 of the 607 firms listed on the NSEL had their accounts prepared and audited to international standards in 1997.

The NSEL has created a market structure that encourages enterprises to make extensive, high-quality financial information available to investors. This effort began with the opening of the official list in April 1997. The current (divided into groups A and B) and official trading lists on the NSEL create an incentive for companies to improve their financial disclosure. Companies graduate from the B to the A to the official list by applying international standard accounting rules and obtaining an international-standard audit, in addition to meeting other requirements, such as profitability and liquidity. Entry into the official list confers respectability on a company, makes it more attractive to foreign portfolio investors, and tends to lower its cost of capital. Thus, there is an incentive for the more forward-looking managers to meet the official list requirements. While so far only seven companies have done so, several more have realized the benefits and intend to meet the requirements. The NSEL and the Securities Commission are to be commended for creating the right incentive structure.

Nevertheless, a problem of accounting and auditing practice in Lithuania remains. The current listing rules of the NSEL cannot specify a domestically applicable set of accounting standards or auditing practices because the domestic accounting profession is not sufficiently developed to adopt such standards. Nor is there a legally sanctioned standard. Local accountants are trained and experienced in the accounting methods of the centrally planned economy, but they have little or no experience in preparing accounts in a market economy.

For this reason, the NSEL listing rules for the official list require that "an *international* accounting firm" prepare the accounts and carry out the audit "in line with *international* practice." This is a reasonable approach in the short-term, but it needs to be followed up with medium-term actions to develop *domestic* accounting and auditing practices. Typical listing requirements in developed markets specify the domestic accounting and auditing standards to be applied. This is important, because there is a relatively small number of officially agreed—or enforceable—international standards, and what really counts are the domestically established standards. In the modern world of international finance—and of the European Union—these standards are converging, but they remain largely a domestic matter.

Nonfinancial Information. Disclosure of nonfinancial, price-sensitive information is a second cornerstone of securities market efficiency. This is often referred to as *continuous disclosure* to distinguish it from the periodic disclosure of financial information (semi-annual and annual accounts). Continuous disclosure requirements are typically part of securities law and the listing rules of stock exchanges. They are aimed at keeping securities markets fully informed at all times, and they usually require officeholders of companies with shares traded on a public securities market to immediately disclose to the market any information that may materially affect the price of the company's securities.

The enforcement of such requirements is taken very seriously in all developed securities markets. They are the basis of fairness and transparency and are directly linked to improved corporate governance. Without such requirements, insiders can easily manipulate the securities market to take advantage of information unavailable to the public.

The legal requirement and the regulations for such disclosure are in place in Lithuania, but enforcement is still weak, notwithstanding that 1,300 notices of material events have been filed since the Securities Commission adopted regulations on such disclosure in June 1996. The time limit for informing about material events is five days, which is too long (in most EU countries such events have to be reported immediately) and is frequently exceeded.[6] Sanctions are applied, but are apparently too mild to be effective.

---

6. On 15 May 1998, the Securities Commission shortened the time limit for disclosure to 24 hours. Equally important is that this new rule is strictly enforced.

Efficient Price Setting. The NSEL moved to continuous trading on 12 April 1998, for the securities traded on the official list and the fifty-one most-traded securities on the current list. Other securities will be transferred to continuous trading if trading in such securities becomes active.

POWERS AND OBLIGATIONS OF MANAGERS

The powers and obligations of managers in relation to the affairs of public companies are established first under the framework of company law, and second within the terms of the articles of association or charter of a company.

The traditional American approach to these topics has been considered the most favorable to good corporate governance. The details vary from state to state, but the basic framework in the United States provides that managers must (i) manage the company in the interests of all shareholders, not in their own interest or that of selected shareholders; (ii) conduct the company's affairs within the terms of the company's charter; and (iii) convene and conduct a general meeting of shareholders according to set procedures in order to report to the shareholders and put to a shareholder vote such matters as appointment or removal of board members or auditors, acquisition or disposal of an asset that represents a significant percentage of total assets (variously expressed as between 15 and 30 percent of total assets), a change in the nature of the business conducted by the company as described in its charter, and so on.

In the last three years, Russia has provided an interesting example of an approach to these issues in a climate where managers are generally considered to be too entrenched, backward-looking, and unconcerned with shareholders. Under the Russian law on joint-stock companies, managers are required to strictly adhere to the terms of a company's charter and must report to, and gain the approval of, a general meeting of shareholders in all matters typically required in U.S. practice, but with stricter voting requirements (for example, a three-quarter voting majority is needed to pass a measure rather than 51 percent) or lower thresholds (such as requiring approval for sale or acquisition of assets representing 10 percent of total assets). The net result is that the powers of managers are significantly reduced compared with those of U.S. managers, and the obligations of managers to consider the interests of shareholders and to report to them are increased.

In Lithuania, the Company Law of 1994 and Law on Enterprises of 1990 include minimal provisions governing the powers and obligations of managers. This is a cause for concern by policymakers and is being addressed through the law reform program of the Securities Commission.

The commission is mindful of Lithuania's desire to join the European Union (EU). Although there is no specific EU directive on the topic, the commission wishes to ensure that its approach is acceptable within the European context. This is a reasonable approach in the circumstances, but it may not be appropriate to take a wholly "European" approach. The European tradition has been to give more discretion to managers and to require less scrutiny and approval by shareholders than has been the case in the United States, and certainly less than now applies in Russia. The European tradition has relied on a two-tiered management structure—a supervisory board oversees the work of the management board—and on close involvement of creditors and major shareholders, especially banks, in management decisions. The public securities market has traditionally been relatively small, and the number of minority shareholders has also been small. But the Lithuanian corporate scene has more in common with the circumstances in Russia and the United States than with those typical of Europe. For example, there are many listed companies and many small shareholders; the local universal banks are not as well placed to play a supervisory role as they are in much of the rest of Europe; and the mangers of many Lithuanian companies are perhaps as entrenched and backward-looking as many in Russia. The Russian and U.S.

models are thus very relevant, and it would be wise to consider them in amending the Lithuanian law.[7]

PROXY SOLICITATION AND CORPORATE TAKEOVERS

An important way in which the securities market contributes to improved corporate governance is through the discipline imposed on managers by shareholders through the threat of company takeovers or through motions at general meetings that are organized through proxy solicitations. Such avenues of action are usually provided for in the companies and securities laws. In Lithuania, they are mentioned in law, but the rights of the parties and the procedures to be followed are unclear and lack detail, and their effectiveness is thus greatly diminished.

The ability to call a general meeting and pass motions that require managers to do or not do specific things is one of the most important disciplines shareholders can impose on managers: it represents a direct intervention by shareholders in the running of a company. For example, if managers are not performing as they should, shareholders can propose motions directing them to undertake specific actions or to remove them from the board of management and replace them with representatives who the shareholders expect to perform better. For this to be an effective discipline, the procedures for calling general meetings, soliciting proxies, and voting by proxy need to be very clearly specified. This is not the case in Lithuania, and the companies law should be amended or a regulation should be promulgated to introduce detailed rights and procedures. The Russian model provides an good example of a strongly shareholder-favorable approach (beyond even the U.S. approach), while the German model provides a more management-favorable strategy. As already mentioned, it is probably the Russian/U.S. end of the spectrum that best suits Lithuania's present circumstances.

Corporate takeovers represent the ultimate securities market discipline on managers; they involve a new controlling shareholder using the securities market to unseat the existing major shareholders and managers. It is often argued that the mere threat of a takeover is a significant discipline on managers in the same way that monopoly practice is thought to be tempered by the mere threat of a new entrant into a contestable market.

For the threat of takeover to be effective, the securities or companies law must specify, in detail, the rules governing takeovers, and thus make it possible for new controlling shareholders to emerge. In Lithuania, this is not the case. The law needs to be amended to set out the triggering events and processes that allow takeovers to occur and to specify the rights and obligations of the parties during a takeover, including those of the person making the takeover bid, the target company managers, and the other shareholders of the company. The Securities Commission approved rules on tender offers both on and outside the NSEL in February and May 1998.

The frequency of unsolicited corporate takeovers, as opposed to friendly corporate mergers, varies greatly from market to market. The highest rate of takeovers has traditionally been in the United States, but the United Kingdom and other developed markets such as Australia and Canada have not been far behind. Continental Europe and Japan, in contrast, have traditionally not had a high level of corporate takeover activity. Proponents of the European and Japanese models argue that a heightened concern

---

7. Raphael La Porta, Florencio Lopez de-Silnes, and Andre Shleifer, "Law And Finance," Working Paper 5661 (Washington, D.C.: National Bureau of Economic Research, July 1996), provides a useful summary of the level of investor protection and the balance of rights between managers and owners under common law and civil law regimes and compares French and German civil law protections with those applying in the United Kingdom and the United States.

about takeovers leads managers to focus too much on short-term returns so that the share price remains high and predators are discouraged. They argue that this focus depletes the long-term viability of companies because it discourages investment in research and development or other costly activities that pay off only in the long term. There are some indications that this may now be changing, but it is too early to say what the trend will be. In Lithuania's case, the entrenched ownership and management structures that have risen out of the privatization process lead to concern that too limited a scope for takeover activity may simply serve to shield managers from an important market discipline.

ACTIVE SHAREHOLDERS

The preceding discussion has focused on rebalancing the rights of managers and majority shareholders and the rights of minority shareholders so that minority shareholders can play an active role in monitoring and influencing the performance of companies. For such a rebalancing to have any effect in practice, there must be minority shareholders that are able to exercise the rights available to them under the law. There are two categories of shareholders that can play such a role: minority shareholders with a substantial holding and institutional investors.

Substantial Shareholders. A holding of between 10 and 30 percent of a company's shares is typically considered a substantial minority shareholding.[8] Substantial shareholders can be an important influence on company management, and small minority shareholders rely considerably on substantial shareholders to lead the way in monitoring management performance and in protecting the interests of all shareholders.

Substantial minority shareholders usually lead the market and carry smaller investors with them. They have more at stake and are able to apply more resources to protect and enhance their investment by monitoring a company's management performance and assessing the company's prospects. In doing so, their actions serve as a signal to other investors. In their efforts to monitor and improve corporate governance, substantial shareholders can call on smaller shareholders as allies against entrenched management. For example, it is usually a substantial shareholder who initiates a proxy solicitation and seeks to marshal smaller shareholders to support resolutions at general shareholders' meetings.

In Lithuania, many firms are classed as public companies and are listed on the NSEL, even though they are closely held by a relatively few shareholders. The Company Law generally prohibits restrictions on the transferability of shares. Certain restrictions, however, can be imposed on employee-owned shares. Such rights and restrictions on transfer make it difficult for a substantial minority shareholder to emerge, because any transfer of title to securities must, in effect, be approved by the controlling shareholders of the company. The very reason that such restrictions are common in Lithuania is that insiders have sought to entrench their positions in many companies following privatization.

While there is no good policy reason for a blanket prohibition on a company's members being able to agree to impose restrictions on transfer of securities if they so desire, there are good policy

8. The actual percentage that is considered a substantial holding varies from country to country and company to company. It depends on the structure of share ownership. If shareholding is very dispersed, relatively small holdings, such as 5 percent, may be sufficient to have a significant influence over the affairs of the company. Usually, however, a substantial minority holder needs upwards of 10 percent to exercise any influence. In many markets, a holding of 15 to 20 percent would lead to the holder being asked to nominate a representative to the board of management of the company. Holdings above 30 percent usually begin to be considered majority holdings rather than substantial minority holdings.

reasons for excluding such companies from characterization as public companies and from inclusion on the stock exchange. The very essence of listed public company status should be that the securities are freely tradable. The benefits of listing should be possible only for companies without preemptive rights agreements and should accrue only to freely tradable securities, and if such rights or restrictions exist or are introduced, such shares should be excluded from listing and should preferably be known as closed corporations (or some similar title) rather than as public companies.[9] The main reason for taking such an approach is simply to allow the market to operate efficiently: investors should have the certainty of being able to assume that the securities of all listed public companies are freely tradable. An important ancillary benefit of this is that new substantial shareholders will be able to build up holdings without restriction, and thus have the potential to discipline existing controlling shareholders and managers.[10]

Institutional Investors. Institutional investors such as pension funds and investment companies can play an important leadership role in the effective exercise of minority shareholder rights. They also bring other important benefits to the securities market.

Pension reform is discussed in Chapter 10 of this Policy Note. Briefly stated, in relation to the securities market, if pension reform in Lithuania involves the creation of a funded, defined contribution component, a significant pool of savings will be created that will be partly invested in the securities market. Chile and Argentina introduced pension reforms of this kind, which became operational in 1981 and 1994, respectively. In their first year of operation, they achieved long-term capital accumulation rates (contributions minus expenses) of 0.7 percent of GDP in Chile and 0.5 percent of GDP in Argentina. In the fifteen years to the end of 1996, the Chilean pension funds had accumulated long-term savings equivalent to 43 percent of GDP. The figure for the three years of operation of the Argentine pension scheme is 2.5 percent (in Chile, at the three-year mark, it was 3.5 percent).[11] These savings pools have been directed to the securities market in the following proportions: corporate equities, 30 percent in Chile and 15 percent in Argentina; corporate bonds, 10 percent in Chile and 8 percent in Argentina; and the balance is largely invested in government securities. In the early years of its operation, the Chilean pension scheme devoted a relatively modest percentage of investment to private sector securities, comparable to Argentina's present rates. This is because of an appropriately conservative approach to risk management by the pension funds under the regulations imposed by their supervisory agencies. Even so, over time, the impact of pension funds on the liquidity of the securities market in both countries has been very marked because the size of the savings pool has been so large.

The impact of the pension funds on the securities market has been manifest in a number of ways, not just through increased liquidity. For example, in Argentina, both the securities and the securities markets that the pension funds are allowed to invest in must be approved by the Securities and Exchange Commission. The commission uses this authorization power to raise standards of practice for both securities issuers and market providers. It does so by setting very high standards of transparency for

---

9. On 17 April 1998, the Securities Commission adopted a rule that only securities with no restrictions on transferability could be listed on the official list.

10. Substantial shareholders typically have to disclose their identity and the size of their holding when it rises above a specified threshold, such as 5 percent. They may also be required to make a takeover offer if their holding rises to 30 percent or so. These requirements serve to give the existing majority owners and the remaining minority shareholders protections from covert takeover of a company. But protections such as disclosure and mandatory takeover offers do not restrict the ability to actually acquire a substantial holding.

11. See the Policy Note on pension reform for projections of capital accumulation under various scenarios in Lithuania.

securities issuers and markets that want to be included on the list of authorized investments for pension funds. Because the potential pool of savings is so large, issuers and market providers have an incentive to meet the commission's standards, and transparency has improved notably, as has the commission's overall stature and influence in the market.

Another manifestation of the positive impact of pension reform on securities markets is its effect on corporate governance. In both Chile and Argentina, the professional management of the portfolio of securities created by investment of the accumulated pension funds requires the pension fund managers to monitor the performance of the companies in their portfolios and the performance of the market generally. The fund managers invest and disinvest according to their assessment of the future potential return on their securities investments, and they compare their own investment performance with that of their competitors. They also report directly to each pension fund participant or account holder on the returns on investment for their account. The pension funds have thus fostered a very active interest in market transparency and investment performance.

In considering pension reform, Lithuanian policymakers should bear these benefits in mind. They are not the primary motivation for undertaking pension reform, but they are important secondary reasons.

Apart from pension funds, the other institutional investor likely to be important in the Lithuanian securities market is the investment company. There are no such companies yet, but there is an investment company law, and the government would like to see these companies develop. Like pension funds, they could come to play an important part in adding liquidity to the market and improving corporate governance. There are currently two legal impediments to the growth of investment companies in Lithuania. Until both impediments are removed, none will develop.

First, the present tax treatment of investment companies is discriminatory; in practice, it makes them unviable. In Lithuania, income and capital gains from financial investments in the hands of individuals are not taxed, but such gains by companies are treated as a contribution to profit, and are therefore subject to a 29 percent profit tax. Investment companies would therefore be liable to the profit tax on the income and capital gains earned from their investments. This means that investment in investment companies would be unattractive compared with investment in other financial instruments. The investment companies could only overcome this disadvantage by earning a return high enough to offset the tax liability and still pay their investors a rate comparable to, or better than, that available from other investment instruments. Because this is essentially impossible, they are unviable.

In most countries, investment companies (or unit trusts or mutual funds) are exempted from this kind of tax liability as long as they act only as pass-through investment vehicles. A pass-through investment vehicle—a company or unit trust—is a legal entity that accumulates income and capital gains from its investments solely for the purpose of passing them on to its investors. This could be achieved in Lithuania by exempting investment companies authorized under the investment company law from the profits tax. This is the most common approach in eastern Europe and Russia, which instituted the practice early this year.

The second factor impeding development of investment companies arises from the Investment Company Law itself. The present law imposes restrictions on related-party activity, which makes it impossible for any existing domestic intermediaries to establish and manage a pooled investment vehicle. These restrictions were imposed to protect against conflicts of interest among the investment company, the investment company manager, and broker/dealers acting on the instructions of the investment company manager. Protecting against such conflicts is a reasonable policy objective, but the current prohibition is too broad-ranging as a policy instrument. It means, in effect, that the securities market intermediaries most able and willing to establish and manage investment companies are prohibited from doing so.

A solution to this problem would be to replace the current prohibition with a more refined set of provisions governing conflicts of interest. These could be written to allow a broker-dealer to act in two or more capacities, but also to impose a duty to act in the best interests of clients in each capacity. The provisions could be strengthened with specific restrictions on the payment of management fees and the handling of client assets. In this way, the existing broker-dealer community in Lithuania would be eligible to establish and manage investment companies, but would be subject to close supervision to avoid conflicts of interest.

Absorptive Capacity

The second set of issues that links the securities market with privatization and pension reform can be grouped under the heading of absorptive capacity. There are two main issues: the first relates to legal uncertainties and the second to coordination between privatization and pension reform and securities market development.

Privatization and pension reform have the potential to bring a greatly increased supply of securities and investment to the securities market. This increase will have an impact on both the primary and secondary securities markets. In the case of the primary market, privatization could bring from fifteen to thirty significant new securities issues to the public over the next three years. In the case of the secondary market, the addition of fifteen to thirty good-quality stocks to the NSEL trading list would add significant and badly needed breadth to the market, and if pension reform proceeds with a funded component, a large pool of savings would be available over the long term for investment in securities, which would add greatly to the depth of the market.

Lithuania has already achieved a good deal in a short time in creating its securities market, but to handle the increased depth and breadth expected from privatization and pension reform, work in two areas is necessary:

- The planning and implementation of privatization and pension reform must be coordinated with development of the securities market to ensure that the securities market is able to fulfill the role expected of it.
- Uncertainties in the law regarding the application of the securities law to shares issued under cash privatization and the concept of nominee shareholding as it is applied to custodian services for foreign institutional investors need to be remedied.

PLANNING AND COORDINATION

It is important for the success of the privatization that the increased supply and distribution of securities is absorbed in an orderly manner. Problems could arise in a number of ways. If promotion and distribution of the public offer subscription form is poorly managed, there could be complaints that segments of the population were excluded from participating or that they were defrauded by the intermediaries involved. If the pricing of the offer is far above or below reasonable expectations, it could cause major undersubscription or oversubscription. Also, if the subsequent entry of the securities onto the trading list of the stock exchange is not well managed, there could be speculative pressure on the price in the secondary market. All of these events could jeopardize not only the success of the privatization program itself, but also the stability of the securities market and the trust placed in it.

The same sorts of considerations arise with respect to the increased supply of investment funds that may accumulate under a reformed pension scheme. Even if only a small proportion of the pension funds' investment portfolio is allowed to be invested in the domestic securities market, as is likely under prudential rules for such funds, the volume of available savings could easily outstrip the supply of quality securities. Extrapolating from the experiences of Argentina and Chile, pension-driven demand for securities could increase demand by up to 30 percent of current market capitalization in the first three years of pension reform. Although there currently appears to be an oversupply of securities, it must be remembered that many of these would not meet the investment criteria that a prudent pension fund (or a prudent investment company manager) would follow in building a sound portfolio. The privatization program will help to alleviate this problem, but the balance between supply and demand should be managed carefully to ensure that the market is not distorted or disrupted.

Coordination between the development of the securities market's absorptive capacity and the implementation of privatization and pension reform will not be a linear process. It is not possible to map out a simple progression of steps at the outset. This is especially the case now, when important structural details of the pension reform are yet to be decided and the privatization program is not yet fully developed. The best approach, therefore, is to establish a mechanism to plan and coordinate activities as they evolve. It may be that the informal relationships between the decisionmakers and administrators involved in the three areas in Lithuania can achieve much of the coordination required. The number of people involved in the issues at a senior level is relatively small, and they are well known to each other. Nevertheless, some form of coordinating committee is probably a better choice.

The exact nature of such a committee will be determined by the usual practices of Lithuanian public administration, but some general points can be made about its structure. First, its function should be coordination of implementation, not development of policy. Second, its membership should include representatives from the Securities Commission, NSEL, CSDL, the Privatization Agency, and the Ministry of Social Security and Labor (in relation to pension reform). Third, its objective should be to identify any securities market aspects of privatization and pension reform implementation and to plan and organize all necessary steps to ensure that the securities market is fully able to facilitate the privatization and pension reform agenda.[12] The NCEL plans to introduce a requirement that all companies in the current list file annual accounts—prepared and audited in accordance with international standards—with the NSEL, starting with 1998 accounts.

PENDING LEGAL ISSUES

The are two current legal uncertainties that should be remedied as a matter of priority in order to put the securities market on a sound footing in advance of privatization and pension reform.

Application of Securities Law. The present Article 3, Clause 4, of the Law on Public Trading of Securities appears to exempt any securities issued as part of cash privatization from the application of the law. This is clearly untenable, because it would mean that all of the requirements of the law governing disclosure and investor protection would not apply to the most important tranche of securities likely to be listed on the securities market in the next ten years. The probable intention of the arrangement was to

---

12. There is already a standing committee of the Seimas on "reform of the financial system," but it has a wide-ranging agenda and is too policy-oriented for the purpose outlined here.

exempt *private placements* of securities under the privatization program from the full prospectus disclosure requirements. This would be a reasonable policy position, but the effect of the article as it is currently written appears much broader than this.[13]

Nominee Ownership. As is the case in other Napoleonic law countries in transition from communist economic and legal arrangements, Lithuania's civil code lacks a clear definition of the concept of nominee ownership in contrast to direct or beneficial ownership.

In a modern securities market, there are many instances when persons or institutions hold securities on behalf of others. This agency role is captured in the common law concept of *nominee*. An important example is the local custodian for securities against which depository receipts are issued or through which foreign institutional investors protect and manage their securities holdings. Such custodians act as the agent of the beneficial owners and, although their names may appear on the securities register, they do so only as the nominees of the beneficial owner. Many foreign institutional investors, especially in the United Kingdom and the United States, are subject to stringent regulation in their home country regarding the safeguarding of their assets, and an important part of this regulation establishes certainty regarding the nominee role of the local custodian. The present Lithuanian law does not give sufficient certainty to such investors.

Policy Recommendations

This section presents recommendations that deal with each of the points raised in the "Key Issues" discussion. They are again grouped under two headings: corporate governance and absorptive capacity.

Corporate Governance

INFORMATION AND PRICING

Financial Information. The transparency of the Lithuanian securities market and its contribution to improved corporate governance would be increased if a domestic accounting and auditing profession with training and experience in modern methods were developed and if there were sufficient incentives for the adoption of better accounting and auditing practices. The Securities Commission and NSEL are well placed to take the lead role in this area. Two things are needed: training and certification for accountants and auditors that is oriented toward modern practice and adoption by the accounting and auditing profession of standards and practices that are in accord with those in Europe and the United States, but are applicable to the specifics of Lithuania's situation. By requiring, for example, list A companies to disclose their financial information using the upgraded accounting standards, and to be audited accordingly, the Securities Commission and the NSEL can create a powerful incentive toward better accounting and auditing in Lithuania, an incentive that is likely to spread.

Nonfinancial Information. The transparency of the securities market and its contribution to improved corporate governance would also be greatly enhanced by tightening the rules, and in particular by improving enforcement of the requirements for disclosure of price-sensitive information by listed public companies. The recently shortened time limit for disclosing such information should be strictly enforced, and penalities to both the companies and their responsible officers should be tightened.

---

13. According to the Lithuanian Securities Commission, this exemption is intended to apply only to situations where an investor in a privatization acquires more than 50 percent of the shares of a company, and under normal rules would then have to offer to buy the rest of the shares.

Repeated failure to report price-sensitive information in a timely manner should lead to temporary or permanent delisting, and fines imposed on officers should be sufficiently high and strictly enforced to strongly discourage noncompliance.

POWERS AND OBLIGATIONS OF MANAGERS

The fairness of the securities market and its contribution to improved corporate governance would be enhanced by amendment of the companies and securities laws to impose more specific and stricter requirements on company managers to protect the interests of minority shareholders. Typical provisions of this kind require, among other things, that managers must (i) manage the company in the interests of all shareholders, not in their own interest or that of selected shareholders; (ii) conduct the company's affairs within the terms of the company's charter; (iii) convene and conduct a general meeting of shareholders according to set procedures in order to report to the shareholders and put to a shareholder vote such matters as appointment or removal of board members or auditors or acquisition or disposal of major assets.

In considering how to draft the detailed provisions for Lithuanian law, policymakers should consider the Russian and U.S. examples. These are stricter than is typical in western Europe, and they are likely to be more appropriate to the structure of ownership and management of post-privatization firms in Lithuania than the more management-friendly approach common in western Europe.

PROXY SOLICITATION AND COMPANY TAKEOVERS

The contribution of the securities market to improved corporate governance would be greatly improved if the companies and securities laws provided more fully developed procedures for proxy solicitation and company takeovers. The procedures for calling general meetings, soliciting proxies, and voting by proxy need to be clearly specified. The rules on tender offers recently issued by the Securities Commission should be bolstered and incorporated in legislation. The Russian model provides a good example of a strongly shareholder-favorable approach (beyond even the U.S. approach), while the German model provides a more management-favorable strategy. As already mentioned, it is probably the Russian/U.S. end of the spectrum that best suits Lithuania's present circumstances. Similarly, the law needs to be amended to set out the triggering events and processes that allow takeovers to occur and to specify the rights and obligations of the parties during a takeover, including those of the person making the takeover bid, the target company managers, and the other shareholders of the company.

ACTIVE SHAREHOLDERS

Substantial Shareholders. The contribution of the securities market to better corporate governance would be improved by facilitating the emergence of substantial shareholders who could take a leadership role in protecting the rights of all shareholders. In Lithuania, the emergence of such shareholders is constrained by the ability of listed public companies to have preemptive rights agreements and, in the case of companies with employee ownership, to place certain restrictions on the transfer of their securities. Such restrictions allow entrenched managers to stop unwelcome substantial shareholders from obtaining title to securities. The recently introduced rule prohibiting the listing of securities with restricted transferability on the official list should be extended to all listed securities.

Institutional Investors. The development of institutional investors, such as pension funds and investment companies, could bring many benefits to the securities market. They could play an important leadership role in promoting increased liquidity, improved transparency, and enhanced corporate governance. They are currently prevented from doing so by two impediments to their development.

First, the present tax treatment of pooled investment vehicles is discriminatory. In practice, it makes them unable to compete with other investment vehicles that do not face the same tax burden. The solution to this is to treat all investment instruments equally for tax purposes. This could be achieved by exempting, as is done in other countries, authorized investment companies that act only as pass-through investment vehicles from the 29 percent profit tax.

Second, the present law governing investment companies imposes a prohibition on related-party activity that makes it impossible for domestic intermediaries to establish and manage an investment company. A better approach would be to replace the current prohibition with a detailed set of provisions governing conflicts of interest that allow a broker-dealer to act as an investment company manager, but would also impose a duty to act in the best interests of clients. In this way, the existing broker-dealer community in Lithuania could build domestic asset management capabilities, but would be subject to close supervision to avoid conflicts of interest.

In addition, to ensure greater availability of shares to institutional investors and the public at large, privatization authorities should be obligated to earmark, as a rule, a significant allocation of shares for public subscription in companies being privatized.

Absorptive Capacity

Privatization and pension reform have the potential to greatly increase the supply of securities and investment in the securities market. It is important that the increased supply be absorbed into the market in an orderly manner. Work in two areas would help ensure this outcome: developments in the securities market must be coordinated with implementation of privatization and pension reform, and two existing legal uncertainties require remedy.

PLANNING AND COORDINATION. Coordination is needed between the development of the securities market's absorptive capacity and the implementation of privatization and pension reform. This will not be a linear process, and some form of interagency coordinating committee is probably the best method of managing it. The committee's function should be coordination of implementation, not development of policy, and its objective should be to identify any securities market aspects of privatization and pension reform implementation and to propose, plan, and organize all necessary remedial steps.

LEGAL UNCERTAINTY. In Lithuania, there are two areas where weaknesses in the legal framework might jeopardize the synergies among securities market development, privatization, and pension reform. First, it appears from Article 3, Clause 4, of the Law on Public Trading of Securities that securities issued to the public under a privatization program may not be subject to the disclosure or shareholder protection provisions of the law. This is apparently not the intention of the article, but it appears to be the effect. The resultant uncertainty should be remedied by amending the law so that the private placement of securities under cash privatization is exempted from the full prospectus disclosure requirements, but that in all other respects the law applies to securities issued under the privatization program. Second, Lithuania's civil code lacks a clear definition of the concept of nominee ownership. This is an impediment to efficient and secure securities transfer (one that acts as an especially perverse deterrent to foreign investors) and should be remedied through legal amendment to introduce such a concept.

ANNEX

Figure 11-1. Sources and Uses of Investment in the Lithuanian Securities Market, 1996

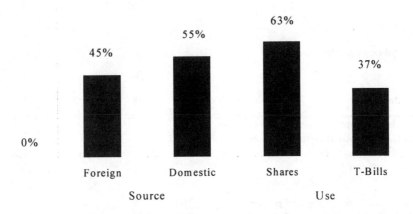

Source: National Stock Exchange of Lithuania Survey of Brokerage Companies, End-1997.

Table 11-1. Lithuanian Securities Market Growth, 1993–97

Item	1993	1994	1995	1996	1997
Total market capitalization, US$million	—	62	159	920	2,200
Annual turnover, US$million	0.31	20	128	130	366
Number of listed companies, year-end	44	183	351	460	607

Source: National Stock Exchange of Lithuania Securities Market Annual Report 1996.

Table 11-2. Average Size of Listed Companies, Selected Countries (market capitalization, US$m)

Country	Average size
United States	894
United Kingdom	677
Philippines	287
Indonesia	280
China	130
Poland	70
Hungary	57
Czech Republic	10
Bulgaria	9
Lithuania	4

Source: International Finance Corporation, *Emerging Stock Markets Factbook 1997* (Washington, D.C., 1997); National Stock Exchange of Lithuania Securities Market Report, 4th Quarter 1997.

Table 11-3. Shareholding Structure for Lithuanian Public Companies by Sector

Sector	Government holdings	Private sector holdings	Total	Small shareholders[a]	Other shareholders[b]	Total
Manufacturing	41	59	100	37	63	100
Chemical	10	90	100	32	68	100
Agricultural and food processing	29	71	100	47	53	100
Construction and construction materials	36	64	100	66	34	100
Energy	84	16	100	17	83	100
Paper and printing	2	98	100	51	49	100

a. Small shareholders own 5 percent or less of a company.
b. Other shareholders own more than 5 percent.
Source: Central Securities Depository of Lithuania Research Group Survey of Top 100 Companies.

Table 11-4. Structure of Ownership of NSEL

Type of shareholder	Number of shares	Percent
State (Ministry of Finance)	110	45
Brokerage companies	39	16
Banks	16	6
Other Lithuanian legal persons	69	28
Private individuals	9	4
Foreign companies	3	1
Total	246	100

Source: Annual Report, 1996, NSEL.

Table 11-5. NSEL Member Firms: Volume and Value of Business, 1997

Rank by percentage of total market turnover	Number of firms	Total number of transactions per firm (average)	Total value of transactions per firm (average), US$m
Top 3 firms	3	8,789	132
Next twelve firms	12	2,309	21
Remainder of firms	41	635	2

Source: National Stock Exchange of Lithuania, Trading Results, Fourth Quarter 1997.

12

THE MACROECONOMIC FRAMEWORK

Despite the progress that Lithuania has made in its transition to a market economy led by the private sector, a wide range of structural problems remain to be managed. These second-generation problems are largely sectoral in nature, and the preceding chapters have analyzed them and made sectoral policy proposals. It is the task of this chapter to place these proposals into a consistent macroeconomic context—that is, to show their aggregate effect on the economy's growth, stability, and financing prospects.

The Lithuanian economy now faces a critical macroeconomic choice. It can maintain the moderate speed and coverage of its current reform program, achieving a respectable growth rate, but continuing to face a variety of bothersome problems. Or, with a more vigorous and comprehensive reform initiative, it can move into a more rapid and sustainable growth path. In other words, Lithuania could remain a relative laggard at the fringes of the European Union or become a major performer in the region with enhanced chances of European integration. Whether Lithuania's growth takes off depends on whether it implements a structural reform agenda that accomplishes two objectives: the elimination of the remaining sources of fiscal imbalance in sectors associated directly or indirectly with the state, and the generation of a major private-sector-led increase in efficiency and investment.

The first goal of the new reform agenda should be to control the fiscal drains associated with the quasi-public sector, defined to include the general government, the public energy sector, strategic public enterprises, the agriculture sector, and other interest groups that are financially dependent on the state. This quasi-public sector deficit is far larger than that posted in the general government accounts, some 4–5 percent of GDP rather than the 2 percent of GDP currently observed in the formal budget. A quasi-public-sector deficit of this size is an immediate fiscal threat to the balance and stability of the macroeconomy. Its measurement, fiscal impact, and the method of its elimination are a central focus of this chapter.

The second macroeconomic goal (an overall enhancement in efficiency) will, in effect, result from the deepening and completion of the adjustment process associated with transition. The state will complete its withdrawal from centrally planned, protected economic activity to make room for private sector initiative in a competitive market environment. The accelerated structural reforms are expected to facilitate growth in the size and efficiency of private investment, which will be the key engine of enhanced growth.

Lithuania's Financial Evolution Since Independence: A Flow-of-Funds View

Because of the key role played in Lithuania's macro framework by investment and by the various deficits—government, foreign, and private—it is essential to examine the current state of these factors.

This can best be done by a review of the financial system as presented in flow-of-funds accounts (which are expressly designed for this purpose). This section will examine how the major economic sectors have financed their deficits in the 1993–97 period. The analysis will come to focus on the finance of private investment and its relationship to both the fiscal and balance of payments deficits and to the monetary and banking system.

The examination of Lithuania's financial performance begins with an outline of its saving-investment process. In figure 12-1, the economy is analyzed, separated into columns for three sectors: the general government,[1] a comprehensive private sector,[2] and rest-of-the-world. For the general government and the private sector, a surplus/deficit or net lending/borrowing curve is derived as the difference between each sector's investment (gross capital formation) and saving. Since the rest-of-the-world does no capital formation for Lithuania, its column contains only its saving (Lithuania's balance of payments current account deficit) and its surplus, rest-of-the-world net lending to Lithuania. The banking sector, which does little saving or nonfinancial investment, is omitted. Looking crosswise at the bottom of figure 12-1 reveals the basic structure of financial flows that has governed the Lithuanian economy: the net lending of the rest-of-the-world finances the net borrowing of the two domestic sectors. The relatively stable—as a percentage of GDP—general government deficit has been financed steadily from abroad. And the higher borrowing need of the private sector since 1995 has been financed by the new, higher level of rest-of-the-world lending. The 1995 and 1996 stability in the curves suggests a flow structure in which a current account deficit of 5 percent of GDP provides for the finance of the government of about 2 percent of GDP, and of the private sector of about 3 percent of GDP. The 1997 projection has maintained this pattern.

These aggregate lending and borrowing flows can be broken down to show a more detailed view of the intersectoral financial process. Since the start of its stabilization program in early 1994, Lithuania has, under IMF sponsorship, been implementing a contraction in the general government deficit. Current policy aims to balance the budget by the year 2000. Control of this deficit has been an essential part of the stabilization program, contributing to the reduction of inflationary expectations and to confidence in the maintenance of the Currency Board–anchored exchange rate. A good indicator of the success of this policy is the general government's surplus of current revenue over current expenditure. Government saving has been constant at about 2 percent of GDP since 1994, except for the 1996 dip, the result of a general shortfall of revenue that is not expected to repeat in 1997. That saving, however, has been consistently insufficient to cover both the very modest level of investment (more on this later) and the authorities' policy of lending to its satellite institutions. This is shown in figure 12-2, where the government's total borrowing curve, running between 4 percent and 5 percent of GDP from 1994 to 1996, is much larger than needed to cover the budget's financial deficit. The additional borrowing provided for the on-lending that has been some 2 percent of GDP in recent years. For 1997, however, the lending is projected to decline, and this, together with the deficit decline, would permit a decline in total borrowing from 4.5 percent to 3.3 percent of GDP.

---

1. The general government includes the state and municipal government, plus the social security, health insurance, and privatization funds.

2. The private sector is a residual sector including all sectors other than the general government, banking, and rest-of-the-world sectors. It includes public enterprises, nonbank financial institutions, and nonprofit institutions, as well as households and all private business organizations.

Figure 12-1. Sector Investment, Saving, and Surplus/Deficit
(Flow data as percentage of current GDP)

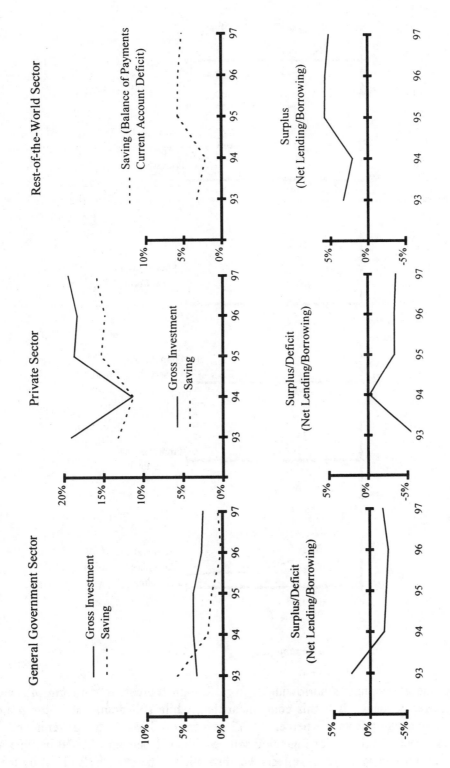

Note: 1997 data are projected.

Figure 12-2. General Government Sector Finance
(Flow data as percentage of current GDP)

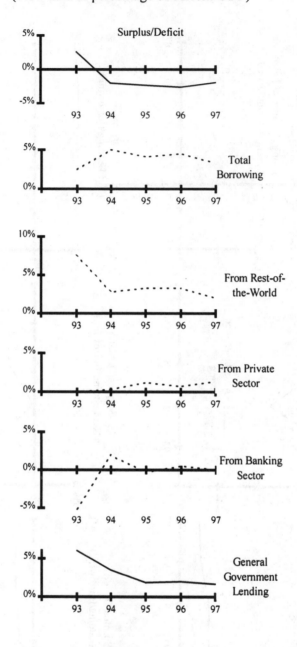

Note: 1997 data are projected.

The bulk of the government's borrowing is from foreign sources, in the form of medium- and long-term foreign currency loans. It is this component that, while still dominant in the projection for 1997, falls with total borrowing from 3.3 percent to 2.3 percent of GDP. In the government's domestic borrowing, the private sector is the major financing source—about 1 percent of GDP in 1995 and 1996. The rising trend of this curve (figure 12-2) reflects the absorption of treasury bills (TBs) by the nonbank sectors. This absorption has been an important institutional development during transition. The start of the Currency Board arrangement in 1994, which greatly limited government borrowing from the central bank, coincided with a short-term government financing need. This stimulated the development of TB auctions managed by the Bank of Lithuania (BoL). The first participants were mainly commercial banks, but later, nonbank institutions in the private sector began to participate to the tune of about 1 percent of GDP yearly.

Figure 12-3. Rest-of-the-World Net Lending to Lithuania
(Flow data as percentage of current GDP)

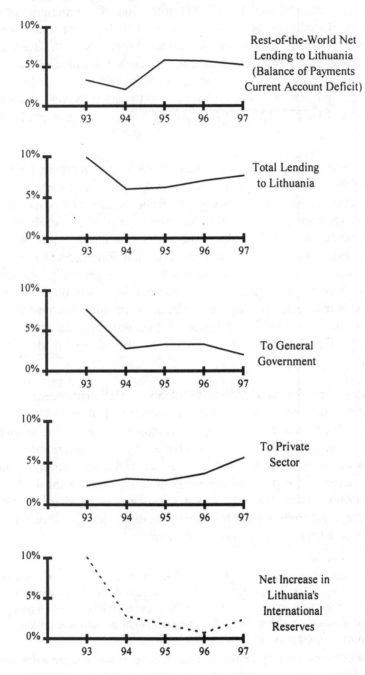

Note: 1997 data are projected.

The rest-of-the-world net lending to Lithuania is broken down in figure 12-3.[3] While total foreign lending rises steadily from 6 percent of GDP in 1994 to 7 percent in 1996, the breakdown of this curve reveals the large but rather steady flow to general government (which was seen as government net borrowing on figure 12-2), accompanied by a sharply rising flow to the private sector, running up to 3.7 percent of GDP in 1996. Somewhat more than half of the private sector flow takes the form of direct foreign investment, concentrated in the services sector and light manufacturing. An improving regulatory climate for such investment, as well as the recent economic growth, underpin further rapid growth in the private sector flow to 5.6 percent of GDP in the 1997 projection. The remainder of the flow to the private sector consists primarily of medium- and long-term loans. This flow of about 2 percent of GDP has been partially supported by Lithuanian government guarantees (especially in the state-controlled enterprises). A residual pattern—combining the impact of the current account deficit and the inward lending flows— imposes itself on the banking sector's international reserves at the bottom of figure 12-3. This measures the overall balance of payments surplus/deficit, and in most years it shows comfortable reserve increases of 1 percent to 2 percent of GDP. The current stock of gross reserves covers about 2.5 months worth of imports.[4]

An analysis of the private sector's financial flows is presented in figure 12-4. It is here, of course, that the bulk of the economy's capital formation takes place, and here that it must be financed. In order to separate the business activity of this sector from that of its households, we make the broad assumption that the private saving of Lithuania's households is placed entirely in the sector's acquisition of money and other financial assets. The rest of the sector's saving thus represents business saving, the funds retained by enterprises that are used to finance capital formation (the internal finance curve on figure 12-4). The growth of this estimate of business saving has generally kept pace with the growth of investment since 1994. Nevertheless, there is a wide gap between them that represents a borrowing need, a demand for funds that is met by the rest-of-the-world, banking, and government sectors. The curves for private borrowing from these three sectors in figure 12-4 combine into the total private borrowing curve. The steady decline in that flow (as a percent of GDP) from 1993 to 1996 is almost entirely attributable to the banking sector curve.

In 1993 the flow of private bank credit—swollen by inflationary needs—was 12 percent of GDP, and the primary vehicle in the financing of private investment. But in 1994–96 that flow grew so little that, as a percentage of GDP, it declined precipitately down to zero. The stagnation of bank lending during the banking crisis in 1996 is understandable, but the deterioration began much earlier. Fortunately, the stable flows from abroad (and from the general government) could partially replace the loss of bank lending. Even in the midst of the banking crisis, about a third of private investment was financed from these flows. Bank lending currently indicates a recovery in 1997; together with an expected increase in the flow from abroad (especially in direct foreign investment), this would enable total borrowing to finance nearly half of private investment.

---

3. Like several of the economies in transition, since 1993 Lithuania has had a continuously growing trade deficit. By 1995 and 1996, it was up to about 8 percent of GDP. The trade deficit is accompanied by offsetting surpluses in services and transfers, which combine to yield current account deficits of about 6 percent of GDP for 1995 and 1996, and which our projection continues in 1997. The movement of the trade deficit, however, sets the pattern of movement for the current account as a whole.

4. It should be noted that Lithuania's external position appears quite strong in comparison with such other transition economies as Latvia, Estonia, the Czech Republic, and Poland. Lithuania's exports exceed 40 percent of GDP and are growing strongly. Lithuania's merchandise trade deficit is lower than that of all these countries except Poland. External debt is only 12 percent of GDP. And in recent years the exchange rate has been maintained with no great difficulty.

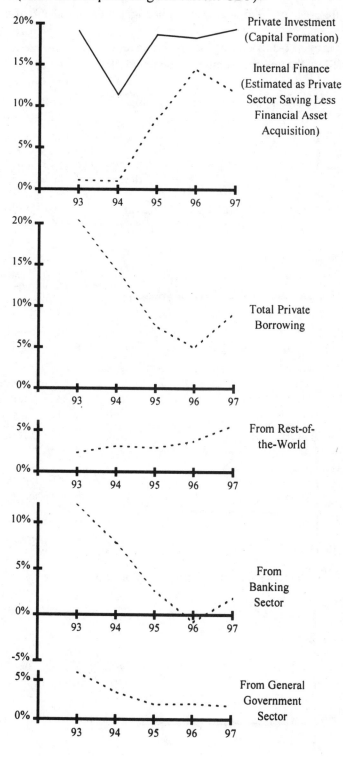

Figure 12-4. Private Sector Investment and Financing
(Flow data as percentage of current GDP)

Note: 1997 data are projected.

Further analysis of the banking sector's (Bank of Lithuania, plus the commercial banks) macroeconomic flows is presented in figure 12-5. These flows are clearly dominated by the sharp declines in both the broad money increment and the acquisitions of private claims. They both descend, so to speak, into the banking crisis of 1996, and they both suggest earlier roots of trouble. The commercial

Figure 12-5. Banking Sector Finance
(Flow data as percentage of current GDP)

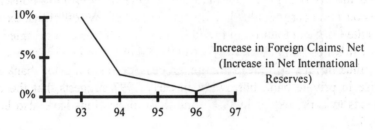

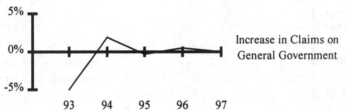

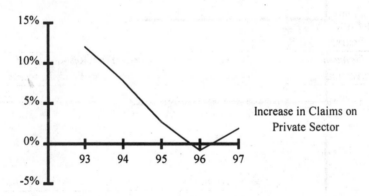

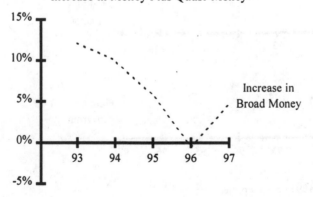

Note: 1997 data are projected.

banking system of Lithuania is a very recent creation, dating only from the late 1980s. The system has been highly concentrated in a few state-controlled banks. Before the crisis, management had little experience in commercial bank operation; bank capital bases were thin; political intervention in lending decisions was common; and many loans were nonperforming. The central bank was not a vigorous supervisor; its attention was focused on international reserve management. The rise in currency outside banks in 1994 and 1995 suggests eroding confidence in the banks. In these years, a number of the smaller banks entered bankruptcy proceedings. In the fall of 1995, both liquidity and solvency problems surfaced. In December, the Bank of Lithuania suspended the operations of Innovation Bank, the country's largest, and the crisis began. During 1996, a quarter of existing household deposits left the system, interest rates on TBs nearly doubled, and significant outflows of foreign exchange occurred. The reserve outflows resulted in a contraction in broad money, which was accompanied by a credit crunch in bank lending. All of this lies behind the two sharply declining curves in figure 12-5. The government and the Bank of Lithuania are still deep in the process of restoring the banking system to health. Nevertheless, the rise in private bank borrowing in early 1997 suggests that the banks will be able to respond to credit needs to some extent in 1997, and these indications have also been put into the 1997 projections in figure 12-5.

The sector accounts discussed above can be placed in matrix form for a given year, as in table 12-1, to show the horizontal balances of the borrowing and lending flows, as well as the vertical sector account balances. With each of its flows expressed as a percentage of the current GDP, table 12-1 reveals the financial flow structure of the economy's macro financial system. Data for 1995 were used to avoid the unusual credit flows of the 1996 banking crisis. The table contains some notable features. The gross investment total of 21.3 percent of GDP is a respectable figure, but one that needs to be higher.[5]

Table 12-1. Flow-of-Funds Matrix, 1995
(actuals as percentage of current GDP)

	General government		Banking sector		Private sector		Rest-of-the-world		Total	
	U	*S*	*U*	*S*	*U*	*S*	*U*	*S*	*U*	*S*
Investment	2.6[a]				18.7				21.3	
Saving		0.2[a]				15.3		5.8		21.3
Surplus/deficit[b]	-2.3				-3.4		5.8			
	ΔFin. assets	*ΔFin. liab.*	*ΔFin. assets*	*ΔFin. liab.*	*ΔFin. assets*	*ΔFin. liab.*	*ΔFin. assets*	*ΔFin. liab.*	*ΔFin. assets*	*ΔFin. liab.*
ΔForeign claims			1.8					1.8	1.8	1.8
ΔGeneral government debt		4.1	-0.3		1.2		3.3		4.1	4.1
ΔPrivate credit	1.9		2.7			7.6	2.9		7.6	7.6
ΔMoney and quasi money				5.7	5.7				5.7	5.7
ΔMisc. and discrepencies		0.2		-1.5		2.7	1.4		1.4	1.4
Total	5.8	5.8	4.2	4.2	25.6	25.6	7.6	7.6	43.2	43.2

a. Figure is adjusted downward by 1.3 to be more representative of five recent years.

b. Sector net lending/borrowing.

5. The gross investment of general government of 3.9 percent of GDP in 1995 is unusually high, although dismal for international standards, and in table 12-1 it has been lowered to 2.6 percent, a figure more representative of the recent period.

With the rest-of-the-world saving at 5.8 percent and government saving at 0.2 percent, the estimated private sector saving is 15.3 percent, and our crude estimate of internal finance is 8.4 percent, a somewhat modest support to the private sector's investment of 18.7 percent of GDP. The basic surplus/deficit structure thus shows the rest-of-the-world surplus of 5.8 percent financing the general government deficit of -2.3 percent and the somewhat larger private sector deficit of -3.4 percent, a relationship seen in figure 12-1.

Sector Policy and the Quasi-Public-Sector Deficit

To put the Lithuanian economy on a path of rapid and sustainable growth, it is necessary, *inter alia*, to eliminate the most serious fiscal imbalances in sectors of the economy that are still dependent on the government, such as banking, energy, agriculture, and social security. This can be seen in the aggregate as the elimination of the deficit of a broadly defined quasi-public sector. This aggregative view is taken here in order to consider the effects of sectoral policy on the general government budget and the macroeconomy as a whole. In this section, the major parts of this deficit are identified and, where possible, estimated.

The root causes of the expanded operating deficit of the quasi-public sector lie in two interrelated areas. The first is the formal budget of the general government. The ongoing stabilization program has, since 1994, called for a reduction in the general government deficit. As noted above, this effort has kept the deficit under 3 percent of GDP and is projected to maintain this level in 1997. But as inflation tax revenues receded, less funding was available to finance items such as subsidized heating, enterprise tax arrears, and cheap agricultural credit. In effect, tighter expenditure policies were shifting expenditures from the general government budget to other sectors.

A major example of expenditure shifting is found in the energy sector. In order to reduce direct consumer subsidies for heating, the government forced the state-owned Lithuanian Power Company (LPC) to sell below cost and to create a liability against the state for the difference. That liability has been estimated at about Lt 800 million, or 3 percent of 1996 GDP, and it grows at about 1 percent of GDP each year. In effect, government expenditures have been transformed into an LPC deficit.

The second root cause lies within the banking sector. The 1994 establishment of the Currency Board procedures, together with the EFF-related debt ceilings, considerably restricted general government's borrowing options. In response, a new form of expenditure shifting arose: informal political intervention to direct bank credit allocations toward state-controlled or state-favored enterprises, regardless of their ability to repay. Such intervention was facilitated by the state's role in bank ownership (the government owns at least a minority holding in banks covering 95 percent of the deposit totals, and fully controls banks accounting for about half of those deposits) and by a less than strict enforcement of banking regulations. This practice added a large new layer of loans, now classified or defaulted. The general government was, in effect, disbursing the capital stock of the banking system in order to shift enterprise subsidies away from the fiscal budget.

As of the summer of 1997, the quasi-public-sector deficit included a range of disparate elements from various sectors, such as the losses of LPC and the newly decentralized district heating companies; different forms of payment arrears; government bond issues in support of bank capital and as compensation for deposit losses; several restitution and compensation schemes (such as allowances for apartment renters) in buildings expropriated during Soviet times; contingent expenses implicit in a large array of government guarantees; and the remaining forms of agricultural subsidy. Below, estimates are made of the aggregate government expenditures and the deficit that would result if those elements were brought into the formal fiscal accounts. The implications of this aggregate of added expenditures will then be considered in the context of the country's projected macroeconomic outlook.

BANKING SECTOR. The restructuring of the banking system has been under way since the crisis of early 1996. The BoL faced a situation in which about three-quarters of the system's liabilities were in insolvent or seriously undercapitalized banks. By late 1996, the government had decided on a plan to recapitalize, restructure, and then privatize two of the three state-controlled banks—the State Commercial Bank and the Savings Bank. The private banks, several of which were under moratorium (Innovation, Litimpex, and Vakaru), were required to recapitalize with private funds to meet prudential regulations or were liquidated. In parallel, both the regulations and the intensity of supervision have been strengthened. Two main features of the banking industry restructuring process involved government financing: the recapitalization of state-controlled banks and the compensation of depositors in liquidated banks.

By the time the 1996 banking crisis broke out, the State Commercial Bank had been insolvent for at least a year. The bank soon lost more than a third of its deposits and had to receive liquidity support from the BoL, and in the second half of that year, from the government (mainly through ordering budgetary organizations to transfer their deposits to the bank). In late 1996, the government finally recapitalized the bank, contributing Lt 165 million, primarily through an issue of ten-year government bonds that would replace the nonperforming bank portfolio. Some Lt 78 million in "bad" loans was also transferred to the state-owned "work-out" unit (Turto Bank). The State Savings Bank—holding a fifth of the system's deposits— has a similar story. A disastrous loss in 1995 drained more than 75 percent of its capital. The bank was recapitalized by the government with a capital contribution of Lt 40 million, a combination of government bonds and a convertible loan. The liquidation of the Innovation Bank, a large (15 percent of total deposits) private bank that had been under moratorium since December 1995, has raised the issue of depositor compensation in the liquidation of private banks. At the time, the Seimas had quickly passed a law pledging a full state guarantee for all Innovation's creditors. After unsuccessful attempts at rehabilitation, in April 1997 the Seimas approved a law for the bank's liquidation. The law calls for a write-off of government deposits; the cash compensation of private clients during 1997 and 1998 at a cost of about Lt 100 million; and the issuance of bonds (Lt 275 million) to compensate all others, to be redeemed in 1999–2002. Seimas has also passed legislation creating a partial protection scheme for deposits in private and state-controlled banks. The scheme has yet to be fully funded, however, which leaves the government in the role of deposit insurer.

Our estimate of the banking sector's portion of the quasi-public-sector deficit consists primarily of assembling the estimates of cash outflows for depositor payoffs in 1997 and 1998 (Lt 148 and Lt 177 million, respectively) and the recapitalization-bond servicing and payoffs in later years. Some Lt 250 million in bonds will fall due in 2006 and in the decade following. The resulting series starts at Lt 225 million and tapers to Lt 50 million after the year 2000 (see table 12-2). Although the total cost of bank restructuring is estimated to be over Lt 1 billion (3.2 percent of 1997 GDP), the financial devices adopted have spread the cost over the next ten to twenty years.

ENERGY SECTOR. The largest element in the quasi-public-sector deficit is that associated with the energy sector. Three problems must be addressed to eliminate this portion of the deficit: (i) the restoration of the financial viability of LPC and Lithuanian Gas prior to privatization, (ii) the strengthening of payments discipline among energy consumers; and (iii) the elimination of budgetary subsidies for energy, except for necessary support of low-income households.

The newly established Energy Pricing Commission, in June 1997, approved price increases of 10 percent for electricity and 25 percent for district heating and the elimination of preferential pricing for agricultural and industrial customers, measures designed to bring prices to cost-recovery levels. In addition, the government made a large (Lt 776 million) financial settlement with LPC in 1997 in relation to prior unpaid production subsidies that involved the takeover of LPC debt and the cancellation of LPC tax arrears. (These measures, together with the decentralization of district heating, should restore LPC to profitability by 1998.)

Table 12-2. The Quasi-Public-Sector Deficit
(Lt million)

Item	1997	1998	1999	2000	2001	2002	2003	2004	2005	2006	2007
Energy sector	750	500	480	400	370	300	270	250	250	250	250
Bank reform	225	200	35	35	35	35	55	55	55	300	0
Municipal gov't.	300	300	200	200	200	200	200	200	200	200	200
Total	1,275	1,000	715	635	605	535	525	505	505	750	450
Memo: revenue from improved tax administration		—	200	400	600	100	—	—	—	—	—

Source: Staff estimates.

Nonpayment of energy bills has been a serious financial problem for LPC and Lithuanian Gas for several years, and it has caused arrears from LPC to Lithuanian Gas, and consequent delays in payments to foreign gas companies. State and municipal budgetary authorities are a major part of the problem. Consumer energy arrears to LPC and Lithuanian Gas were 1 percent of GDP at the end of 1995. During 1996, measures were introduced to deal with delinquent customers, including increased use of cutoffs and improved budgeting for budgetary organizations, and arrears dropped by half. But by March 1997, the arrears had risen again, to 0.8 percent of GDP. In 1997, the government made arrangements to pay LPC directly on behalf of municipalities whose debts exceeded 30 days of billing and to remove the necessary amounts from their budgetary transfers. Other disciplinary measures included fining the heads of delinquent budgetary organizations and the disconnection of customers. In addition, Lt 100 million that can be used to clear the energy arrears of budgetary organizations was included in the budget. It is expected that the impact of such measures will substantially reduce energy arrears in the second half of 1997, which will improve the cash flow to LPC and Lithuanian Gas. (In the first quarter of 1997, LPC was able to clear its arrears with Lithuanian Gas, which, in turn, was able to reduce its arrears to foreign suppliers.) Also, the increase in energy prices to cost-recovery levels should remove the need for further producer subsidies in the government budget. These increases, however, will simultaneously create additional social safety net needs for low-income consumers. The 1997 budget contains Lt 200 million to address this need.

Our estimate of the energy sector's contribution to the quasi-public-sector deficit—to cover remaining producer subsidies and energy arrears settlements—thus starts at Lt 750 million for 1997 (2 percent of projected GDP). It drops to Lt 500 million in 1998, and tapers steadily down to Lt 250 million after 2003 (see table 12-2).

MUNICIPAL GOVERNMENT. The rationalization and modernization of the system of municipal finances will play a significant role in placing Lithuania's quasi-public accounts on a sustainable path. About a quarter of the consolidated general government expenditures takes place at the municipal level, and such key public services as public utilities, education, and health are primarily the responsibility of local government. Although municipalities have the power to collect fees for the services they provide, the critical element in balancing their budgets is currently the revenue that they receive as a transfer from the central government. Recent years have seen a steady restriction of these transfers, forcing service reductions and the postponement of urgently needed infrastructure investment. The reform of municipal finance that began in 1993–94 has slowed. The authorities are considering some major changes, including ending revenue sharing under the personal and corporate income taxes, paired with the elimination of state transfers, an arrangement that would initially favor municipal governments. Such key issues as the degree of independent revenue authority and the nature of available borrowing authority of municipalities, however, remain undecided.

Meanwhile, the municipalities have resorted to the buildup of arrears as a means of finance. In April 1997, their arrears for electricity and heat were the equivalent of 86 days and 190 days worth of billing, respectively. They also have allowed arrears to build up in the forwarding of their income tax withholdings to the state. Added financial pressure will result as the state forces the municipalities to discharge energy arrears.

The transfer of the district heating system from LPC to municipal ownership and control in mid-1997 will be an additional financial burden for municipalities. The losses of the LPC heating business in 1996 were some Lt 420 million, the bulk of it in district heating. Even with the 25 percent price increases projected—and if these are implemented—it will probably take some time before losses of this size are erased. The operating efficiency of municipal control remains to be seen. In addition, the renovation of district heating, badly needed as an energy conservation measure, will be a major financing problem.

Unfortunately, from the many uncertainties surrounding the financial framework, only a crude estimate can be made for this component of the quasi-public-sector deficit. Table 12-2 shows that municipalities will need Lt 300 million in 1997 and 1998 to cover transfer losses and district heating losses. The subsequent amounts of Lt 200 million are for continuing district heating losses and the restoration of the service level (through minimum investment outlays) to that of recent years.

AGRICULTURAL SECTOR. The thrust of the agricultural reform program is threefold: rationalization of the existing agricultural support mechanisms, increasing the role of the private sector in agriculture, and further opening the sector to international trade. It is the first of these, with its focus on the agricultural subsidy programs, that is most closely tied to the quasi-public-sector deficit. The government's agricultural subsidy program has been the main mechanism for the transfer of massive amounts of financial resources to agriculture.

In 1996, the government began the reduction of subsidies with a 5 percent real reduction in agricultural subsidy expenditures. For 1997, in the context of the new Rural Support Fund (RSF), which will now encompass all subsidy and public agriculture-related investment programs, a variety of reforms have been made. Fewer products are eligible for support, support prices are reduced in real terms, and limits on the volume of production that will be eligible are being tightened. These steps will continue the reduction of budgetary subsidy expenditures in real terms. At the same time, a second component of the RSF, its targeted investment programs, will be expanding. Subsidized credit through the state-controlled Agricultural Bank will be discontinued and replaced by a system of competitively allocated capital grants, which will target high-quality seed production, cooling tanks for dairy products, and a range of programs that focus on infrastructure and agricultural services.

It is not possible at this stage to estimate the effect of all these changes on the government budget. On the whole, the reforms seem most likely to be a reorganization of the existing expenditures for agriculture rather than a reduction. It appears that the subsidy reductions will be roughly balanced by added expenditures for the new investment programs. This process of budgetary transformation will, in effect, gradually reduce the share of the quasi-public-sector deficit attributable to agriculture within the formal budget. For this reason, an estimate for agriculture has not been included in table 12-2.

CONTINGENCIES. A new savings restitution plan (SRP) is under consideration to compensate state bank depositors for losses incurred during 1991 and 1992. The compensation is to be financed from privatization revenue as it becomes available in coming years. As planned, the SRP does not place any burden on the formal budget, but the overall compensation is large, perhaps 10 percent of 1996 GDP. Privatization revenue will appear slowly, and public pressure may mount to make the disbursements quickly. Rapid SRP payments would constitute a large additional increase in the quasi-public-sector deficit, and the effects would pose a serious new threat to macroeconomic balance.

A second contingency is the future financial state of the social insurance fund (SoDra). The current financial position of SoDra is not strong, and projections indicate deficits after 2000 as the proportion of the elderly in the population grows. The government is planning a number of near-term remedial steps, including increasing the retirement age, reducing pension indexation, and improving social security tax coverage and the timeliness of tax payments. These steps should solve SoDra's immediate financial problems. In the medium term, a framework for private pensions is under consideration, which might involve a reduction in SoDra's revenue. The program is still in the planning stage, however, and will take some time to implement and take effect.

Table 12-2 assembles the estimated components of the quasi-public-sector deficit. Estimates, although rough, have been possible for the banking, energy, and municipal government sectors. As explained above, estimates were not possible for the agricultural sector, and are not included for the contingencies. The total series starts at Lt 1.3 billion in 1997, about 3.5 percent of the current GDP, and tapers down to Lt 0.6 billion in three years, less than 2 percent of GDP. In other words, the estimated quasi-public-sector deficit is more than half again as large as the budgeted deficit represented in the formal accounts of the state. The rapid decline results from the early concentration of structural reform expenditures in banking, and in the energy sector, of expenditures for the cleanup of arrears and for producer subsidy programs that have not yet been eliminated.

A Policy Choice: Two Macroeconomic Scenarios for Lithuania

Two contrasting longer-term views of Lithuania's future were proposed at the start of this chapter. The first one, representing the impact of continuing, moderate policy action, projects an economy growing in real terms at 3 percent yearly. The second view projects the impact of more vigorous and rapid implementation of the sectoral reforms. The growth rate in this scenario is 6 percent annually. The key factor in the projections causing the difference in growth rates is *the size and efficiency of the economy's investment*. In the one case, private investment responds weakly given the persisting constraints in the private sector environment. In the other case, private investment responds with confidence to the new profit possibilities inherent in the reforms, and investment not only grows faster, but also is able to incorporate increased efficiencies. To explore the implications of these two contrasting views, this section develops two projection scenarios for Lithuania that look a decade ahead, through 2007.

The two projections are derived from the World Bank's RMSM-X model, adapted to Lithuania's current situation. This model is not to be understood as an endogenous-growth econometric model. Rather, each projection begins with assumed growth rates for major economic variables such as production, investment, and exports. These assumptions are essentially judgmental projections. Making use of these assumptions, the model carries the base period national accounts into the future. In the context of RMSM-X, such projections of the government budget, the balance of payments, and the monetary accounts, together with the basic national accounts, permit the derivation of the private sector and its finance. This, in turn, permits an examination of the consistency of patterns of saving, investment, and finance (especially external finance) over the term of the projection.

A Moderate Growth Outlook

The moderate-growth scenario is summarized in table 12-3. The real GDP growth rate is assumed to be 3 percent yearly, in contrast to the 6 percent real growth rate of the high-growth projection. This lower growth scenario is seen to be the result of slower progress in the reduction of the quasi-public-sector deficit and in such growth-related policy areas as privatization, the business environment, and pension and security market reform. A key factor in setting the 3 percent growth rate is the similar growth rate of gross domestic investment, a pace that maintains—but does not increase—its 21 percent of GDP proportion throughout the projection. A number of elements will retard investment. The slow pace of policy reform and the moderate fiscal tightness suggest a slow development of business confidence in macroeconomic stability, and bank lending rates will remain high. Needed infrastructure improvements will lag as government investment falls from its current rate of 2.6 percent of GDP to 2 percent over the decade. With only a moderate growth in overall investment, and weak structural reform performance, the productivity improvements essential for the modernization of Lithuania's economy will not appear. This is symbolized in the projection by the incremental capital output ratio (ICOR) rise from 5.8 to 6.8 over the decade. Nevertheless, while not stellar, an annual growth rate of 3 percent—the rate of recent years—can be regarded as quite satisfactory; it maintains a per capita consumption growth rate of 2.8 percent in the moderate projection.

A problem portrayed in this projection is a lingering annual inflation rate of some 18 percent over the next decade. The Currency Board arrangement that was adopted in 1994 has undoubtedly been effective in reducing inflationary expectations, but the government plans to withdraw from this arrangement in 1998 to facilitate more flexibility in central bank policy. Meanwhile, substantial inflationary forces remain. Lack of sector-based structural reform, in particular, keeps the fiscal accounts in a persistent and substantial deficit (4–5 percent of annual GDP). The inflation requires a steady yearly devaluation of 15 percent in the US$/litas exchange rate (from the present 4.0 to 18.0 in 2007) to maintain the present level of the real effective exchange rate. Some loss of monetary credibility undoubtedly results.

With respect to external trade, the projection assumes a continuation of the current robust growth in real exports to the West until the millennium, tapering off to an annual growth rate of 3 percent by the end of the forecast period. Real exports to the East also continue their strong growth into 1998, but fall off more rapidly than exports to the West, reaching a 3 percent growth rate by 2007. Modest economic growth, coupled with robust growth in exports, yields a rise in the ratio of exports to GDP from 52 percent to 61 percent over the forecast period. Imports are expected to increase at a more moderate pace, resulting from the slower real GDP expansion, and one positive consequence of this scenario is that the resource-balance deficit (exports - imports) declines from -8.2 to -2.4 percent of GDP over the forecast period.

Yet the outflow of net factor income (especially that of debt servicing) will grow rapidly enough to preclude any real improvement in the current account deficit, which will decline as a share of GDP from about 8 percent to 5 percent in 2007. Thus, the rest-of-the-world will continue to be a major lender to Lithuania, supplying an inflow of some 7 percent of GDP annually, eventually pushing the debt/GDP ratio from under 15 percent in 1996 to over 40 percent by the end of the forecast period. The projection assumes a continuing—and more than satisfactory—growth in international reserves (including those of

Table 12-3. Moderate-Growth Projection
(percent and US$ million)

Indicator	Estimated 1996	1997	Projected 1998	1999	2000	2001	2002	2003	2004	2005	2006	2007
Real annual growth rates (1993 prices)												
GDP at market prices	3.6	3.6	3.3	3.0	3.0	3.0	3.0	3.0	3.0	3.0	3.0	3.0
GNP at market prices	3.5	3.5	2.8	2.5	2.6	2.7	2.7	2.7	2.7	2.7	2.7	2.8
Gross domestic income	..	3.7	3.6	2.7	2.8	2.9	3.0	3.1	3.1	3.1	3.1	3.1
GNP per capita	3.7	3.5	2.8	2.5	2.6	2.7	2.7	2.7	2.7	2.7	2.7	2.8
Consumption per capita	2.4	1.8	3.3	1.4	1.5	2.7	2.7	2.8	2.7	2.6	2.8	2.8
External debt outstanding and disbursed and debt service												
Debt outstanding and disbursed (DOD)	1,129	1,502	1,953	2,320	2,639	3,003	3,396	3,748	4,214	4,669	5,135	5,643
DOD/GDP	14.5	19.9	24.0	26.8	28.7	31.0	33.2	34.6	36.9	38.7	40.3	42.0
Debt service (US$ millions)	139	281	255	240	385	410	469	523	638	704	799	884
Debt service/XGS	3.3	6.7	5.5	4.7	7.0	6.9	7.4	7.7	8.9	9.2	9.9	10.4
Debt service/GDP	1.8	3.7	3.1	2.8	4.2	4.2	4.6	4.8	5.6	5.8	6.3	6.6
National accounts (percent of GDP at current market prices)												
Gross domestic investment	21.0	21.0	20.8	20.6	20.6	20.5	20.5	20.5	20.5	20.5	20.5	20.5
Gross domestic fixed investment	20.1	20.3	20.1	20.0	20.0	20.0	20.0	20.0	20.0	20.0	20.0	20.0
Gross domestic savings	11.4	12.8	13.4	14.8	16.1	16.5	16.8	17.0	17.3	17.7	17.9	18.1
Gross national savings	12.8	13.5	13.7	14.6	15.4	15.4	15.4	15.3	15.3	15.3	15.3	15.2
Government investment	2.6	2.5	2.3	2.1	2.0	2.0	2.0	2.0	2.0	2.0	2.0	2.0
Government savings	0.1	0.3	0.1	-0.1	-0.3	-0.4	-0.6	-0.6	-0.7	-0.8	-0.8	-0.9
Private investment[a]	18.4	18.5	18.5	18.5	18.6	18.5	18.5	18.5	18.5	18.5	18.5	18.5
Private savings	12.7	13.2	13.6	14.7	15.7	15.9	16.0	15.9	16.0	16.1	16.1	16.1
ICOR[b]	5.84	5.84	6.36	6.93	6.87	6.85	6.83	6.82	6.82	6.82	6.82	6.82
General government accounts[c] (percent of GDP at current market prices)												
Current revenues	29.8	31.1	30.8	30.7	30.7	30.7	30.6	30.6	30.6	30.5	30.5	30.5
Current expenditures	29.7	30.8	30.7	30.8	31.0	31.1	31.2	31.2	31.3	31.3	31.4	31.4
Capital revenues	0.0	0.0	0.0	0.0	0.0	0.0	0.0	0.0	0.0	0.0	0.0	0.0
Capital expenditures	2.6	2.5	2.3	2.1	2.0	2.0	2.0	2.0	2.0	2.0	2.0	2.0
Investment	2.6	2.5	2.3	2.1	2.0	2.0	2.0	2.0	2.0	2.0	2.0	2.0
Overall balance (– = deficit)	-4.7	-4.2	-4.3	-4.3	-4.3	-4.6	-4.7	-4.8	-4.8	-4.9	-5.0	-5.1
External accounts												
Total export volume, annual growth rate (percent)	..	4.0	7.4	6.8	5.7	4.8	4.1	3.7	3.5	3.5	3.1	3.1
Export/GDP (percent)	52.4	53.9	54.9	56.8	58.4	59.4	60.0	60.3	60.6	60.8	60.9	61.0
Total import volume, annual growth rate	..	1.3	6.5	3.8	3.4	4.2	3.6	3.4	3.1	2.9	2.8	2.8
Import/GDP	62.1	62.2	62.2	62.6	62.8	63.4	63.7	63.8	63.7	63.6	63.5	63.3
Current account (US$ millions)	-641.7	-563.9	-578.2	-521.3	-470.5	-4921	-522.1	-559.4	-593.8	-615.6	-661.1	-706.7
Current account/GDP	-8.2	7.5	-7.1	-6.0	-5.1	-5.1	-5.1	-5.2	-5.2	-5.1	-5.2	-5.3
Prices												
Inflation rate (period average)	25.0	10.0	15.0	16.0	17.0	18.0	18.0	18.0	18.0	18.0	18.0	18.0

a. Includes changes in stocks. b. Fixed investment only. c. General government includes central government, municipalities, and extrabudgetary funds.

the deposit money banks) of 2 percent of GDP yearly. The stock of international reserves, as expressed in months of imports, will grow from 2.2 to 4.5 months.

The fiscal policy expressed in the projection is only moderately tight; the current general government deficit of some 2.5 percent of GDP continues through the decade. The considerable resistance in Lithuania to raising taxes—despite their low level in international comparisons—is reflected in current revenues that remain at about 30 percent of GDP despite an upward creep of current expenditures from 30 percent to 31 percent. Government saving declines continuously, from near zero to -0.9 percent of GDP. Lending operations, largely a reflection of the passing on of government borrowing from abroad, have been maintained. In order to keep government borrowing down to 5 percent of GDP, however, capital expenditures have been rationed. They start at the already very modest level of 2.6 percent of GDP, and soon decline to 2 percent. In effect, the failure of the current budget to generate savings is hindering the government investment effort (see table 12-3). Also, any eventual privatization revenue (capital revenue) is assumed to be directly passed through to beneficiaries of compensation schemes (as currently determined by law), and thus is not reflected in the budget.

We turn now to the private sector and the financing of the main portion of the economy's investment. In 1995, private sector investment was about 19 percent of GDP. As explained above, the growth of private investment is moderate in this projection, and its percentage of GDP remains unchanged over the decade; the growth of saving behaves in the same manner. With the large current account deficit—that is, the large rest-of-the-world annual saving of 5.3 percent of GDP—the domestic saving available to the private sector is only 16.0 percent of GDP (see table 12-4). By our crude estimate, the portion of this amount that comprises internal business financing might be some 7 percent of GDP, while the capital formation to be financed is nearly 19 percent. If this is so, private sector borrowing to finance such real investment would have to be about 12 percent of GDP. In the moderate projection, the estimated proportion of private borrowing to private investment thus rises from a reasonable 41 percent in 1995 to a quite large 63 percent in 2007. This projection can be characterized as a heavy-borrowing scenario.

That borrowing and lending relationship becomes clear if the implicit flow-of-funds accounts are examined in matrix format with the banking sector represented, as in table 12-4. The line for the issue of general government debt (5.1 percent of GDP) shows that 2.3 percent is absorbed by the rest-of-the-world and 1 percent by the private sector. The remaining 1.8 percent of GDP is taken by the banking sector. Similarly, of the private credit issue of 11.6 percent of GDP that is necessary to finance private sector investment, 4.9 percent is absorbed by the rest-of-world, 2.2 percent represents on-lending from government, and the remaining 4.5 percent is bank borrowing. In this projection, the borrowing needs are sufficiently high that even with the large flow from abroad (2.3 percent and 4.9 percent, stemming largely from the current account deficit of 5.3 percent of GDP), major borrowing needs have to be met by the banking sector (1.8 percent of GDP for government and 4.5 percent of GDP for the private sector). The projection thus assumes that the banking sector will be restored to health over the next few years and will be able to accommodate these major credit demands.

If we compare the financial flow structure at the end of the projection (table 12-4 for the year 2007) with that at the start (table 12-1 for 1995), we can see how that structure evolves over the decade. The lines for investment, saving, and surplus and deficit are not greatly changed. The moderate-growth scenario maintains a structure in which the balance of payments current account deficit provides a major rest-of-the-world surplus that finances the deficits of the general government and the private sector. But the borrowing and lending structure does change. Borrowing grows substantially—for the government, from 4.1 percent of GDP to 5.1 percent, and for the private sector, from 7.6 percent of GDP to 11.6

percent. This expanded lending is provided mainly by a rapidly growing banking sector, which will provide bank portfolio growth (including international reserves) from 4.2 percent of GDP annually to 8.4 percent, and the necessary increase in the broad money stock from 5.7 percent of GDP annually to 8.2 percent. It is this shift in the borrowing and lending structure toward increased borrowing that makes the moderate-growth projection a heavy-borrowing scenario.

Table 12-4. Moderate-Growth Projection, Flow-of-Funds Matrix, 2007
(percent of current GDP)

	General government		Banking sector		Private sector		Rest-of-the-world		Total	
	U	S	U	S	U	S	U	S	U	S
Investment	2.0				18.5				20.4	
Saving		-0.9		0.1		16.0		5.3		20.4
Surplus/deficit[a]	-2.9		0.1		-2.4		5.3		0	
	ΔFin. assets	ΔFin. liab.	ΔFin. assets	ΔFin. liab.	ΔFin. assets	ΔFin. liab.	ΔFin. assets	ΔFin. liab.	ΔFin. assets	ΔFin. liab.
ΔForeign claims			2.1					2.1	2.1	2.1
ΔGeneral government debt		5.1	1.8		1.0		2.3		5.1	5.1
ΔPrivate credit	2.2		4.5			11.6	4.9		11.6	11.6
ΔMoney and quasi money				8.2	8.2				8.2	8.2
ΔMisc. and discrepencies		*		0.2		*	0.2		0.2	0.2
Total	4.2	4.2	8.4	8.4	27.6	27.6	7.4	7.4	47.6	47.6

a. Sector net lending/borrowing.

Lithuania is currently not a highly indebted country, either internally or externally, but the borrowing flows of this projection do carry the debt stock and money stock figures to rather high levels over the next ten years. The steady current account deficit of some 5 percent of GDP causes the external debt stock to rise from 14 percent to 42 percent of GDP, and debt service payments to increase from 1.8 percent to 6.6 percent of GDP. The steady government borrowing of some 5 percent of GDP causes the government debt stock to grow from 7 percent to 39 percent of GDP. The acceleration of banking sector growth leads to the growth of private plus government bank credit from 11 percent to 26 percent of GDP. And finally, the broad money stock grows from 18 percent to 38 percent of GDP. While these figures are not yet alarming—especially given the projection's annual inflation rate of 18 percent—they may well be worrisome and affect business confidence in a country that has recently experienced a major banking crisis.

As indicated above, to move toward a sustainable high-growth path for Lithuania's economy, the first necessary—but not, by itself, sufficient—step is the elimination of the quasi-public-sector deficit. If this step were carried out, how would the projection be affected? In table 12-2, the total of additional expenditures associated with government-directed policy start at Lt 1,275 million for 1997, decline to Lt 635 million by the year 2000, and then slowly decline over the decade to Lt 450 million, except for the Lt 750 million figure for 2006, when the bank recapitalization bond issues fall due. For the first three key years of expenditure, these figures are equivalent to 3.5 percent, 2.8 percent, and 2.0 percent of GDP, respectively. Thus, the true deficit of the state and its financially dependent sectors for these years is not the steady 2.2 percent of GDP posted by the general government, but 5.7 percent, 5.0 percent, and 4.2

percent of GDP. And, if the added expenditures were put into the budget with no other changes, the projected issue of government debt for 1997–99 would be worth 7.7 percent, 7.0 percent, and 6.2 percent instead of 4.2 percent of GDP.

The government debt line on table 12-1 provides a summary of the impact of such added borrowing. If the government debt issue were raised from 4.1 percent to 7.1 percent, the added 3 percentage points would have to be placed with the other three sectors. Any additional government borrowing from abroad (assuming no change in the current account deficit) would squeeze private borrowing from abroad, which might well retard investment. Alternatively, the private sector might seek to borrow more from banks—or the government might do so directly—with a consequent additional further growth in the flows of bank credit and the money stock. The latter outcome—because the amounts involved are large—would compromise the appropriate tight monetary and credit policy in the face of ongoing inflation and a balance of payments current account deficit. It is also unlikely in the current institutional environment that the government could greatly increase its direct borrowing from the private sector.

What is then implied by the quasi-public-sector deficit problem is a need for a greater tax effort. As table 12-3 indicates, the moderate growth projection includes little growth in general government current expenditures relative to GDP—from 29.7 percent to 31.3 percent—and the growth that does take place is entirely the result of rising interest costs. Current revenue grows even less, from 29.8 percent of GDP to 30.5 percent. Given the low level of taxes in Lithuania compared with its neighbors and the Organization for Economic Cooperation and Development (OECD) countries, there appears to be room for an increase of 2–3 percent of GDP in the VAT and/or taxes on companies and individuals. The government has already launched reform measures in tax administration that might add 1–2 percent of GDP over a few years (see table 12-2). These resources could eliminate or greatly reduce the quasi-public-sector deficit. The government is currently reluctant to raise tax rates, but the need to eliminate the quasi-public-sector deficit makes an urgent case for doing so.

In sum, the moderate growth scenario presents a continuation over the next decade of the current twin deficits—that of the balance of payments current account, and that of general government. The posted government deficit that would accompany slow revenue growth makes the necessary elimination of the quasi-public-sector deficit difficult. And the continuing external deficit that would accompany sluggish export growth necessitates a large flow of capital into Lithuania. So far, this flow has been plentiful enough to meet the need, based no doubt on confidence established by the Currency Board arrangements and the government's short-term stabilization policies. Should this confidence diminish, and if foreign borrowing were to become difficult, financing of the foreign deficit could become a major problem. The projection, however, has assumed a plentiful capital flow. Finally, this moderate growth— but high borrowing—projection contains strong private borrowing pressure on a banking system that is just now emerging from a very weakened state.

High Growth and Major Reform Impact

Given a substantial reduction in the quasi-public-sector deficit, vigorous implementation of needed sector policy reforms could well place the Lithuanian economy on a sustainable high-growth plateau. This vision is embodied in the high-growth projection scenario presented in this section. It is characterized by strong export behavior and rapid growth in capital formation, both driven by enhanced confidence and the efficiencies to be derived from improved institutions and incentives. Table 12-5 sets out the main features of the projection.

Table 12-5. High-Growth Projection
(percent and US$ million)

Indicator	Estimated		Projected									
	1996	1997	1998	1999	2000	2001	2002	2003	2004	2005	2006	2007
Real annual growth rates (1993 prices)												
GDP at market prices	3.6	3.6	4.0	4.5	5.0	5.5	6.0	6.0	6.0	6.0	6.0	6.0
GNP at market prices	3.5	3.5	3.5	4.0	4.6	5.2	5.8	5.9	5.9	6.0	6.0	6.0
Gross domestic income	..	3.5	4.4	4.4	4.9	5.5	6.1	6.1	6.1	6.1	6.2	6.2
GNP per capita	3.7	3.5	3.5	4.0	4.6	5.2	5.8	5.9	5.9	6.0	6.0	6.0
Consumption per capita	2.4	1.8	2.9	2.3	2.7	3.7	5.2	5.1	5.3	5.8	6.0	6.0
External debt outstanding and disbursed and debt service												
Debt outstanding and disbursed (DOD)	1,129	1,461	1,887	2,223	2,449	2,666	2,864	2,936	3,054	3,170	3,294	3,426
DOD/GDP	14.5	18.9	22.6	24.7	25.1	25.3	25.0	23.6	22.6	21.6	20.6	19.8
Debt service (US$ millions)	139	282	255	237	385	405	439	466	542	536	551	554
Debt service/XGS	3.3	6.6	5.4	4.5	6.6	6.3	6.2	6.0	6.3	5.7	5.3	4.9
Debt service/GDP	1.8	3.6	3.0	2.6	4.0	3.8	3.8	3.7	4.0	3.6	3.4	3.2
National accounts (percent of GDP at current market prices)												
Gross domestic investment	21.0	21.5	22.0	22.5	23.0	23.5	23.5	23.5	23.5	23.5	23.5	23.5
Gross domestic fixed investment	20.1	20.8	21.4	21.9	22.5	23.0	23.0	23.0	23.0	23.0	23.0	23.0
Gross domestic savings	11.4	13.0	14.5	16.4	18.4	19.8	20.5	21.3	21.9	22.3	22.5	22.7
Gross national savings	12.8	13.9	14.8	16.2	17.7	18.8	19.2	19.8	20.2	20.5	20.5	20.6
Government investment	2.6	2.5	2.6	2.8	2.9	3.1	3.2	3.4	3.6	3.6	3.6	3.6
Government savings	0.1	0.4	0.6	1.3	1.7	2.1	2.3	2.6	2.7	2.8	2.8	2.8
Private investment[a]	18.4	19.0	19.4	19.8	20.1	20.5	20.3	20.1	19.9	19.9	19.9	19.9
Private savings	12.7	13.5	14.2	15.0	16.0	16.7	16.9	17.2	17.5	17.7	17.7	17.9
ICOR[b]	5.84	5.84	5.38	4.59	4.50	4.18	3.92	3.91	3.91	3.91	3.91	3.91
General government accounts[c] (percent of GDP at current market prices)												
Current revenues	29.8	30.9	31.1	31.4	31.7	31.9	32.1	32.3	32.4	32.4	32.4	32.4
Current expenditures	29.7	30.5	30.5	30.1	29.9	29.9	29.8	29.7	29.7	29.6	29.6	29.6
Capital revenues	0.0	0.0	0.0	0.0	0.0	0.0	0.0	0.0	0.0	0.0	0.0	0.0
Capital expenditures	2.6	2.5	2.6	2.8	2.9	3.1	3.2	3.4	3.6	3.6	3.6	3.6
Investment	2.6	2.5	2.6	2.8	2.9	3.1	3.2	3.4	3.6	3.6	3.6	3.6
Overall balance (- = deficit)	-4.7	-4.2	-3.9	-3.5	-3.2	-2.9	-2.8	-2.8	-2.7	-2.7	-2.7	-2.6
External accounts												
Total export volume, annual growth rate	..	6.5	7.3	7.3	7.7	7.5	7.5	7.5	7.6	7.6	6.9	6.9
Export/GDP	52.4	53.8	54.7	56.2	57.7	58.8	59.6	60.5	61.5	62.5	63.1	63.8
Total import volume, annual growth rate	..	4.2	6.1	4.8	5.2	5.9	6.4	6.4	6.7	7.3	6.8	6.8
Import/GDP	62.1	62.2	62.2	62.3	62.3	62.5	62.6	62.7	63.0	63.7	64.1	64.6
Current account (US$ millions)	-641.7	-592.4	-599.5	-566.7	-518.3	-495.2	-486.5	-457.1	-434.8	-438.3	-466.1	-488.6
Current account/GDP	-8.2	-7.6	-7.2	-6.3	-5.3	-4.7	-4.2	-3.7	-3.2	-3.0	-2.9	-2.8
Prices												
Inflation rate (period average)	25.0	12.3	10.0	8.5	7.5	7.0	6.5	6.0	5.5	5.0	5.0	5.0

a. Includes changes in stocks. b. Fixed investment only. c. General government includes central government, municipalities, and extrabudgetary funds.

In the high-growth projection, real annual GDP growth rises from the current 3.6 percent to 6 percent by 2002, and remains at 6 percent to the end of the projection period in 2007. Gross investment follows an identical path. Both GDP and investment grow at double the rates in the moderate projection. This high rate of investment will be a direct result of energetic sectoral reforms, although a simple quantitative translation is not possible. Nevertheless, for a number of reasons the policy impact on investment is assumed to be large. The increased pace of privatization, a more favorable (and accountable) private sector development environment (through better tax administration, judicial systems, and mechanisms for corporate governance), sounder and more efficient financial systems (both in banking and in security markets), and the development of longer-term sources of funding from banks and pension-based investment funds can trigger a major, permanent improvement in confidence. This, in turn, could drive an increase in investment, and in its efficiency. The major improvements in efficiency are symbolized by the ICOR drop from 5.8 to 3.9 over the projection decade. In parallel, real per capita consumption attains an annual 6 percent growth rate, in contrast to the 2.8 percent annual rate of the moderate-growth scenario, making the overall economic framework more socially sustainable.

Furthermore, in the high-growth scenario, it is assumed that inflation continues to decline, with the annual rate falling steadily from the current 12 percent to 5 percent by 2007. This decline (and the lessening current account deficit discussed below) creates a much easier situation for the monetary authorities. The real effective exchange rate can be kept constant with only a moderate devaluation of the US$/litas exchange rate, from 4 to 6.75, in sharp contrast with the previous scenario. In turn, the authorities will be able to maintain lower long-term interest rates, further encouraging investment.

Both exports and imports rise more rapidly in the high-growth scenario. Export volume grows to 7.5 percent annually, remains there through 2005, and ends the forecast period at 6.9 percent yearly, over double the rate used in the moderate-growth scenario. Despite this difference, the proportion of exports to GDP rises from 52.4 percent to 63.8 percent, only 2 percentage points higher than the moderate-growth setting. This is the result of the cumulative effect of the increased output of the economy. Imports grow more slowly, and end the forecast period at 64.6 percent of GDP, only 1.3 percentage points higher than the moderate-growth scenario. Consequently, the current account deficit falls steadily, from -8.2 percent of GDP in 1996 to -2.8 percent of GDP in 2007, in marked contrast to the virtually unwavering -5.2 percent current account deficit of the moderate-growth projection.

The lower current account deficit in this projection, coupled with the increased output of the economy, elicits a drastically lower level of required international financing. As a consequence, the proportion of external debt to GDP rises from 14 percent to only 20 percent over the projection period, half the level of the moderate-growth scenario. Not surprisingly, the proportion of debt service payments to GDP increases from 1.8 percent to only 3.2 percent, approximately half the 6.6 percent level of the moderate-growth scenario.

In fiscal policy, a tighter stance is presented in the high-growth scenario. Current expenditures are kept level at 29.7 percent of GDP, in contrast to a growth to 31.4 percent in the moderate-growth projection. VAT increases boost current revenues from 29.8 percent of GDP to 32.4 percent, nearly 2.0 percent more than in the earlier scenario (see tables 12-3 and 12-5). The upshot is a rise in general government saving to 2.8 percent of GDP, which is available to finance the growth in government investment from 2.6 percent to 3.6 percent of GDP. Finally, the general government deficit tapers off sharply in the high-growth projection, from the initial -2.5 percent of GDP to about -1.0 percent from 2001 to 2007. The government deficit, like the balance of payments current account deficit, is considerably smaller here than in the moderate projection.

This tighter fiscal policy should help in the management of the quasi-public-sector deficit. This clearly occurs after the year 2000, when the deficit has fallen to -1.0 percent of GDP and the additional quasi-publicily generated 1.0–2.0 percent of GDP could be borrowed, if necessary. But there is a timing difficulty in the earlier years, 1997–99, when the greatest financing is needed—3.5 percent, 2.7 percent, and 1.9 percent of GDP, respectively. In these years, the posted deficits, although falling, are still large, at 2.1 percent, 2.0 percent, and 1.5 percent of GDP. The implication is similar to our finding in the moderate projection. Added tax revenue will be necessary in the early years, but because indirect taxes have already been raised, the burden would fall on direct taxes.

Table 12-6 shows the financial flow structure of the high-growth projection at its end in 2007. (This table can be compared with table 12-1, the current structure.) The higher government saving figure of 2.8 percent permits growth in government investment to 3.6 percent. (Government investment, which is currently at 2.6 percent, declined in the moderate projection to 2 percent.) With the smaller deficit of -0.8 percent, the overall government borrowing need would only be 2.6 percent of GDP, largely to cover the on-lending of 1.8 percent. The issue of government debt to be placed is thus much smaller in the high-growth projection. The debt is placed in the following manner: 1.2 percent with the rest-of-the-world, 0.5 percent with the private sector, and 1.0 percent with the banking sector.

Table 12-6. High-Growth Projection, Flow-of-Funds Matrix, 2007
(percent of current GDP)

	General government		Banking sector		Private sector		Rest-of-the-world		Total	
	U	S	U	S	U	S	U	S	U	S
Investment	3.6				19.9				23.4	
Saving		2.8		0.2		17.7		2.8		23.4
Surplus/deficit[a]	-0.8		0.2		-2.2		2.8		0	
	ΔFin. assets	ΔFin. liab.	ΔFin. assets	ΔFin. liab.	ΔFin. assets	ΔFin. liab.	ΔFin. assets	ΔFin. liab.	ΔFin. assets	ΔFin. liab.
ΔForeign claims		2.2						2.2	2.2	2.2
ΔGeneral government debt		2.6	1.0		0.5		1.2		2.6	2.6
ΔPrivate credit	1.8		1.8			7.5	3.9		7.5	7.5
ΔMoney and quasi money				4.4	4.4		*		4.4	4.4
ΔMisc. and discrepencies		*		0.4		-0.4	*		*	*
Total	5.4	5.4	5.0	5.0	24.8	24.8	5.0	5.0	40.2	40.2

a. Sector net lending/borrowing.

Table 12-6 also shows relatively low rest-of-the-world saving (2.8 percent of GDP) being placed into net lending to Lithuania. Even with the 2.2 percent accumulation of foreign reserves, the total rest-of-the-world lending is only 5.1 percent—1.2 percent into government debt and 3.9 percent into private credit. The 5.1 percent capital inflow represents a decline from 6.2 percent over the decade of the projection.

In the high-growth projection, total investment as a percentage of GDP grows substantially, from 21.3 percent to 23.4 percent, and private sector investment increases from 18.7 percent to 19.9 percent. The private saving figure of 17.7 percent of GDP is high as well, reflecting the projection's high levels of profits. Our crude estimate of business saving, or inside financing, is also high, at 12.8 percent of GDP, so that by 2007 only about a third of the private real investment has to be financed by borrowing. This proportion of borrowing would leave businesses in a much sounder financial position than the nearly two-thirds proportion at the end of the moderate projection. With the volume of private borrowing falling in this projection to 7.5 percent, and even with less foreign lending available, the private sector's call on the banking system is only 1.8 percent of GDP, a decline from 2.7 percent at the start of the projection. The banking system thus expands much more slowly than in the earlier projection, and the stock of domestic bank credit rises only to some 20 percent of GDP. Similarly, monetary expansion is more modest: the annual increment falls over the projection period from 5.7 percent of GDP to 4.4 percent, and the stock of money rises to only 32 percent of GDP. In this high-growth scenario, with its smaller key deficits, more comfortable, less demanding use is made of the financial system.

The broad purpose of our two projection scenarios has been to map out two plausible, policy-determined paths for the Lithuanian economy. As a final contrast and summary of the endpoints of the two projection paths, tables 12-4 and 12-6 can be compared. The high-growth projection carries investment to 23.4 percent of GDP, the moderate projection to 20.4 percent. The surplus/deficit structure differs sharply, with the high-growth rest-of-the-world surplus at 2.8 percent of GDP (rather than 5.3 percent) and the government deficit at -0.8 percent of GDP (rather than -2.9 percent). In the high-growth projection, government borrowing is smaller, at 2.6 percent of GDP (rather than 5.1 percent), and so is private borrowing, at 7.5 percent of GDP (rather than 11.6 percent), and the smaller demand for borrowing by both sectors in the high-growth projection reduces the flow of bank credit to the two sectors to 5.0 percent of GDP (rather than 8.4 percent), and the money stock increment to 4.4 percent of GDP (rather than 8.2 percent). The high-growth scenario is a low-deficit, low-borrowing scenario. It will leave the financial system, and ultimately the economy, in a far healthier position.

Some Concluding Policy Recommendations

The purpose of this chapter has been to place the sector reform proposals of this volume in a macroeconomic context and to consider the macromanagement policies that would support the effectiveness of the reform proposals. The central macropolicy task is the elimination of the quasi-public-sector deficit in the near future. Once this is achieved, vigorous implementation of the sector reforms can place Lithuania on a high-growth plateau. In this context, the projections have shown the importance of improved government revenue performance, a firm growth path for exports, and the restoration of the health of the banking system as the key macro areas needed to support the reforms.

ELIMINATION OF THE QUASI-PUBLIC-SECTOR DEFICIT. The estimates of the quasi-public-sector deficit for 1997–99 of 3.5 percent, 2.8 percent, and 2 percent of GDP, which then continue on at about 1.5 percent of GDP, confirm the large size of that sector's deficit. In neither of our projections could these early years be properly managed by increased general government borrowing—improved revenue performance would be necessary in either case. General government current revenue is now 29.8 percent of GDP. This would need to be raised by 3 percentage points of GDP in 1997–99 to finance the quasi-public-sector deficit. This is not an unreasonable increase given Lithuania's low level of taxation relative to OECD countries (especially in income and profits taxes). It is too soon for Lithuania to be considering general tax reduction.

EXPORT SUSTAINABILITY. Lithuania's merchandise exports were up 21 percent and export volume was up 13 percent in 1996. The question is, will such rapid growth continue? Indicators that suggest sustainability of exports—such as the high and growing export-to-GDP ratio and the lack of persistent pressures on the exchange rate in either direction—appear favorable for Lithuania. Our high-growth projection thus assumed a continuous growth in annual export volume of 7 percent, which was an important cause of the reduction in the current account deficit. Continuing export growth is a major force impelling Lithuania's progress on the rapid growth path.

HEALTH OF THE BANKING SYSTEM. The Lithuanian banking system—restructured and privatized—will still have had very little experience in commercial banking as a business; that is, in making viable and regular short-term business loans. This commercial bank function will need support and strengthening. As the projections show, the growing borrowing needs of the private sector will be met largely by the banks. If the banking system is unable to extend the credit demanded over the next decade, would-be borrowers may well not be able to finance desired investment. A high-growth path will require a properly functioning commercial banking system.

Distributors of World Bank Publications

Prices and credit terms vary from country to country. Consult your local distributor before placing an order.

ARGENTINA
Oficina del Libro Internacional
Av. Córdoba 1877
1120 Buenos Aires
Tel: (54 1) 815-8156
Fax: (54 1) 815-8354
E-mail: olilibro@satlink.com

AUSTRALIA, FIJI, PAPUA NEW GUINEA, SOLOMON ISLANDS, VANUATU, AND SAMOA
D.A. Information Services
648 Whitehorse Road
Mitcham 3132
Victoria
Tel: (61) 3 9210 7777
Fax: (61) 3 9210 7788
E-mail: service@dadirect.com.au

AUSTRIA
Gerold and Co.
Weihburggasse 26
A-1011 Wien
Tel: (43 1) 512-47-31-0
Fax: (43 1) 512-47-31-29

BANGLADESH
Micro Industries Development
  Assistance Society (MIDAS)
House 5, Road 16
Dhanmondi R/Area
Dhaka 1209
Tel: (880 2) 326427
Fax: (880 2) 811188

BELGIUM
Jean De Lannoy
Av. du Roi 202
1060 Brussels
Tel: (32 2) 538-5169
Fax: (32 2) 538-0841

BRAZIL
Publicações Técnicas Internacionais Ltda.
Rua Peixoto Gomide, 209
01409 Sao Paulo, SP.
Tel: (55 11) 259-6644
Fax: (55 11) 258-6990
E-mail: postmaster@pti.uol.br

CANADA
Renouf Publishing Co. Ltd.
5369 Canotek Road
Ottawa, Ontario K1J 9J3
Tel: (613) 745-2665
Fax: (613) 745-7660
E-mail: order.dept@renoufbooks.com

CHINA
China Financial & Economic
  Publishing House
8, Da Fo Si Dong Jie
Beijing
Tel: (86 10) 6333-8257
Fax: (86 10) 6401-7365

China Book Import Centre
P.O. Box 2825
Beijing

COLOMBIA
Infoenlace Ltda.
Carrera 6 No. 51-21
Apartado Aereo 34270
Santafé de Bogotá, D.C.
Tel: (57 1) 285-2798
Fax: (57 1) 285-2798

COTE D'IVOIRE
Center d'Edition et de Diffusion Africaines
  (CEDA)
04 B.P. 541
Abidjan 04
Tel: (225) 24 6510;24 6511
Fax: (225) 25 0567

CYPRUS
Center for Applied Research
Cyprus College
6, Diogenes Street, Engomi
P.O. Box 2006
Nicosia
Tel: (357 2) 44-1730
Fax: (357 2) 46-2051

CZECH REPUBLIC
USIS, NIS Prodejna
Havelkova 22
130 00 Prague 3
Tel: (420 2) 2423 1486
Fax: (420 2) 2423 1114

DENMARK
SamfundsLitteratur
Rosenoerns Allé 11
DK-1970 Frederiksberg C
Tel: (45 31) 351942
Fax: (45 31) 357822

ECUADOR
Libri Mundi
Librería Internacional
P.O. Box 17-01-3029
Juan Leon Mera 851
Quito
Tel: (593 2) 521-606; (593 2) 544-185
Fax: (593 2) 504-209
E-mail: librimu1@librimundi.com.ec

Codeu
Ruiz de Castilla 763, Edif. Expocolor
Primer piso, Of. #2
Quito
Tel/Fax: (593 2) 507-383; 253-091
E-mail: codeu@mpsat.net.ec

EGYPT, ARAB REPUBLIC OF
Al Ahram Distribution Agency
Al Galaa Street
Cairo
Tel: (20 2) 578-6083
Fax: (20 2) 578-6833

The Middle East Observer
41, Sherif Street
Cairo
Tel: (20 2) 393-9732
Fax: (20 2) 393-9732

FINLAND
Akateeminen Kirjakauppa
P.O. Box 128
FIN-00101 Helsinki
Tel: (358 0) 121 4418
Fax: (358 0) 121 4435
E-mail: akatilaus@stockmann.fi

FRANCE
World Bank Publications
66, avenue d'Iéna
75116 Paris
Tel: (33 1) 40-69-30-56/57
Fax: (33 1) 40-69-30-68

GERMANY
UNO-Verlag
Poppelsdorfer Allee 55
53115 Bonn
Tel: (49 228) 949020
Fax: (49 228) 217492
E-mail: unoverlag@aol.com

GHANA
Epp Books Services
P.O. Box 44
TUC
Accra

GREECE
Papasotiriou S.A.
35, Stournara Str.
106 82 Athens
Tel: (30 1) 364-1826
Fax: (30 1) 364-8254

HAITI
Culture Diffusion
5, Rue Capois
C.P. 257
Port-au-Prince
Tel: (509) 23 9260
Fax: (509) 23 4858

HONG KONG, CHINA; MACAO
Asia 2000 Ltd.
Sales & Circulation Department
Seabird House, unit 1101-02
22-28 Wyndham Street, Central
Hong Kong
Tel: (852) 2530-1409
Fax: (852) 2526-1107
E-mail: sales@asia2000.com.hk

HUNGARY
Euro Info Service
Margitszigeti Europa Haz
H-1138 Budapest
Tel: (36 1) 350 80 24, 350 80 25
Fax: (36 1) 350 90 32
E-mail: euroinfo@mail.matav.hu

INDIA
Allied Publishers Ltd.
751 Mount Road
Madras - 600 002
Tel: (91 44) 852-3938
Fax: (91 44) 852-0649

INDONESIA
Pt. Indira Limited
Jalan Borobudur 20
P.O. Box 181
Jakarta 10320
Tel: (62 21) 390-4290
Fax: (62 21) 390-4289

IRAN
Ketab Sara Co. Publishers
Khaled Eslamboli Ave., 6th Street
Delafrooz Alley No. 8
P.O. Box 15745-733
Tehran 15117
Tel: (98 21) 8717819; 8716104
Fax: (98 21) 8712479
E-mail: ketab-sara@neda.net.ir

Kowkab Publishers
P.O. Box 19575-511
Tehran
Tel: (98 21) 258-3723
Fax: (98 21) 258-3723

IRELAND
Government Supplies Agency
Oifig an tSoláthair
4-5 Harcourt Road
Dublin 2
Tel: (353 1) 661-3111
Fax: (353 1) 475-2670

ISRAEL
Yozmot Literature Ltd.
P.O. Box 56055
3 Yohanan Hasandlar Street
Tel Aviv 61560
Tel: (972 3) 5285-397
Fax: (972 3) 5285-397

R.O.Y International
PO Box 13056
Tel Aviv 61130
Tel: (972 3) 5461423
Fax: (972 3) 5461442
E-mail: royil@netvision.net.il

Palestinian Authority/Middle East
Index Information Services
P.O.B. 19502 Jerusalem
Tel: (972 2) 6271219
Fax: (972 2) 6271634

ITALY
Licosa Commissionaria Sansoni SPA
Via Duca Di Calabria, 1/1
Casella Postale 552
50125 Firenze
Tel: (55) 645-415
Fax: (55) 641-257
E-mail: licosa@ftbcc.it

JAMAICA
Ian Randle Publishers Ltd.
206 Old Hope Road, Kingston 6
Tel: 876-927-2085
Fax: 876-977-0243
E-mail: irpl@colis.com

JAPAN
Eastern Book Service
3-13 Hongo 3-chome, Bunkyo-ku
Tokyo 113
Tel: (81 3) 3818-0861
Fax: (81 3) 3818-0864
E-mail: orders@svt-ebs.co.jp

KENYA
Africa Book Service (E.A.) Ltd.
Quaran House, Mfangano Street
P.O. Box 45245
Nairobi
Tel: (254 2) 223 641
Fax: (254 2) 330 272

KOREA, REPUBLIC OF
Daejon Trading Co. Ltd.
5 Bangalore Town
Sharae Faisal
PO Box 13033
Karachi-75350
Tel: (92 21) 446307
Fax: (92 21) 4547640
E-mail: ouppak@TheOffice.net

Daejon Trading Co. Ltd.
P.O. Box 34, Youida, 706 Seoun Bldg
44-6 Youido-Dong, Yeongchengpo-Ku
Seoul
Tel: (82 2) 785-1631/4
Fax: (82 2) 784-0315

LEBANON
Librairie du Liban
P.O. Box 11-9232
Beirut
Tel: (961 9) 217 944
Fax: (961 9) 217 434

MALAYSIA
University of Malaya Cooperative
  Bookshop, Limited
P.O. Box 1127
Jalan Pantai Baru
59700 Kuala Lumpur
Tel: (60 3) 756-5000
Fax: (60 3) 755-4424
E-mail: umkoop@tm.net.my

MEXICO
INFOTEC
Av. San Fernando No. 37
Col. Toriello Guerra
14050 Mexico, D.F.

Mundi-Prensa Mexico S.A. de C.V.
c/Rio Panuco, 141-Colonia Cuauhtemoc
06500 Mexico, D.F.
Tel: (52 5) 533-5658
Fax: (52 5) 514-6799

NEPAL
Everest Media International Services (P) Ltd.
GPO Box 5443
Kathmandu
Tel: (977 1) 472 152
Fax: (977 1) 224 431

NETHERLANDS
De Lindeboom/InOr-Publikaties
P.O. Box 202, 7480 AE Haaksbergen
Tel: (31 53) 574-0004
Fax: (31 53) 572-9296
E-mail: lindeboo@worldonline.nl

NEW ZEALAND
EBSCO NZ Ltd.
Private Mail Bag 99914
New Market
Auckland
Tel: (64 9) 524-8119
Fax: (64 9) 524-8067

NIGERIA
University Press Limited
Three Crowns Building Jericho
Private Mail Bag 5095
Ibadan
Tel: (234 22) 41-1356
Fax: (234 22) 41-2056

NORWAY
NIC Info A/S
Book Department, Postboks 6512 Etterstad
N-0606 Oslo
Tel: (47 22) 97-4500
Fax: (47 22) 97-4545

PAKISTAN
Mirza Book Agency
65, Shahrah-e-Quaid-e-Azam
Lahore 54000
Tel: (92 42) 735 3601
Fax: (92 42) 576 3714

Oxford University Press
5 Bangalore Town
Sharae Faisal
PO Box 13033
Karachi-75350
Tel: (92 21) 446307
Fax: (92 21) 4547640
E-mail: oxford@oup.co.za

Pak Book Corporation
Aziz Chambers 21, Queen's Road
Lahore
Tel: (92 42) 636 3222; 636 0885
Fax: (92 42) 636 2328
E-mail: pbc@brain.net.pk

PERU
Editorial Desarrollo SA
Apartado 3824, Lima 1
Tel: (51 14) 285380
Fax: (51 14) 286628

PHILIPPINES
International Booksource Center Inc.
1127-A Antipolo St, Barangay, Venezuela
Makati City
Tel: (63 2) 896 6501; 6505; 6507
Fax: (63 2) 896 1741

POLAND
International Publishing Service
Ul. Piekna 31/37
00-677 Warzawa
Tel: (48 2) 628-6089
Fax: (48 2) 621-7255
E-mail: books%ips@ikp.atm.com.pl

PORTUGAL
Livraria Portugal
Apartado 2681, Rua Do Carmo 70-74
1200 Lisbon
Tel: (1) 347-4982
Fax: (1) 347-0264

ROMANIA
Compani De Librarii Bucuresti S.A.
Str. Lipscani no. 26, sector 3
Bucharest
Tel: (40 1) 613 9645
Fax: (40 1) 312 4000

RUSSIAN FEDERATION
Isdatelstvo <Ves Mir>
9a, Kolpachniy Pereulok
Moscow 101831
Tel: (7 095) 917 87 49
Fax: (7 095) 917 92 59

SINGAPORE; TAIWAN, CHINA; MYANMAR; BRUNEI
Asahgate Publishing Asia Pacific Pte. Ltd.
41 Kallang Pudding Road #04-03
Golden Wheel Building
Singapore 349316
Tel: (65) 741-5166
Fax: (65) 742-9356
E-mail: ashgate@asianconnect.com

SLOVENIA
Gospodarski Vestnik Publishing Group
Dunajska cesta 5
1000 Ljubljana
Tel: (386 61) 133 83 47; 132 12 30
Fax: (386 61) 133 80 30
E-mail: repansekj@gvestnik.si

SOUTH AFRICA, BOTSWANA
For single titles:
Oxford University Press Southern Africa
Vasco Boulevard, Goodwood
P.O. Box 12119, N1 City 7463
Cape Town
Tel: (27 21) 595 4400
Fax: (27 21) 595 4430
E-mail: oxford@oup.co.za

For subscription orders:
International Subscription Service
P.O. Box 41095
Craighall
Johannesburg 2024
Tel: (27 11) 880-1448
Fax: (27 11) 880-6248
E-mail: iss@is.co.za

SPAIN
Mundi-Prensa Libros, S.A.
Castello 37
28001 Madrid
Tel: (34 1) 431-3399
Fax: (34 1) 575-3998
E-mail: libreria@mundiprensa.es

Mundi-Prensa Barcelona
Consell de Cent, 391
08009 Barcelona
Tel: (34 3) 488-3492
Fax: (34 3) 487-7659
E-mail: barcelona@mundiprensa.es

SRI LANKA, THE MALDIVES
Lake House Bookshop
100, Sir Chittampalam Gardiner Mawatha
Colombo 2
Tel: (94 1) 32105

SWEDEN
Wennergren-Williams AB
P.O. Box 1305
S-171 25 Solna
Tel: (46 8) 705-97-50
Fax: (46 8) 27-00-71
E-mail: mail@wwi.se

SWITZERLAND
Librairie Payot Service Institutionnel
Côtes-de-Montbenon 30
1002 Lausanne
Tel: (41 21) 341-3229
Fax: (41 21) 341-3235

ADECO Van Diemen EditionsTechniques
Ch. de Lacuez 41
CH1807 Blonay
Tel: (41 21) 943 2673
Fax: (41 21) 943 3605

THAILAND
Central Books Distribution
306 Silom Road
Bangkok 10500
Tel: (66 2) 235-5400
Fax: (66 2) 237-8321

TRINIDAD & TOBAGO AND THE CARRIBBEAN
Systematics Studies Ltd.
St. Augustine Shopping Center
Eastern Main Road, St. Augustine
Trinidad & Tobago, West Indies
Tel: (868) 645-8466
Fax: (868) 645-8467
E-mail: tobe@trinidad.net

UGANDA
Gustro Ltd.
PO Box 9997, Madhvani Building
Plot 16/4 Jinja Rd.
Kampala
Tel: (256 41) 251 467
Fax: (256 41) 251 468
E-mail: gus@swiftuganda.com

UNITED KINGDOM
Microinfo Ltd.
P.O. Box 3, Alton, Hampshire GU34 2PG
England
Tel: (44 1420) 86848
Fax: (44 1420) 89889
E-mail: wbank@ukminfo.demon.co.uk

The Stationery Office
51 Nine Elms Lane
London SW8 5DR
Tel: (44 171) 873-8400
Fax: (44 171) 873-8242

VENEZUELA
Tecni-Ciencia Libros, S.A.
Centro Cuidad Comercial Tamanco
Nivel C2, Caracas
Tel: (58 2) 959 5547; 5035; 0016
Fax: (58 2) 959 5636

ZAMBIA
University Bookshop, University of Zambia
Great East Road Campus
P.O. Box 32379
Lusaka
Tel: (260 1) 252 576
Fax: (260 1) 253 952

ZIMBABWE
Academic and Baobab Books (Pvt.) Ltd.
4 Conald Road, Graniteside
P.O. Box 567
Harare
Tel: 263 4 755035
Fax: 263 4 781913

Tel: (92 42) 628-6089
Fax: (52 5) 624-2822
E-mail: infotec@rtn.net.mx